D0712803

Culture and Identity in a Muslim Society

SERIES IN CULTURE, COGNITION, AND BEHAVIOR

SERIES EDITOR
David Matsumoto, *San Francisco State University*

SERIES ADVISORY BOARD
Deborah Best, *Wake Forest University*
Michael Harris Bond, *Chinese University of Hong Kong*
Walter J. Lonner, *Western Washington University*

The Middle East: A Cultural Psychology
GARY S. GREGG

Culture and Identity in a Muslim Society
GARY S. GREGG

Culture and Identity in a Muslim Society

Gary S. Gregg

UNIVERSITY PRESS

2007

OXFORD
UNIVERSITY PRESS

Oxford University Press, Inc., publishes works that further
Oxford University's objective of excellence
in research, scholarship, and education.

Oxford   New York
Auckland   Cape Town   Dar es Salaam   Hong Kong   Karachi
Kuala Lumpur   Madrid   Melbourne   Mexico City   Nairobi
New Delhi   Shanghai   Taipei   Toronto

With offices in
Argentina   Austria   Brazil   Chile   Czech Republic   France   Greece
Guatemala   Hungary   Italy   Japan   Poland   Portugal   Singapore
South Korea   Switzerland   Thailand   Turkey   Ukraine   Vietnam

Library of Congress Cataloging-in-Publication Data
Gregg, Gary S.
Culture and identity in a Muslim society / Gary S. Gregg.
    p. cm.—(Series in culture, cognition, and behavior)
Includes bibliographical references and index.
ISBN-13 978-0-19-531003-0
ISBN 0-19-531003-9
1. Identity (Psychology)—Morocco—Case studies. 2. Ethnopsychology—Morocco—Case
studies. 3. Personality and culture—Morocco—Case studies. I. Title. II. Series.
BF697.G74 2006
155.20964—dc22   2006001435

9 8 7 6 5 4 3 2 1

Printed in the United States of America
on acid-free paper

ACKNOWLEDGMENTS

I owe deep thanks to my colleague Alison Geist for six years of collaborative research in Morocco, and to Robert LeVine for his long support of this investigation. Thank you to Douglas Davis, Susan Davis, and Susan Miller for their excellent research in Morocco and for many discussions of this study. Also thanks to my first teachers of "culture and personality," Theodore Schwartz and Robert Levy, to my colleagues in the Society for Personology, especially Bertram Cohler, Ruthellen Josselson, Revenna Helson, Avril Thorne, and Dan McAdams, and to George Rosenwald, Elliot Mishler, Hubert Hermans, and Chris Latiolais for crucial discussions of interviewing, narrative analysis, and theories of identity. Thank you to the many Moroccan research assistants who patiently tutored me in Arabic and worked with me translating the interviews. Above all, I thank Mohammed, Hussein, Rachida, Khadija, and the other Moroccans who narrated their life-stories to me and patiently taught me their language and culture. This research was supported by a Fulbright Research Fellowship and a grant from the National Science Foundation.

CONTENTS

NOTE ON TRANSLITERATION
OF ARABIC TERMS

Moroccan Arabic is an unwritten dialect, with pronunciation that varies among regions of the country. In many cases, there is no officially correct spelling in English letters. My thanks to Hamid Ouali at the University of Michigan's Department of Linguistics for helping with transliterations of the Arabic terms. For the letters that do not have close English equivalents, we have used the following transliterations:

ت	t
ط	ṭ
د	d
ض	ḍ
ه	h
ح	ḥ
س	s
ص	ṣ
ع	ʿ
غ	gh
خ	kh
ء	ʾ

When I have quoted or paraphrased works by other authors that contain Arabic terms in English letters, I have kept the transliterations these authors have used.

Culture and Identity in a Muslim Society

This book presents an investigation of the cultural shaping of self or identity. Unlike most psychological and anthropological studies of culture and self, it directly studies individuals by using "study of lives"-style interviews with young adults living in villages and small towns in southern Morocco. It analyzes the life narratives of two men and two women and builds a theory of culture and identity that differs from prevailing psychological and anthropological models in important respects. In contrast to modernist theories of identity as unified, the life narratives show individuals to articulate a small set of identities, among which they shift. But in contrast to postmodernist theories that claim people have a kaleidoscopic multiplicity of fluid selves, the narratives show a small set of identities, integrated by repeated use of culturally specific self-symbols, metaphors, and story plots. Perhaps most important, the life narratives show these young Moroccans' self-representations to be pervasively shaped by the volatile cultural struggle between Western-style "modernity" and authentic Muslim "tradition."

Culture and Self ✿

In the last fifteen years, psychologists have rediscovered culture and its influence on emotion, thought, and self and focused especially on how cultures vary in their "individualist" versus "collectivist" orientations and on how these differences give rise to "egocentric" versus "sociocentric" selves. The results of these studies appeared to converge and produce a consensus that:

1. the world's cultures can be ranked on a dimension of individualist versus collectivist, with Western cultures falling at the individualist end and non-Western cultures at the collectivist end, and

2. individualist cultures give rise to "independent" selves that have solid boundaries that separate them from others, so that Westerners think and act autonomously, while

3. collectivist cultures foster "interdependent" selves with permeable boundaries that embed non-Westerners in social relationships, so that they think and act relationally.

Most social psychology textbooks now include a section on "culture" that highlights these conclusions, and many programs designed to promote intercultural understanding teach them as the foundation for successful study-abroad experiences and international business relationships.

There have been criticisms of this theory. Anthropologists with extensive fieldwork in supposedly "collectivist" cultures have warned that neither Westerners' individualist ideology nor non-Westerners' collectivist ideologies should be mistaken for the experience people actually have of themselves.[1] They also have pointed out that the new "we're egocentric, they're sociocentric" view disturbingly echoes the old stereotype that the autonomous, conscience-directed individual was the crowning creation of Western civilization and that non-Westernized peoples were submerged in family and tribal relationships, their behavior not governed by conscience but by sensitivity to social shame.[2] Psychologist Harry Triandis, one of the pioneers in the study of individualism and collectivism, has long argued that neither cultures nor selves can be ranked on a single "I"–"C" continuum.[3] And Turkish psychologist Cigdem Kagitcibasi has argued that collectivism in some social spheres is quite compatible with individualism in others.[4] These cautions have had little impact on the gathering consensus, however, and textbook writers have felt free to use dubious photos to illustrate collectivist versus individualist orientations (one juxtaposes Asian schoolgirls wearing uniforms for a festival with American students lounging about their campus).[5]

In 1999, the *Asian Journal of Social Psychology* published a literature review[6] and a meta-analysis[7] that concluded that the simple "I versus C" contrast does not hold for America and Japan, long considered the archetypal cases. *Psychological Bulletin* gave its entire January 2002 issue to a comprehensive meta-analysis of I versus C studies[8] that found only limited support for this generalization concerning all Western versus non-Western cultures, and included extensive comments by cross-cultural researchers who argued that the I versus C approach needs to be drastically revised or abandoned.[9] In 2004, *Human Development* published an even sharper critique of this line of research that urged cross-cultural psychologists to study individuals and how they experience and represent their cultures.[10] Together, these reviews, meta-analyses, and commentaries have undermined the seemingly solid consensus about I versus C cultures and selves.[11] They bring the study of culture and self to a crisis point, casting doubt on core findings and research methods. The danger looms that psychologists may respond as they did several decades ago to ethnocentric oversimplifications in studies of "national character": by turning away from the study of culture. But the doubts also open opportunities to rethink the relation of culture and self, to use a greater variety of methods, and to develop more complex models of how culture influences selves.

This book presents an alternative to the I versus C approach, based on direct study of individuals—of young adults living in towns and villages in southern, "pre-Saharan" Morocco. After studying more than 100 families in the area, I conducted six- to eighteen-hour "study of lives" interviews (in Moroccan Arabic) with each of eleven individuals to investigate the cultural shaping of identity. The first chapter discusses the theories of identity that guided the study and reviews writings on identity in North African societies. The second provides a brief introduction to the "cultural geography" of Moroccan society, and chapters 3 through 6 analyze the life narratives I elicited from two men and two women. These four studies build a theory of culture and identity, which chapter 7 summarizes.

The theory developed from these life-narrative studies differs from prevailing psychological and anthropological models in important respects: in viewing culture as distributed among the members of a society, rather than as shared by them; in viewing cultures and selves not as individualist or collectivist, but as animated by tensions between group loyalties and personal ambitions; and in viewing self as having three levels of psychological organization, each subject to different cultural influences that exert their main effects in successive developmental periods. With regard to self-representation, the life narratives show identity to be defined not just by clusters of self-attributions or hierarchies of self-schemas but by a set of identity-defining *discourses*, which articulate often contradictory values and expressive styles. People continually shift among these discourses—sometimes smoothly, sometimes in distress and confusion—but their contrasting self-representations appear integrated by repeated use of *culturally specific self-symbols*, *metaphors*, and *story plots*. This model converges with other important lines of cross-cultural research, especially that on emotion (which shows universal emotions shaped by culturally specific display rules) and that on acculturation (which shows widespread shifting between alternative "cultural frames").[12] Perhaps most important, the life narratives show these young Moroccans' identities to be pervasively shaped by the volatile identity politics that pits Western-style modernity against authentic Muslim tradition.

I did not design this study to investigate individualism versus collectivism, but Morocco provides an especially appropriate setting because Clifford Geertz's often-cited contrast of the relationally defined, "mosaic" Moroccan self with the "bounded" Western self helped inspire much of the I versus C research.[13] And Oyserman and associates' meta-analysis found that in comparison with the United States, Middle Eastern samples were as collectivist as East Asian ones, and even less individualist.[14] The interviews, however, clearly show a mixture of strong sociocentrism *and* egocentrism, as Cigdem Kagitcibasi,[15] Suad Joseph,[16] and Charles Lindholm[17] have noted of Arab-Muslim societies.[18] The textbook author who put in the margin by his I versus C section "*If you cut off the ties of blood, you will have to worry on your own.*—proverb from Morocco (a collectivist culture)"[19] neglected to add other proverbs like *aqarib agarab*, or "close relatives are scorpions," which cynically mock homilies about filial loyalty and warn that one must look out for oneself. The Lebanese imam who delivered the powerful sermon on familial loyalties recorded by Richard Antoun had disobeyed his father's orders to leave school, moved out of his house so he could keep studying, and then became imam when he strode up to the mosque pulpit at the same time as the old imam and out-orated him to the villagers' acclaim.[20] As the narratives indeed show, most Moroccans sustain extended family loyalties that most Americans do not, and this has important psychological consequences. But this makes neither their culture nor their selves collectivist, and it does not prevent them from thinking of themselves as individuals or acting with often bold initiative. What proves to be much more important to the psyches and selves of the young Moroccans I interviewed are the conditions of economic and political underdevelopment in which they live and the unavoidable challenge of responding to the Western influences that now permeate their society.

The young Moroccans I interviewed in 1987 and 1988 were born into relatively traditional village settings. They all received some high school education and have or want careers as functionaries, technicians, or teachers rather than as farmers or herders, but beyond this, their paths to modernity diverge in often contradictory ways. They belong to Morocco's first post-Independence generation, a generation with huge hopes and frustrations that observers often cite to account for their increasing support for "fundamentalist" Islam. The news magazine *Jeunne Afrique* insightfully characterized them as "*entre cora et Quran,*" torn between their passions for soccer and religion. At school, they took half their classes in Arabic and half in French, so they speak both languages fluently. Some also speak Tashelhait Berber and some a little English or Spanish. They say their modern educations and visits to relatives in Morocco's big cities "opened" their minds and vistas of possibility, inviting them as teenagers to dream grandly about their futures. When I interviewed them in their twenties, most were reconciling themselves to smaller or dashed dreams or struggling to keep dreams alive. That is likely to be the story of their generation: dramatic population growth, the absence of raw materials for industrialization, and, many would say, rampant corruption have forced them into lives that are neither traditional nor modern but something quite else, which the term *underdevelopment* at least names.

I designed this research to apply study-of-lives methods in a non-European society in order to test and extend a model of identity developed from American life narratives and presented in my *Self Representation*. Henry Murray and his colleagues developed these methods in the 1930s, 1940s, and 1950s by combining intensive interviews, projective tests, and observations, in the belief that detailed examination of individual lives would yield important information about the structure and development of personality. Works like Murray's *Explorations in Personality*,[21] Robert White's *Lives in Progress*,[22] M. Brewster Smith and colleagues' *Opinions and Personality*,[23] and Erik Erikson's *Childhood and Society*[24] laid the groundwork for nearly all subsequent studies of life-course development. Robert Levy's landmark *Tahitians*[25] showed how productively a similar method could be used in a non-Western society and yielded important insights about the cultural patterning of development and emotion. The method certainly has limitations, especially because the small number of individuals who can be studied cannot be a "representative" sample. But it directly studies individual selves, and its enduring strength lies in its ability to provide a rich source of data in which the *representational* linkages of social structure, culture, and personality can be explored in near-microscopic detail.

Study-of-lives research has become especially important to cultural psychology for several reasons. Studies of culture and self by cross-cultural psychologists typically use paper-and-pencil measures of traits, values, or self-schemas to test for differences between group means.[26] Anthropologists studying the cultural construction of self usually rely on inferences about what public performances—in ritual, speech, and etiquettes of self-presentation—imply about the selves who enact them. Most writings on self in Arab-Muslim societies—including Geertz's article on the Moroccan "mosaic" self,[27] Jon Anderson's analysis of self in Afghanistan,[28] and Steven Caton's work on Yemeni selves[29]—analyze these sorts of data. The line of research missing from nearly all of this literature, however, has been that on individual lives (with Katherine Ewing's studies of Pakistani life histories an important exception[30]). Because the study-of-lives approach examines selves in an order-of-magnitude greater detail than any of these methods, it can play a crucial role in resolving the current debates over egocentric versus sociocentric selves and in moving beyond the current impasse created by reliance on either aggregated or public performance data.

Developments in semiotic theory, discourse analysis, and narrative psychology now provide tools for finer grained analyses of narratives than have been done in the past. Life histories can now be not just treated as cultural documents that indicate major life-cycle events but examined for patterns of culturally shaped feelings and thoughts. Complementarily, decades of ethnographic work on Mediterranean and Middle Eastern societies now make it possible to trace variations in social organization and culture with a precision that earlier researchers could not achieve. These advances enable a researcher to identify the cultural region associated with characteristics observed in a life narrative and to move from global statements about culture and self to more nuanced inferences about the role of overlapping and intersecting culture areas in shaping specific features of personality and identity. My analyses focus on turns of phrase and shades of meaning, in the conviction that the structures that organize personality and identity appear distributed through the details of representation and cannot be discovered in smaller samples of thought or behavior, in aggregate data, or in the main themes of individual biographies. By almost microscopically tracing the symbolic routes these individuals follow as they transform feelings of pollution into purity, shameful fear into honorable courage, or deprivation into bounty, the narrative analyses map how each of these young Moroccans selects elements from their culture to fashion identities and orchestrate their emotional lives.

Perhaps most important in light of the West's current "clash of civilizations" with the Arab-Muslim world, the detailed study of these lives points beyond the simplistic and often ethnocentric national character interpretations of Middle Eastern cultures that continue to be published.[31] These have been incisively criticized[32] but continue to have enormous influence: The 2002 edition of Patai's 1973 *The Arab Mind* contains an introduction by the director of Middle Eastern Studies at the JFK Special Warfare Center and School, who writes: "At the institution where I teach military officers, *The Arab Mind* forms the basis of my cultural instruction."[33] Few alternatives exist to these national character interpretations (though see my *The Middle East: A Cultural Psychology*), and psychological studies of Middle Eastern societies remain fragmented. By distinguishing three levels of personality organization and by tracing patterns seen in the narratives to the overlapping cultural regions that have shaped my respondents' lives, this book will show the struggles of these young adults to embrace both Western-style modernity and features of their Moroccan-Muslim heritage.

Background, Methods, Biases ❀

I had lived in the Ouarzazate area for three years when I began these interviews. During this time, my colleague Alison Geist and I studied the agropastoral Imeghrane confederation[34] in conjunction with a rangeland conservation project. As part of that research, we studied three villages in depth and closely followed two rich and two poor households in each village over that period. I interviewed the senior men in 90 of the 115 households in the foothills village of Toundout where we lived, 40 of 75 in the mountain village of Tamzrit, and 30 of 35 in the plains village of Assaka, charted each household's history, diagrammed its kinship ties, and traced major decisions about family members and resources. In addition to providing background on the organization of relatively traditional households, many of these turned into informal life history interviews. I also wrote notes on life histories from the many conversations I had with young men in these villages (and quite a few women, in my colleague's company) and with perhaps a score of other Moroccans we came to know well, including technicians, veterinarians, and research assistants with the Agriculture Ministry; shopkeepers and neighbors in Ouarzazate, where we kept a small apartment; and administrators in government bureaus. This information proved crucial for conducting and analyzing the interviews, especially for understanding some of the broader and subtler implications of the life stories I heard.

I sought respondents for formal taped interviews by explaining my research to acquaintances and asking for introductions to people in their twenties who had at least a year of high school education. All eleven recorded life narratives came from friends or relatives of these acquaintances. They lived in Ouarzazate, the provincial capital, or in Skoura or Agdez, both of which are clusters of villages with small administrative and market centers located about an hour's drive to the east and south of Ouarzazate, respectively. Some of the interviews took place in the living room of our apartment in Ouarzazate, some in the guest rooms of respondents' family homes, and a few in cafés and on riverbanks. They usually lasted between one and two hours and totaled from six to eighteen hours with each person.

I told prospective interviewees that I was a psychologist who studies "personality development" and emphasized that I taught at a university and was not a psychotherapist. I said I wanted to compare the lives of Moroccans to those of Americans I had interviewed, and I explained that I would tape-record the interviews, keep their words in confidence, disguise their identities in print, and give them copies of the tapes.[35] I asked them to serve as "my teacher" about Moroccan society, but because I could not guarantee the security of the tapes, I cautioned against saying anything that could "cause problems" for them. I then followed the study-of-lives[36] semistructured interviewing style I had used with Americans: open-endedly asking about experiences, relationships, and beliefs and following with associative questions[37] that invited respondents to elaborate their accounts. I asked about colloquial and classical Arabic phrases I did not fully understand, and this often elicited rich explanations of concepts and descriptions of social life. I included a set of projective tests (Rorschach, Thematic Apperception Test, sentence completion, and early memories protocol), which I interpret qualitatively and use to support or cast doubt on inferences I initially draw from the life history portions. I do not seek to reconstruct developmental histories of their lives but to analyze each verbatim text as a set of self-representational "story segments"[38]—75 in Mohammed's narrative, 178 in Hussein's, 135 in Rachida's, and 142 in Khadija's—which I examined one at a time for their affective content and for their conceptual and symbolic organization.[39]

My interviewees' motives for participating were complex, never clear to me, and probably not obvious to them. Our long residence in the area and work with the highly regarded Ministry of Agriculture gave us reputations as outsiders who liked Morocco and respected Moroccans but never quelled suspicion about our objectives or the mixture of envy and resentment that privileged Westerners evoke. As an American and a *professeur*, my gaze always had great power to threaten and to affirm, which my respondents' gaze cast upon me did not. Complex forms of transference and countertransference developed in all of these interactions, but I did not try to bring these up as topics of discussion, and so I can only speculate about their character and influence. I believe I conveyed a sense of engaged interest and "unconditional positive regard," which, together with my outsider status, created relationships in which some respondents talked about experiences they had never before discussed—and this may have had some beneficial effect for them. In two instances, when interviewees voiced discontents they had no means to resolve, I suspect it had detrimental effects. All narrated their lives in a space of moral and motivational ambiguity that feels at once comfortable and unsettling—as do "depth" interviews in one's own culture.

All four of the lives described in this book show a good deal of emotional distress and conflict, which I sometimes use clinical terms to describe. But this is not a clinical study, and it is important to keep in mind that all lives are to some extent organized around turmoil and distress. As Erik Erikson repeatedly emphasized, health lies not in the absence of conflict but in the ability to make it meaningful. Narratives of ordinary Americans show abundant psychological conflict and struggles for meaning, though I believe poverty, malnutrition, and poor health care intensify forms of distress for rural Moroccans that most Americans, with their greater material resources, can ameliorate.

The four young adults whose life narratives I analyze in this book are

- Mohammed: A respected manager of a local cooperative and father of three, he describes going "wild" as a bright but delinquent teen. After a troubling stint in the army and a spiritual rebirth, he has returned home to live a "clean," devoutly religious life in his father's home in Skoura—with which, it turns out, he feels deeply dissatisfied.
- Hussein: After failing his second-year university exams, he sits at home "with neither work nor rest," alternately keeping alive his dream of an urbane, urban life, retreating into what he imagines was the healthy, natural life of tribal tradition, and listening with increasing interest to Islamist preachers.
- Rachida: A devoutly religious teacher, she has used her career success to fend off marriage proposals and remain at home, where she has carved out a remarkable degree of independence within her interde-

pendent extended family. She alternately argues passionately for women's equality with men and claims that women are prone to chaotic emotions and need male authorities to control them.

• Khadija: A bank secretary with a bad reputation, she says she is split into a "French Khadija," who drinks, smokes, wears pants like a man, and has "love affairs," and a "Moroccan Khadija," who dreads the Judgment Day, regrets all that the French Khadija thinks and does, and yearns for forgiveness.

And the others with whom I recorded life histories:

• Mohammed K: A twenty-seven-year-old agricultural "engineer" with a master's degree in soil science from a French university, he was marking time in Ouarzazate while hoping for a transfer to a larger Moroccan city. He had grown up in a rural farming family, and after several unsuccessful "modern"-style courtships, he had recently asked his mother to find a spouse for him from his home village.

• Ahmad: A twenty-eight-year-old tenured high school science teacher, he was living in a large wing of his parents' home in Ouarzazate, where, with his education and income, he acted as the effective head of his household. The first boy from his neighborhood to pass the baccalaureate and attend college, he had traveled extensively in Europe and was the most modern of those I interviewed. He also was the most traditional, in that he was emerging as a religious leader in his community and was arranging to be married to a prestigious family's eldest daughter, whom he did not know.

• Said: A twenty-two-year-old university student from a poor farming family in a hamlet of Skoura, he was a professed agnostic who felt estranged from much of Moroccan tradition but also from Western materialism. His father was old and ill, and he had decided to drop out of school to work and support his mother and two younger siblings, both of whom were doing well at school but couldn't continue without a family income.

• Mohammed B.: A nineteen-year-old high school junior from one of the most conservative religious families in Skoura, he was struggling with secular worldviews he finds increasingly appealing and with the lure of Ouarzazate's vices, available to him because he lives away from home in the school's dormitory.

• Nasser: A rather conventional twenty-one-year-old, he had been forced to repeat his senior year of high school in Ouarzazate for the second time and so quit school and came home to Agdez. There his father had him unhappily working in the family's fields and in the marginally profitable café his older brother ran near the highway. A heavy smoker and sometimes drinker, he felt he hadn't taken school seriously enough and alternately blamed himself for letting down his family and his father for failing to understand his problems. Shudder-ing at the future Agdez seemed to hold for him, he felt he didn't now know how to get out.

- Mebarik: A thirty-two-year-old farmer, he was the oldest and least educated of those I interviewed. Married and the father of three, he was an agricultural innovator in Skoura but also a controversial figure because he had installed gasoline engines to pump water from deep wells that farmers farther down the slope believed would have flowed into their unmechanized wells. Probably because of these disputes, he found ways to make himself unavailable to all but social visits after the second taped interview.

- Naima: A high school–educated, twenty-six-year-old, full-time mother of four, she had been abused as a child. As a teen, she became addicted to watching French movies on TV and dreaming that a hero would step out of the screen and spirit her away. One day, something like that happened. A young Frenchman came to Agdez with a health care project and fell in love with the region, the language, and Islam. His Sufi *sheikh* (master) told him he needed to marry, and a friend suggested he propose to Naima, whom he did not know. She ac-cepted. To her alternating contentment and dismay, she soon found herself living a few doors from her mother and becoming a more traditional wife and mother than many of her high school friends. Recollections of abuse turned overwhelming in the second interview, and she asked to do no more.

On Writing about Lives ❀

Freud set the literary standard for writing case histories by infusing clinical description with the rhetoric of mystery novels and casting himself as a de-tective hunting down the clues that would solve his patients' symptoms.[40] More recently, psychiatrist Robert Coles has written an evocative series of books about the psychological struggles of ordinary people caught up in so-cial strife[41] and living on the margins of mainstream America.[42] He eschews technical terms and detective work in favor of literary portraits of people and their landscapes. Few ethnographers have written more beautifully about the textures of daily life than Lila Abu-Lughod on Bedouin women[43] or Unni Wikan on women in urban Cairo.[44] Other ethnographers—such as Kevin Dwyer[45] and Ruth Behar[46]—have relied on their respondents' words, some-times working with them to edit their interview texts into coauthored auto-biographies.

My writing differs from all of these styles, most of all in its focus on the analysis of verbatim interview texts. I have not written biographies, nor have I let my respondents tell their own stories (with the brief exception of Khadija in chapter 6), nor do I set up mysteries to be solved. I am especially concerned to show the evidence on which my inferences rest, so I often include passages that may seem repetitive. The imperative of providing evidence also leads me to discuss details I would happily omit from a biography, a detective story, or a life told in the respondent's own words. I hope the absence of literary devices makes it easier to follow and evaluate my interpretations. But I also hope that evocative life portraits will emerge from each chapter and that the narrative passages will enable readers to hear these young Moroccans speak for themselves. Four individuals can hardly represent Morocco, let alone the vast area and varied cultures of "the Middle East." But I believe their life narratives nonetheless show important dimensions of what Erik Erikson termed the *task* of identity development throughout the region.

Oyserman and colleagues express the view of many psychologists when they write that "cultural psychology's goal is to identify cultural contingencies that moderate individuals' thought and behavior, *not to provide a rich description of a specific culture, or a communal farmer within a culture.*"[47] Comparing group averages on values or self-attributions certainly helps identify psychologically important "cultural contingencies," but a cultural psychology based *only* on group averages yields precisely the false picture of uniformity currently being taught by many textbooks. Rich descriptions of specific cultures are no less essential to building cultural psychology than are rich descriptions of the geology of Mars to building a theory of planetary evolution—which is why the MER rovers are digging through Martian rocks as I write. No one studies a communal farmer's life or self just to describe it richly. The study-of-lives objective is to microscopically examine the interaction of culture and psyche. Science progresses by devising methods for getting orders of magnitude closer to the phenomena, which is what telescopes, microscopes, planetary probes, and life history interviews accomplish. Cultural psychology needs large sample surveys, laboratory experiments, and depth studies of lives to play complementary roles. One studies a communal farmer or a devout schoolteacher or a secretary with a bad reputation or an unemployed young man "sitting with neither work nor rest" in order to build more sophisticated theory. Sometimes, however, it's also possible to richly describe individuals struggling for meaningful lives and perhaps make it easier for Westerners to understand why "they" come to embrace or reject "our" way of life.

Theory

Men on the Moon; Girls on the Beach

Brahim-n-Ait Ali ou Hamou, an illiterate farmer in the pre-Saharan foothills of Morocco's High Atlas mountains, lectured us often about the traditional life he lived and the modern one he sought. One day we discussed these matters over tea and almonds in the guest room of his rambling and frayed rammed-earth home, as his fellow tribesmen gathered across the dry riverbed at the tomb of the village's patron saint to celebrate the Prophet's birthday. Each region was bringing its contribution: barley and olive oil from the plains, a ram from the mountains, shrubby firewood from what was left of the forest. All morning the men chanted in the mosque, and the women came in small groups to make personal offerings and pleas to the saint.

At midday, the paths and rooftops crowded with spectators, and the ram was led into a cluster of white-robed men and tossed onto its back. Four teen-aged boys grabbed its legs, the men chanted a prayer, the imam slashed its throat, and the race was on: to run the blood-spurting ram through the neighborhood of the saint's lineage to the irrigation canal, where in order to bring bountiful water in the following year, the young men must dunk it before it expires, mingling its blood with the water, both of which are rich with baraka, God's bounty or blessing. Children ran to snatch tufts of baraka-filled wool for their mothers and sisters, who burn it in charcoal braziers and inhale its baraka-rich fumes. Then the ram was butchered, and the saint's descendants prepared couscous to share its baraka-rich meat with the lay villagers surrounding them. A ritual of reciprocity, like those staged in so many traditional societies: the products of the preceding year drawn in to make a sacrifice for the approaching one and then dispersed as a collective meal that celebrates the unity before God of the social segments nested within segments, which formerly—and occasionally today—were set at each other's throats. The saint's descendants act as a kind of Leyden jar that collects baraka from the chain of holy ancestors and ionizes all the local products that pass through it in the ritual state.

"No," Brahim said, "I'm not going over there. I don't have time. Look, America's gone to the moon and we're still dunking sheep in the canal? That won't get us anywhere. We've got work to do." Break the reciprocity[1]— break the chain that ties not only the saint to the Prophet but also Brahim to the three acres of terraced fields that he must cultivate by hoe and harvest by hand yet yield only half the barley he needs to keep his family in bread and cous-cous. Those precious strips of deep green chiseled into the rocky wastes that used to yield such baraka now give Brahim endless, Sisyphean labor. But he had plans. The bumpy dirt road to his village was soon to be paved, and this would bring tourists to the café he owned on a little hill above the weekly market site. In the meantime, he had begun to sell butane-fueled ovens, shipped from his brother in Casablanca, to the local families with incomes from sons working as "guests" in Europe. If he prospered, he said, he would move to Casablanca, to a concrete-block house with electricity, running water, and a bathroom.

Far to the north, in Tangier, the Hajj Mohammed lives in a concrete-block house with electricity, running water, and a bathroom. A decade older than our friend Brahim when anthropologist Henry Munson[2] interviewed him, he, too, had wanted a modern life. He left his boyhood village for France, where he worked in a mine and made each hour what a Casablanca factory worker makes in a day. He made the pilgrimage to Mecca and became "the Hajj," but then his fortunes turned. His uncle cheated him of his inheritance, and the Hajj was too generous and too easily conned to keep his money. So today he scrapes by, peddling "the junk of Christians" in the Tangier flea market, leaning on the charity of his wealthy brother, and fuming with resentment:

> We thought that once we obtained independence everything would be wonderful. We thought we Muslims would live the way the Christians live, with villas, cars, and servants. But now we are no better off than we were under the Christians. Now the Fassis [wealthy merchants from Fes] rule as the Christians used to. They have villas, cars, and servants. But those of us who toil for a mouthful of bread have gained nothing since independence. . . .
>
> And the Fassis and the other rich Moroccans have forgotten their religion. They have become like Christians. Sometimes they speak French among themselves. They send their children to French schools. They marry French women. And even their Muslim wives and daughters bare their bodies like Christian whores. They wear bikinis at the beach and short skirts and low-cut blouses in the streets.[3]

In his remote hamlet of adobe castles, Brahim sees an astronaut land on the moon and turns against tradition. In the bright lights of Morocco's most international city, the Hajj watches young people aping the French and seethes against modernity:

> *Why does God allow the Christians to live like sultans in our land while we are like slaves in their land? This is God's punishment. And this is God's test. Muslims have left the path of Islam. . . . Until we return to the path of Islam, the Christians will continue to control our stores, our factories, our hotels, our mines, and the minds of our young people. . . . Some day, God willing, we shall arise and cleanse the house of Islam of all Christian filth.*[4]

Brahim's and Mohammed's views reflect a pervasive debate on the values of tradition and modernity, on backwardness and development, and on the worth of indigenous versus Western ways. This debate goes on in surprisingly similar ways from Morocco to Pakistan, and it spares no detail of daily life. It has become impossible *not* to declare one's stance by one's dress, speech, table manners, hygiene habits, and scores of other outward signs. Tunisian sociologist Aziz Krichen evocatively describes how, in the decades since Independence, education and media have intensified European influence and turned North African societies into worlds of duality:

> Dualism in the economy with the traditional sectors and modern sectors . . . dualism of urban spaces with the contrast between the medina and the European-style city . . . dualism of administration, justice, education, religion, press, artistic and sports activities. . . . Even foolishness was affected . . . with psychiatrists on one side and sorcerers and witch doctors on the other. . . .[5]

The constantly disputed terms of this dualism form a "rhetoric of development" that permeates the culture of Morocco and of much of the Middle East.

A theory of "culture and self" must take account of how pervasively this duality shapes the self-presentations and self-perceptions of those who live in it. And the duality influences not only the identities fashioned as individuals enter adulthood but also the entire course of psychological development. For beneath the volatile debates about tradition and modernity, Moroccans have since birth been enmeshed in relationships and social institutions that have mixtures of traditional and modern features, sometimes creating developmental discontinuities and defining important "developmental tasks" that differ from those typical of life courses in America, Japan, India, and other cultures.

This chapter outlines the theoretical model I use to analyze the life narratives and to describe the psychological effects of Morocco's distinctive mixture of North African–Muslim tradition and Western-style modernity. The first section sketches the model of personality organization I took into the field. It begins by reviewing social psychological models of self, Erik Erikson's theory of psychosocial identity, and the distinction between personality genotype and phenotype developed by Kurt Lewin, Gordon Allport, and Robert LeVine. It then outlines the model of multiple identities developed in my *Self Representation*, based on life-history interviews with Americans. The second section examines three lines of research on North Africans carried out by American ethnographers: studies of the cultural construction of persons by Clifford Geertz, Lawrence Rosen, and Dale Eickelman; a 1950 study of acculturation in Algeria by Horace Minor and George DeVos; and Vincent Crapanzano's studies of the Hamadsha, a religious brotherhood that practices trance dancing and the healing of spirit-related disorders. I leave discussion of most Moroccan and Middle Eastern theorists for the narrative chapters, but the third section of the chapter, "Cultural Dualities," summarizes accounts from other regions of the Middle East that show how public disputes about Western-style modernization can influence the formation of personal identities. It ends with consideration of the complex role that identification with the Other plays in the formation of identity; for the Moroccans I interviewed, this means both the modern Other living in Casablanca and France and the traditional Other living in the pre-Saharan hinterlands.

Theories of Identity ❀

Anthropologists who study the cultural construction of self tend to assume it is formed either in accordance with a culture's "concept of personhood" or by its rituals and etiquettes of social interaction. Clifford Geertz's influential analysis of self-construction in Morocco takes this approach.[6] Those influenced by postmodern theories, by contrast, view culture as comprised of conflicting discourses and regard the self as a "site" where discourses typically intersect, producing fluid, continually shifting selves. Janice Boddy's analysis of Sudanese women who join spirit-possession cults takes this approach, viewing the women as developing selves defined by the hegemonic (official and dominant) discourse of orthodox Islam, and "antiselves" defined by the counterhegemonic discourse of spirit possession.[7] Most cross-cultural psychologists take approaches that differ from both of these and adopt information-processing models that assume individuals form clusters of self-attributions or hierarchies of self-schemas based on the (often biased) inferences they make about their dispositions and regularities in their social behavior. Some of these self-schemas may come to have traitlike permanence and guide an individual in nearly all situations; others may be elicited for transient use in particular social contexts.

The 1990s saw an explosion of research by both anthropologists and cross-cultural psychologists on the formation of "independent" selves in "individualist" cultures versus "interdependent" selves in "collectivist" cultures. The way was led in the early 1980s by Hofstede's worldwide survey of IBM employees, which found evidence that cultures could be ranked on a dimension of individualist versus collectivist values (or "I versus C"),[8] by Shweder and Bourne's contrast of "sociocentric" Indian versus "egocentric" American selves,[9] and by Geertz's discussion of the Moroccan "mosaic" self, in which he made the following often-quoted observation:

> The Western conception of the person as a bounded, unique, more or less integrated motivational and cognitive universe, a dynamic center of awareness, emotion, judgment, and action organized into a distinctive whole and set contrastively both against other such wholes and against its social and natural background, is, however incorrigible it may seem to us, a rather peculiar idea within the context of the world's cultures.[10]

Markus and Kitayama developed this contrast in their 1991 "Culture and Self" but mixed two models of self that actually differ in important ways.[11] On the one hand, they followed Geertz in suggesting that Western independent selves have solid boundaries separating them from others, whereas Asian interdependent selves have permeable boundaries that enmesh them in social relationships. This notion surprisingly echoes earlier ethnocentric views that Western civilization evolved to a higher level than "primitive" cultures by hatching the autonomous individual from its long incubating immersion in kinship relations. In the same paper, Markus and Kitayama proposed a "repertoire of schemata" model of self, according to which people in all cultures have independent *and* interdependent self-schemas, but cultures differ in which they frequently elicit.

Sharp criticisms have been leveled at both anthropological and psychological studies of culture and self. In 1990, Robert LeVine objected to the resurgence of "Eurocentric social evolutionism" in the new wave of studies, which seemed to embrace the view that "the world's peoples can be divided into those who rely on psychic organization and those who rely on social organization for the fulfillment of the basic ego functions."[12] He insisted that even seemingly simple cultures can have "specific behavioral domains" that entail differing principles of self-organization. In 1993, Melford Spiro criticized the notion that a culture's social etiquettes or "concept of personhood" reflects the selves of its members and insisted that individuals often don't think of themselves—or experience themselves—in the ways their culture prescribes, so that it is possible for few or even no members of a culture to develop selves congruent with their culture's construction of self.[13] The view advanced by many psychologists—that cultures can be ranked on a scale of individualism versus collectivism and that these orientations shape egocentric versus sociocentric selves—has been repeatedly criticized for misrepresenting both Western and non-Western cultures.[14] Matsumoto marshals evidence that this does not hold for the United States and Japan, which are typically cited as the archetypal contrast.[15] Triandis has repeatedly argued that individualism should not be equated with the Western form of modernity and pointed out that hunter-gather cultures tend to be individualist and that collectivism appears most strongly associated with peasant agricultural societies rather than simply with non-Western ones.[16] As Spiro noted, the premier Western theorists of self—William James, G. H. Mead, and Erik Erikson—all propose thoroughly sociocentric models, matching Markus and Kitayama's diagram of the *interdependent* self.

A number of researchers have moved beyond the simple contrast of I versus C, and a consensus appears to be emerging that people in all cultures develop multiple self-conceptions and that all cultures have multiple domains that elicit different self-schemas.[17] Other studies by Markus and her colleagues have emphasized the "repertoire of schemata" rather than the "boundary permeability" formulation, some investigating relationships among "possible selves."[18] As early as 1989, Triandis proposed that individuals have "private," "public," and "collective" selves and that the frequency with which each is elicited depends not only on a culture's I versus C orientation but also on its degree of complexity and on the tightness versus looseness of its social norms.[19] Many researchers have followed his lead and used "priming" experiments to study how cultural contexts "sample" schema from these three selves.[20] These views converge with recent theories of acculturation, which have moved away from viewing it as a unidimensional process, in which individuals gradually lose their immigrant or minority identities as they develop a majority culture identity, toward an "alternation"[21] model that recognizes the prevalence of multiple "bicultural"[22] and "hybrid"[23] identities. Inspired by the writings of W. E. B. DuBois and Malcolm X, researchers studying ethnic identity have long recognized that disadvantaged minority status readily sets up dualities of identity, as individuals internalize both their in-group's standards and the majority group's stereotypes of them. Most models of ethnic identity development hypothesize dramatic shifts in reference groups and identities, ideally progressing toward a bicultural maturity.[24] Studies by Hong and colleagues[25] and Verkuyten and Pouliasi[26] demonstrate that bicultural individuals can master and shift identities between cultural frames with relative ease. These developments may even signal convergence with discourse and narrative approaches, which have long recognized the self's multiple voices.

Narrative Theories of Identity

Recent studies of identity within the framework of "narrative psychology" have yielded models that differ on key points from the information-processing models adopted by most social psychologists. Narrative theories reject the prevailing information-processing notion that identity can be mapped as a collection, cluster, or hierarchy of self-schemas, in favor of the view that it is organized as a story, in which plots, characters, dialogues, and symbols serve as the crucial elements.[27] Narrative psychologists share the conviction of many cognitive psychologists that the human brain/mind has evolved to automatically construe aspects of experience via story structures,[28] a view that converges with the argument by some phenomenologists that humans cannot order experience without plot structures, regardless of whether lives or human history "really" have any order.[29] Narrative theories differ, however, in which features of story structure they emphasize. Jerome Bruner sees *plot structure* as bringing coherence to the multitude of characters and actions animating a life story.[30] Hubert Hermans draws on Bakhtin's theory of the "polyphonic" novel to account for the way a person's self appears distributed among the characters in his or her life narrative, such that "the" self does not coincide with any single figure but is organized as the *dialogue* among them.[31] My model emphasizes the crucial role played by key *symbols* and *metaphors* in orchestrating plots and dialogues, and especially in eliciting emotions and linking them to conceptual interpretations.[32] In what remains perhaps the most complete account, Dan McAdams incorporates many of these narrative elements, and his own work investigates *themas* and *scripts*—constructs he develops from Henry Murray and Sylvan Tomkins, respectively.[33]

Narrative studies of identity use a variety of data-collection and analysis methods. McAdams often takes a *nomothetic* approach,[34] using coders to scale features of life stories so that he can explore their statistical associations with other characteristics (e.g., gender, ethnicity, personality traits). Others use variants of the *idiographic* procedure[35] George Kelly devised as an adjunct to life-history interviews.[36] Kelly theorized that people develop a relatively small number of "personal constructs"—which now would be termed *schemas*—that define their identities and relationships with others. Unlike schema models, however, Kelly believed personal constructs take the form of bipolar contrasts. His Role Construct Repertory (REP) test is a grid on which the subject describes ways significant people resemble and differ from one another; he or she then gives a numeric rating to each individual for each similarity-difference contrast. The resulting matrix can be factor-analyzed to yield a small set of underlying bipolar constructs unique to that individual. Seymour Rosenberg and his colleagues have devised a similar idiographic procedure that uses semistructured interviews to elicit a matrix of identities by features (traitlike personal attributes) and then employs a clustering technique to yield a map of the hierarchical organization of multiple identities.[37] Hubert Hermans and Peter Raggatt have developed idiographic structured-interview methods for identifying selves in dialogue,[38] and Bruner, I, and many others use extended life-history interviews and narrative analysis techniques.

Few narrative theorists are concerned with the accuracy of life stories. Most view them as mythic, not only in the sense that they may depart from what objective observers would assert to be "the facts" but also more fundamentally in their design. Myths and stories inherently reach beyond the facts, neglecting and distorting them for the sake of creating deeper meanings and emotionally exciting or calming, inspiring or comforting story lines. It is the mythic characters and story lines animating life narratives that structure identities and carry out the crucial work[39] of linking an individual's life trajectory with predominant mythic themes from his or her culture. When researchers who take information-processing approaches ask individuals to fill out paper-and-pencil scales, they essentially ask them to lay templates atop their mythic story lines and extract features in the form of clusters or hierarchies of self-schemas that the researchers then compare across cultures. This approach may identify important cultural differences, but the extracted schemas may provide an inadequate and misleading account of identities fashioned as mythic story lines. And at the present time, faced with a global resurgence of ethnic, ultranationalist, and fundamentalist identities, the "cold" information-processing models appear to be of little help in understanding the "hot" emotions driving quests for mythic story lines to live, kill, and die by.

In spite of recent advances in recognizing the multiplicity of identity and the complexity of cultures, many researchers studying culture and self continue to use *self* in imprecise ways, often within a single publication: as prevailing cultural values, as a culture's "concept of person," as an egolike structure with solid versus permeable boundaries, as clusters or hierarchies of self-schemas, as a culturally shared "sense of self," as a collection of explicit self-concepts or social stereotypes, as metaphoric self-symbols or implicit story scripts. They also differ in whether they view the self as constructed afresh from situation to situation or as an internal structure with its own developmental history. And they differ in whether they regard the self as one component of personality or as the totality of a person's "character." Discourse theorists, who have been most attentive to the self's multiplicity, have had difficulty formulating a theory of its organization, with some following Michel Foucault in suggesting that the self has dissipated into fragments in postmodern conditions.[40] Most disturbing, textbook writers continue to present only the simple contrast of I versus C or egocentric versus sociocentric selves, often with ethnocentric illustrations.

The present research employs a narrative model that differs from those adopted in most studies of culture and self. In fact, the self is not its central construct. Rather, it investigates the organization of *identity* and its crucial role in integrating an individual's *personality* and in creating meaningful engagements with that person's cultural environment. It regards both of these—integrating one's personality and fashioning a meaningful life in one's society—as challenging developmental tasks that take work to achieve and sustain and that take different forms in successive life stages. It therefore emphasizes the ways identity is designed to manage emotional and motivational tensions within personality, tensions often created in the process of adapting one's temperament to prevailing cultural values. It views development as requiring individuals to amplify some emotions and motives and to suppress others—a process that may go smoothly or create turmoil. This emphasis on emotion distances my narrative approach from prevailing schema models and brings it closer to studies of culture and emotion, which affirm the universality of core human emotions *and* the cultural specificity of the display rules to which their expression is adapted.[41] It nonetheless differs from culture-and-emotion research in examining how styles of emotional regulation organize personality and identity.

In line with the early "configurationist" theory of culture and personality, the approach taken in this book recognizes that cultures selectively favor particular emotions and motives from what Ruth Benedict termed the "great arc of human possibility"[42] and ignore or condemn others, which leaves many individuals whose personalities do not closely fit their culture's predominant values struggling for meaningful lives. This approach also recognizes Erik Erikson's observation that rapid social change can disrupt the continuity of child-adolescent-adult development, intensifying the personality-culture misfit for what seems like an entire generation. And when young people's struggles to fit themselves to their culture turns into a struggle to create a culture that fits them, they sometimes change the course of history—which appears to be occurring in many Middle Eastern societies.

Erikson's Theory of Identity

My notion of identity builds directly on Erik Erikson's work.[43] The place of "psychosocial identity" in his eight-stage scheme of development is well known: The consolidation of an identity appears as the focal developmental task of late adolescence and makes possible an acceptance of adult challenges and responsibilities. This reorganization of personality begins in mid-adolescence, triggered by (1) the bodily and emotional changes associated with puberty, (2) the social assignment of new institutional and interpersonal roles, and (3) the cognitive acquisition of formal operational thought (the ability to manipulate systems of abstractions), which converge to disequilibrate a late childhood self-regulatory system. The prolonged adolescence of modern societies often makes this a period of psychosocial moratorium, in which the individual no longer remains a child but has yet to make commitments to adult roles. This intensifies the challenge of integrating new features of life into an ego structure that will provide a self-regulatory system for adulthood. The task of identity formation typically takes shape in the form of deep and often troubling questions: Who am I? What do I believe in? What will I live for? The answers to these questions, at least when confirmed by one's community, consolidate an ego identity that enables an individual to move from what often appears as a rather narcissistic concern with creating himself or herself to the young adult tasks of forging bonds of intimacy with others and building a world through one's work.

But how does identity provide a system of integration and self-regulation? Here Erikson develops two crucial theses that summarizers of his theory often fail to note. Both are entailed in his view that identity consists not just of an image of one's self, or of a group of qualities attributed to one's self, but of a global value system that requires construction of a world enlivened with personal relevance in such a way that authentic ideals and defensive distortions become complexly interwoven. First, Erikson formulates the eight developmental ages as stages of ego integration, not of identity development per se. Identity per se does not come into existence until the fifth stage, because the biosocial experiences and cognitive operations required to construct it have not yet developed. Who one perceives oneself to be may indeed change during any stage, but identity per se develops through three successive structures: introjection, identification, and identity proper.

According to Erikson, introjection—the "primitive" fantasy or sense of fusing with an object by incorporating it—operates during infancy. As a child passes through the phases of separation and individuation that occur in the second and third years of life, identification—imagining or wishing to be like someone, usually a parent or sibling—begins to replace introjection as the primary orienting and self-regulating attachment. In adolescence, formal operational thought makes possible new forms of abstract thinking, and these fashion value and ideological systems in which other individuals come to function as *symbols* of abstract qualities. Identifications do not disappear, but their incorporation into more comprehensive and subtler value systems transforms their psychological character. As symbols, identifications come to stand for principles and styles of life—so that the Jesus of a ten-year-old is not that of a twenty-year-old, which is why we balk at describing a ten-year-old as a Christian, no matter how much the child admires or even prays to Christ.

The second point is that identity takes shape as an *ideology* in the political sense of the term. An identity reintegrates a disequilibrated ego by linking a young person's new body, with its new sexual, physical, and intellectual powers, to valued and devalued positions in the adult social order. That is, it organizes personality by orienting it toward a place in the world and a life trajectory through the social order. I use the terms *place* and *trajectory* to distinguish this notion from *role* because Erikson's work emphasizes the fact that identity is not simply a constellation of roles (lawyer, father, runner, etc.), but a way of life that transcends specific roles by interpreting their significance, by judging them, and by integrating them within a larger framework. American life narratives indeed show roles to be important, but as symbolic embodiments or betrayals of one's values and as public statements of one's personal worth or worthlessness. They also show that personal values tend to be represented—as Erikson believed—in terms of macrosocial symbols rather than of microsocial roles, building identities around what it means to be male or female, white or black, a professional or a worker, and other factors. Identity takes ideological shape not only because it employs politicized symbols of a person's place in the social order but also because it represents a strategy for achieving, mastering, and defending one's place. A person enacts or *deploys* an identity as a kind of propaganda[44] to present a self to others—as Erving Goffman has so elegantly shown[45]—to convince others of one's talents and of the legitimacy of one's pursuits. But of even greater psychological importance, a person deploys his or her identity as a kind of internal propaganda: at times as self-justification, at times as a moral self-critique, at times as an exhortation to strive, endure, or resist temptation.

As a value system and political ideology, then, an identity must differentiate and judge the new powers of a young adult's body and mind and represent them in terms of concepts, images, and symbols that simultaneously label and evaluate the range of possible stances a person might take in the adult social world. To differentiate and judge means that some of one's impulses (or desires, fantasies, emotional reactions, etc.) will be positively valued, represented as associated with admired figures, and embraced as one's own, and others will be negatively valued, represented as associated with feared or despised figures, and often rejected as not being one's own. Again and again, Erikson shows how identity tends to be structured as a system of usually positive self-representations (embraced as "Me") set in opposition to usually negative self-representations (rejected as "not-Me") that have been disowned and rendered "ego dystonic" by being projected across the boundaries of gender, race, religion, and nationality, where they coalesce into stereotypic representations of out-groups.[46] His biography of Martin Luther,[47] for example, describes three identity "elements": a "mute," who falls silent before religious authorities as had Martin as a child before his father; the rebel "spokesman" son, who posted his theses on the Wittenberg church door as a challenge to the pope; and the "father," who argued that rebellious peasants were "not worth answering with arguments. . . . The answer for such mouths is a fist that brings blood from the nose,"[48] much as Martin's father had bloodied him with his fists. Luther's identity, Erikson writes, consists of a configuration of these elements, each a relation or dialogue between figures of authority and rebellion.

This symbolic structure facilitates affective self-regulation by recruiting the powerful pressures of group membership and community support to the intrapsychic struggle to cultivate positive impulses and resist temptations to indulge the negative. Thus a hard-driving high-achiever's yearning for nurturance and dependence may become easier to resist when represented (that is, "projected") as the sloth that destines the poor to their lives of indulgence, filth, and despair (see chapter 7 of my *Self Representation*). Erikson's deep concern for the ideological consequences of normal identity consolidation—ethnocentrism versus an embracing of plurality—pervades his work. He repeatedly seeks to distinguish "wholistic" consolidations of identity that incorporate all of the potentially contradictory elements of one's personality from "totalistic" ones that leave individuals like Luther despising groups that come to represent elements they try to excise. Yet he never fully comes to grips with the implications of his theory. Erikson's anthropological outlook led him to see the social function of identity as binding young adults to their in-group and made him reluctant to term ethnocentric identities "pathological." But as a refugee from the Holocaust and as a clinician who had seen that identity *can* coalesce around nonethnocentric distinctions, he also remained reluctant to term ethnocentric identities "healthy."

Self Representation

The model I took into the field combines Erikson's view of identity's role in integrating personality with "structuralist" theories of narrative, especially Claude Lévi-Strauss's analyses of myth.[49] It emphasizes the centrality of Erikson's insight about the ways people use fictional figures, social stereotypes, and real others to narratively represent both the ideals they embrace and aspects of their personalities they deny, disown, and project. In structuralist or semiotic terms, Erikson shows identity to be organized as a system of binary *Me* versus *not-Me* representations, such that a researcher cannot know what a *self*-representation means without also knowing the *not-self* or *antiself* representation(s) that defines it by contrast. He also shows that the signs and symbols that anchor the differentiation of inner states by linking them to *Me* versus *not-Me* oppositions tend to be drawn from a society's map of hierarchy and inequality: race, gender, class or caste, religion, and the like. Story-by-story analyses of American life narratives show these boundary-marking signs to be central to self representation. Parallel *Me* versus *not-Me* oppositions typically appear in accounts of adult relationships, early memories, Thematic Apperception Test stories, and political opinions. The temporal axis of the stories making up a narrative has a melodic character, in which transformations of *past-Me* representations into *present-Me* and *future-Me* representations are played again and again, in differing contexts and differing periods of time. The stories also set up a harmonic axis, which defines *Me* representations in opposition to *not-Me* Others at each "beat" of time, and these contrasts parallel those of the melodic axis. Even when life narratives focus on face-to-face relationships, these tend to be figuratively represented in terms of concepts and tropes drawn from a stereotypic map of the macrosocial order. And even an individual's earliest memories often encode ethnic, political, and religious meanings in ways that suggest they have been selected and revised in accordance with structures of adult identity, as if to establish a set of Kuhnian exemplars to show how one's world paradigmatically works.

As should be clear, this model of identity also draws on Freud's famous paper "Negation,"[50] in which he argues that primary process thought knows no negation, which secondary process thought accomplishes by affixing a distorting negation sign that renders a motive or self representation unrecognizable as one's own. A frightening or immoral wish thus may appear clearly in a person's conscious thought but as belonging to another person, whose otherness signifies negation. Here my model also draws on *The Authoritarian Personality*,[51] which treats ethnocentric stereotypes (of race, religion, gender, social class, etc.) as society's basic lexicon of negation signs. That study regarded *rigid* personality constellations as employing these to semiotically disown what Freud termed *incompatible ideas*. In other words, what the anti-Semite dislikes about Jews are his or her own negated (and then projected) qualities. A close reading of that work, however, suggests that the use of social categories to represent identity in *Me* versus *not-Me* oppositions may be a universal process, among democratic as well as authoritarian types (see chapter 2, *Self Representation*). Although rigid personality constellations do appear to produce rigidly ethnocentric identities, life narratives indicate that most (and perhaps all) individuals draw on group stereotypes to define themselves by contrast to *not-Me* representations. The difference between authoritarian and democratic personalities appears to lie less in the *use* of stereotypes than in *which* stereotypes one employs, in *how rigidly* one holds them, in whether one identifies or disidentifies with traditionally scapegoated groups, and in whether one wishes to destroy or protect the *not-Me* Other.

My model of identity also incorporates G. H. Mead's theory that the self is organized as a social structure, which arises from imaginatively taking the perspective of Others on one's self in progressively more global, macrosocial contexts. Mead suggests that as a member of a sports team comes to see his or her role within the whole field of the game's positions and strategies, so an individual develops a self as a position and set of roles within a social structure. He believed that this process developmentally differentiates and integrates the self in the sort of encompassing manner Erikson would term *wholistic*. But he also struggled to reconcile this optimism with his disturbing recognition that individuals often experience the greatest coherence of self when they identify with the Generalized Other of their national or ethnic in-group, in hostility to an out-group (see chapter 8 of *Self Representation*). It is this intersubjective process[52] of seeing one's self from shifting social perspectives that so deeply internalizes a stereotypic map of the macrosocial order and structures an internal dialogue about who one is—between "I" and "Me" poles of the self, for Mead—in terms of societal stereotypes. Indeed, the primary value of life narratives derives from their potential to reveal *structures of dialogue*[53] and to show identity not simply as a set of values or hierarchy of self-concepts but as an orchestration of shifting social positions and stances in continual dispute.

And if, as G. H. Mead maintained, the self has a social structure,[54] then should not different social structures pattern identities—and the integration of personality—along different lines? If gender, class, and ethnicity emerge as the central symbolic axes of self-representation from American life narratives, what dimensions might organize those of young Moroccans living in the villages and towns around Ouarzazate?

Levels of Personality Organization

As Kurt Lewin, Gordon Allport, and Robert LeVine have urged, the model of identity I use makes a fundamental distinction between *genotypic* and *phenotypic* levels of personality. This derives from a straightforward analogy to the biological findings that genetic traits may or may not be expressed in an organism's morphology or behavior and that a gene may be expressed in dramatically different phenotypic forms, depending on the organism's environment during development.[55] Psychological theory, these researchers argue, must similarly distinguish an underlying genotype-like structure of traits, affects, or drives from the phenotype-like motives and behaviors an individual actually exhibits. A person may engage in socially prescribed actions that have no corresponding deep motivation or may suppress strong feelings or wishes so that they never see the light of day. More important, one may express a trait ("need for achievement," for example) as behavior X in one situation and behavior Y in a second, and then engage in behavior Y in a different setting as an expression of a competing trait (perhaps "need for affiliation"). To infer that either behavior X or Y necessarily and always manifests a need for achievement would be to make the error that has nourished a long and senseless debate about the stability of traits and the power of situational stimuli to control behavior.[56]

The important point is that psychological models must take account of the "generative" processes that transform genotypic characteristics into phenotypic ones, that take deep characteristics to the surface or map deep structures onto surface structures. The Freudian defense mechanism *reaction formation* provides an excellent example: an aggressive impulse toward a loved one surfaces as a representation portraying the person as endangered by some other (*not-Me*) source, so the individual represents himself or herself as experiencing only a desire to protect the loved one. Freud's famous "Rat Man" patient thus complained of obsessive ideas that a horrible rat torture might be inflicted on his father or his lover and felt compelled to perform prayers and other nonsensical rituals to protect them (see chapter 1 of my *Self Representation*). The aggressive wishes thus emerged from his genotypic-level personality but were transformed by being construed as issuing from others, so that at the phenotypic level the Rat Man represented himself as a protector. Jung's theory of archetypes similarly describes how one's wishes or fears may be encountered in the world as *projections*, eliciting responses that do not appear to stem from one's own motives.

For example, a politically liberal factory worker I interviewed defined himself both in contrast to his macho, ethnically prejudiced, and conformist coworkers and in opposition to his dictatorial managers, against whom he waged a running "guerilla war" of clever insults and practical jokes (see chapter 6 of *Self Representation*). But he also talked at length about his fascination with tyrannical dictators—Napoleon, Hitler, Idi Amin, and others—who appeared to coalesce into a shadow archetype representing his own capacity for evil. Thus his own genotypic-level aggression was represented as issuing from dictator figures, against whom his phenotypic-level identity set him in opposition. In both of these examples, deep aggressive feelings undergo crucial transformations as they come to the surface, where they appear to emanate from malicious others and thereby represent all that Freud's Rat Man patient and my interviewee strive *not* to be. I do not believe that the psychoanalytic typology of defense mechanisms adequately names or explains such transformations, especially in that all rhetorical devices can accomplish them. But life narratives provide data in which this kind of rhetorical and hence psychological transformation can be traced.

Following Erikson, then, I view identity as "working" to facilitate self-regulation by mapping transformations of genotypic characteristics into phenotypic ones. I endorse no particular theory of genotypic personality, however, nor seek to construct one. The genotype-phenotype distinction can be operationalized in many ways: as biological temperament versus overt behavior or, following Paul Ekman[57] and David Matsumoto,[58] as biologically based affects versus culturally shaped display rules. Robert Levy's notion that each culture systematically *hypercognizes* some emotional states (facilitating their conscious experience and communication) and *hypocognizes* others (effecting something like repression) also accounts for patterned disjunctions between levels of experience.[59] Daniel Stern[60] and Mardi Horowitz[61] also propose layered psychological models that help account for genotype-phenotype transformations. I will follow Robert LeVine's formulation.[62] Personality genotype, he writes,

> refers to a set of enduring individual behavioral dispositions that may or may not find socially acceptable expression in the customary (or institutionalized) behavior of a population. Its major characteristics are early acquisition (through the interaction of constitution and early experience); resistance to elimination in subsequent experience; and capacity for inhibition, generalization, and other transformations under the impact of experiential pressures. . . .
>
> Three broad classes of dispositions comprise the personality genotype:
>
> (1) Basic, probably genetically determined, parameters of individual functioning, such as general activity level and thresholds for perceiving, discriminating, and reacting to stimuli (e.g., arousal and irritability thresholds). . . .
> (2) The motivational residues of early experience. The child's representations of his wishes and fears concerning other persons in his early life provide unconscious prototypes

for his emotional response to others in subsequent environments. . . .

(3) Adaptive organizations that monitor and regulate responses to stimuli coming from the external environment and from internal needs.[63]

By contrast, personality phenotype

refers to the observable regularities of behavior characterizing an adult functioning in the variety of settings comprising his environment. . . . If the individual is functioning normally, his phenotypic personality is a stable organization of characteristics that affords him satisfaction of his perceived needs, enables him to meet social demands and take advantage of sociocultural opportunities, and protects him from excessive anxiety. . . .

One of the most important integrating characteristics of the personality phenotype is a self-concept, an internal mental representation of the self that includes boundaries between, and identities with, the self and other individuals, groups, and ideologies. In his functioning as a member of society, the individual uses this enduring self-concept to monitor his own behavior and to determine the extent to which each of his behavior patterns is ego-syntonic, that is, consistent with his image of himself.[64]

As for the relationship of phenotype to genotype, LeVine explains that:

The phenotype is not independent of the genotype; in a sense, it *is* the personality genotype modified by prolonged normative experience, through the deliberate socialization by parents and through direct participation in the wider social system. . . . In their phenotypic expression, genotypic dispositions may be suppressed and disguised for purposes of social adaptation and conformity, but are not thereby eliminated.[65]

In practice, then, I assume nearly everyone to be capable of experiencing the full range of human emotions but that each person finds himself or herself chronically engaged in struggles with a distinctive configuration of emotional tensions—which I seek to identify from narrative and projective test data as "genotypic-level personality." Provisionally, I draw on psychodynamic terms to describe these affects and some of the highly automatic transformations that operate on them like defense mechanisms. The crucial point is that I will regard genotypic personality as an affective and object-relational pattern rather than a conceptual one. Consisting of diffuse states of arousal, feeling tone, and mood, affects require interpretation and representation for the individual experiencing them to decide what they are and what to do about them. Phenomenologically, a person finds himself or herself "thrown" into a body and nexus of social relations that repeatedly *feel* certain ways; she or he must develop a representational system that interprets and facilitates the management of these chronic tensions. As a value system and ideology, an identity does the work of interpreting, representing, and configuring genotypic affective tensions into a phenotypic personality organization.

Like Lewin and Allport, LeVine distinguishes genotypic and phenotypic levels as an analogy, not literally to refer to genetic endowment versus behavior as modified by experience. But because it remains difficult not to read the terms literally, I will use the term *core personality* to refer to LeVine's genotypic level and *identity* to refer to his phenotypic level. In fact, my analysis of these life narratives convinces me that an important third level of personality organization must be postulated, in a sense "between" core personality and identity. Admiring the parsimony of a two-level, genotype-phenotype model, I resisted this for a long time. But culturally distinctive structures of feeling and relationship schemas appear in at least several of the Moroccan narratives that show too much organization to regard them as core characteristics but that also do not define identities. I gradually came to recognize these as what G. H. Mead describes as a "social self" and Bourdieu as a "habitus."[66] I use the term *social personality* or *social persona* for this intermediary level. These three levels—core personality, social persona, and identity—parallel the three levels of personality organization proposed by McAdams: Level I personal dispositions, Level II needs and motives, and Level III an identity anchored in a life story.[67] I suggest that these levels are mainly shaped in successive developmental periods (early childhood, late childhood, and adolescence–early adulthood) under the influence of different features of a person's culture.

A final point about genotype and phenotype, or core personality and identity: My analyses of the symbolic organization of self representation in American life narratives was strongly influenced by Paul Ricoeur's *Freud and Philosophy*.[68] In that work, Ricoeur showed that the interpretation of a symbol system (such as a religion) requires two readings, both of which he sees entailed by Freud's theory of sublimation. One reading shows how such systems vicariously gratify and defend against deep, often unconscious motivations (I will say *core-level affects*), and so interpretation proceeds by following a path of *regression*, peeling away existential, moral, and aesthetic meanings as defensive distortions that conceal the underlying impulses and conflicts. God, to cite a common oversimplification, emerges from such analysis as a father "writ large."[69]

Ricoeur insists that this strategy tells only half the story, however, and in many respects, the less important half. The other half must be ascertained by reversing direction and following the path of *progression*, by which deep motivations are developed through rhetorical and aesthetic devices to serve as vehicles for the articulation of authentic, sublime meanings—meanings that cannot be explained as defenses against what they indeed defend against.

Thus the fact that God compensates or protects one from deep feelings about one's father may harness the emotional power that enables God to represent sublime and authentic truths. And it may be the fact that God represents sublime and authentic truths that enables Him to function so effectively as a defense. In my view, this double or dialectical interpretive strategy must be followed in the analysis of a life narrative. The product of the first movement, a description of core personality, may show identity as a system of compensations and defenses, but this does not fully *explain* either the genesis of identity or the meanings it encodes. Identity develops from what a person does with the givens of his or her core characteristics—how she or he uses existential reflection, moral judgments, and aesthetic techniques to differentiate, transform, and integrate them. And so a description of identity requires the second, progressive movement.

In the introduction to his *The Work of Culture*,[70] Gannanath Obeysekere notes that he similarly had been freed of the reductionist character of psychodynamic theory by Ricoeur's book on Freud. He explains that his title refers to the progressive movement—not just of the interpreter but of individuals' developmental use of cultural symbol systems to transform and give new meanings to deep motivations. An individual's cultural heritage provides myriad routes by which core features of personality can be transformed into public performances, life projects, and identities. And however strongly authorities attempt to impose these, individuals retain an important degree of latitude to improvise and create. In the model I propose, identity emerges from core personality and social persona by an appropriation and reworking of cultural symbols that closely parallels Obeysekere's notion of the "work of culture."

Discourses, Symbols, and Multiple Identities

Identity appears constructed in life narratives in one or more *discourses*. A discourse can be characterized as a model for enacting a certain type of character, in relation to other characters and in a range of settings. A discourse defines identity by locating Me versus not-Me representations in narrative space and time and in a nexus of feelings, motives, and moral sentiments that serve as causal forces and provide the reasons people act as they appear to. That is, it sets out a narrative configuration of the elements of an identity—like Luther's "son," "spokesman," and "father" figures. Only rarely do discourses have simple story structures, however; typically, they appear as value systems or worldviews that encompass many stories, often with varying plots and morals. Sociolinguist James Gee's definition of *discourse* takes account of its fundamentally ideological character and recognizes that it entails not just language but performative style:

> It's not just *what* you say or even just *how* you say it, it's also what you *are* and *do* while you say it. It's not enough just to say the right

"lines," one needs to get the whole "role" right (like a role in a play or movie). . . . A "role," as I am here using the term, is a combination of saying the right sorts of things in the right way, while engaging in the right sorts of actions and interactions, and appearing to think and feel the right way and have the right sorts of values. I call such integral combinations of sayings—doings—thinkings—feelings—valuings "Discourses."[71]

Importantly, a discourse is neither a self nor a personality, though it may organize several subselves or senses of self. A life narrative may set out two or more discourses (though in my studies, rarely more than three), each of which configures the narrator's core-level affective tensions into distinctive identities.

The model I adopt entails two additional theses about the units of self-representation. First, identity simultaneously differentiates and integrates core-level affects. How? At critical points in the architecture of identity, it does so by employing *structurally ambiguous* symbols to represent positive and negative manifestations of the affect. A structurally ambiguous symbol, similar to the well-known figure-ground reversible optical illusions, has a set of features that mean X and another set of features that mean Y, so that the affect it represents can be interpreted as X in one context and Y in another.[72] As an example, we can consider the life narrative of "Sharon" (see chapter 5 of *Self Representation*). Sharon describes herself at the outset as "a New Age type person," and she concretely anchors this abstract notion in the key symbol *tofu*. She explains that she came into her own at the age of twenty when she discovered the New Age way of life—especially the tofu-based "nondairy" vegetarian diet she practices—which lifted her out of a depressive "rut" into which she had fallen after deciding not to go to college. She began making tofu, then selling it, and now runs a large and successful tofu-making cooperative. She says she aspires to become a "master of tofu" as described in *The Way of Tofu*[73] and sees her promotion of tofu as helping build a "natural," "simple," "spiritual" counterculture as an alternative to the "chemicalized," "complex," "material" world of mainstream America. As tofu symbolizes her New Age identity, "chemicalized" synthetic foods, and specifically dairy products ("the chemicals that are used in meat, and especially in dairy—it's not a grass-fed cow that gives you milk, it's factory-produced milk"), symbolize all that she opposes and strives not to be.

The tofu versus dairy opposition turns out to be a highly personal one, as well as embodying wide social significance. She says her lifelong struggle with lethargy and mental ruts has entailed a tendency to overeat, all of which suggest to her a troubling likeness to her mother, who was overweight and twice hospitalized for depressive "nervous breakdowns." In particular, she says she experiences especially strong cravings for unhealthy dairy products—

milk, ice cream, cheese—that she now keeps in check by turning to tofu-based and other natural substitutes:

> I've been eating a lot of soy 'cause with soy milk if you've got a craving for milk, you can sort of flavor it up so it'll give you that same taste, so it'll satisfy that urge. And you can make ice cream out of soy milk, so you can satisfy your munchies for ice cream. And I eat a lot of nutrition yeast which has a real cheesy taste, so it satisfies my urge for cheese.

She summarizes her life history as a story about nurturance. She began as a thoroughly loved child who had "a warm, cozy, still-in-the-womb type of existence," but her mother's hospitalization and classmates' taunts about her chubbiness thrust her out into a hostile, "frustrating" world. Now, with her discovery of the New Age counterculture, she says, "I'm nurturing myself, and thinking of ways to create those feelings again." This clearly suggests that her cravings for dairy—whether or not they have biological underpinnings—represent cravings for nurturance, satiety, and security. Her childhood memories and projective test protocols strongly support this view: her earliest memory is of her mother putting hot pepper on her thumb to make her stop sucking it: "I got a burned mouth, and I just remember crying and screaming ... thinking, you know, this burns, why'd she do this?" This memory thus provides a kind of origin myth, an ur-exemplar warning that her food-focused craving for nurturance can lead to poisoning and rage. The tofu-versus-dairy opposition thus organizes an identity by differentiating her core-level craving for nurturance, satiety, and security into a natural, healthy, empowering form *versus* an artificial, unhealthy, draining form.

How does this work representationally? The tofu-dairy relation is a structurally ambiguous one, a relation of *identity-in-difference*. Tofu and dairy foods share textures, tastes, and appearances that make them sufficiently similar for her to substitute one for the other and satisfy her urges. At the same time, they differ in all-important features of origin, manufacture, packaging, and chemical-spiritual ingredients, and these differences set them in diametric opposition. The similarity enables both dairy and tofu to represent nurturance, satiety, and security, but the opposition enables tofu to represent vitality, health, and autonomy and dairy to represent lethargy, obesity, and frustrating dependence. The structured ambiguity thus enables her to use the symbol pair to differentiate her core-level craving into healthy versus unhealthy forms and to integrate her identity as a New Age–type person in contrast to a materialistic-type person whose chemicalized diet inclines to violence or mental ruts.

Because both symbols are concrete and their shared taste, color, and texture features can evoke and be evoked by emotional responses (probably according to classical conditioning principles), dairy and tofu can represent affective states. Because they can simultaneously establish a conceptual similarity and a contrast, they can differentiate affective states by giving the essentially "same" affect contradictory interpretations in different contexts. The features that mean nurturance are differentiated to mean X (unhealthy) in one context ("it comes from chemical-fed cows") and to mean Y (healthy) in another ("it comes from soybeans"). Because they can organize this kind of figure-ground differentiation of affects, structurally ambiguous symbols play a privileged role in the "information processing" that constructs self representation. They link affect and cognition, bringing emotion under the control of thought—however ineffective or illusory such "alchemical" control may be. Elaborated into mythic worldviews, such structurally ambiguous symbols—and often rituals that evoke and enact them—provide a technology for interpreting and transforming affective states or, as it is more frequently experienced, for moving one's self from one emotional terrain (e.g., lethargy-inducing desires for "chemicalized" dairy foods) into another (e.g., energy-inducing desires for "natural" soy foods).

The second thesis about units of self-representation concerns the observation that life narratives typically articulate alternative identity-defining discourses, each symbolically "orchestrating" core-level affective tensions into different identities. On closer analysis, the self-representational inconsistency that saturates all life narratives shows itself to be patterned: narrators typically move by quantumlike shifts among a small number of often contradictory discourses. This may take a variety of forms, but it usually involves either a literal or metaphorical repositioning of the subject to a different stance or location within the same symbolic space or reversing the figure-ground features of key symbols in order to position the subject in a different but homologous representational space. To again present an American example, a young sales executive named "Faith" from an Italian working-class family described herself as "a diamond in the rough" and narrated her life as a Pygmalion-like story in which she struggled to become cultured as she moved up in the corporate world (see chapter 7 of *Self Representation*). She portrayed her childhood milieu as a "shit-hole" and a "sewer" and then told of how in high school "a couple of gentlemen discovered me" and "cleaned me up," inspiring her to go to college and "shoot for the stars," which she continues to do in her fast-track career.

The stories she tells repeatedly employ symbols of dirt and gems, dark and light, to articulate both their melodic themes and their harmonic tensions. The melodic theme consists of the cycles of *Me → not-Me → Me* reversals, which she endlessly repeats as she describes how failures leave her feeling worthless, dirty, and wounded and her successes raise her out of the muck and into the gleaming light of stars and gems. In some stories, she moves through these cycles over the course of a few minutes or hours, in others over the course of a love affair of several years, and in others over the course of her entire life. The harmonic tensions are the relationships she establishes between herself and important others (*Me versus not-Me*) at each point in these cycles: when she is gem, she portrays herself as *not* like her ignorant and crude "dumb Dago" siblings or like lazy inner-city blacks, who know only how to "have kid after kid after kid"; when she slips and commits a "crude" faux pas or shoots off her "foul mouth," she portrays herself as failing in the eyes of her refined, white, upper-class colleagues.

In other stories, however, a different order of shift occurs, as she indicts the white, upper-class world for its phoniness and defends her working-class and ethnic roots—and to do so she employs the "same" symbols as those by which she narrates her Pygmalion-like transformation. In the stories of this inverted discourse, she describes herself as "earthy" and quotes approvingly her father's dictum that "a man who gets his hands dirty, you know he's going to be a good guy." She says she's not the sort of person who cares "should I wear gold or silver," accuses her colleagues of having a haughty "I'm so clean and my skin's so white" attitude, and condemns one wealthy ex-boyfriend as having been "born with a silver spoon in his mouth." Essentially, the *Me* = gem = cultured versus *not-Me* = dirt = crude identity inverts to a *Me* = dirt/earth = authentic versus *not-Me* = gem/plastic = phony identity. In *Self Representation*, I suggested that these shifts resemble musical key changes in which structurally ambiguous symbols serve as modulating chords.

One advantage of using a musical analogy to describe these structures is that it avoids many of the more controversial notions associated with psychoanalytic and structuralist theories. It also links the model to contemporary work in cognitive science, such as that of Lehrdahl and Jackendoff,[74] who have incorporated much of Heinrich Schenker's generative theory of music composition. Their theory emphasizes that a listener nonconsciously performs simultaneous multiple interpretations on the surface score of a composition. At any point in time, a "selection function" (similar to what Jackendoff believes operates in linguistic and visual processing as well) "compares the current possibilities and designates one as salient . . . [and] this one will be heard as the structure of the music up to this point, and it will generate anticipations of what is to come." Disconfirmation of an anticipation results in neither a breakdown of interpretation nor a resort to defensive maneuvers as predicted by many theories but instead produces a shift by which one of the alternative interpretations is designated as salient, so that "suddenly the whole previous passage changes structure like a Necker cube." The affective meaning of a composition thus derives in part from "the realization or violation of one's expectations" and in even larger part from "all the tensions engendered by the unconscious presence of conflicting structures."[75] As Jackendoff[76] later points out, this model parallels Dennett's[77] "multiple drafts" view of consciousness, and it closely fits the nature of self-representational meanings and the kinds of identity shifts I have observed in all the life narratives I have analyzed.

A key question in the analysis of the four narratives will be: What culture has shaped these lives? Is it Arab culture? Islamic culture? Mediterranean culture? Moroccan culture? The narratives yield no single answer but suggest that particular features of personality and identity have been organized by patterns characteristic of intersecting regions, decreasing in size from those just named to that of pre-Saharan Morocco. Thanks to a century of research by hundreds of scholars, we now know a great deal about the geographical distribution of Great and Little traditions in the Middle East, and this makes it possible to study their interweaving in narratives in a way that could not be done even a couple of decades ago. For an overview of cultural influences on psychological development, see my *The Middle East: A Cultural Psychology.* Here I will review writings on culture and self in North Africa by American anthropologists.

The Geertz-Eickelman-Rosen View of Culture and Self

Fieldwork conducted in the 1960s and 1970s by Hildred and Clifford Geertz, Dale Eickelman, and Lawrence Rosen defines a remarkably coherent view of Moroccan society, which Eickelman summarized in the first edition of his text on the Middle East as follows:

> I worked with the initial assumption, shared for the most part with . . . Clifford Geertz, Hildred Geertz, Lawrence Rosen and Paul Rabinow—that Morocco's social structure was best conceived with persons as its fundamental units . . . [and that] persons are not arranged in layerlike strata or classes but are linked in dyadic bonds of subordination and domination which are characteristically dissolved and reformed. The relatively stable element in this type of social structure is not the patterns that actual social relations form, but the culturally accepted *means* by which persons contract and maintain dyadic bonds and obligations with one another.[78]

Hildred Geertz's excellent study of a prominent household in the town of Sefrou[79] shows that Morocco's large extended-family groups cannot be considered lineages (she terms them "patronymic associations") because of their frequent loss of kin and incorporation of nonkin and because even when their relationships follow kinship lines, they remain flexible and open to continual negotiation of the sort characterizing nonkin patron-client relations.[80] Clifford Geertz's study of the town's commercial sector[81] shows the importance of "*nisba* types"—terms of reference and sometimes of address built by adding an -*i* to a person's occupation, place of origin, religious order, nickname, or the like—to identifying and evaluating persons in the ongoing negotiations of daily social interaction. (A resident of the town of Sefrou, for example, would be a *Sefroui*.) Rosen presents rich examples of how the negotiation of patron-client relations proceeds at all levels of society. He, too, insists that Moroccan social structure does not consist of corporate groups: "Reality for the Moroccan is the distribution of ties that he or she possesses to others. And that reality is achieved through a process of negotiating the meaning of the terms and relationships of which it is composed."[82] Like C. Geertz, Rosen seeks to identify a cluster of flexible core concepts—general notions of truth, time, and so forth—that he believes organize the negotiations. In *Moroccan Islam*, Eickelman similarly argues against corporate groups: "Social institutions are subjectively held ideas about social relations shared by members of a given society. The existing social order is a manifestation of this texture and meaning."[83] And he, too, seeks to identify a cluster of terms that guide the negotiation of relationships—*qodret Allah*, God's will; *ᶜaqol*, reason; *teḥashem*, propriety; *ḥaqq*, obligation; *ᶜar*, compulsion[84]—centering on the flexible determinations of degrees of social *qaraba*, closeness.

The Geertz-Eickelman-Rosen view opposed and effectively countered the then-traditional view that Middle Eastern society is in fact organized as its folk ideologists say it is, into kinship groups—extended families and segmentary lineages. The segmentary view was advanced for Morocco by the French social anthropologist Robert Montagne,[85] the British Ernest Gellner,[86] and the American David Hart,[87] all of whom studied Berber tribal groups in more remote regions of the country. As we saw in our own research on the agropastoral Imeghrane tribe of the High Atlas,[88] social groups in such "traditional" regions do have a more corporate character than they do in the towns studied by Eickelman, Rosen, and the Geertzes. But even in the most remote, "premodern" regions, the permeability of these groups and the room for individual negotiation are surprisingly great. The Geertz-Eickelman-Rosen view that social relations are not so much ascribed by birth as built up through constant dyadic negotiation captures an essential feature of social relations in Morocco, one that historically has enabled individuals to move between remote villages and urban centers with surprising ease.

Yet where American anthropologists have tended to emphasize the importance of the cultural *means of negotiation* by which, as Eickelman put it, "dyadic bonds of subordination and domination" are continually "dissolved and reformed," Moroccan investigators have emphasized the fact that relationships so pervasively take the form of *subordination and domination*. Indeed, classlike layers objectively exist and lead to the pervasive formation of hierarchical patron-client networks. In the three villages we studied, few families lack property, but most cannot come close to meeting their own subsistence needs, because roughly 10 percent of the households own 60 to 80 percent of the productive resources. (These estimates match those of Ministry of Agriculture surveys in many villages and reports of economic anthropologists throughout many parts of the rural Middle East.[89]) This distribution of wealth means that the top 10 percent chronically lack the labor they need to produce from their resources and that the two thirds who cannot meet their subsistence needs have to enter into clientage relations with wealthy patrons (as shepherds, sharecroppers, wage laborers, or voluntary helpers) to get access to the resources they need. The wealthy 10 percent also tend to get control of government development projects and opportunities for urban and overseas employment, with the consequence that access to these modern resources continues to be negotiated in quite traditional patron-client terms. It is not clear that the Geertz-Eickelman-Rosen view of social relations requires rejecting the existence of classlike layers, as they repeatedly insist, or ignoring the degree to which "bonds of *subordination* and *domination*" (emphasis added) depend on the military and police support that local elites receive from centers of political power.[90]

Still, it is essential to understand that although Moroccans are highly sensitive to disparities of wealth and poverty, the classlike layers did not traditionally form the distinctive cultural layers they do in feudal or industrial societies; they neither join layermates into social groups nor prominently mark them by dress, speech, taste, or the like as distinct from members of other layers. Traditional neighborhoods mix rich and poor with little outward sign of whether any particular door leads to a palace or a hovel. Families like those studied by H. Geertz have both wealthy and desperately poor branches. Patron-client relations typically form within families, lineages, and neighborhoods and are articulated in familistic terms that also extend to define patron-client relationships among nonkin as well.[91] In addition, families, households, and larger patronymic associations remain the fundamental integrative units and seek to strategically distribute their members throughout different occupations and political factions in order to create an organized system or, in some cases, a kind of miniconglomerate. It is not unusual to encounter a Ouarzazate-area household with a merchant father living in town, his clientlike brother farming ancestral lands in Imeghrane, one of his sons an illiterate shepherd in the mountains, another a miner in Lyons, another a factory worker in Casablanca, and a daughter a local elementary school teacher. Their control of extensive resources objectively places them in a particular classlike layer, but their occupational specializations put them in different cultural worlds, and little or no class identification develops. Culturally, then, traditional Morocco was not a caste society, a feudal society, or a class society, and even though people have become much more aware of the sort of class distinctions typical of industrial societies, it still would be misleading to term it a class society. Yet the fact that most young people have to continually negotiate "relations of domination and subordination" can profoundly affect the development of both personality and identity, as Abdullah Hammoudi recently has argued.[92]

The Geertz-Eickelman-Rosen view is especially important to this investigation of identity because they present their analyses of the means of negotiation as describing not just social relations or cultural etiquettes but selves, identities, and concepts of the person—terms they often use interchangeably. For example, in Eickelman's essay "Traditional Islamic Learning," he initially sets out an interesting distinction between *individual* and *person* as follows:

> "Individual" refers to the mortal human being, the object of observation and self-reflection. . . . "Person" refers to the cultural concepts that lend social significance to the individual. . . . The notion of "person," to paraphrase Jean La Fontaine, is society's confirmation that an individual's identity has social significance.[93]

He then presents a fascinating analysis of several *tarjama*s (semiofficial biographies) of religious scholars he studied in Morocco and Yemen, showing how these were fashioned and used to legitimate their elite social status. In his conclusion, he makes a number of interesting observations about the effects of recent social changes on individuals and personas, which he glosses as "consequences for conceptions of self and person." He notes that tribal or colonial situations create competing "identities" that may be left out of the *tarjama* biography (that of collaborator with the French, for example) or left implicit in it (such as that of tribal leader). And he notes that although "full personhood is still confined to a limited number of individuals . . . the way in which individuals achieve full personhood is much more open than in the past,"[94] and so the traditional *tarjama*-legitimated persona has been eclipsed among the younger generation by "the persona of the sincere, religious-minded believer."[95] He sees that these sociological changes have important psychological consequences, but the sudden displacement of the individual-versus-person distinction in his analysis by the undefined terms *persona, identity, full personhood*, and *conceptions of self and person* leave it unclear precisely what those consequences may be. I think it significant that this ambiguity arises precisely at the point Eickelman seeks to move from analysis of his data—individual lives—to speculation about what the spread of new politico-cultural styles (especially political or fundamentalist Islam) among the younger generation might imply about their "conceptions of self."

C. Geertz devotes much of his well-known essay "From the Native's Point of View" to a discussion of the Moroccan *concept of person* or *sense of self*—terms he uses interchangeably. Geertz advocates taking a semiotic rather than psychological approach to investigating a culture's concept of person, arguing for "experience-near" descriptions, which means using terms like *fear* rather than *phobia, love* rather than *object cathexis*, and the like. "The trick," he says, "is to figure out what the devil they think they are up to."[96] The main means Moroccans use "to sort people out from one another and form an idea of what it is to be a person," he says, lies in the construction of *nisba* labels to link people to multiple and overlapping social groups, activities, and contexts. Nisba constructions add an *i* (male) or *iya* (female) suffix to a term to associate a person with it; a person from Rabat thus becomes a *Rabati* or *Rabatiya*.

In Geertz's view, "nisbas render men relative to their contexts, but as contexts themselves are relative, so too are nisbas, and the whole thing rises, so to speak, to the second power: relativism squared."[97] He then characterizes the Moroccan view of the self as a "composite," well suited to life in a "mosaic social organization," in contrast to the Javanese concept of the self as a "persona" and to the Balinese concept of the self as a "point in a pattern."[98]

Although I have not conducted fieldwork in Java or Bali, I am convinced that these contrasts capture important differences in the cultural means by which individuals size up each other and in the cultural etiquettes by which they negotiate their relationships. But I am not convinced they describe concepts of person or senses of self. One reason for my hesitation derives from several of the observations Geertz makes en route to these conclusions. First, while emphasizing that "the social contextualization of persons is pervasive" in Morocco, he asserts: "As individualistic, even willful, as the Moroccans in fact are, their identity is an attribute they borrow from their setting."[99] Second, he continues to note that the social pattern "produces a situation where people interact with one another in terms of categories whose meaning is almost purely positional, location in the general mosaic, leaving the substantive content of the categories, what they mean subjectively as experienced forms of life, aside as something properly concealed in apartments, temples, and tents."[100] And third, he sums up this line of argument by inferring: "Selfhood is never in danger because, outside the immediacies of procreation and prayer, only its coordinates are asserted."[101]

Note that these are psychologically deep interpretations: that Moroccans are "individualistic," that the *nisba* system defines their "identities" rather than just their concept of person (and perhaps one among many?), that the "substantive content of the categories" of identity is concealed in privacy, and that "selfhood is never in danger" are all strong assertions that essentially profile a Moroccan "national character." All but perhaps the last are at least potentially researchable hypotheses, but Geertz offers no data about them in any of his writings. We might let the first go (that Moroccans are "individualistic, even willful") as an offhand characterization not meant as a psychological hypothesis, but he puts forward the others precisely as inferences about psychological qualities based on his analysis of the experience-near terms organizing social relations. There are serious problems with this analysis, two of which I will mention.

The first concerns his assertion that the substantive content of the categories of identity is concealed. In the Ouarzazate area, to identify a man with the *nisba* term Imeghrani or Skouri provides useful information about his origins (a Berber mountain tribe or an Arabic-speaking oasis community), his language, his way of life, whose taxi he'll prefer to take home, and even his likely political connections. In this case, Geertz has it absolutely right: the substantive meaning of these terms remains largely private. But to term a man a Dra'oui, which ostensibly refers straightforwardly to someone from one of the villages lining the Dra'a River, essentially labels him a "nigger." It immediately evokes the richly elaborated stereotypes of the pre-Saharan cosmology,[102] according to which the region's "white" Berbers are strong, free, and favored by God and the "black" former slaves who continue to do most of the sharecropping labor in the Dra'a oases are weak, unfree, and marked with the color of divine disapproval. Like all ethnocentric stereotypes, it protects one man's clearly vulnerable selfhood by putting another's in danger. I once watched the Berber village headman insult a passing Dra'oui sharecropper: "Which is worth more," he said loudly to everyone, "a she-goat [black in that area] or a ram [the prized sacrificial and culinary animal, and white in that area]?" The Dra'oui responded by repeatedly asking why we were all sitting in the hot sun instead of drinking tea in the shade of the headman's large and well-appointed house—endangering the selfhood of the headman, who had fallen on hard times and couldn't afford to entertain in the manner expected from someone of the stature he claimed. These examples not only cast doubt on Geertz's psychological inferences but also do so precisely at the point at which a minor skirmish in an ancient ethnic war broke out (the headman could not get his gun and use the Dra'oui for target practice, as Hart reports the neighboring Ait Atta tribesmen boasted they did in the past[103]). They also show how *nisba* terms may link into broader and less composite symbolic and metaphoric systems that ultimately draw a good deal of their power from purporting to reveal just what goes on in the privacy of "apartments, temples and tents."

I find it surprising that Geertz does not move into that terrain to analyze *self* in Morocco, especially in light of his earlier essays "Religion as a Cultural System" and "Ethos, World View and the Analysis of Sacred Symbols."[104] In the first, he makes the important distinction between indigenous models "of" reality, which map the world as it appears to present itself, and "for" reality, which provide instructions for building a world. As a map for reality, Geertz argues that religion, with its sacred symbols and rituals, creates an emotional, moral, and motivational order, sustaining "a basic congruence between a particular style of life and a specific (if, most often, implied) metaphysics,"[105] or, as he phrases it in the second essay, "by fusing ethos and world view, [religion] gives to a set of social values what they perhaps must need to be coercive: an appearance of objectivity."[106] These accounts of how religious systems produce order by linking affect and cognition into a model for a way of life offers an excellent description of the cultural construction of identity. And if the *nisba* terms, or the clusters of concepts identified by Rosen and Eickelman, define a flexible, relativistic mosaic without substance, might not Islam provide the stable order, the "appearance of objectivity," the "substance" of personhood? Geertz fails to consider this possibility.

The second problem concerns Geertz's incomplete analysis of naming practices, a strategy he used so effectively to describe the Balinese construction of selves.[107] He does not explore the fact that Moroccans have (1) a family/

lineage name, which links them to the patrikin-based ethic of honor; (2) a given name typically drawn from the cast of Muslim religious figures (Mohammed, Ali, etc.) or from the ninety-nine names of God (Abdallah, Abdelkrim, etc.), which links them to the religion-based ethic of piety; and (3) a nickname, which acknowledges idiosyncrasies and individuating characteristics.[108] As several Middle Eastern scholars have observed, a core tension animating personality or self is that between kinship loyalty elaborated in terms of the honor-modesty code and a Muslim religiosity articulated in practices for managing body and affect (especially cycles of pollution and purification) and in etiquettes for staging public self-presentations. Family and personal names thus define crosscutting spheres of attachment and obligation, and often antagonistic values and contradictory identities—perhaps much the way attachments to career and family differentiate contradictory organizations of self for many Americans.

Nicknames then add a layer of individuating terms, often referring humorously to physical characteristics (e.g., "the bald one") or likening people to unusual animals, and so present an informal, impolite contrast to the weightiness of family and religious names. This naming system yields no "relativism squared" mosaic that leaves the essence of self private and protected. Instead, it reflects chronic struggle over loyalty, principle, and conscience that puts the essence of a man[109]—his honor and piety—always at public risk. Even a more thorough analysis of cultural data, then, suggests an encoding of distinct patrikin-centric, religion-centric, and egocentric selves in Moroccans' names and points toward the need to investigate how these components may get organized and elaborated.

Finally, the Geertz-Eickelman-Rosen view of Moroccan culture and self is distinctive for its highly cognitive emphasis. None of these ethnographers pursues questions about how Islam or other Moroccan symbol systems render affect meaningful and manageable—the question that makes Geertz's work on Bali so rich. It may help to recall Gregory Bateson's (1958) distinction between eidos and ethos and suggest that the Geertz-Eickelman-Rosen view may provide an admirable account of the eidos, the logic of Moroccan social relations, but not of their ethos, their affective tuning. Geertz does venture into this territory in his *Islam Observed*, where he explores the life of a sixteenth-century Moroccan saint to contrast the affective tuning of cultures at the Western and Eastern poles of the Islamic world, [110] but he does not draw this analysis into his discussion of the Moroccan concept of person. In *Moroccan Islam*, Eickelman notes that reflections of pervasive patron-client types of relations appear in Moroccans' emotional involvements with saints, but he then declines to weave these sorts of observations into his various accounts of social identity.

The Geertz-Eickelman-Rosen line of inquiry has yielded nuanced accounts of the cultural categories with which Moroccans negotiate personal relationships. But in spite of their sense of self and concept of person terminologies, they do not give accounts of identity or self. Nor do they give accounts of those features of social life—most prominently, those concerning honor and religion, tradition and modernity—in which central aspects of self are made manifest and identity publicly contested.

Oasis and Casbah

Two explicitly psychological studies have relevance to culture and identity in Morocco. The first embodies much that was wrong with the "basic personality" approach worked out by Abram Kardner and his students in the 1930s and 1940s. *Oasis and Casbah* reports Horace Minor and George DeVos's study of the psychological effects of rural-to-urban acculturation in neighboring Algeria. Conducted in 1950, the project shows little evidence of the work on attachment-separation and on identity that greatly broadened psychodynamic theory in the 1950s. Minor and DeVos asked a Rorschach expert unfamiliar with North Africa to formulate a series of predictions about personality differences between men living in a southern oasis community (much like those in the Ouarzazate area) and their neighbors who had moved to urban Algiers. They hired French-speaking Algerian assistants to administer Rorschach tests and conduct brief life-history interviews with twenty men in the oasis and twenty-six in Algiers. They then had the Rorschach protocols blind-scored and coded for the relevant traits, and statistically tested their hypotheses.

Though Minor did fieldwork in the sites, neither researcher spoke Arabic, and by current standards, they had little familiarity with Middle Eastern or Islamic cultures. Perhaps as a consequence, the book is rife with what today appear as orientalist inferences, phrasings, and asides (e.g., the Algerians exhibit "a tendency . . . toward illogical, rather than systematic thought"[111]). Still, it proves to be an interesting work, and although it does not directly concern itself with identity (Erikson's *Childhood and Society* appeared in 1950), it is most interesting for the suggestions it contains about this feature of adult personality. When statistical tests confirmed only a chance percentage of the predictions about rural-to-urban acculturation, Minor and DeVos wisely concluded that a range of religious and social attitudes can change (for the city-dwellers did espouse generally more "modern" views in a number of areas) without concomitant changes in underlying personality organization. They then proceeded to identify several Algerian-versus-American and rural-versus-urban psychological differences and wrote a series of capsule case histories to illustrate the diversity of personal adaptations.

First, they report finding more signs of psychological distress and constriction among Algerians than among "normal" Americans. This may reflect only the Eurocentric norms of Rorschach interpretation and the greater anxiety experienced by the Algerians in the testing situation. But populations that experience chronic malnutrition, a 20 to 30 percent childhood mortality rate, a high prevalence of chronic and debilitating diseases without adequate medical care, and a century of despoliation and military oppression by a colonial power may indeed be expected to experience higher levels of psychological distress and constriction—though Minor and DeVos cite none of these factors. They also found greater use of externalizing and projective defenses among Algerians, which may again reflect Eurocentric norms but might be predicted as responses to greater physical suffering, emotional loss, and military oppression.

Second, contrary to one Rorschach expert's predictions, they found an association between *dis*belief in supernatural forces (*jinn* spirits, the evil eye, ogres, and the like) and higher levels of psychological distress (especially on scales of hostility and bodily preoccupation), mostly among residents of Algiers:

> The attenuation of traditional beliefs among the urbanized Arabs is related to increasing intrapsychic tensions. . . . The minority position of the more acculturated urban Arab is reflected in his perception of the social environment as hostile and threatening.[112]

Even if we provisionally assume that these measures *might* have some validity, this association still could be an artifact (life in Algiers could expose the men both to modern beliefs and to new risks and threats). But Minor and DeVos suggest that the two are directly related: "The decline of supernatural beliefs decreases the protection from stress which they provide in the oasis."[113] I note this in large part because most of the lives I studied show prominent struggles to find nonsupernatural explanations for the disturbing experiences traditionally attributed to spirit beings or sorcery (nightmares, "hysterical" paralyses, accidents and injuries, impotence). It indeed may be, as Minor and DeVos suspect from their failure to find predicted acculturation differences, that some modernizing processes, especially formal education, change attitudes and identities without affecting core-level characteristics and create developmental disjunctions and "adaptational" difficulties in the process.

As brief and clinical as their eleven case histories are, they suggest precisely that. Minor and DeVos don't employ the concepts identity, self, or even the older term *ego ideal*, yet what clearly captures their attention is the range of attempts these Algerian men were making to work out niches in the colonial world—in particular, how they define themselves in terms of symbols of Frenchness and Algerianness. They describe "Ali" as traditional in most features of his personality and beliefs, but after he had worked for four months in France,

> we see him as a teen-aged, oasis youth who intensely desires to identify with the French way of life. He uses a mixture of European and Arab dress and is vain about his wristwatch, a certain mark of French contact. He wears a fez like an Arab urbanite and swears that he will

never wear the more rural turban. . . . Beneath the clothes and speech, however, we find a core of cultural belief which is characteristically like that of the unacculturated oasis Arabs.[114]

"Ahmed" spent only a few years in the local French school but more skillfully blends French and Arab elements (again, "His wristwatch remains the most obvious symbol of French contact"[115]). Now an innovator in the oasis community, he shifts from emphasizing one style or the other, according to circumstances. "Benazouz" was a young nationalist they suspect perished in the subsequent Algerian war of independence. They describe him as having an "ambivalent" social identity, as "looking both ways in his acculturation." By this, they mean that while highly Westernized in many respects, he vehemently defends Arab culture and orthodox Islam, "looking down on groups he considers primitive or simple," which include "backward" Arabs, the "Negro" ("Dra'oui"?) heads he perceives in one of the Rorschach ink blots, and American Indians.

These and other case studies show that Minor and DeVos were most struck by the struggle for identity they saw being carried on in terms of French versus Arab cultural concepts, styles, and symbols. Their capsule portraits outline the binary (*Me* versus *not-Me*) and shifting nature of self-representation. Ali strives to be solidly "French, not-Arab"; Ahmed mixes cultural genres and shifts flexibly between "French, not-Arab" and "Arab, not-French"; and Benazouz vehemently asserts himself to be "Arab/Muslim" and "not French" in some contexts and "not-primitive" in others. The case portraits provide precious few details, just enough to see that prominent self-symbols (e.g., clothes, manners of speech, stereotypic group representations) sometimes mean French versus Arab, sometimes Muslim versus heathen, sometimes modern versus primitive. Minor and DeVos discuss these not just as attitudes or beliefs that individuals may "hold" but as they provide compensations for, defenses against, and vehicles of expression for underlying impulses and tensions. So, in sharp contrast to the Geertz-Eickelman-Rosen view, this study suggests that identity—as it provides a "model for" an organization of personality—takes shape as a political-religious structure, drawing heavily on symbols arising from the colonial encounter and the sacred symbols of Islam.

Spirit Possession and Identity

A second inquiry relevant to culture and identity in Morocco is Vincent Crapanzano's psychoanalytically inclined studies of the Hamadsha religious brotherhood.[116] The Hamadsha provide some of the most spectacular examples of folk or popular Islam: its members believe themselves to be possessed by the widely feared *jinniya* (female spirit) Aisha Qandisha. In periodic trance-dancing sessions, they slash their heads or otherwise mutilate themselves, which placates the *jinniya* and may cure others of illnesses she has inflicted on them. The order is organized along the lines of the many Sufi religious brotherhoods in North Africa, dedicated to a religious path set out by a saint and passed on through lines of descendants or chains of teacher-student transmission (the orders are called *tariqas*, which means "ways" or "paths"). Because they are the least orthodox of the North African brotherhoods, many Moroccans regard the Hamadsha and the similar Aissawa orders with embarrassment and accuse them of engaging in backward, un-Islamic practices.

Crapanzano focuses on explaining the Hamadsha order and ritual as therapy and not on describing Moroccan personality or identity in general. But he does portray the rituals through which he believes a Hamdushi (the Hamadsha member's *nisba* term) symbolically becomes feminized and/or suffers mutilation and in the process acquires a sense of masculine empowerment from the saints (who act as vehicles of power descending from God through the Prophet) as a pattern that draws on prominent cultural themes. Although he primarily employs psychoanalytic terms (Aisha Qandisha "seems to function as a sort of externalized superego"[117]), he shows how structures of self-representation oscillate between what Erikson would term identity elements: powerless outcaste, powerful but malevolent *jinniya* (demoness), and powerful and benevolent saint. Again, he does not label or analyze this as a structure of identity, but he has identity in mind when, in his essay "The Self, the Third, and Desire,"[118] he argues from a Lacanian perspective that self inevitably takes on a triadic structure.

Crapanzano's discussion of circumcision in Morocco[119] also has relevance for research on identity. Male circumcision in the Middle East remains something of an ethnographic puzzle: conceptually and ritually defined as making a man of a boy and purifying him in preparation for marriage, it is typically performed between the ages of three and seven. It is not staged as a test of a boy's courage or endurance but treated as a regrettable necessity that must be forcibly performed on an unsuspecting, misinformed, or deliberately deceived child. Many boys experience it as sheer terror, though some older children recall the gifts and celebration honoring them. Crapanzano argues that it would be wrong to view it as a "rite of passage," for it entails no passage, only a return to the world of women to await a later, more gradual entrance into the world of men, unmarked by any distinct ritual. The rite itself conveys "a series of contradictory messages that remain unresolved, at least in the ritual immediate. What resolution, if any, comes with time, . . . "[120] probably with marriage (with which circumcision is explicitly associated) and perhaps with fatherhood and a son's circumcision. In general, he observes, such culturally imposed inflictions of separation, mutilation, and pain "serve as symbolic orientation points for the articulation of personal history, ultimately of self."[121]

I read in this account the intriguing suggestion that the disjunctive features of the experience raise a question (i.e., they put manhood in question) that must be addressed recurrently through the life cycle and to which the ritual's conceptual and symbolic construction—manhood achieved via the purifying annulment of a feminization or mutilation—provides a schematic answer. That is, the ritual doesn't masculinize when it is performed but provides a template for masculinization that may be gradually comprehended and enriched in meaning during subsequent discussion, observation, and reflection. The actual course of an individual's development remains open, but the template provides, in Geertz's terms, a "map for" constructing a man or, in Obeysekere's terms, a blueprint for the masculinizing "work of culture."

Crapanzano's studies thus show the importance and problematic nature of *masculine* identity development, which does not appear prominently in the Geertz-Eickelman-Rosen view. They also describe a cultural schema of masculinization that Abdullah Hammoudi recently developed in detail.[122] More broadly, the notion that disjunctive experiences can pose developmental questions that cultural templates later answer is a useful one, especially because Moroccan culture appears to pattern several points of disjunction and to provide multiple templates. This is why it is so important to distinguish levels of personality organization: core personality may develop into various identity templates and indeed shift between identity discourses (e.g., French modernist to Arab traditionalist; disempowered black to malevolent demoness to benevolent saint), depending on circumstances.

Cultural Dualities ❀

The Illusion of Wholeness

Many writings on identity in other Middle Eastern societies emphasize how the "clash" of traditions with Western-style modernization has created pervasive duality and dispute. Katherine Ewing has been one of the few anthropologists to investigate the cultural shaping of self by studying individual life histories and to show the importance of multiple, often contradictory self-representations. In "The Illusion of Wholeness," she analyzes interviews with Shamim, a Pakistani woman studying for her PhD and struggling to both chart her own life and remain a dutiful daughter. [123] These show her "rapidly shifting self-representations" between "two self-images based on inconsistent premises."

> At some moments she presents an image of herself as a good, obedient daughter who will, hopefully, become a good wife. At other times her self-representation is that of a "politician" who can employ various strategies to meet her personal needs and wishes.[124]

The first is rooted in the sociocentric concept of personhood familiar throughout South Asia, Ewing writes, "in which persons are regarded, not as individuals with personal needs, but rather as units of the social order." This is articulated in terms of Muslim principles of filial piety and control of *nafs* (desire) by ʿ*ql* (reason/social maturity).[125] The second draws on an egocentric cultural model of everyday political maneuvering, according to which "each person operates to maximize his or her advantage (or that of his or her family) vis-à-vis others in order to realize personal or familial wishes and goals."[126] These juxtaposed "good Muslim" and "clever politician" models—that roughly parallel the contrast I will draw between "piety" and "honor"—cause conflict and guilt for many Pakistanis, Ewing observes, and lead Shamim and others to see the same qualities and acts from contrasting perspectives:

> The good Muslim may explain manifestations of "political" action as the excessive indulgence of a person's *nafs*. Alternatively, from the political standpoint a person's actions, though proper behavior for a good Muslim, might be branded as "boorish" or stupid or, more benignly, labeled "simple." . . . [127]

Ewing notes that when Shamim changes self-images, she also changes her images of her parents and the personal memories that go with them, so that each of the two self-representations comprises a whole frame of reference. Because she generally remains unaware of her shifts, each frame of reference creates a feeling—or illusion—that the self is whole:

> People construct a series of self-representations that are based on selected cultural concepts of person and selected "chains" of personal memories. Each self-concept is experienced as whole and continuous, with its own history and memories that emerge in a specific context, to be replaced by another self-representation when the context changes.[128]

In a subsequent paper, Ewing shows how educated Pakistanis may develop contrasting modern and traditional self-representations and how dreams of Sufi *pirs* (masters) may bring about a reorganization of the prominence given to each. In postcolonial Pakistan, she writes:

> Many people are forced into situations in which they must organize strands of their lives that are highly inconsistent with one another. Many Pakistanis have found that self representations developed in a traditional Muslim family are difficult to reconcile with those formed in British-dominated educational, governmental, and business settings.[129]

She presents the life histories of two Western-educated professional men for whom the duality had become conflict, though she points out that many individuals shift so smoothly between even "radically inconsistent" self-representations that they do not notice themselves doing so or become troubled by the contradictions. These men, however, struggled consciously with the conflict and ultimately resolved them in favor of traditional religion by means of a centuries-old cultural schema in which they dreamed of a Sufi master and then became his disciple. Where they previously gave priority to their Westernized self-representations, the dreams served as catalysts for reversing the emphasis and bringing their religious selves to the forefront of their daily lives. The dreams thus enabled them

> to bridge what they had felt was a chasm between, on the one hand, their concepts of themselves and their relationships in a working world that has been significantly shaped by the postcolonial situation of modern Pakistan, and, on the other hand, their experiences of self and relationships in the context of their religious lives.[130]

Together, these papers and her *Arguing Sainthood* show how contrasting cultural models—"good Muslim" versus "clever politician" and "Westernized modernity" versus "traditional religiosity"—may be internalized as contrasting identities.

Ewing's work was followed in 1998 by an issue of *Ethos* devoted to the theme "Communicating Multiple Identities in Muslim Communities." Using diverse approaches to differing sources of data, the contributing ethnographers demonstrate "overlapping and otherwise multiple identities" in Morocco, Algeria, Niger, Bangladesh, and Turkish Cyprus. Together, these studies show that self-representations are shaped both by local ethnic, religious, and gender contrasts and by the global duality of Westernized modernity versus traditional religiosity.

Westernization

The twentieth-century histories of Turkey and Iran are often taught as case studies of the conflict of tradition and Westernization that has shaped identities throughout the Middle East. In the 1920s, the nationalist government of Turkey, led by Mustafa Kemal ("Ataturk"), set out to modernize the country along European lines. Writing in the 1950s, Daniel Lerner praised Ataturk's attack on "the 'oriental mentality' which interdicted republican development."

> Ataturk aimed at nothing less than reshaping a traditionalized society by transforming the daily deeds and desires of the people—first the new elite, then the ancient mass. . . . His model was the "modern Western style" and his method was the production of "new Turks."[131]

In addition to adopting a new legal code modeled on the Swiss, creating a compulsory public education system, building a network of roads, providing villages with radios, and closing down religious shrines and brotherhoods, Ataturk set out to modernize the fine details of dress. In 1925, the "Hat Law" prohibited men from wearing the traditional fez and designated European-style hats as the official headwear. Ataturk explained:

> Gentlemen, it was necessary to abolish the fez, which sat on the heads of our nation as an emblem of ignorance, negligence, fanaticism, and hatred of progress and civilization, to accept in its place the hat, the headgear used by the whole civilized world, and in this way to demonstrate that the Turkish nation, in its mentality as in other respects, in no way diverges from civilized life.[132]

The law also allowed women not to veil, and Western-style dress soon became the norm for urban men and women.

The desire to demonstrate the attainment of Western-style civilization led Turks to transform the minutest details of their comportment, as sociologist Nilufer Gole writes, "as if European eyes are watching over their daily lives."[133] She cites the writings of Ahmet Tanpinar as capturing the psychological duality introduced by Westernism, at times intensifying into a "psychosis" affecting the "inner self." "We have moved toward the West with a will reinforced by the requirements of history," Tanpinar wrote, "yet at the same time, we own a past such that it is impossible to close our ears once it starts to talk to us with all its quality." The duality of inner voices ties life into a "knot," so that the Turk lives "in the middle of two different but overlapping worlds, unaware of each other."[134] In popular speech, the duality came to be known by borrowed French terms: *alafranka* (European) ways versus *alaturka* (Turkish) ways.[135]

The Kemalists maintained one-party rule until the 1950s, and as historian Hugh Poulton describes, "the continuing Islamic sensibilities of the large majority of the population began to make themselves evident."[136] In the 1970s, cultural and political strife grew intense, with leftists, rightists, and religious activists attacking the Western-oriented government and conflict intensifying between the Kurdish minority and Turkish majority and between the Alevi (Shi'i) minority and Sunni majority. Nearly all features of dress became political symbols, and "by the end of the decade," Emelie Olson writes, "even the curve or droop of a man's mustache was carefully calibrated for its political significance."[137] As street violence escalated toward civil war, the military seized power in 1980 and used force to impose order. To defuse the explosive identity politics, it issued a "Dress and Appearance Regulation" for public employees that prohibited men from wearing mustaches, beards, or long hair, and women from wearing short skirts, low-cut dresses, and headscarves.

In 1984, newspapers carried stories about the valedictorian of the University of Ankara medical school, who was not allowed to give a graduation address because she insisted on wearing a headscarf, and then about an engineering professor threatened with dismissal because she wore a headscarf while teaching. These set off what came to be known as the "headscarf" dispute, as surprisingly large numbers of women students demonstrated to win the right to veil. Westernized students and professional women opposed the pro-veil protestors, and the entire nation debated the matter. As Gole explores in *Forbidden Modern*, paradoxes abound: that women's bodies have reemerged as the focus of morality and politics shows the strength of tradition beneath decades of state-imposed modernism, but that the Islamist women are taking active roles in public politics shows that modernism has triumphed. Though defending the authenticity of tradition, the activists condemn truly traditional veiling styles as not Islamic, and they themselves veil as a fully modern statement of fashion-based identities and political commitments.

"Westoxication"

In 1925, the year of the Hat Law in Turkey, the commander of Persia's Cossack Brigade, Reza Pahlavi, became shah of shahs—king of kings—and began a similar program of modernization in the nation he insisted be called Iran. He first built a modern army and used it, often brutally, to settle the nomads, crush resistance, and mobilize the population for government projects. Taking many of Ataturk's reforms as examples, he put in place new Western-style legal, financial, and education systems and began building an infrastructure of roads, communications lines, and factories. In 1929, his government ordered men to dress in Western clothes and in 1936 became the first to outlaw veiling. His soldiers and police enforced these rules, sometimes tearing veils off women in the streets. There was one religious protest, which the Shah's troops machine-gunned and silenced.[138]

The shah and his followers also developed what historian Roy Mottahedeh calls a "cult" of Iran's pre-Islamic past to provide a nationalist, non-religious identity on which Western ways might be grafted. The shah's regime celebrated the heroes of the national epic, "The Book of Kings," and new public school texts gave pride of place to the sixth century B.C. kingdom founded by Cyrus. Zoroastrian motifs were revived, and Arabic words purged from the language in favor of "pure" Farsi. Mostafa Vaziri writes:

> The constitution of a national memory of the glorious past was a central element of Pahlavi policies designed to give a distinct sense of identity to the people of Iran. Pre-Islamic Zoroastrian emblems appeared on government agencies and buildings and special attention was paid to Zoroastrian festivals—all in order to revive the past and to connect with it.[139]

Mottahedeh tells how the naming of children inscribed the hopes of modernization in new identities:

From the 1930s on, middle- and upper-class Iranians, duly impressed by the role of Iran in ancient history, gave their sons such names as Cyrus and Cambyses, names that would have been outlandish and virtually meaningless to Muslim Iranians before the translation of modern European books in the nineteenth century. In fact, by the next generation, when the Cyruses of the 1930s had grown up and had named many of their children after ancient Iranians, the newly engrafted historicist cult seemed to have taken.[140]

After the Second World War, Mohammad Reza Pahlavi continued his father's programs and in 1971 celebrated the 2,500th anniversary of Iranian kingship: "the shah stood before the tomb of Cyrus and proclaimed, 'sleep easily, Cyrus, for we are awake.'"[141] Then:

> In the boldest gesture of all, the government changed the calendar from the Islamic era to an era based on the supposed date of the foundation of Iranian kingship by Cyrus. In 1976 Iranians found themselves no longer in 1355 of the Islamic era but in 2535 of "the era of the King of Kings."[142]

In spite of this massive propaganda, Mottahedeh writes that "the third generation of Cyruses does not seem to have been significantly larger than the second. . . . Something had gone sour. . . ."[143] The most influential diagnosis came from Al e Ahmad, an educator from a rural village who studied in Moscow and at Harvard. He saw an authenticity in village life that had been lost in the new modern cities and in 1962 wrote a book titled *Gharbzadegi* (literally, "West-stricken-ness") to describe the "illness" that afflicted Iran: "I say that *gharbzadegi* is like cholera [or] frostbite. But no. It's at least as bad as sawflies in the wheat fields. Have you ever seen how they infest wheat? From within."[144] Mottahedeh explains the term:

> To be "stricken" in Persian means not only to be afflicted with a disease or to be stung by an insect but it also means to be infatuated and bedazzled; "West-stricken-ness," therefore, has sometimes been translated as "Wextoxication." But a less outlandish word, "Euromania," captures enough of the sense of the Persian to be a passable stand-in for the nearly untranslatable Persian original.[145]

Al e Ahmad wrote that Satan's modern incarnation is the machine, manufactured in the West, which enslaves those who consume its products. Even more powerful forms of enslavement come from the superficial cravings Westernization implants in Iranian minds and the way Iranians come to see and know themselves through the gaze of Europeans. He compares Iranians to the crow in a popular Sufi folktale: The crow sees a partridge walk by and is amazed at the measured elegance of the partridge's gait. After long and painstaking practice, the crow forgets how to walk like a crow but never learns how to walk like a partridge. In the end, he concludes, the Euromaniac "has no personality—he is an object with no authentic origin."[146] In spite of his personal dislike for the religious elite, Al e Ahmad came to believe that traditional Islam remained the reservoir of Iranian authenticity.

Westoxication struck responsive chords in many circles. In the following two decades leading to the 1979 revolution, it provided much of the language adopted by opposition groups, from leftists to Islamic militants. Pre-revolutionary Iranians thus could opt for Western-style modernization in opposition to "backward" and "superstitious" traditions or "fanatical" religious movements, or they could choose "authentic" tradition rather than the soulless materialism of Euromania. Vaziri describes this as a form of "cultural schizophrenia."[147] Mottahedeh suggests that a "love of ambiguity" long enabled the majority of Iranians to "shift roles from devotee to cynic," from Cyrus (the pre-Islamic king) to Hosein (the Shi'i martyr), from the modern to the traditional—a "freedom" he believes the revolution brought to an end. Morocco has followed a less extreme path toward modernization, but Al e Ahmad's critique of Euromania still rings true for many of the post-Independence generation. Whether or not they love ambiguity, they certainly make lives and identities in an atmosphere of West-strickenness that easily turns into feelings of alienation and inauthenticity.

On Identification and Alterity

As Erikson emphasizes, identity is much more than an individual's identifications, but it is still anchored in identifications. I use the term *identification* much as it has entered our own folk psychology: as a process or relationship that yields something like role models that we look up to and that thereby shape our personalities for better or worse. But we need to give identification a second thought, as it turns out to be complex, subtle, and rather mysterious, a special case of *mimesis*, of imitating or making a copy of an Other. Michael Taussig[148] recently has drawn on the writings of Walter Benjamin, Theodore Adorno, and Max Horkheimer to explore the mimesis set into play in the colonial encounter, in particular, the use made by Latin American Cuna Indian healers of wooden *nuchukana* figurines carved of Europeans but believed to embody native spirits and the therapeutic use by poor European colonists of images of Indian devils. "The wonder of mimesis," Taussig writes, "lies in the copy drawing on the character and power of the original." Humans evince a "compulsion to become the Other," he says, from which they sense they can capture an alien power.[149]

Identification seeks to make the self resemble an Other to share in its power, entailing "sympathetic" magic insofar as it strives for resemblance and "contagious" magic as it seeks contact. "And what does such a compulsion to become Other imply for the sense of Self?" Taussig asks, specifically of the Cuna's figurines of Europeans: "Why are they Other, and why are they

Colonial Other?"[150] To add yet another order of complexity, Taussig points out that copies diverge from originals not only because of poor attention to detail or sloppy craftsmanship but also because the copying is driven by projection, by imaginings of the Other colored by one's own wishes and fears. What a remarkable process, then, is identification, either when one seeks to share in the Other's power by becoming it, or when one seeks—through disidentification—to master the Other's power by controlling or even destroying the original, as the Nazis did the Jews. Adorno and Horkheimer's insight, following Freud's writings on negation, was that disidentification (as seen in anti-Semitism) entails an identification established before the negating *dis-* may be prefixed.

In Taussig's view, it is this mysterious process of mimesis, the compulsion to become Other, that creates identity:

> Mimesis registers both sameness and difference, of being like, and of being Other. Creating stability from this instability is no small task, yet all identity formation is engaged in this habitually bracing activity in which the issue is not so much staying the same, but maintaining sameness through alterity.[151]

In his 1890 *Principles of Psychology*, William James explored the normal multiplicity of selves and pondered "mutations of the self" in which alter selves uncannily step forward in multiple personality, trance states, automatic writing, and spirit mediumship. Almost as an aside, he noted:

> One curious thing about trance-utterances is their generic similarity in different individuals. The "control" here in America is either a grotesque, slangy, and flippant personage ("Indian" controls, calling the ladies "squaws," the men "braves," the house a "wigwam," etc. are excessively common); or, if he ventures on higher intellectual flights, he abounds in a curiously vague optimistic philosophy-and-water, in which phrases about spirit, harmony, beauty, law, progression, development, etc. keep recurring. It seems exactly as if one author composed more than half of the trance-messages, no matter by whom they are uttered. Whether all sub-conscious selves are peculiarly susceptible to a certain stratum of the Zeitgeist, and get their inspiration from it, I know not; but this is obviously the case with the secondary selves which become "developed" in spiritualist circles.[152]

It wasn't just spirit mediums who captured power from Native American alterity in Victorian America. Historian Mark Carnes reports that nearly a quarter of the male adult population in the 1890s belonged to fraternal orders, including the Freemasons, the Odd Fellows, and the Knights of Pythias, whose meetings were devoted mainly to initiating members through elaborate levels of hierarchy.[153] In some of these, men became figures in Old Testament landscapes, in some Greek or Roman warriors, in some medieval knights, and in many they became Indians—and then went to their mostly professional and white-collar jobs the next day. Lewis Henry Morgan, the pioneer of American ethnography, began studying the Iroquois in 1845 to devise rituals for his fraternal order, whose initiates were ritually reborn as adopted "Red" warriors while a chorus chanted for the destruction of white men. As Morgan became a serious student of the Iroquois, he drifted away from his "boyish" fraternity brothers and was adopted into a real(!) Iroquois clan.

What power were these men capturing in their copies? Noting that these were male fraternities and that the initiations emphasized warriorhood and the bestowal of ranks by elders on their new "sons," Carnes suggests that the orders symbolically built a kind of rugged masculinity that was disappearing from office work, from comfortable domestic life, and from the gentler brands of Christianity ascendant in Protestant churches. We can ask, after Taussig, why the colonized Other, as imagined by whites far from the frontier, should come to provide identificatory role models for middle-class masculinity, in precisely the decades when the originals were being destroyed? How was this captured "primitive" power carried back into Victorian-era offices and homes, somehow "maintaining sameness through alterity"?

And what of the mimesis of the colonized? In an early chapter of Orhan Pamuk's 1990 novel *The Black Book*, a journalist writes a column on the history of mannequin making in Turkey, telling the story of Master Bedii, "the patron saint of mannequin making," and his son who learned his art. The spectacularly lifelike mannequins Master Bedii made for the first national naval museum were removed after the "narrow-minded Sheikh of Islam . . . threw a fit" at his blasphemous competition with God's power of creation, and for the next twenty years he worked modestly from his basement. Then one day:

> He noticed that those famous haberdashers in Beyoglu began to place mannequins in their store windows when, during the excitement of the initial wave of Westernization in the early years of our Republic, gentlemen discarded their fezzes in favor of Panama hats and ladies peeled off their veils and slipped on high-heeled shoes. When Master Bedii first saw those imported mannequins, he thought that the moment of victory he'd anticipated for years had arrived. . . .

He "bolted out of his underground workshop" to sell his mannequins to the storeowners, but "one by one," they all rejected him:

> Apparently, the mannequins he made didn't look like the models from the West who taught us style; instead, they resembled our own people. "The customer," one of the store owners said, "doesn't want the topcoat shown on the back of a mustachioed, bowlegged, dark and skinny citizen who's seen every day by the tens of thousands in

the streets; he wants to slip into a jacket worn by a new and beautiful person from a distant and unfamiliar land, so that putting on the jacket he can believe he, too, has changed and turned into someone else." . . . A more laconic store owner pointed out that his customers did not buy an outfit but, in truth, bought a dream. What they really wanted to purchase was the dream of being like the "others" who wore the same outfit.

Master Bedii's son took the journalist to see the masterpieces collected in their cellar and explained his father's belief:

Above all, we must pay attention to the gestures that make us who we are. . . . In those years, his father believed that a nation's lifestyle, history, technology, culture, art, and literature could change, but there was no chance that the gestures could be altered. . . . He kept pointing out again and again the gestures of the mannequins, their postures, and the essence that was "us" in those stances, as they waited for the hour of eternity when they'd be animated at last.

As they walked the streets, however, father and son began to notice that people's gestures and movements "had changed and lost their authenticity."

At first, they couldn't figure out who the man in the street modeled himself after, given that he saw nobody other than himself and those who looked so much like him. . . . Some time later, as the father and son worked on a line of mannequin children, it all became clear to them: "Those damn movies!" cries the son. . . .

He tells the journalist: "My father never lost hope that someday mankind would achieve the felicity of not having to imitate others." At the end of the essay, though, the journalist confesses:

I'd been thinking that this crowd of mannequins was also dying to get out of this bleak and dusty dungeon as soon as possible and, like myself, emerge on the face of the earth, to observe other people under the sun, to imitate them, and live happily ever after like ourselves by trying to become someone else.[154]

This book will not quite get to the heart of all this "othering" and of the magical transfers of power that occur as selves find—and lose—themselves in reflections that bounce across the light-bending boundaries of history, geography, and social distinction. But this concern lies at the heart of my inquiry, and with an extended analogy to narrative's musiclike orchestration of experience, it will explore the ways four Moroccans selectively use their culture's repertoire of themes, motifs, and Others to create themselves by rich mixtures of classical form and contemporary improvisation.

2

A Cultural Geography

When I wrote *Self Representation* about the life narratives of young Americans, I assumed my readers shared my respondents' culture and easily would grasp what it meant when one described herself as a New Age–type person and another said he'd once tried to style himself after the Beat writers. I didn't hesitate to use familiar cultural terms, describing one respondent as living a counterculture lifestyle and another as narrating a Pygmalion-like life story. Even while I was emphasizing the role of culture in shaping my respondents' identities, I never recognized the way every step in my interpretations depended on the cultural understandings I *presumed* respondent, writer, and reader all shared. This book cannot rest on that presumption and presents daunting difficulties about how to provide enough background on North African culture for readers to understand my respondents' words and evaluate my interpretations of them. I have struggled with how much information to present and whether to present it in a didactic style ("I'm the expert, and here are the basics you need to know") or let subtler understandings emerge from my respondents' varied points of view and inner dialogues. After drafting and rejecting several approaches, I have settled on a compromise.

I will leave most of the background for the narrative chapters and explain cultural practices and meanings when the texts require it. I hope this invites the reader to ask continually: "What do I need to know about the culture to understand what this person feels and means?" I also hope this helps show the myriad ways culture patterns the voicing of a life and that it shows culture not just as shared understandings or norms but as disputed meanings and values. At the same time, I believe that many readers will appreciate a sketch of Moroccan society before moving on to the life narratives. So I have written this "cultural geography" in a rather old-fashioned, author-as-expert style. It describes some of the physical and cultural landscapes in which my respondents live, moving from Casablanca to Marrakech, through the High Atlas Mountains, and to the towns and villages of the pre-Sahara. It reviews the major historical events that shaped their parents' and their lives and presents a few facts and figures that set the parameters of their life prospects. And because my respondents' life stories are so permeated by contrasts of "modern" and "traditional" styles of life, I occasionally take license to describe some of the ways these clash, converge, and braid together, especially through the ubiquitous presence of Western tourists.

I write in this chapter (and in the rest of the book) in the "ethnographic present"—as I observed Moroccan society in the late 1980s and on a follow-up visit in the mid-1990s. Changes in the ensuing decade—especially the death of King Hassan II and ascent of his reform-minded son, Mohammed VI, and the continued expansion of the electricity grid, schools, and health clinics into rural areas—have altered details of the cultural geography. But a 2003 visit showed the overall portrait to remain much the same, especially with regard to the cultural dualities from which young Moroccans forge their identities.

Casablanca ❀

Young Moroccans love *dar beyḍa*—"the white house," Casablanca—for many of the reasons tourists usually despise it. Searching for the exotic backdrop to Bogart and Bergman's romance in the movie *Casablanca*, tourists find but a pale copy of a Western industrial city, and beyond the gardens of the Hilton or Hyatt, much of it looks dirtier, shabbier, and more congested than those they know at home. There are so few signs of the scenes and styles that drew Henri Matisse, Edith Wharton, Paul Bowles, and Mick Jagger and so many drab and dented commodities dumped on Third World markets when no Westerners wanted them. *Dar beyḍa* is a modern city, without ancient architectural wonders, tombs of legendary rulers, medieval fortresses, or quaint "old medina" quarters with labyrinthine alleyways and entrancing scents of African spices. Most tourists find their way to the lovely restaurants and nightclubs on the seaside Corniche but discover nothing more exotic than "credit card welcome" carpet and souvenir shops staffed by young men wearing their idea of what tourists expect dashing Saharan tribesmen to wear.

Moroccans mostly come to *dar beyḍa* from poorer, dustier, truly "backward" places—the places tourists seek out as authentic, exotic, real Morocco. To Moroccans, the big city gleams and bustles with excitement. In its great expanses of working-class or *populaire* neighborhoods, dense mixtures of three-story apartment buildings, shops, schools, mosques, cafés, and cinemas set stages for the young, educated, multilingual Moroccans who are busily creating a new culture. From hip street slang, to new businesses serving multinational corporations, to Euro-Arab fusion rock, to human rights, union, and feminist activism, to cultural satire theater troupes, to local brands of militant Islam, the city pulses with new culture animated by old energies and old culture infused with new spirit. *Dar beyḍa* eclipses Tangier as Morocco's gate-

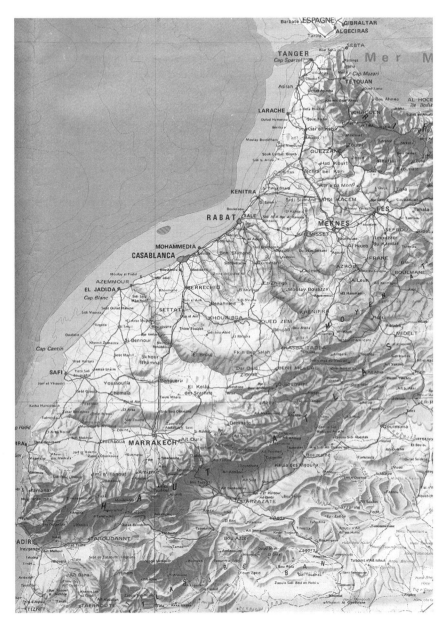

Morocco: Principal cities and High Atlas mountains

way to the world and Rabat, home to one of the world's longest-reigning monarchs,[1] as the gateway to Morocco's future. Many of those I interviewed glimpsed that future when they came to *dar beyḍa* as children to visit relatives. Most felt exhilarated by what they saw and returned to see their homes and hometowns with fresh eyes.

The Dual Economy ❀

A two-lane highway leaves Casablanca past walled bidonvilles (shantytowns or slums), and heads south toward Marrakech. It is crowded with buses, Mercedes "grand taxis" squeezing in six passengers with the driver, and trucks laden with household goods and canisters of Butagaz, the butane fuel most urban Moroccans use for cooking. It takes only a few kilometers to get into the countryside dotted with farmhouses: modest one-story adobe buildings with little iron-grilled and shuttered windows, usually encircled by an adobe wall to form a family compound. After an hour, the terrain turns increasingly arid, and djellaba-clad men can be seen driving donkey carts along the roadside, plowing behind a camel yoked to an ox, and herding sheep on the stubble of wheat. Then come the more arid "phosphate plains," with dusty new towns that process Morocco's main export. Then there are more farms, poorer ones, with adobe houses, cactus-walled compounds, and herds of goats grazing the untilled hillsides.

Like many so-called underdeveloped nations, Morocco can be said to have a dual economy: a modern, capital-intensive economy in which companies vie for international and domestic markets and a traditional, labor-intensive economy in which households provide much of their own subsistence. Casablanca thrives as the center of the modern economy, but the subsistence sector is visible a few kilometers past the city limits. More than half the population lives in rural communities, and every city-hinterland region replicates this duality.

These economies operate according to sharply contrasting principles: in the modern sector, labor and materials are purchased, technology is used to boost productivity, and products are sold; in the subsistence sector, resources and labor are acquired largely by traditional rights, most labor is done by hand, and products are distributed among family members or circulated as gift and countergift among neighbors and kin. Some products may be sold at local weekly *suq-s* (markets), on a sort of sliding scale of bartered prices by which the affluent often pay more than the poor. The traditional sector also includes the thousands of small craft producers, shopkeepers, and traveling merchants from whom the populace buys most of its goods; they rely on highly personal relationships rather than on modern business practices. The coexistence of modern and subsistence economies means that "modern" and "traditional" ways of life are not just matters of taste but solidly rooted in contrasting processes of production and distribution and in the family and social relations organized to carry out each.

These are, of course, ideal types, and reality is more complicated. A good many city-dwellers have left the subsistence sector but failed to gain a foothold in the modern economy, and so they live marginal or slum-bound existences in neither. And the modern sector permeates the rural, in the form of government agencies that administer and "develop" it, of urban landlords who own much of the better farmland, and of corporations that market basic commodities. In addition, most families cannot be said to be solidly in one or the other and typically have members in each. Most families strive to break into the modern sector while conserving their subsistence base as a springboard and insurance policy, and they shuffle people and resources from one to the other as opportunities expand and contract—creating much more flux and instability than first meets the outsider's eye. Most young Moroccans of the generation I interviewed grew up in families with one foot in the modern economy and one in the subsistence sector—and have carried their families' hopes that they would have fully modern, "white collar" careers.

Marrakech ❀

The tourist brochures proclaim Morocco "a land of contrasts," and nowhere do the modern and the traditional stand more brilliantly juxtaposed than in *ma-raksh* (emphasis on the second syllable) or Marrakech. An island of date palms, red adobe, and adobe-hued concrete, this former capital of an empire that stretched from Granada to Timbuktu sits bathed in sunlight in the arid red-clay plain at the foot of the snow-capped Atlas Mountains. Date palms wave everywhere against vibrant blue skies, and among them the city's beauty unfolds in nuances of red—ocher, sepia, pink, dusky orange—and in nuances of modernity and tradition combined with a startling sleight of hand. The road from *dar beyḍa* (Casablanca) first enters the *ville nouvelle*, the "new city" of tree-lined neighborhoods of private family villas, wide boulevards, art deco architecture, luxury hotels, shops, cafés, bookstores, restaurants, and nightclubs. Tourists mix with young Moroccans, many in stylish Western dress, often strolling together or riding mopeds as couples, enjoying a public freedom that defies stereotypes of Muslim cultures.

In the middle of the Boulevard Mohammed V (named for the king who led the country to independence in 1956) sits the seven-story Hotel Renaissance (*nahaḍa* in Arabic, which means "renewal" and was a slogan of the early anticolonial movement), with curving art deco terraces on its roof topped with a neon sign that reads "bar." In late afternoons, the tables fill with Moroccans and a few tourists, who chat and gaze out on the red city, the red desert plain, and the 14,000-foot Jebel Toubkal, which rises in the distance. A mile down Boulevard Mohammed V, the dark minaret of the fifteenth-century

Marrakech: main boulevard in the "new city"

Koutoubia mosque towers over the landscape, marking the way to the medina, the walled "old city" of curving, forking, reed-shaded alleyways, too narrow and crowded with people and donkeys for cars to pass. At the entrance to the medina stands another mosque, where a dozen blind beggars sway and sing or chant suras (verses) from the Quran in eerily beautiful tones. Beyond the beggars stretch lines of seemingly identical *hanut*s (small one-merchant shops) displaying plump dates and yard-long cords of dried figs. Further in, veiled women in djellabas clamor over brightly colored rolls of cotton and brocade; around a corner sit shops with barrels, bags, and bottles of unfamiliarly scented spices; down another alleyway, the butchers set out rows of cows' hooves and goats' heads and ineffectually whisk flies away from chunks of beef and mutton. And always the sounds of Moroccan Arabic, shot through with refrains of Middle Eastern popular music and Quranic recitations, echo from the shopkeepers' stalls, mixing with children's shouts, clattering donkey hooves, and rusty bicycle bells. Authentic, exotic, real Morocco.

*Marrakech: twelfth-century Koutoubia mosque, just
outside the walls of the "old city"*

Between the Koutoubia mosque and the keyhole-shaped gates to the
medina sits the clattering, jostling *jameᶜ l-fna* (Place of the Dead), where the
heads of executed rebels and criminals once were displayed and where now a
non-stop carnival of acrobats, musicians, storytellers, monkey trainers, snake
charmers, dream interpreters, astrologers, orange juice and kabob vendors,
and "Saharan" hawkers of magical paraphernalia draws surging crowds of
tourists and Moroccans. Tiny Renault taxis ferry hurried Moroccans between
the old and new cities, and horse-drawn British-style carriages take tourists
on leisurely, romantic tours. Across the street from the Koutoubia minaret
sits the Marrakech Club Med; a block behind it is the palatial Mamounia Hotel
and Casino; somewhere concealed in the medina are the vacation homes of
Mick Jagger, Yves St. Laurent, and others. Ringed with affordable hotels and
restaurants that fill with European youth, the *jameᶜ l-fna* is Marrakech's

premier attraction. Each hour, dozens of charter buses disgorge their tour groups to join in the scene, snapshotting and shopping their way into the medina.

Tourists and Guides ❁

For young Moroccan men, there's real money to be made guiding tourists through the medina's mazes, often to carpet and jewelry stores whose owners give them hefty commissions. The competition grows so intense that strolling tourists get no more than a minute's peace after one would-be guide angrily departs and another offers his services, and they quickly take offense at the "pushy" Arabs who don't "respect their rights."[2] Encouraged by the tourism ads, a good many foreigners treat the *jameᶜ l-fna* square and medina alleyways like a theme park rather than residential and shopping neighborhoods. They waste little time reflecting on the appropriateness of wearing shorts, undershirts, and halter tops in a Muslim country or of photographing anyone who looks picturesque. The young guides perceive that tourists feel their money permits them any sort of loutish or racist behavior, and on this score, they're astute ethnographers. At the same time, though, the young foreigners project a vigorous image of freedom that many Moroccans find tantalizing. A good number come with sincere curiosity and meet Moroccans who invite them to their homes for meals and to late-night discussions in cafés, where real questions get asked and debated. When they put it all together, the pushy guides usually develop far more nuanced understandings of Westerners than the Westerners ever do about Moroccans.

Then there is sex. Enough Europeans take Moroccan lovers—for a night or a week or occasionally for life—that most young Moroccan men have at least one friend who has "had" a *Fransia* or a *Deutschlandia* or an *Americania*. There's nothing to lose by asking, so women traveling alone get asked and asked and asked, and many leave cursing "Arab" men. The Arab men mostly go home without scoring, turn on the TV, and find themselves again confronted with blond-haired, blue-eyed, bikini-clad babes, striking sultry poses in French-dubbed American dramas or pitching Pepsi and Coke between news of the Palestinian intifada and World Cup soccer. If they read the *New York Times Sunday Magazine*, they could have stared at a full-page ad of blond supermodel Jerry Hall in a bikini, standing among dark women concealed in Iranian-style chadors (not worn in Morocco), with the caption, "Jerry Hall's swimwear raised a few eyes in Morocco."

In the blink of an eye, the spectacular view from the rooftop Renaissance Bar can turn into a neocolonialist theater, in which the guides' unnerving, slow-boiling rage seems all too natural in light of the humiliating treatment they accept—these educated unemployed speakers of five and six languages— as they hawk the most backward features of their cultural heritage to foreigners eager to buy authentic Morocco. Questions flare like fireworks. Those who've bedded Europeans: Have they tasted freedom? Proved their equality? Turned themselves into exotic rides in the theme park? The veiled, djellaba-clad woman carrying home bread from the public oven: Is she an embodiment of authentic Moroccan family values? Or a sign of Moroccan backwardness? And the young Moroccans on afternoon dates in the *ville nouvelle*: Are they cultural pioneers creating a Moroccan future? Or merely what the French termed *evolved natives*, a privileged elite whom the fundamentalists view as having sold their souls to ape the Europeans? A young Moroccan at the Renaissance orders a cold beer (Stork brand, the symbol of sainthood), opens a pack of cigarettes (Koutoubia brand, with a picture of the minaret on the package), and reads the latest news of the intifada and the war in Iraq.

Economic Dependency ✾

It is often said that the Middle East can be divided into a set of nations with oil and small populations and a set with large populations and no oil (Iraq and Iran being the exceptions with both). Morocco falls in the latter group and must import nearly all its energy for household consumption, transportation, and manufacturing. This means the government must choose between going deeper into debt to subsidize energy costs and risking popular anger if it allows market prices to push the cost of electricity and cooking fuel out of reach. Electricity and Butagaz are already too costly for many in the countryside, where dependence on the traditional energy source—fuelwood shrubs gathered by women and girls[3]—contributes to the deforestation of rangelands and keeps girls too busy to attend school. The lack of energy, combined with a lack of metals, wood, and water, makes industrialization expensive and difficult.

The country's development depends primarily on three sources of income: the wages of the nearly half-million Moroccans working in Europe, tourism, and the export of phosphates.[4] Commercial fishing and export agribusiness (citrus fruit and olives grown on some of the country's best farmland, taken from Moroccans by French and Spanish colonists and now operated by Moroccan businessmen) make smaller but important contributions to the national income. And as a "moderate" and "friendly" Arab state strategically located at the entrance to the Mediterranean, Morocco receives significant foreign aid from France and the United States that has helped build the country's impressive infrastructure of roads, schools, telecommunications, airports, and health care facilities and also subsidized the building of a modern army and its two-decade war in the western Sahara.

Improvements in nutrition and public health have significantly lowered mortality rates, and the population quadrupled in the twentieth century from around 7 million to an estimated 25 to 30 million. The annual growth rate remains high at about 2.5 percent, and nearly half of the population is under age fifteen—a catastrophic situation for planners, who cannot see how more than a fraction of these will find ways to support themselves as adults.[5] The leading sources of national income seem precarious: the first Gulf War dropped tourism to nearly nothing for a few months, and political events in Europe could easily culminate in a gradual or sudden end of "guest worker" programs. So although this generation and their parents have seen dramatic improvements in their life expectancies and standards of living, they stare into an uncertain future of possibly shrinking opportunities. The number of well-educated but unemployed young people like Hussein (chapter 4) has been growing alarmingly. Many move into the cities in hopes of catching hold of a new government development project or some part of the tourist trade. Some persevere and succeed; some lose themselves in delinquencies; some turn to fundamentalist indictments of Western decadence and Moroccan corruption.

Tribes ❀

A five-hour drive takes one south from Marrakech over the High Atlas Mountains to Ouarzazate. This is the first leg of the "route of the *qasbah*s," whose landscapes and architecture have provided backdrops for *The Black Stallion*,

Marrakech, High Atlas, and Ouarzazate regions

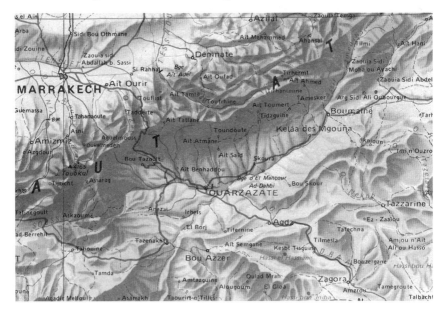

The Jewel of the Nile, The Sheltering Sky, Kundun, Hidalgo, and a dozen other feature films.[6] An hour into the foothills, the tractor-plowed farms owned by wealthy *marrakshi*s give way to isolated Berber villages with tiny terraced fields scattered along riverbanks—plowed, irrigated, and harvested by hand. Another half hour yields breathtaking vistas of interior valleys, where three- and four-story crenellated-towered fortresses built during the "tribal" and colonial eras still stand majestically on strategic promontories. These mountains are home to two closely related Berber groups, the Tashelhait-speaking Masmouda tribes astride and to the west of the highway, and the Tamazight-speaking Sanhaja tribes to the east, beginning roughly where the High Atlas broadens into the Middle Atlas. Most Moroccans are, in fact, Berber in origin, but well more than half—mainly those in the plains and cities—have become Arab in culture, language, and identity. Along with the Rif Mountains on the Mediterranean shore, the Atlas Mountains and some pre-Saharan areas remain preserves of Berber culture. Most Berber men have traveled to the cities and learned Moroccan Arabic, but many women have not.

The High Atlas villagers continue to practice an agropastoral way of life termed *transhumance,* in which most members of a household grow subsistence and cash crops near their homes, and a shepherd branch lives on the ranges and walks a herd of sheep and goats (and sometimes camels) through a yearly sequence of pastures: up into the mountains in the summer and down onto the plains in the winter. Villages typically have twenty-five to seventy-five households, belonging to three or four patrilineages, which historically

High Atlas: village on the Marrakech-Ouarzazate Road

were united in collective defense of their water sources, maintenance of their irrigation systems, and performance of religious rituals. A handful of villages typically united to form a *taqbilt*, or "tribal fraction," that managed and defended territories, water resources, and pastures. These tribal fractions typically combined into larger *taqbilt*s termed *tribes* or *confederations* by ethnographers. These were mainly political groupings organized to manage and defend larger territories and to deal with state authorities.[7]

Ethnographers have noted that the system resembles a "segmentary lineage system," as famously described by Evans-Pritchard for the cattle-herding Nuer of Sudan.[8] Tribal groups throughout the Middle East were long described as segmentary lineage systems, with levels of smaller units nested in larger units (households in lineages, lineages in tribal fractions, etc.). Tribes living beyond all but the most determined reach of state authorities were thought to have their "acephalous" structure preserved by counterbalanced feuds and alliances at each level. Ethnographers have subsequently demonstrated that tribal groups often don't organize themselves according to their map of kinship segments, which provides more of a model or idiom for social relations than a flowchart of how groups actually form and split. The segments comprising these High Atlas tribes are built of territorial and political alliances as well as kinship groupings, and tribespeople construct plenty of social relations that cut across kinship segments.

But a "tribe" nonetheless consists of a system of segments nested within segments, with conflicts fracturing and uniting groups at varying levels. Two ecological factors underlie this: (1) already-scarce resources shift unpredictably (the villagers we studied never knew which of four springs might dry up or which fields would be washed away when rain fell), often leading to strife; and (2) every household functions with a chronic imbalance of person power and resources, requiring all sorts of provisional arrangements within and between them. These set in motion a personalistic "politics"—frequently violent in the past—aimed both at weaving together social groups along and across the lines of segmentation and at provoking and resolving conflicts.

Traditionally, then, this was a world of shifting lines of cooperation and strife, in which every male tribesman was a soldier—potentially for his family, his multifamily household, his lineage, his village, his tribal "fraction," his tribal "confederation," or even, on occasion, for Islam or the nation. A collection of unwritten laws provided principles that could be used to mobilize cooperation, warfare, and peacemaking, but it was still incumbent upon a man to demonstrate his physical prowess, courage, and cunning and give weight to his word by backing threats and promises with action. Women, junior men, and dependent "clients" were to be kept obedient and loyal by a judicious mixture of intimidation, protection, affection, and generosity. But strife often tore into the heart of households and families, with diverging interests pitting even brother against brother, as in the apocryphal story of Abel and Cain. The "Legend of the Bani Hilal," North Africa's best known oral epic,[9] is driven by the tragic conflict of kin loyalty and betrayal, crystallized by punning wordplay with *ikhwan* and *khawan*—brothers/brotherhood and betrayal—that performers typically weave through it to evoke a tragic sense of their intimate linkage.

The strategies, etiquettes, and ethics associated with this segmentary politics show a remarkable similarity in circum-Mediterranean rural societies, and ethnographers have described them as an "honor code."[10] As we will see, many observers mistakenly viewed this as a clear-cut and widely shared code of conduct and have failed to appreciate the importance of regional differences in its character. But the household, village, and tribal politics of southern Morocco's resource-scarce segmentary societies give rise to an ethic of masculine honor *achieved* by demonstrations of prowess and generosity and of feminine honor *achieved* by hard work, fertility, and modesty. These themes appear prominently in the life histories I elicited, even though the young Moroccans I interviewed were no longer living off the land.

Lords of the Atlas ❀

Farther up, the High Atlas turns into jagged granite, with spectacular peaks and cliffs, and the precarious road switchbacks up the side of a narrow arm. Finally, it crests and levels into a beautiful grassy meadow, a prized pasture in the yearly transhumance cycle. The rise at the end of the meadow is marked as the Tizi-n-Tichka pass, and a two-hour descent to Ouarzazate begins, through more pastures dotted with the stone huts used by shepherd families. The only paved turnoff leads in a half hour to Telouat, site of the once-sumptuous fortress of the el Glaoui *taqbilt* and eponymous family of sheikhs (Arabic) or *amghar*s (Berber), the greatest and most infamous of the "lords of the Atlas."[11] Supported by the French, who found them expanding their power in the early decades of the century, the el Glaoui did much of the dirty work of conquering and pacifying the independent *taqbilt*s of southern Morocco. Every tribal group initially resisted the el Glaoui and French forces, but the Foreign Legion's demonstration of the ease with which rifled artillery could tear apart adobe fortresses quickly brought the surrender of most. In many cases, villages had long been split into feuding clans when the el Glaoui forces arrived, and one clan sided with their external enemy (the el Glaoui) in order to vanquish their internal enemy (the rival clan). But the fearsome nomadic Ait Atta confederation rallied resisters to fight an effective guerrilla war and held out until 1933, when the Legion finally surrounded their fighters on a barren plateau in the rugged Saghro Mountains and brought in airplanes to bomb them.[12]

Following the strategy of indirect rule, the French helped the el Glaoui leaders exercise direct rule over Marrakech, much of the High Atlas, and most of the pre-Sahara until independence in 1956. Thami el Glaoui governed

Telouat: qsar (fortress/palace) of the el Glaoui tribal sheikhs who ruled southern Morocco during the colonial era

Marrakech as *pasha*, with the help of neighborhood *mqedem*s (headmen) and Foreign Legion soldiers. His fellow tribesmen built *qasbah*-style fortresses in Ouarzazate and other strategic centers, they installed a *khalifa* (lieutenant governor) and contingent of el Glaoui soldiers in each, and the French set up legion bases nearby. Then they built a fortress at the heart of each tribe and installed a *caid* (tribal ruler) with a contingent of el Glaoui tribesmen as soldiers. These *caid*s, in consultation with French "indigenous affairs" officers and backed by Foreign Legion troops, picked the tribes' sheikhs and *mqedem*s. This whole apparatus then deployed whatever violence and coercion was needed to extract as much surplus as possible from the region's meager subsistence and cash crop production, which impoverished local populaces for two decades. Villagers and tribespeople were assessed arbitrary taxes on all of their yields, required to assemble great "gifts" to their el Glaoui masters, and taken off to perform corvée (conscripted and unpaid) labor on building projects. Any who resisted were beaten, thrown into the dungeon cellars of the el Glaoui fortresses, or saw their families ruined. As locals still describe it, "the south was like a cow: the French held the horns while the el Glaoui milked it."

The parents of my respondents grew up and into adulthood under Foreign Legion-backed el Glaoui rule and continue to resent the repeated despoliations that prevented them from rising above mere subsistence. Two periods of drought and hunger, known colloquially as "the year of rice" (1936)

Telouat: interior of the el Glaoui qsar

and "the year of rationing" (1945), added to the collective misery and sent many young men fleeing to cities in northern Morocco and Algeria in search of work, as did Hussein's father. In the early 1950s, some signed on with the French and fought in Indochina, as did Khadija's father. Many joined the nationalist cause, and like Hussein's father, returned after Independence (1956) with determination to help build a new nation. And like Hussein's and Khadija's fathers, many prospered as employees of the French and came home with money and skills that boosted them into local elites.

When independence came, el Glaoui leaders fled into exile, and the Liberation Army rounded up Marrakech's pro-Glaoui neighborhood headmen, shot them, and burned their bodies outside one of the gates to the old medina. In the south, the el Glaoui *khalifas*, *caids*, and soldiers fled unharmed, and the local sheikhs and *mqedems* they had appointed were deposed. But as the monarchy struggled to rehabilitate the rural aristocracy as a conservative counterbalance to the pro-democracy urban liberation forces, they gutted the power of the newly elected rural assemblies, installed new *caids* (tribal governors) and government paramilitary police in the old el Glaoui fortresses, and reinstalled most of the sheikhs and *mqedems* who had grown rich and powerful as part of the el Glaoui–French rule.[13] In Morocco's Sous Valley region to the west of Ouarzazate, the colonial-era *caids* and sheikhs were removed and marginalized, and stunning economic development followed. In much of Ouarzazate province, local elites have remained entrenched into third and fourth generations, maintaining their exploitive relationships. There they continued to milk successful entrepreneurial efforts and cornered the benefits of government development projects. Economic development has lagged and depended mainly on external forces: guest work in Europe (roughly 10 percent of rural families have a member working in Europe), expansion of tourism, and every couple of years, the windfall of a feature film.

Ouarzazate ✿

The road out of the High Atlas descends into dry desert heat, follows a nearly dry riverbed through a rocky barren plain for another hour, passes the new dairy cooperative and the tennis club for government employees, and then enters the town of Ouarzazate. New neighborhoods of modest cement houses block out older ones of adobe, and the road passes a new tiled square with an ice cream parlor and a car rental agency. After another half kilometer it arrives "downtown": three blocks of cafés, banks, and shops, two small and inexpensive hotels, and Dimitri's Supermarche and Café, run for more than fifty years by a pair of brothers who came with the Foreign Legion and stayed. Ouarzazate has the province's only hospital and airport, the largest of its two high schools, one of its two movie theaters, the Agricultural Ministry offices that manage huge development projects, and all of the region's administrative offices: the provincial government, the post office, the police and gen-

Ouarzazate: traditional neighborhood overlooking the dam that regulates water flowing south to the Drᶜa River oases

darmes, the Highway Bureau, the courts, the Ministry of Education, and more. Yet it still feels a bit like a "last outpost" kind of place, because few of the villages even five kilometers out of town have running water, electricity, sewers, or telephones.[14]

As sleepy as it can sometimes appear in the heat of an August afternoon, Ouarzazate also bustles with trucks of goods, grand taxis and buses of Moroccans, busloads and cars full of tourists, government workers in Land Rovers and trucks, and scores of Moroccans on mopeds. It is a crossroads town, where the highway from Marrakech (one of three over the High Atlas) intersects with the only east-west road south of the mountains, and it has grown as a cultural crossroads as well. There are tribesmen from the hinterlands with their heads wrapped in white scarves, rural women whose shawl designs designate their tribe, townspeople in traditional djellabas and Western coats, soldiers in their fatigues, officials in business suits, high school students boisterously jostling along the street, beggars, a pair of American Peace Corps volunteers, a French family in their car, and a half-dozen young Germans with backpacks. There's little to see or do in the town itself—no historical sights, no enchanting old medina, no glittering new city—and most of the Moroccans have come for business, are passing through, or going about their daily work.

It is, however, a hub on the "route of the *qasbah*s," and on a plateau toward the south end of town sit three of six luxury hotels, overlooking an old picturesque walled community and the fortress of the El Glaoui rulers, which has been turned into a tourist attraction with a carpet and souvenir shop on either side. In the distance, the Dades and Ouarzazate rivers join and then cut through a gorge in the rugged, dark Saghro Mountains and flow down the Drᶜa valley into the Sahara. The Saghro gorge was dammed in the 1970s to smooth out the ancient flood and dry cycles along the Drᶜa, and the Hotel Azghar and the Club Med—where Khadija (chapter 6) worked as a secretary—have stunning vistas of the lake, which can turn a deep turquoise blue beneath a clear desert sky. Some Westernized Moroccans come to the hotels to dine, to drink in privacy with friends, and to dance at the discos, as occasionally does Khadija. At the other end of town, the downscale Gazelle Hotel's almost hidden bar fills each afternoon with less privileged local men, mostly teachers and functionaries, surreptitiously throwing back a few beers.

In spite of the southern tribes' legendary battles against the Foreign Legion in the 1920s and 1930s, Ouarzazate and the whole southern region have a reputation for being "softer" or more tranquil than other parts of Morocco, especially the conservative and "tough" north. Only a few of the tour group tourists venture into town, and they are more likely to encounter curious young Moroccans who want to chat with them than would-be guides. Many of Ouarzazate's teachers, technicians, functionaries, and hotel employees are young, have come from big cities on their first postings, and bring modern styles and attitudes with them. The large number of students, many living in the high school's dormitory and in twos and threes in rooms rented by their parents, add to the quantity of young people free of their parents' supervision. When the heat eases and the dust storms quiet down, there's plenty of modernity and freedom for young people like Mohammed (chapter 3) to be lured off the straight path and into delinquency and, like Khadija, to dream herself French.

The Pre-Sahara ❀

Ouarzazate Province is something of a mini culture area of its own. Roughly the size of Belgium, it encompasses several distinct ecological and cultural zones (see Map 2.2): the southern slopes of the High Atlas Mountains, the Dades River Valley, the Saghro Mountains, and the Drᶜa River Valley. Settlements in all of these areas are sustained by water from the High Atlas snowpack, which flows both underground and aboveground along a number of riverbeds. These meet at Ouarzazate and then flow down the Drᶜa River until it disappears in Saharan sand. Villages line the Dades and divert into their fields the waters that flow year-round. Skoura (where I interviewed Mohammed and several others) is a date palm oasis on a gently sloping plain that draws its water from an intricate system of wells. Clusters of date palm hamlets also line the Drᶜa River all along its nearly hundred-mile descent into the Sahara. The paved road south from Ouarzazate meets the Drᶜa River at Agdez (where I interviewed Hussein and Rachida). Irrigation traditionally depended on floodwaters, but the dam now provides more regular flows of water to the Drᶜa cultivators. Dades-Drᶜa civilization is an ancient one, and land and water rights have evolved into baroque, labyrinthine configurations. Equal inheritance by sons fragments fields into tiny patches of land. Combined with the preference for owning parcels in each area of a village's fields (because one rarely knows which will receive water at the end of the summer or which will flood in winter rains), this has led households to own many small, widely distributed plots. In some areas, different families own the land, the palm trees, and the water rights on each parcel. The Agriculture Ministry's project of surveying and "rationalizing" cultivation along the Drᶜa gives every appearance of stretching into a decades-long endeavor.

For centuries, the pre-Sahara was home to Berber-speaking tribes of the Masmouda (western) and Sanhaja (eastern) groups, with important client groups of Jews and African-origin "blacks." From the fifteenth century, Bedouin Arabs fought their way into the area and settled, part of the great migrations of the Beni M'guil across North Africa. For the past two to three centuries, the region has been a checkerboard of Berber-speaking and Arabic-speaking groups, with the pastoralists of the mountains dominating the agriculturalists and craftsmen settled in oasis and riverside villages on the plains. Many villages became official clients to one or another of the pastoralist tribes, who then "protected" them from the attacks of other tribes. The protector tribe often settled a few families in fortified dwellings in each client village, camped near the village during the winter portion of their transhumance circuit, and as the price of protection, traded with the villagers on terms most favorable to the tribesmen. In some cases, the tribesmen came to own fields, date palms, and water rights in the villages and worked out sharecropping arrangements by which villagers labored on them.

In spite of their homogeneity of outward appearance, most villages were highly stratified by both ownership of resources and social prestige. Many were dominated by the descendants of a *marabout* or *wali* (holy man or saint), who owned most of the land. A numerically larger group of landless blacks, originally brought from sub-Saharan Africa as slaves, farmed the land as share-croppers. Many oases also had small communities of landless Jews, who worked as craftsmen and traveled the region as merchants, at least some of whom prospered. Pre-Saharan villages tended to have between fifteen and seventy-five households and differed in the proportions of these groups. In the High Atlas, pastoralism predominated, and nearly everyone was a "free" tribesman. Often, there were no saintly lineages and few or no blacks or Jews. In the cluster of foothills villages comprising Toundout (where we lived while studying the Imeghrane), the majority of residents were tribesmen, but there also were several marginal saintly lineages and three small, separate villages of blacks who worked throughout the area as blacksmiths, sharecroppers, and house builders. There had also been a Jewish *mellah* with about twenty fami-lies. Along the Dades and Drᶜa rivers, saintly lineages were much more nu-merous and prominent, and tribesmen tended to be in the minority. Blacks often were the majority of households and Jews a significant minority.

Skoura ❀

Most tourists take the route of the *qasbah*s east, toward the imposing gorges of Todgha, where they'll be feted at a mock Berber wedding they won't be told is mock. Leaving Ouarzazate, they see desert too dry for cactus, camel herders in the wintertime, and groups of men, women, and donkeys from villages that were relocated when the dam was built, trudging back to fields they cultivate along its shore.[15] Then they pass Skoura, a five-kilometer stretch of sparsely planted date palms, a few with fields of barley planted beneath them, and occasional hamlets of ten to thirty households. Toward the east-ern edge of the oasis, the palms and green fields become denser, and tourists can catch glimpses of spectacular three-story, crenellated-towered *qasbah*s, with colorful residents coming and going from their mysterious interiors. Buses occasionally stop on the roadside so tourists can pour out and take photos, and the children come racing across the dry riverbed to beg, usually for ballpoint pens ("*donnez-moi un stylo, monsieur?*"). Then the buses keep going, and most days no more than a private car or two pulls off the highway into Skoura's two-block-long town center.

The Centre abuts the walled square where the souk (weekly market) is held on Wednesdays, and most of the shops—dry goods, butchers, moped and bicycle repair, cafés—open only on that day. A couple of small shops and cafés open every day, along with the bureau of the *caid* (rural area governor), a post office, an infirmary, an agriculture station, a *collège* (junior high school), and the stand where Peugeot station wagon grand taxis wait to fill up before setting off for Ouarzazate or, at dusk, up into the villages in the foothills. Dusty dirt roads lead off in all directions and show how huge is this Arabic-speaking island in the middle of the Berber Imeghrane confederation, and how hard three years of drought have hit it. Perhaps half its fields sit untilled, a quarter of its estimated 15,000 residents have left, and the rest are getting by on money sent from relatives in Marrakech, Casablanca, or Europe.

At the northern edge of the oasis sits a cluster of saints' tombs with domed adobe roofs, and Skoura's *khettara* irrigation system comes into view: lines and lines of five-foot-high piles of dirt, about fifteen feet apart, angling across the desert toward the snow-capped mountains. The underground flow of water nears the surface beneath Skoura, and villagers begin building a *khettara* by digging a shallow channel that lets it flow into a field. Because this yields only a small amount of water, they continue the channel upstream until the sides get too deep to hold. Then they dig a well, about twenty feet angled upstream from the open channel, and connect it by a tunnel to the channel, then another well and tunnel, another well and tunnel, and so on, until enough water has been tapped to irrigate a hamlet's fields. Skoura has more than eighty lines of *khettara*, most with a hundred or more wells (twenty-five to thirty feet deep at the upslope end), all dug and maintained by hand—an astonishing sight, as parts of the desert turn into a cratered moonscape. Each of the many hamlets has its own complicated system of rights and turns that regulate how the water and maintenance of the *khettara*s are shared, though most of the labor is done by blacks who live as clients, sharecroppers, and house builders for wealthier families. Mohammed and three of the other Moroccans I interviewed grew up in different hamlets of Skoura. After going to school in Rabat and Ouarzazate and serving in the army, Mohammed has returned to live in his family home, next to one of the dramatic *qasbah*s photographed by tourists and near an experimental solar panel–powered pump mounted on a well by the Agriculture Ministry.

Agdez ❀

From Ouarzazate, another paved road runs south along the Dr^{c}a River to Mhamid, which once was a terminal point of caravan trade to West Africa. For centuries, salt from mines in the Atlas foothills was traded for gold across the Sahara, and the proprietor of a mine in Toundout still sends a dump truck load of salt rocks down the Dr^{c}a River to be sold at the weekly circuit of souks. The road winds through the rugged, desolate, sometimes breath-taking Saghro Mountains and, after a half hour, joins the Dr^{c}a River at Agdez, home to four of those I interviewed. Since their births, Agdez has grown into a small town around its administrative center, marketplace, junior high school, and a cluster of fast-food brochette stands, cafés, and souvenir shops. Most houses now have running water and electricity, which the surrounding villages do not. A steady trickle of tourists take the side trip down the Dr^{c}a to Zagora, Morocco's date capital, which offers spectacular views of date palm oases, walled villages, and towering qasbahs, some of which can be seen in Bertolucci's film of Paul Bowles's Sheltering Sky. A few go farther to the sand dunes to tour the ancient library at Tamegrout or to snap photos of themselves by the "Timbuktu 67 Days" sign at Mhamid. Many pause at Agdez for snacks, cold drinks, and perhaps one of the ceramic model qasbahs made by a renowned folk artist.

Hussein's father grew up in a picturesque village a few bends in the river upstream from Agdez, but ten years ago, he built one of the new-style cinderblock houses between the tourist shops and the administrative center where he works. His and the other Dr^{c}a villages sit on the riverbank, just above the river's flood line, and most consist of two to four lineage groups, each with its own neighborhood or quarter of dwellings. Rachida's family has lived for generations in a traditional adobe house in a hamlet of "blacks" that has gradually become a neighborhood of Agdez. The town has grown around the road, built largely by enterprising villagers who have moved there to market souvenirs to tourists, to sell urban goods to villagers, or—like Hussein's and Rachida's fathers—to work in government bureaus. It has a handful of neighborhoods, and most lack more than a shadow of the lineage-based organization of the traditional villages. Some households consist only of part families whose members move between Agdez and a village home, depending on seasonal labor needs. An increasing number are families who have moved permanently —like Hussein's and Rachida's—their ancestral fields now worked by sharecroppers.

The town is a hot, dusty place that can one moment feel remote from civilization, and the next fully enmeshed in all things modern. The decaying Foreign Legion garrison sits on a hillside above the town, its buildings now housing government offices, and every fall, the nomadic herders of the still-powerful Ait Atta confederation camp a half mile out of town in their black goat-hair tents. Many of the idle young men—though rarely Hussein —pass their time in the cafés, reading Jeunne Afrique, listening to the latest Casablanca bands, and watching World Cup soccer and international news on TV.

Saints and Zawiyas ✤

At Agdez, the narrow paved road rejoins the Dr'a River and snakes beside it into the desert. The riverbed widens and narrows, sometimes bordered by nothing but rocky brown soil, sometimes by vast fields of date palms. The hamlets of crenelated-tower *qasbah*s around Agdez give way to rectangular walled villages, with mosque towers rising above the roofs within. Djellaba-clad men and women wrapped in dark shawls carry farm tools, water, bundles of fuel shrubs, and children in and out of the shadowed gates to the villages. A two-hour spellbinding drive beneath a cloudless blue-domed sky takes one to Zagora, the only "real town" south of Ouarzazate, with an upscale tourist hotel, a high school, blocks of cafés, and a large cooperative that processes and packs dates. The paved road continues south, passing more walled villages and groups of women draped in navy blue cotton shawls embroidered with scattered starburst designs in dayglow colors and sparkling silver spangles. A half hour later, it reaches the village of Tamegrout and the Nasseriyine *zawiya*.

A *zawiya* perhaps resembles a monastery in being a religious sanctuary, usually associated with a *marabet*, or saint. The saint's tomb may be part of the *zawiya* compound, a neighborhood that houses descendants or prominent followers of the saint, who may themselves have reputations as saintly figures. Many *zawiya*s also serve as a kind of lodge, meetinghouse, and meditation center for a *tariqa* (religious order or brotherhood) that follows the spiritual teachings and *treq* (path or way) of the saint. Some *zawiya*s operate

Dr'a Valley: zawiya at Tamegrut, with saint's tomb and Quranic school

religious schools, teaching the Quran to children and training older students in the religious sciences they need to become village imams or *fqih*s. (A *fqih* is a religious specialist, who may serve as the imam, or prayer leader, at a mosque and also may teach children at a Quranic school.) Some *zawiya*s also serve as *horm*s, or sacred sanctuaries where people in trouble can seek refuge and request help from religious leaders in solving their difficulties. The Nasseriyine *zawiya* combines all of these features and was the home and sometimes headquarters of the Nasseriyine *tariqa,* a Sufi brotherhood that has followers throughout Morocco and North Africa. Founded in the sixteenth century, it once housed one of the most prestigious religious universities and extensive libraries in North Africa, and the government has helped it put some of its beautifully calligraphed and illustrated manuscripts on display. Though the most precious and fragile have now been removed to an archive in Rabat, a multilingual guide takes tourists through the many marvelous works that remain, including pages from a seventeenth-century Quran written on gazelle skin.

Next to the library, a classroom of adolescent boys chant the Quran, under the direction of a gray-bearded scholar. Around the corner and down a dusty alleyway sits the tomb of Sidi Mohammed ben Nasser, the primary saint of the Nasseriyine order. Unlike the disappointingly drab buildings of the *zawiya* compound, Sidi ben Nasser's imposing tomb has a beautiful green-tiled roof, engraved arched portico, and massive inlaid wooden door. Many Moroccans take this trip down the Dr^{c}a in a bus or grand taxi to make a *ziyara* (pilgrimage) to the saint. Members of the brotherhood come to see the founder's home and pray, chant the order's mantralike *dikr* (litany), and leave an offering or donation. Others make the pilgrimage because they have become *mrabet* (tied) to the saint, who serves as their intercessor with the prophets and God. This sort of relationship to a saint can be acquired from family tradition, through the advice of a friend or a *fqih* (religious specialist), because the saint has visited one in a dream, or because one has been stricken with an illness that the saint's *baraka* (divine blessedness) is reputed to cure. Pilgrims may bring an offering (sugar, tea, coins), pray to the saint, and make a plea and a vow to be performed if their plea is granted. They may sacrifice a chicken, goat, or ram at the tomb, consume some of the meat that then bears the saint's healing or empowering *baraka,* and leave the remainder to the saint's descendants or *zawiya* brothers as an offering. They may take something from the tomb—a bit of earth that they ingest or rub on their skin, a bit of wool from a sacrificed animal that they burn in a brazier and inhale the smoke—that similarly infuses their bodies with the saint's *baraka.* Others sleep at the tomb and pray for the saint to visit them in their dreams and relieve them of their troubles—often to drive out jinn spirits or make them pregnant. Sidi ben Nasser is especially renowned for curing madness (usually attributed to jinn possession), as are a couple of well-known saints in Skoura and the vicinity of Agdez.

This sort of saint-focused religiosity is especially prominent in North Africa, with domed saints' tombs scattered across the landscape in every direction. In the Atlas Mountains and pre-Sahara, a typical village of fifty households will have a dozen or more spots in its vicinity associated with saintly *baraka*—some of them tombs of named persons with hagiographies, some of them grave markers of unknown persons, some of them rock outcroppings or springs associated with the travels of a local or great holy man. *Zawiya*s like that at Tamegrout are rare and stand out as major features of the region's sacred landscape. It was in a *zawiya* like this one that Mohammed's father found refuge from poverty, learned the Quran, became a *fqih* (religious specialist), and acquired his first spouse. No central authority or institution regulates saintly places and practices, so some fall into disuse, and others emerge and grow in popularity. Rachida's deceased grandfather—a religious leader of her community during the colonial–el Glaoui period—has come to be venerated by some for his *baraka* and may become a new "saint."

Saint "worship" and pilgrimage is an important feature of circum-Mediterranean societies that has been incorporated into Catholicism on the European shore. Many of the practices associated with it, including pilgrimage, sacrifice, vows, and "incubation" (sleeping in a saint's tomb to be visited by the saint in one's sleep and healed or made pregnant), are ancient features of Mediterranean religious "cults." But with large portions of North African populations living in tribal societies beyond the control of central governments, saints and *zawiya*s took on important political roles as well. Charismatic holy men often served as mediators in intertribal and intratribal feuds, and most of the prominent *zawiya*s in southern Morocco are located on the boundaries of traditionally hostile tribes. Weekly markets were held on *horm* (sacred or protected) ground near a saint's tomb at tribal or subtribal boundary points, and tribesmen laid down their arms and suspended active hostilities when they entered. At important historical junctures, holy men emerged as political leaders who unified tribal groups against the predations of sultans or incursions of foreign colonizers.

The Pre-Saharan Cosmology ❀

Tribesmen, blacks, Jews, and holy men are the social groups that outline the contours of a distinctly pre-Saharan cosmology.[16] At the top of the chain of being are the light-skinned Berber tribesmen (and later-arriving Arabs), who name themselves *amazigh* (the free people), who historically contrasted their political autonomy to the "submission" of most urban and agricultural peoples north of the High Atlas to the authority and taxation of the sultans and who continue to contrast themselves to the unfree clients who live among them. Until their pacification in the 1920s and 1930s, they governed themselves by a body of unwritten tribal customs, and in many areas by a "five fifths" system of political organization and leadership. According to this system, tribes, tribal fractions, and sometimes villages were divided into five roughly equal groups—along lines often held to be natural but frequently were gerrymandered to achieve balance. Rights and responsibilities were allocated equally among the fifths, and in many tribes, the elder household heads met once a year to elect an *amghar-n-oufella* (top chief). Typically, four of the fifths chose the chief from the other one, and these rotated so no fifth could provide the top chief for more than a year at a time. Many village and household tasks—especially women's work in larger households—continue to be organized by the principle of rotation among putatively equivalent units.

At the bottom of the chain were the dark-skinned African-origin *ḥraten*—a derogatory term that can mean either "people of the plow" or "free secondarily" (i.e., second to the free Berbers or Arabs). In addition to sharecropping, blacksmithing, and house building, they served as barbers, circumcisers, and musicians. These occupations brought them into close contact with nature and dangerous, perhaps polluting forces, a contact that was perceived to signal not only divinely ordained inferiority but also access to forces (Satan, jinn spirits, saints, and God) that could prove either benevolent or beneficent. Across North Africa, poor blacks made up most of the members of the less orthodox religious brotherhoods. These include the Hamadsha, who are "married" to the Sudanese *jinniya* (demoness) Aicha Qandisha (or to her male counterparts) and slash their heads with knives at her behest at the peak of their trances, and the Aissawa, who are possessed by animal spirits and so can charm snakes and heal poisonous bites.

The Jews, who emigrated to Israel in the 1970s, occupied an ambiguous status as light-skinned non-Muslims who were neither free nor enslaved. Their lower, client status was clearly recognized and marked by dress and residence, but their relative prosperity and freedom of movement often gave them considerable covert power. They were often highly respected for their personal dignity and religious devotion, but they also appear in many folktales as archetypally sinister characters who practice sorcery or to whom accursed princesses are mistakenly betrothed. In addition, the world of jinn spirits is believed to mirror that of humans, so there are Muslim jinns (who can be mischievous, easily affronted troublemakers), Jewish and Christian jinns (who have subversive intents and cause more serious harm), and atheist jinns (who are the most malevolent). Images of Jews have probably become more stereotypic and ethnocentric since they departed and anti-Zionism intensified among younger Moroccans who support the Palestinian cause. The teenage niece of one of our Toundout neighbors fell into a seizure one day while in the bathroom of her Marrakech home, and when she regained consciousness she began speaking in a strange language. The *fqih* (religious specialist) called in to exorcise the jinn possessing her ascertained that it spoke Hebrew and was, in fact, an Israeli commando spirit. Her parents insisted she shun her

Western-style dress and start observing the daily prayer cycle in order to prevent a recurrence.

Perhaps surprisingly, religious personages—saints, their descendants, and *fqihs*—also have an ambiguous status, and alongside awe at their spiritual powers, suspicions of hypocrisy and hucksterism run deep. More than a few jokes circulate about unscrupulous holy men, particularly those who solve fertility problems. Childless women sometimes sleep in saints' tombs in the hope that the saint will visit in the night and make them fertile, but it is said that the saints' living descendants may act as intermediaries. And *fqihs* are not infrequently reputed to use their esoteric knowledge to perform sorcery for the right price. Some of the ambivalence toward religious figures may stem from the harsh treatment Quranic schoolteachers often mete out to their seven- to ten-year-old students. Many parents as well as *fqihs* believe an atmosphere of fear to be a prerequisite for memorization, and cruel beatings the proper punishment for inattention to God's words.

In addition, there are many scoundrel-saints held in great affection and esteem throughout North Africa. Humans become saints by gifts of *baraka* that often proves itself in heroic feats of devotion, miraculous humiliations of tyrannical sultans, and scandalous violations of social conventions that otherwise might look like madness. We met one such figure in a Dades River village said to be home to a lineage of not just a saint's descendants but descendants of the Prophet. Popular belief holds that a great saint's *baraka* passes to one person in each generation of his descendants, and even to outsiders Si Mohammed was clearly the one: he radiated charisma, spoke eloquently, had a photographic memory, and was said to have a reputation as a religious healer throughout the south. His neighbors had elected him to the local rural council, and he succeeded in getting a modern health center built, staffed, and equipped near his cluster of villages. He also had built a café-lunch stop for tourists and truck drivers on the Ouarzazate-Er Rachidia highway. He was obviously eccentric: he had painted a nursing gazelle on the long wall of his guest room in violation of Islam's prohibition of representational art, and we once were served there by a teenage girl who physically climbed across him to reach the other side of room and then sat with her elbow on my knee and stared up into my eyes. Si Mohammed nonchalantly commented that he had just bailed her out of jail, as if that explained her comportment. We later learned that his café doubled as a house of prostitution, which finally put our experience with his teenage tea server in perspective. Villagers we knew cursed him but laughed at the same time, admitting that he really "had something" that somehow excused the scandal.

No clear line separates orthodox from unorthodox religious practices, and Moroccans intensely debate where the boundary should be drawn. Many orthodox Muslims condemn as blasphemous saint "worship" and the exuberant styles of chanting and trancing practiced by some religious brotherhoods. The orthodox tend to be higher status and male, and many observers have noted that men have an Islam of the mosques and women an Islam of the saints. And as in our own society, the poor and dispossessed tend to prefer worship that values emotional exuberance rather than self-restraint. To make matters more complex, many advocate orthodox Islam as "modern," in opposition to "traditional" forms they believe have contaminated the Quran and the Prophet's teachings with backward folk beliefs and superstitions.

Moroccans also dispute how much emphasis should be placed on legalistic versus mystical features of Islam: on conformity to the rules spelled out in the Quran and *ḥadith* (sayings or deeds of the Prophet) versus spiritual self-realization that may come by a kind of oceanic immersion in divine light. Although some of the Sufi *tariqa*s (brotherhoods or paths) emphasize ecstatic union with God over sober conformity to rules, many of the orthodox also study esoteric or mystical knowledge. Poetic evocations of spiritual illumination and radiance effuse the rich imagery of popular Islam in North Africa. In addition, most members of *tariqa*s carry a string of ninety-nine prayer beads, one for each of God's ninety-nine names, which they use to count the repetitions of their own chant or litany. The string of beads is called a *tasbih*, which refers to the phrase *subhan Allah*, or "Glory to God." It is believed that every being—animate and inanimate—has a natural vibration, and when it settles into the calmness of its natural vibration, it utters, in its own form but in resonance with all other beings, *subhan Allah*. The Sufi paths lead beyond the limitations of earthly strife, toward the illuminated resonance of the divine within and the divine spread through the great multiplicity of the world's beings. Though none of the young Moroccans I interviewed belonged to Sufi brotherhoods, images of luminous blessedness, cast in pre-Saharan hues, appear as fonts of meaning in many of their narratives.

The Rally ✤

Every year we lived in the Ouarzazate area, modernity unexpectedly reached into the desert in dramatic and disruptive ways: a feature film, a visit of the king, a drive to collect "contributions" to build the world's largest mosque in Casablanca. One year, it was a horse rally. For a few days, no one quite knew what the news meant, and we suspected it was another confused and distorted rumor. A whole lot of "rich Europeans," said to be "princes and princesses and people like that," were coming to race their horses through the Dades Valley and then across the Atlas Mountains to Marrakech, where they'd have a "big party." Like a good many confused and unbelievable rumors, this one turned out to be true: there was to be a five-day route-of-the-*qasbah*s horse rally, with one night to be spent in our home village of Toundout. It was never resolved, however, whether the horses were flown to Morocco from Europe, because only European thoroughbreds would do, or provided by the king, who had far finer horses than any European.

Because princes and princesses don't stay in villagers' homes, drink water from irrigation canals, sleep in flea-infested bedrolls, pass evenings without electricity, or defecate outdoors in the ruins of crumbled *qasbahs*, it soon became clear that this event was going to take work. The provincial governor sent his lieutenants to meet with the *caid* who governs the Imeghrane, the *caid* met with the sheikhs who head the *taqbilt*s (tribal fractions) of the Imeghrane, and then the sheikhs met with their *mqedem*s (village headmen), their relatives, and their clients. Within two days, the cluster of villages known as Toundout was buzzing with activity. The army rolled in and took charge of constructing a bivouac of colorful festival tents on a small plateau between two of the villages. Cartons of sterile bottled water were stockpiled for the riders, and a pair of water trucks were positioned on the edge of the plateau to provide them with showers after their long day's ride. A line of portable toilets was installed above a gulch, and a generator truck parked behind the tents to provide them with lights. Miniskirted, halter-topped members of the advance team flirted with the more gregarious sheikhs and *mqedem*s as they oversaw the layout of the campsite, counted and recounted provisions, and chatted endlessly with their bosses on mobile phones. The *caid*'s contingent of *mokhazni*s (paramilitary police) were sent out to requisition trucks from local merchants and then to round up any able-bodied men sitting in their usual clots of friends and haul them up to the plateau to aid in the construction work. It's "hospitality," the officials said. "It's the *kulfa* (forced labor, imposed by the el Glaoui tyrants during the colonial era)," muttered many of the men, who suspected the *caid* was pocketing the cash budgeted to pay local laborers.[17]

On the day of the rally's arrival, the army brought up more communications equipment and a small medical detachment and cleared a pad for the helicopters that tracked the riders and stood ready to medevac any who sustained injuries. The ground in and around the tents was covered with carpets requisitioned from local villagers. Chefs from Marrakech hotels arrived from the previous night's encampment and began preparing dinner. In the afternoon, the villagers lined the road leading into the site from the hills, and they were supplemented by truckloads of women brought from other villages to serenade the riders with ululations while a helicopter circled overhead. The "princes and princesses" looked dusty and tired as they arrived but waved appreciatively to their welcomers. From the southern road, merchants' trucks brought from surrounding villages singing and dancing groups, with their arrays of drums and tambourines, to provide *folklorique* entertainment until the late evening chill settled on the encampment.

Two days later, it was all gone. The merchants and perhaps the *caid* were a little richer. No one ever found out what it had cost to put on a fine party for the "people of the horses." But the villagers felt proud they'd shown their guests such exquisite hospitality. "It's our custom," they said.

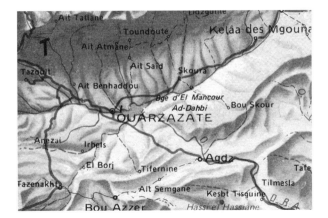

Ouarzazate, Skoura, and Agdez

Families ✿

Mohammed's parents were from Arabic-speaking farming families in the date and olive oasis of Skoura. Hussein's mother and father, and most of the households in his village near Agdez, were "free" tribespeople of the Berber Ait Seddrat tribe; their other neighbors were landless African-origin "people of the plow." Rachida's parents were part of a community of blacks or people of the plow on the edge of Agdez. Khadija's father had been born in one of the mountain groups of the Ait Seddrat but was raised in a French-run orphanage and married a woman from an Arabic-speaking community to the west of Ouarzazate. After Independence, all four fathers—who had attended only Quranic school—got government jobs that gave them regular salaries and freed them from dependence on subsistence agriculture. They all kept their village homes and fields, however, to provide their households with barley, fresh vegetables, and dates, and as insurance policies should a crisis shrink the modern sector and squeeze them back into subsistence. They all saw their sons'—and sometimes daughters'—futures in salaried jobs in the cities, so they sent them to school and pushed them to achieve with all the means they knew, confident there would be no going back to the agropastoral way of life still practiced a kilometer out of their towns, to the delight of tourists and filmmakers.

A Note on the Life Narratives

The following chapters analyze the life narratives of Mohammed, Hussein, Rachida, and Khadija. The narratives were transcribed verbatim into Moroccan Arabic and then translated by me (working from both the tapes and the transcriptions) in consultation with several Moroccan assistants who were highly fluent in English. For the purpose of analysis, I divided each interview into "story segments," roughly corresponding to sociolinguist James Gee's (1991) notion of a *part*: 75 in Mohammed's narrative, 178 in Hussein's, 135 in Rachida's, and 142 in Khadija's. I conducted three separate analyses of each story segment: first of the concepts and conceptual oppositions it employs, second of the affects and relational orientations it depicts, and third of the symbols, metaphors, motifs, and type scenes used in it. I use story segment numbers as references for quotations from the life narratives, which have been archived at the Foley Institute for Human Development at Northwestern University.

Because my interviewees' precise vocabulary is crucial to the analyses, I have left many Moroccan Arabic words and phrases in the excerpts I include, with English translations in parentheses. This will enable Arabic-speaking readers to follow the analyses more closely and give all readers a sense of my interviewees' language. To convey ambiguity and shades of meaning, I often suggest two or more translations for Arabic terms and phrases.

Many Moroccans mix French with Arabic, and I have included their French terms and phrases (with English translations) so readers can follow the shifting of languages. This is especially prominent in Khadija's narrative. I also have included some verbal pauses or "emphatics" in an effort to convey the rhythm and life of Moroccan Arabic: *ṣafi*, which roughly means "that's it" or "that's all"; *raḥ*, which roughly means "indeed," "that's it," or "really"; *gaᶜ*, which means "all" or "at all"; and *nit*, which means "exactly" or "precisely."

Mohammed

I met Mohammed soon after I began working in a hamlet of Skoura called Oulad Yacoub, a couple of kilometers west of the village *Centre*. On the afternoon I came to tape the life story of a blind, aging storyteller named Si Abdullah, Mohammed was one of a half-dozen neighbors who showed up to listen. He worked as the accountant for Skoura's main agricultural cooperative and was the youngest, brightest, and most articulate of the visitors. He also was a forceful "personality" to be reckoned with and interrogated me in a way that was at once suspicious, challenging, curious, and welcoming. I felt that my ability to work in the hamlet depended on building rapport with him, so I offered to come back and talk with him about my research.

A few days later, I found him at home, drinking tea and snacking with his father, a younger brother, and a couple of neighbors. They lived in a traditional rammed-earth house, just behind one of the grand but crumbling *qasbah*s tourists photograph from the highway. Their weathered wooden door resembled every other but opened to a spacious, well-appointed home with comforts rarely found in the countryside. The group was discussing religion, with Mohammed and his father occasionally reciting portions of Quranic suras (verses) and *ḥadith*s (deeds or sayings[1] of the Prophet). I was struck by the lack of formality and distance between the two men, who seemed to enjoy a mutual respect and rapport I had rarely seen between fathers and sons. When I mentioned this later, Mohammed laughed and said yes, many others had commented that they seem more like brothers than father and son.

Mohammed led me to another sitting room, where I explained my research and asked if he would be interested in telling me his life story. He agreed. Some weeks later, during the third long interview, he said he had become increasingly dissatisfied with his life in Skoura, which he saw as going nowhere, and was considering a move to Rabat and a new career. He also said he had been having headaches and stomach pain, which he attributed to eating "she-goat" but feared might be the ulcer for which he had been taking

Skoura: qsar *in the palmerie*

medications on and off for the last seven years. When I returned several weeks later for a final interview, I learned that he had gone to Rabat to have surgery. He recuperated with relatives there for several months, and I did not see him again. I think it likely that our conversations (several hours informally and eight hours on tape) contributed to his growing distress and perhaps also to his illness.

Life History ✿

Ancestors

I began by asking Mohammed to tell me about his family, and he started with his great-grandfather, who was known as sheikh Ali, even though he was neither a religious nor a political official. "My great-grandfather was a *rajel kabir* (a big/important man)," he said, using a term often applied to men who combine wealth, strength, courage, tact, and generosity into an honorable, someone-to-be-reckoned-with persona. He also was a hajj, Mohammed noted, having made the pilgrimage to Mecca, it's said, on foot. In the 1920s, sheikh Ali killed a man in the intervillage feud set off by the arrival of the French-backed forces of the el Glaoui tribe but then was killed by a relative of his victim when he boldly ventured into an enemy hamlet to visit his aunt.

Skoura: moped repair shops in the village center

Mohammed had little to say about his grandfather, Hassan, who quickly "grew tired" of the El Glaoui's oppressive rule and forced labor and "fled" to work for French colonists near Rabat. There he took a second wife, failed to piece together a decent life, and abandoned his family in Skoura. This left Mohammed's father poor and without a champion, but he excelled in the local Quranic school, which was the only form of education at the time. Conditions at school were oppressive, and because his father couldn't pay his full share, the *fqih* (religious teacher) singled him out for harsh treatment. The *fqih*, he says, was

> a good person, but he had a violent nature, he had a Glaoui-like nature. [How's that?] *isti͏ᶜmari schwiya* (He was a little oppressive/exploitative) He worked them hard, he used/exploited the kids. He would take them over to work on the house he was building. . . . And he beat them well, he gave them the stick/whip well. . . . My father *mziyer rasu* (squeezed/confined himself) in the mosque until he memorized the entire Quran. (Story 7)

At the age of fourteen or fifteen, his father, too, "fled" home, against his mother's wishes. Mohammed says: "He saw that his mother was ᶜ*yan* (old/tired/weak), and he left. He figured, 'I have to go and get a position, to make a little money.'" He had no destination but "just left with the idea of wandering around until he found a place to work."

He wandered to a *zawiya* (religious sanctuary) in a remote High Atlas valley, whose sheikh, Moulay Abdelhamid, had become renowned as a man of saintly *baraka* (blessedness) for his religious knowledge, his curing powers, and his political role in settling feuds. He also had rallied the tribes to resist the French-backed El Glaoui forces, and legends still circulate about his miraculous escape from the infamous El Glaoui dungeon at Telouat. Like all saints, he also was famed for his generosity to the poor and persecuted, and the *zawiya* still serves as a sanctuary to which people in trouble flee. The *zawiya* took in his father to teach children at its Quranic school.

Mohammed's father was happy with his new life for a while, until he once accompanied the sheikh of the *zawiya* to visit the *medrassa* ben Youssif in Marrakech, one of the great religious schools in North Africa. He yearned to stay and study there, but the sheikh insisted he return to the *zawiya*. This sowed the seeds of discontent: "He figured he wasn't doing anything there—just sitting, eating, and teaching the children. He got bored of that and left." Mohammed later elaborated, "After a while he realized that he was being exploited." He saw the sheikh spending more and more of his time in Marrakech, and those left behind to run the *zawiya* acted like little more than lackeys. His son, soon to be the *zawiya*'s next leader, was the worst: "He'd just collect all this stuff (gifts from the tribespeople), take it to Marrakech, and waste it." Unlike his father, the son had "no generosity, no *indibat* (self-control/restraint), no fear of God"—the qualities that make an honorable man of religion. The new generation of *zawiya* leaders "were well-off, but they wouldn't give my father this or that, and he just sat, ate, and thought. And he didn't want to just keep sitting there like that."

Before he left, however, "they told him he had to get married," and the *zawiya* elders, acting as senior kinsmen, arranged his marriage to a girl from the saint's lineage. A few months later, "he brought her back to Skoura pregnant, but she died suddenly before giving birth." His widowed father soon found work as the *fqih* (imam and Quranic schoolteacher) to a village of the Ait Abdi, one of the more remote High Atlas tribes. There he took care of the modest adobe mosque, guided the villagers' religious lives, and taught their children the Quran. A little over a year later, he arranged a marriage to a woman from Skoura, and she soon gave birth to Mohammed in Ait Abdi. When independence came, his father came back to Skoura to run his uncle's dry goods shop and also to teach Quranic school at their hamlet's mosque.

Big Men and Saints

This ancestral history conveys three important features of Mohammed's world. First, it testifies to the tenuousness of familial arrangements, the distressing flux and uncertainty that lie behind the cultural ideology of extended family stability. Mohammed's great-grandfather killed and got killed, his grandfather abandoned his family, his father had to find a foster family, and then his father's first wife died while pregnant. Mohammed will add to this his own mother's death when he was seven. In fact, departures, deaths, marriages, divorces, inheritance partitionings, and shufflings of personpower to exploit ever-shifting patterns of resources all lead to a surprising fluidity of family organization.[2] Households rarely remain stable for long, and most experience chronic imbalances between their members and the economic and social roles they must fill to subsist or prosper. The continual need to rearrange families and households gives rise to an intensely competitive interpersonal politics, which often amplifies anxieties about the stability of familial bonds—anxieties that are already elevated because of high mortality rates.

Second, Mohammed's brief account of his ancestors outlines the traditional honor- and religion-centered world into which he was born. Note that he traces only the paternal line, which reflects the patrilineal organization of North African society. And he shows admiration for two contrasting models of manhood: the *rajel kabir* (big man), here in the person of his bold, daring, and reckless great-grandfather, and the *fqih* or sheikh (religious teacher or saint), here in the person of the generous, self-disciplined, God-fearing Moulay Abdelhamid, the man of peace who played a heroic political role when called. As if to highlight these qualities, he sets both in contrast to their dishonorable, scoundrel sons: his grandfather, who abandoned his family, and Moulay Abdelhamid's son, who exploited the tribesmen his father had served and "wasted" the wealth his father redistributed so generously. Mohammed's sketches of these characters could hardly better depict the defining archetypes of the region's honor-modesty system: the tribal big man, daring in war; the divinely blessed, peacemaking saint; and the dishonorable sons, who indulge themselves and abandon or exploit those they should protect.

Third, these stories of ancestors introduce a more personal, psychological tension that runs prominently through Mohammed's narrative: an oscillation of entrapment and flight. Twice he portrays his father as finding himself deprived, exploited, and stuck in an anxious boredom of seemingly endless routines. Missing the figures who might nurture him, sustain him, and promote his interests (his father, his mother, Moulay Abdelhamid), Mohammed says he fled—rebelliously against the advice of his seniors. He depicts most men as acting impulsively and presents all of the turning points in his father's life as coming suddenly upon him. We will see him repeatedly cast episodes of his own life in similarly impulsive terms.

The qualities he emphasizes in these ancestral stories thus outline a tension between two affective or relational orientations: pursuit of a home that provides security, order, piety, fear of God, and self-discipline and impulsive flight from confinement in what he perceives to be patronless, anxiously boring, exploitative environments. This emotional duality also reappears in Mohammed's accounts of the critical junctures in his own life and emerges as the animating conflict of his narrative. The fact that he so prominently casts his father's biography in these terms suggests it forms a kind of emotional lens through which he perceives his world as well as himself. Other narrative passages and the projective tests I gave Mohammed suggest this emotional duality has an obsessive-compulsive character: it typically entails a churning, wrought-up, *mziyer* (squeezed/tense) kind of anxiety that underlies a tension between, as Erik Erikson phrases it, "holding on" and "letting go" styles of impulse control. For Mohammed, this particularly concerns holding on to and letting go of anger fueled by feelings of deprivation and confinement. Terming this tension *obsessive-compulsive* does not *explain* it, but it usefully *describes* a broad feature of his core-level personality organization—an oscillation between a sometimes-rigid, ritualized style of control and an often-impulsive flight from control—that shapes his narrative at nearly every turn.

Mohammed describes his own life as having three fairly distinct phases. His childhood was torn almost as soon as he can remember by his mother's death, after which he became an ideal son and Quranic student known in his hamlet as *niḍam*—which means ordered, organized, responsible, and well-bred. His teenage years were marked by high achievement in public school and delinquency outside it, and his penchant for carousing, drinking, stealing, and fighting escalated until he became *jahel*—which means wild, rabid, and ignorant (the pre-Islamic era is known as the *jahiliya*). His mature adulthood took shape in a solitary reconversion experience, after which he so dedicated himself to piety that his friends now teasingly but admiringly call him *fqih*—which in this context means religious devotee and scholar. The following sections examine these phases and the identities he associates with them. As *fqih*, Mohammed has put his *jahel* (wild/ignorant) period behind him, yet he continues to experience many of the feelings he says drove him to wildness.

A "Well-Bred" Child

Mohammed says his parents were well liked in their mountain village and that when he was born, the Ait Abdi sheikh (political leader) and his wife insisted on naming him.[3] When Skouris pass through, he adds, the sheikh's now-elderly wife still asks about him. His earliest memory—a simple recollection of delight at watching a yellow cat while visiting Moulay Abdelhamid's shrine with his parents (Story 16)—also confers an aura of "auspiciousness" to his beginning. Unlike dogs, cats are relatively rare in the area and have positive religious associations as the Prophet's favorite animal.[4] Mohammed recalls asking his parents what it was and observing it in wonder, and he comments twice, "I *liked* that scene." Effused with good feelings, this memory places him in a holy site and at the center of his family—before he acquired siblings or lost his mother. This memory brings to mind a second:

> There was a dispute between my parents. . . . With the noise of the words between them, I woke up and told my father, "What's this ṣeda‎ᶜ (trouble)? I'm going to *nherris rasik* (break your head)! Get

away from my mother or I'll break your head!" He said, "Get up!" I was little. I got up and a drum fell on me and knocked me back. I was grabbing for it to hit my father.

That's an incident I recall like it's in front of me. . . . I was just little, but I saw them quarreling and I was going to protect my mother. I reached for the drum and it fell on my head [laughing] and they laughed. . . . They stopped their words and laughed and laughed [laughing]. (Story 17)

Mohammed recounted this story with relish because his bold and reckless act brought about such a delightful conclusion. His attempt to attack his father in defense of his mother appears to reflect the prototypic core of the region's so-called honor code: to rise to the defense of one's mother against any threat and even insurmountable odds. The strife that unfolds in the profane space of the family's sleeping room contrasts sharply with the harmonious ambience of the shrine's sacred interior—and these earliest memories evoke the pair of value systems and virtues many scholars have seen at the core of North African culture: religious *baraka* (blessedness) and manly honor.

Mohammed indeed has a hearty sense of humor and often casts his wildness in funny stories that show a gallant kind of impulsiveness. He subsequently recalls an incident in which he screamed in fear of a dog but then felt so embarrassed at his cowardice when he heard the adults running to his rescue that he bit himself and claimed the dog had done it (Story 22). In his next earliest memory of his father, he recalls riding behind him on a bicycle to the village grain mill and getting his foot caught and cut in the rear wheel, for which he felt himself to blame: "I felt like I did something not good—got my foot caught in the wheel. I felt like I had made the mistake" (Story 20). Next he recounted how strongly he yearned to stay beside his father and be a man among the men:

I liked to be with him a lot, and to not be apart at all. I wanted to go with him always: I wanted to sit with him, and if there were people visiting, I never wanted to be apart. He'd say, "Take off," and I'd say, "No. I have to stay. I'm a man and I have to sit/stay with you." (Story 21)

Sometimes his father would let him play near him and his guests, and "I felt tranquil/at ease." When his father sent him away, "*kanteqeleq* (I would become upset), it would make me angry. I would go out and cry." "He'd say, 'There are men here,' and I'd say, 'I'm a man too, I have to stay.' Even when I was little!"

A psychoanalytic interpreter might detect a prototypic Oedipal sequence in these memories,[5] but such an interpretation would reach well beyond Mohammed's words and entail an orthodox Freudian view of personality I do not endorse. Yet early memories often encode a kind of unsystematized origin myth, and these certainly suggest the importance of the daring "manliness" ethnographers have claimed to be characteristic of Mediterranean cultures—which also animates his accounts of his paternal ancestors. Mohammed recalls his two earliest memories as a pair, portraying a contrast of familial blessedness and strife that turns out to represent prototypic forms of good and bad feelings for him. Perhaps most important, they set out a sequence of harmony, rupture, and reparation—which scripts his life history.

When I asked if he ever feared his father, he described how his father once beat him and threatened to "smoke" him above a fire for playing a gambling game with other children:

> He didn't accept cardplaying, and he saw me. I couldn't go home that night, because if I went in he would *slekhni* (skin/beat me). I went to the house of a woman who'd taken care of me when my mother died. . . . He came for me there, but he didn't say anything. I thought that if he's not going to say anything now, he won't. We came back to the house. At night they brought me dinner but I couldn't eat. I was really frightened.
>
> After dinner he said, "You were playing cards and gambling." I said, "Yeah, we were." He said, "I'm going to take you and let you have it." He beat me. He beat me, but what really terrified me was when he grabbed me and said, "Lay flat on your stomach," and I did, and he called out, "Get me a rope!" He held my arms behind my back and said he's going to tie me and hang me from a chain and give me smoke [light a fire under him]. He frightened me. He frightened me good. (Story 23)

Then, he says "some pain seized me in my stomach" and intensified until he had to have an appendectomy "just from that fear."

> That woman who'd taken care of me after my mother died came over and brought me some herbs to drink, but the pain didn't want to go away. Finally they took me to the hospital, and I stayed eleven days from that fear. They took out that—the pain and that *ṣeda* (trouble) that came up, it gave me appendicitis, my appendix swelled up and they cut out my appendix. (Story 24)

It is not clear precisely what took place in this series of events, but they certainly show why Mohammed feared his father. By using the term *selkh* (skin, slang for "beat," but literally referring to animals) and by describing how his father tied and threatened to hang and smoke him, the incident also resembles the ritual sacrifice and butchering of an animal. All butchering in Morocco follows sacrificial rules, but the holiest family celebration in Islam—the *ʿyd al adha* (Great Sacrifice/Feast)—explicitly reenacts the Abrahamic sacrifice, in which the patriarch renews the covenant with God by killing a ram in place of his son. Mohammed's beating thus echoes of sacrifice in a highly ambiguous manner: his father treats him like an animal but in a way that may have religious, even redemptive connotations.

Mohammed concludes this story with a complaint that his father was too harsh:

> He wanted *bn Adam* (a person) to be good and honest and to stay on the straight path. But we weren't ready to consider what he wanted yet, we still had to play and fool around. He had the eye of a big/old man, and we were just small: we have to play, we still have to do a lot of whatever comes to us to do. And he says no. And he did that to me and I went to the hospital. (Story 24)

When I asked if his father apologized, he patiently set me straight on how father-son relationships work in Morocco:

> No, no, he didn't say anything. No, we can't apologize. Like I could make a mistake with my son, but I couldn't come in and say, "Oh, excuse me." We can't do that. No. We say a parent mustn't make mistakes, he mustn't lower/let fall his *shakhsiya* (character) in front of his kids. Even though he's the one in error, he mustn't lower his character in front of them. (Story 24)

He speaks as if he understood this even then, and so "even though that incident happened, there wasn't distance between us. I never tried to distance myself."

Just as we can't know precisely what happened, neither can we know what psychological effects it had on him. It certainly is possible that this incident, and the general atmosphere of restrictive, fearful patriarchal authority, amplified his ambivalence over compliance and rebellion, and the tension between his compliant holding on and rebellious letting go styles of expression. But only the event's narrative/mythic significance can be traced in his interview text. As part of his life history, it helps set the stage for two pivotal events in which he triumphed over his fear: a fight with a neighborhood bully and defiance of an officer in an army interrogation chamber, which we will consider later. It also sets the stage for subsequent accounts of neglect by his father that he blames, in the absence of a mother, for his going wild. Stomach pain also may have become a psychosomatic idiom by which he articulates distress with his father: since returning home as a loyal adult son, he has experienced repeated bouts of abdominal pain diagnosed as an ulcer. This intensified during the months I interviewed him, culminating in his departure for Rabat to have surgery.

Not Forgotten in Sleep or Death

Mohammed ends this memory by honorably rising above resentment, but it leads him to speak of the "other things in my life that, like when my mother died, that were a little difficult—in particular, when he remarried."

His resentment stemmed from the lack of care he perceived from his step-mother and the other relatives who helped run their household, and although the incidents he cites seem somewhat trivial, it is important to keep in mind the extent to which the provision of food conveys caring in the chronically undernourished pre-Saharan world. Mohammed says neglect has left him withdrawn and troubled by ᶜ*ouqed* (complexes) that have prevented him from "succeeding in life":

> We were little, we were five [children], and when he was around, there was no problem. But when he wasn't here, there were problems. You'd come home and have to take responsibility for yourself, you'd have to make your own place to sit, and go look yourself for something to eat—understand? Like you'd say, "Give me something to eat" [and they'd respond:] "Not until your father comes"—like that. And "Why did you do this and that?" There was some ṣedaᶜ (noise/trouble). . . . That sort of thing really affected us.
>
> [What was the effect?]
>
> ᶜ*ouqed* (complexes), it left us with complexes. We would have been more open/extroverted. A person could succeed in life more than he has if there had been some close caretaking. . . . If a person has some intelligence, and does well in his studies, he just needs . . . [trails off]. If he finds someone who takes care of him and, for example, says, "I've wronged you, excuse me, you need this, you need that," oh, that person will reach I don't know where. I don't know *how* far he'll be able to go. But if his situation . . . [breaks off], it changes his direction and has an effect on his ideas, on his mind, and that lasts until now. (Story 25)

Searching for words and shifting to a more distanced third-person point of view, he here imagines that if his father *had* been able to apologize, he would have been able to go "I don't know how far."

Recalling his father's brutal treatment, then, leads him to memories of feeling neglected, and to blame this neglect for his failures. This in turn leads him to tell of his mother's death when he was seven:

> That's the thing that doesn't want to be forgotten in sleep or death. I'll probably always keep recalling that afternoon we were coming home—she was sick—and my father came and carried her from here, and took her to the hospital. I saw her like that, "Where's she going?" I was crying, and I went out and followed them until they were far away and someone grabbed me and took me back, and I kept crying. They said, "She'll come back, she'll come back." Until the day they brought her back from the hospital, ṣafi, she's not going to live.
>
> They told me my mother had come back and I craved a lot to see her. They'd told me when she came back from the hospital I'd

find her on her feet and healthy. I ran to see her and found them carrying her. I asked, "Why's she not walking?" They said, "No, she doesn't walk." I followed them until they brought her into the room here. I came in and sat next to her head. She opened her eyes, and didn't speak. She opened her eyes, and tears came falling. And me, at that time, I didn't weep or anything. But I saw her like that and *ṣafi*. I went out, and when I went out they called me and tried to distract me, said come here, look, this and that, this and that, look here's a little bicycle. And I didn't want those things. I wanted my mother and *ṣafi*.

When she died, I was outside playing soccer until I heard screaming—wa, wa, wa. I said, "What's that?" Someone said, "Your mother's died." I didn't accept it, I told them, no, I didn't want to say, "Yes, my mother died." I came back but they didn't let me in. I said, "Why? I've got to see her." They said, *ṣafi*, and they held me and didn't let me in. They sent me away and I went out wandering about. (Story 26)

Mohammed recalls these events angrily as well as sadly, his anger focused on those who tried to keep him away from his mother, on the doctors and hospital he felt killed her, and on the relative who tried to distract him after her death by telling him she would come back even while he heard her being buried:

I heard them taking her out to the cemetery—"There's no God but God and Mohammed is his Prophet." I said where are they going? They said they're going out, she'll come back. And I waited and waited for her to come back. She'll come back today, she'll come back tomorrow. And so the incident went, like that. It had a *big* effect on me, a *big* effect. (Story 26)

He remembers a neighbor woman taking him in for a while, but the loss and lies together hit him hard: "From that day, I began to feel that I needed *l-ᶜtifa* (affection/compassion), that I needed someone to care for me." By that point, Mohammed seemed surprised to be reliving these events and concluded his account with an attempt to shake off his sadness: "Oh, well, it's not a problem now. That period has passed, and I succeeded."

In the months that followed, he says he put his nose to the grindstone, helped take care of his four younger siblings, and became precociously adult:

I'd get up really early in the morning and get firewood, I'd light a fire, make coffee, wake up my brothers and sisters, and give them coffee. Then I'd study the Quran. I'd recite: *ya Allah, ya Allah, ya Allah*. Then I'd have coffee and go to school. For a *long* time, I kept that up. (Story 27)

Mohammed's father soon remarried, but his stepmother treated him callously, and he continued to take care of his siblings. He especially resented having to light the kitchen fire and heat water at the crack of dawn, which traditionally is women's work. In the ensuing years, he became such a model of devotion and responsibility that he acquired the nickname *niḍam*, which means self-disciplined and well organized:

> I'd get up early and pray and recite the Quran. I'd go to the mosque to read the Quran and all the rest. I was well-bred, so well-bred that they called me here in the hamlet *niḍam*. You know what *niḍam* is? [What?] *niḍam* means that all matters are in order and good, that I follow the correct path. (Story 63)

Mohammed's childhood memories thus sketch a life that originated in mythically special circumstances. His great-grandfather Sheikh Ali and his god-grandfather Moulay Abdelhamid establish descent lines that link him to both martial and spiritual powers, and the leaders of the Ait Abdi treat his birth among them as a special event. His earliest memory makes this tangible, harmoniously joining his family in the ambience of a sacred scene, enlivened by his curiosity about the shrine's cat—the favorite animal of the Prophet, whose name he bears. Subsequent memories shatter the harmony, at first in reparable ways. Then the beating he thinks put him under the surgeon's knife and his mother's death irreparably rupture his world. Mohammed does not make the order of these events clear, but the order of his telling describes a kind of fall from grace that leads him squarely "onto the path" of piety and responsibility but also leaves him with "complexes": the lack of nurturance he believes subsequently led him astray. These themes reappear in his reconversion experience, which brings him, perhaps finally, home.

To Rabat

Mohammed excelled in Skoura's primary school, but because it had no junior high, his father arranged for him to stay with a relative in Rabat and go to school there. He then tells a long, complicated tale about becoming—at the age of twelve—a pawn in a struggle between two groups of relatives. The neighbor who accompanied him to Rabat dropped him off at the house of his maternal relatives, who were then to take him to his paternal aunt, but they refused and insisted he stay with them instead. Caught off guard, he stayed, but soon felt confused, confined, and angry:

> They kept me there, by force. . . . I began to *teghiyer* (get angry), to become a little *meqeleq* (anxious/worried), *mziyer* (uptight/upset). I saw new people, a new style of living and all that, and I just stayed there, watching them. (Story 28)

He still does not know what motivated his hosts, but he felt they weren't acting purely out of kindness. When he brought home better grades than his host's children, he felt them grow envious and make it difficult for him to study. Their harassment peaked when they refused to let him use electricity at night—forcing him to buy and study by candles—which appears particularly symbolic because it echoes his father's new wife's refusal to light a fire for him. Finally, he got fed up, found his paternal aunt's house on his own, and moved in with her as his father had originally planned. Her son quickly became a close friend and introduced him to the city's street life. His schoolmates teased him about being the "country boy," but he excelled in sports as well as in the classroom, and soon they shut up.

Mohammed looks back on his two years in Rabat as a continuation of his "well-bred" period, in which he excelled in his studies and in sports and learned the modern ways of Morocco's capitol. But his account also shows some familiar themes: he finds himself trapped by manipulative relatives and feels *meqeleq* (anxious/worried), *mziyer* (uptight/upset), and *teghiyer* (angered) by his conditions of deprivation until he finally flees. This constellation of confinement and wrought-up, angry anxiety resembles what he portrayed his father as experiencing at his mother's home and then at Moulay Abdelhamid's *zawiya*, and what he says he experienced at home after his mother's death. Then his flight takes him to nurturance, and he prospers.

Honor and Delinquency

Problems began a couple of years later, when Mohammed's brother graduated from primary school, and his father found a room to rent for them in Ouarzazate so they could attend school there. Though just an hour from his home in Skoura, he found himself trapped in greater privation and less able to resist temptation. He actually described this period as a continuation of his account of his first childhood fight, which became a landmark event of rebellion and self-assertion.

> My father used to beat us a lot, like if someone came and complained about me, he would beat us *good*, without checking out why. Kids would come and challenge/offend me or something, and I couldn't fight. I couldn't tell them something/answer their challenge. (Story 31)

Humiliated by a neighborhood bully's taunts, one day he decided he could take no more:

> There was one kid here who always picked on me. I'd be walking along the path carrying something and he'd say, "Hey, give it to me!" And I couldn't hit him because my father would . . . [pause]. One day I decided that's it . . . my father can kill me or do whatever he wants, I have to fight him, so he doesn't keep harassing me like that.

So we went out in front of the *qsar* (building) here, and he met me [and said:] "Come here, show me what you've got!"—like that.

They fought:

We were hitting *good*. I grabbed him and beat him up *good*; I turned him all bloody. . . . He'd get up and I'd hit him and hit him and knock him down. I beat him up *good*. . . . From then on [wiping his hands "finished"], he never again talked to/challenged me. (Story 31)

The fight could have brought demands for payment, threats of vengeance, or violence from the beaten boy's family. But the other boy's uncle watched it all and told the senior men in Mohammed's lineage that the altercation had been his nephew's fault, and his father said nothing to him about it. "From then on," Mohammed recalls, "I had a little spirit in me, and if someone came up and bothered me, I'd fight him. . . . I became courageous." In fact, he says he "got into the spirit of fighting" and began to act as protector to younger boys:

After that I considered myself someone who could fight and win. Some little kids might come along and say someone had done something to them, and I'd say, "Come here, come here, *ghadi ntehorm bik* (I'll give you protection). . . . "What did that kid do to you?" And I'd beat him up. I got into the spirit of fighting. (Story 31)

This account provides a veritable précis of the masculine honor code: risking life and limb, he answers another's challenge and is vindicated by a council of elders; he then embraces the character of "someone who could fight and win" and, using the traditional term for "sanctuary"—*horm*—begins acting as a patron-protector to those weaker than himself.

With a sense of bemusement, then, he recalls other fights. One occurred in a rough neighborhood of Ouarzazate while he was a student there:

Yeah, I got attacked by six once, in Ouarzazate. I was going through a stage, and I got into fighting a lot. One night six ganged up on me, and beat me up *good*. They hit me here with sticks and rocks. (Story 32)

Another took place when he was older:

I had nearly grown up, and I fought with some guy at a bus station. I hit him with a glass of tea, and he hit me with the teapot [laughing], and we fought there in the café. There were three of them, and at first I was hitting him good, but then the others came in from behind. One hit me with a chair and we kept fighting all the way to the bus. . . . One hit me here and hurt my jaw, and I couldn't keep fighting. (Story 32)

Mohammed does not present these later incidents as defenses of honor or principle but as sordid if funny events and as signs of his reckless impulsiveness. I asked if he angers quickly, and this led him to describe what he sees as a wild, misanthropic period in his life:

> Yeah. I get pissed off *tout de suite* (Fr., quickly). A word or two sets me off. [For your whole life?] No, no, not my whole life. I've sometimes gotten a little angry but not until after *teqeleqt shwiya* (I became a little upset/nervous). [When was that?] It must have been when I was sixteen or seventeen. I no longer wanted/liked people. I got to a point where I didn't want anything to do with people, I couldn't stand people. I became, a little, like I was *jahel* (wild/rabid). (Story 32)

He was staying in a hovel of a room—as many poor students do—with his younger brother, cooking and cleaning for themselves (which takes hours without modern kitchen conveniences), and scraping by on the few *dirham*s their father sent them each week:

> My brother and I were in a house in Ouarzazate where there are lots of drunks and fights . . . and *ṣafi*, I began to get pissed: I couldn't any longer stand studying. Sometimes we wouldn't have money left, and we wouldn't have any food to eat, for a day or two—a night or two of hunger, with nothing. . . . And with that burner, it all stank from the gas. I'd get up and go to school and sit in class and still stink from the gas. [laughs]
>
> My father, I don't know what he was intending for me. I would have preferred to go to the dormitory for poor children. . . . It would have been better to go there and be with other students, than stay by ourselves. (Story 33)

The Night of Destiny ✸

Mohammed's simmering anger came to a crisis after three weeks of Ramadan fasting on the Night of Destiny, the holiest day on which God began handing down the Quran to the Prophet:

> The Night of Destiny came and we didn't have a thing to eat. I was fasting, and *there was nothing to eat*! I was hungry and watching people cooking and getting the break-fast meal ready. And we had *nothing* to eat, not even a single dried date. I went down to the fields and searched for fallen fava beans, but I couldn't find enough.
>
> I went back up to our room and I remember grabbing ahold of the beam and I fell. I found myself on the ground. I couldn't see and I felt my hands and legs hitting the ground. I fell, I fainted and fell. I stayed like that for a long time, I don't remember. My eyes were open but I couldn't see, I made out just a little bit of light. I felt like

someone who had been felled by *jnoun* (spirits) or something. After a little, I began to check out how my eyes were, they were burning/shaking. I felt cold. I went to a corner and sat. (Story 34)

In the afternoon, he set out again in search of food, this time to the mosque, but he could not bring himself to beg. He tried to steal some bread but got caught and punched. Again he nearly begged for bread but felt too humiliated. He retreated home and spent the night in hunger, which he describes in terms that echo those he used for the pain that led to his appendectomy: "the pain wanted to kill me. I was grabbed by the pain." He tried again to steal some bread and got caught by a neighbor, who then took pity on him and gave him money to buy food. But it was too late to save his spirit:

> From then it started. I started to get touchy, hard. The slightest thing would set me off. I couldn't stand people anymore. Whenever I'd see people, I started saying people are no good, there's no goodness among people, there's no benevolence/compassion among people. I began to avoid *bn Adam* (people, literally: descendants of Adam). I'd say it's no good, it only creates evil for me. Things stayed like that—my studies kept going along, sometimes without food, sometimes other things, through those years in Ouarzazate. I figured myself sort of strong, and when I'd meet some *m'enser* (a tough guy) I didn't like, just a word or two and I'd fight. I made a lot of noise/trouble. (Story 34)

Alone and agonizingly hungry on the night all Muslims should be spiritually full, Mohammed could hardly narrate a more poignant portrayal of his alienation and despair. He fears he has been possessed by a jinn spirit, but he subsequently becomes something worse: a misanthrope who believed "people are no good." He began to vent his anger by cruising for fights and looking for ways to escape. "I began to tell myself I need something to make me forget all that," he says, and he started drinking, smoking, and visiting prostitutes—"I felt like going *inheref* (bad/delinquent)." He ends up beyond human bounds and bonds: *jahel* (rabid), like an animal, outside of Islam. Counterpoised to the *niḍam* (orderly/responsible) child he was and the *fqih* (pious/devout) adult he will become, his *jahel* (rabid), perhaps even demon-possessed state on the Night of Destiny defines a negative identity, a counterself.

He sees the immediate cause of his delinquency in his pursuit of manly prowess, which he now views as a mistaken notion of honor. When I asked why he thinks he went "off the path," he answered:

> I haven't found any cause, really. People imitate each other, that's all. One couldn't find someone who could help him make his way in life, and at that time we thought a good deal of people who smoked —that those were the real men. We modeled ourselves on those who spent the evening in company [of women] or those who fought and won—those were our heroes. (Story 35)

Later he reiterates his critique of his father, saying again that he lacked adult advice and counsel:

> There was nobody. We were all alone in Ouarzazate. We were young, but not that young. We were immature, and we used to go out and do whatever we wanted, and met people without purpose who only wanted to smoke and drink and quarrel, *ṣafi*. (Story 62)

He now sees that he was following Satan:

> At that time I used to imitate *shitan* (the devil), my own devil. I used to follow him to nowhere. He was leading me nowhere, to Hell, leading me on that road which ends in Hell. (Story 66)

Yet he also makes it clear his deprivation began with his mother's death and then was aggravated by his father's remarriage, increasing distance, and decreasing succor. He repeatedly portrays himself as struggling in darkness, confinement, and hunger for light, warmth, and nurture. He recollects his predawn lighting of the family hearth after his mother's death, returning home from school to be denied food, being forced to light candles at his relatives' home in Rabat, lacking food to cook, and stinking from the gas stove in the dark, cramped room in Ouarzazate. Like so many of the characters in his life story, he felt he had to flee:

> I started smoking. I thought I'd forget with cigarettes, but it didn't help, and I just went on to another level. I'd find someone who was drinking and drink, until I was doing a lot of things. What am I going to do? I have nothing I can do. I decided I couldn't stay in Ouarzazate. My father said, "Stay and study." I was looking for work. I was dying of hunger. He said keep studying. (Story 33)

Again, he explicitly blames deprivation: "If I had just found good living conditions, food and drink and like that, I would have reached I don't know where."

The negative *jahel* (wild/ignorant/rabid) identity—the animalistic, Satan-led antiself he became in Ouarzazate—is as much a cultural construction as his positive identity, his pious, God-fearing, well-bred self. This pair represents a differentiation of contradictory identities, of contrasting "senses of self," or of opposing subselves.

Soldier

As a struggling eighteen-year-old high school senior, Mohammed came home to Skoura to study for the baccalaureate exam, which would grant him admission and financial aid to study at a university. He was still angry and often unable to stand the company even of his family. Then his father became ill and entered a hospital in Rabat, throwing Mohammed into a panic about his future and his role in the family should his father die:

When my father became sick, I began to carry a little bit of responsibility, that if, God forbid, that operation wasn't successful, those
children who are still here need a lot of this and that, and who is going
to take care of the family? If it's God's will, if my father passed away,
it would put the well-being/reputation of the family before the hamlet. (Story 38)

With his reputation for delinquency, he appears to have feared his own in-
ability to head the family, and he imagined the scorn his relatives and neighbors would heap on him if he failed. Impulsively, he enlisted and became an
ᶜskeri (soldier):

I thought: what am I going to do? I'll go and enlist, in order to do
some kind of work. I wasn't drafted, I just signed up. I didn't discuss
it with anybody, I didn't do anything. I just took my own opinion,
and said, what am I going to do? I had nothing to do. So I enlisted.
That was my only escape, so I signed up. (Story 38)

He thought the army might provide the discipline he couldn't bring to his
own life, and he liked the camaraderie and tough physical training at boot
camp. But Morocco's war in the former Spanish Sahara had not yet wound
down, and he was sent, as a gunnery technician, to a base near the fighting:
"There still were difficult times in the war," he says. "The trucks would go
out and there was only death. Whoever went out there died."
 Mohammed didn't fight, but soon after he learned his father had recov-
ered, he had a sudden change of heart about his decision:

One day it all got me angry and started me thinking about home. I
started to think that I've come and wasted my future. Why did I
enlist? Now I've gotten myself stuck here in the Sahara, and I can't
study. . . . [I decided] I've got to find a way to get out and get back
to my way in life. (Story 40)

He then recounts a long and dramatic series of efforts to get out of the army,
which came to a head when he got into a fight with an officer. He was servicing
artillery weapons one day when a lieutenant ordered him to hand over some
new equipment that had been shipped to his commander. Mohammed refused,
the lieutenant slapped him, he punched the lieutenant and then drew his gun
to hold off a contingent of military police. The MPs called the commander:

Finally the *capitaine* came and said what's happening? I told him, "Sir,
a shipment came with your name, and I was about to send it to you
when this person came and said to give him your shipment. I told him
it wasn't in his right to request it from me." He slapped me, and I hit
him with my fist and broke his glasses, and the MPs came to seize me.
I said I wouldn't surrender until the *capitaine* came, and then I saluted
the *capitaine* and I gave him my weapon. (Story 42)

The captain ordered him to jail, and he obediently headed off. Then the captain relented and transferred him to another base, but he made up his mind to get out of the army. His new commander refused to sign the discharge paper he drew up and jailed him when he refused to work.

When he got out of jail, he went AWOL and hitchhiked to Rabat, determined to convince someone at the military headquarters to approve his discharge. There he was threatened with jail in an infamous prison for political criminals, to which he responded with bravado: "No problem, I'll go to jail. It'll be better than going to the Sahara. I'll take jail, *ya Allah* (let's go)!" The officer continued to threaten him and he demanded to see a Colonel K, saying, "I just want to go to the colonel and tell him what's happening to me, and then they can take me and kill me or do whatever they want, he can even cut off my head." He was taken to an interrogation chamber in the building's basement, "a cave with a lot of lights and equipment and stuff. They were trying to frighten me." He again offered to have his head cut off:

> I told him there's nothing that will frighten me. I'm ready. You can even kill me, because I'm going to die anyway in the Sahara. I'm ready to die tomorrow. If you want them to kill me here, you name it! I'd prefer for you to kill me here than have someone else do it. (Story 44)

Mohammed persisted and wore them down: "They finally got tired, and the colonel told me, 'May God calm you, get out of here!'" I asked if he was posturing or really ready to die, and he said he was serious: "I couldn't stand it any more. I wasn't acting. It was in my mind that I wouldn't go back, even if they were going to cut off my head. I had reached that degree: if they were going to kill me, they could kill me." It was the lieutenant's slap, he said, that made him determined to leave the army (Story 44).

Here again, Mohammed casts himself as confined in an anxious state of continual movement that goes nowhere, and again he flees. He again views his actions as reckless and funny, but he also portrays himself as courageously determined to restore his honor after being slapped by the lieutenant for his loyalty to the captain. And he presents the climactic confrontation as taking place in a cavelike torture chamber equipped with bright lights and frightening equipment. This completes the third and most dramatic narrative cycle in which he leaves home, establishes himself as a success, finds himself trapped in deprivation, and after a symbolic crisis in a cavernlike room, flees. The first took place at the house of his relatives in Rabat, the second in the hovel he shared with his brother, and the third here. All echo his descriptions of earlier periods of neglect, and his defiance in the interrogation chamber may well represent a triumph over the fear he felt when his father beat and prepared to smoke him.

Mohammed thus narrates these episodes as variations on a set of core themes, and they trace a developmental trajectory as he moves from a confrontation with his own animality in Ouarzazate to a more honorable victory over the forces of death in Rabat. Here again, he carries out a successful rebellion against authority for the sake of honor—as earlier he recounted rising to his mother's defense against his father and risking figurative death by his father's hand to fight his neighborhood taunter. Here he clearly draws power from offering to have his throat cut—and the Abrahamic sacrifice, echoed in his description of the beating that caused his appendicitis, probably provides a cultural prototype for Mohammed's scripting of this scene. He faces down Fear, and his victory serves to mark the nearly final killing-off of his animalistic, *jahel* (wild/ignorant) self.

Fqih

Having defied death, Mohammed returned to a kind of liminal existence at his family home in Skoura. His discharge papers didn't arrive, and without them he could neither take the baccalaureate exam nor apply for government jobs. His father remained hostile, disapproving both of his impulsive decision to enlist and of his equally impulsive decision to force his discharge (Story 45). Months stretched into two years, and he again grew restless and angry: "I didn't do anything. I used to wander about during the day. At night I started smoking and feeling angry. I wondered what I could do." Finally he took an exam with the Agriculture Ministry and was hired as a clerk, without anyone asking for his discharge papers. His anxiety grew as his first payday approached, but his discharge arrived in the nick of time.

Assigned to keep records at the agricultural station in a foothills village, Mohammed lived alone and, at twenty-two, began to reflect on his life. His reflection led to a rebirth. In our last interview, I asked him how he got out of his misanthropic state of mind and came "to like people again." He began his answer by reiterating that he'd gone off the path as a student in Ouarzazate because he lacked someone to guide him:

> I mean, I feel that I lacked a lot of things, which made me hate people. Because I lived *mekerfes mezian* (in a great deal of hardship), I looked at people and saw that nobody had any compassion, none whatsoever for you, and all that made me give myself over to vice/debauchery. I lacked something, but nobody helped me to get out of that mess in spite of my age. . . . (Story 62)

Now, he says, he knows "I must model myself upon somebody who has good manners and all the rest, and who can help me make my way in life and give me some advice, like my *murshid* (counselor/mentor)." He found his *murshid* late one night in his solitary room:

> I was sitting like this and thinking about how I came into the world: a human being came out of my own mother's belly/womb, and he was clean. A small embryo/fetus that fell on the ground, clean: he

didn't know anything about smoking or drinking or lying or stealing. Why now had I sullied/tarnished myself and filled my head with all these things: I smoke, I drink, I live without purpose, I stay up late at night, I lie, I have become this and that. Why I didn't stay like I was born, clean? Why! From that time I decided *ṣafi*. . . . I used to be good and well-bred and now I have sullied myself with all this. I must stop all this and become clean again.

I was living alone, and I'd sit and think about things. I'd go through my life and my recollections and weigh up the pros and cons. . . . One night I was sitting above a bale of hay, meditating/musing over my life, and I found it not good. . . . I just sat like this and became sick and tired of that life . . . I regretted that life. I'd been born clean, knowing nothing, and being innocent. But when I became older I reached some stage where I sullied myself with all the bad characters, cigarettes, alcohol, and all the rest. Why have I done this to myself? . . .

I asked myself what to do, and I decided to become clean like the first time I came out of my mother's womb. I must give up smoking, drinking, and all that stuff. I must start praying and devote myself to religion, *ṣafi*. (Story 63)

The next day he began to pray:

That was it! I said, "God, put me on the right path." I asked God to put me on the right path and take care of my affairs/business, and keep me away from the bad path. And things have worked out well. . . . I felt better, I was OK, and life was better, too. Whatever plan I made, I carried it out. If I decide, for example, to do this and that and I make a plan, and I'm sure about it, therefore I carry it out, *ṣafi*, no problem. . . . That's what I've done, from that time until now. (Story 63)

Again alone and isolated in a compassionless world, Mohammed meditates on the moment he was born from his mother's womb, and he experiences the sort of transformation Carl Jung termed *apacocastasis*: a reorganization of adult personality based on a *re*conversion to childhood piety. He is reborn figuratively of his mother—"I decided to become clean like the first time I came out of my mother's womb"—and literally of God, the Creator. Here he appears to draw on a powerful cultural model and rhetoric, which Richard Antoun explicates in his account of a village imam's sermon on *rḥam*.[6] The sermon employs derivatives of the *r * ḥ * m* root to rhetorically integrate a vision of the life course: the Muslim begins life with a cutting of the umbilical relation to the *raḥim* (womb) but is sustained through its earthly course by maternal compassion/benevolence and by a broader *silat ar-raḥam* (network of uterine kin), and then at death returns to God, *al raḥman* (the Compassionate), *al raḥim* (the Merciful).

After further describing how, in the mountain village, he sometimes read the Quran and cried over the wrongs he had done, I asked him which passages had so moved him. Images of "betrayal, orphanhood, and poverty," he said. "All these exist in the *sura al-ḍuha* (The Morning Hours)." I asked him to tell me about the sura, and he recited it:

> In the Name of God, the Compassionate, the Merciful
> By the light of day, and by the dark of night, your Lord has not
>   forsaken you, nor does He abhor you.
> The life to come holds a richer prize for you than this present life.
> You shall be gratified with what your Lord will give you.
> Did He not find you an orphan and give you shelter?
> Did He not find you in error and guide you?
> Did He not find you poor and enrich you?
> Therefore do not wrong the orphan, nor chide away the beggar. But
>   proclaim the goodness of your Lord.[7] (Story 66)

He then explained:

> Here God, the Great, the Merciful calls out to the Prophet and instructs him, because the Prophet had been through that state—orphanage and poverty. He calls upon the daylight: by the light of day and by the dark of night, your Lord has not forsaken you, nor does he abhor you. . . . The life to come is better than this ephemeral one which will end. You live 60, 80, 90, 100 years and then you die. But up there, in God's home, the orphan who has lost his parents finds compassion, commiseration, clemency, and kindness. (Story 66)

When I asked about other Quranic suras that have special meaning for him, he recited a verse from *al-infiṭar* (The Cataclysm):

> Oh man!
> What evil has enticed you from your gracious Lord who created you,
> gave you due proportion and an upright form?
> In whatever shape He willed He could have moulded you.[8]

He explains:

> He speaks to everyone: "O man! What evil has enticed you? What evil has enticed you from your gracious Lord who created you, gave you an upright form, and proportioned you?" . . . This means: he has created human being out of a drop of purified water. He made out of that drop a man and a woman, they met and he created the fetus in the mother's belly, [and] the parts were formed gradually, one month, two months, three months. . . .
> How then could you give up God who created you and follow *shitan* (the devil)? This is all blasphemy. Human being is on a dark

path, following the *shitan* (devil), that's all. Why don't I go back to God, the Merciful, who made me out of nothing. (Story 68)

Mohammed portrays himself as thrown off the ordained course of his life by his mother's death and his father's neglect and says he feels a deep "lack"—of compassion, guidance, and succor—which enrages him, turns him against humanity, and in his final view, renders him vulnerable to Satan's temptations. In the Quran, he comes to comprehend his "lack" as an echo of the Prophet's orphanhood and poverty, and he finds in God a home with "compassion, commiseration, clemency, and kindness." Meditating on his birth and death—"I thought how I came out of my mother's belly young and clean, therefore I thought about death"—Mohammed finds God as the creator to whose compassion and mercy he ultimately will return. Again alone in darkness, he finds light—the daybreak—that Quranic commentators say represents the coming into this dark world of the truth. He returned to the path of piety, and his friends and relatives noticed his immediate and dramatic change:

> They noticed a big difference. They realized I had changed to the extreme. They called me *fqih, fqih*—most of the guys, the young ones called me *fqih* (man of religion). Everybody at work or outside people noticed it, my friends in the hamlet, everybody, even up in Rabat. (Story 72)

He also returned to the study of Quranic recitation, the high art of the Muslim world, which requires long training in a system of named tones, cadences, and rhythms as complex and nuanced as those found in Western classical music.[9] He has developed a local reputation for his beautiful, strong, and precisely controlled voice.

Mohammed now defines the righteous path as one of purity, light, and cleanliness in contrast to that of dirt, darkness, and pollution: "When we went to Ouarzazate, it was like black pages—you know what *saouda* (blackness/obscurity) is? . . . I consider that period as some page I've scrawled with dirt, all scrawled with dirt." This imagery establishes a solid link to the practices of Islamic piety that organize daily life into five daily cycles of increasing pollution and ritual restorations of purity preparatory to prayer. The very physiological processes of life steadily increase one's pollution, rendering one increasingly vulnerable to unwholesome emotions and influences, especially to the whisperings of Satan and the mischief of the jinn spirits. Worry and anger may, as some *ḥadiths* (deeds or sayings of the Prophet) state, come from Satan, but they always can be treated with purification and prayer—and Mohammed says he now follows the recommendations of the *ḥadith* when he feels upset rather than turning to vices:

> If I get angry, if I'm upset, I go and perform my ablutions. Then I sit and read the Quran until I feel better. Then, everything is OK. Why

does *ḥadith* advise us to read the Quran, to perform one's ablutions and pray? If people perform their ablutions and pray they won't do something else. . . . If one is distracted and does something, he will do it blindly. But if you perform your ablutions and read the Quran, you won't have time to be upset. . . . So if you get angry, you read the Quran and sit by yourself until that moment of anger passes away. (Story 73)

If Mohammed now manages the cluster of emotions that comprise his delinquent, misanthropic, sullied subself by ritual purification and Quranic recitation, he representationally distances himself from them by locating them both in his personal past and in the distant future, at the end of history. He explains another *ḥadith* about the signs of approaching *ṣeraᶜ* (ruin, destruction):

[When you hear] people boast and brag that they've built seventeen- or eighteen-story buildings . . . when you see women all naked or dressed with transparent linen so you can see their bodies, and you see them fooling around and gossiping in the street in order to steal away people's hearts, and you see above their head their hair like the hump of a camel—these are all signs of *ṣeraᶜ* (apocalypse). (Story 68)

The term *ṣeraᶜ* means "shock," "fall" (as in epilepsy), "madness," and "rabid" —the same sort of terms he uses to describe himself in his *jahel* (wild/rabid) days.

With this configuration of religious concepts and images—the Prophet as impoverished orphan, God as the merciful and compassionate creator, cycles of pollution and purity, and the divine light of daybreak—Mohammed defines his primary and "official" identity and takes the Prophet, his namesake, as his model. From an opposed set of representations—abandonment to the temptations of devils, dirt, darkness, and wildness/animality—he symbolizes the complex of deprivation, anger, and impulsiveness that led him off the pious path and into an inhuman anti-identity. He resolutely condemns the second, but his humorous presentation of his delinquent actions and impulsive decisions betrays a good measure of warmth and admiration for the character he was—the sort of admiration he conveys for his great grandfather, the big man who recklessly wandered into his enemy's village, and the sort of warmth he feels for himself as a little boy, trying to attack his father in his mother's defense.

Psychologically as well as culturally, his pursuits of honor and piety led him on diverging developmental paths, the first toward a personality consolidated around an impulsive, letting-go style of expression and the second toward a personality organized by a restrained, holding-on style of self-control. These appear in his narrative as contrasting subselves or identities. Mohammed now feels he mindlessly sought a sullied form of heroism, and his *fqih* (devoutly religious) identity rests on defining the impulsive, indulgent, rebellious side of his character in terms of a negative *jahel* (wild/rabid) identity that helps him disintegrate it. These terms and story lines help him "hold on" with techniques of purification, emulation, and worship before his feelings of neglect, anger, and flight can assemble into a coherent, active self. Other portions of his narrative, however, show that he has hardly banished these from his experience.

Husband, Father, and Still Son

Mohammed studied for the baccalaureate exam as he worked in the mountains and passed it as a "free" candidate, which gave him the right to enroll at a university. He wanted to pursue Islamic studies, at which he excelled, and registered at the new university in Agadir. But because the universities were overcrowded, the ministry stopped providing scholarships to those already employed, and Mohammed could not afford to pay his own way. So he returned to his post, disappointed but committed to making a good life in the countryside. A transfer to Skoura was approved, and he returned to live in his father's house and work as the accountant for a new agricultural cooperative. Then twenty-four, with a steady job, a home, an intense piety, and other marks of maturity, he needed to marry—and two years later he did. But his long, meandering account of his marriage entails all of the familiar themes of indecisiveness and impulsiveness, entrapment and escape, submission and rebellion against his father's wishes that appear in so many other contexts. Everything about his life had changed yet, in psychologically important ways, stayed the same.

> When I was working in the mountains, I wanted to marry Zahara. She was my cousin's daughter, and we lived in the same house when I was studying in Rabat. I got to know her *caractère* (Fr., personality) and she got to know my *caractère*. We agreed to get married. When I quit school and went into the army, she stayed in school in Rabat. When I came back for a visit, she asked me if we were still getting married. I didn't know what to say to her. I was in the army, in the desert, and with all the transfers and not being settled, I couldn't tell her if we were still going to get married. I didn't know what I was going to do. . . . (Story 49)

By the time he was back in Skoura, he says, another problem developed:

> My father lives in the *bled* (countryside), and he's made sacrifices for me, and he wants me to be in the *bled* near him. So how can I get married and run away from him and go to Rabat? I'm not like that. I wouldn't be at ease/feel comfortable if I went away from him. . . .
>
> I said to myself that my father did everything for me when I was young, he educated me and helped me, he had a hard time and all

that, so I can't go away from him. . . . If I run away, I wouldn't be worthy of his name. I have to please him and to be near him, and even if there are problems. . . . So I told her I can't tell you if we're going to get married or not. (Story 49)

Finally he asked her to leave Rabat and live with him in Skoura, but she refused. She then had a good job with an insurance company and suggested he move there. He declined, citing two reasons: the duty he felt to his father and his fear that he might fail in Rabat or again find himself distracted by the temptations of urban life. Construing marriage to Zahara as a flight from responsibility that might open the door to impulsive "problems," he decided "to marry here in the *bled* (countryside)." But now he views his decision *not* to marry her as an impulsive mistake, which occurred because "I didn't think about things carefully."

> When the news reached them [Zahara's family] that I'd made up my mind to marry here in the *bled*, they were angry and made a great fuss. They said I was no good because I didn't marry her. . . . She got married, and she's OK, she's become really well-off. . . . I just didn't know what to do, so I got married. . . . Indeed, if I had married her, if God wanted, we would have been better off, much better than this life I live now. (Story 49)

Mohammed's search for a local marriage quickly grew complicated, created strife with his father, and threw him into endless vacillations and so "swelled my brain" that he finally agreed to let his father contact a local family who had a daughter named Aisha:

> I never knew their house was even on the map. Because of all that *ṣedaᶜ* (noise/trouble), the men of my family came and said you must do this and that. I told them, *ya Allah* (go ahead) sir, you do whatever you want. . . . They went to see the girl, and when they came back, they told me she was good and her parents were all right. I said, God bless us. . . . So one day I went to see her. . . . She greeted me like this, *salem, salem* (Hello, Hello), and retraced her steps. I came back and said, do it, there's no problem. That was that. We settled the matters with them, made all the arrangements, and agreed on a wedding date. (Story 56)

To escape the *ṣedaᶜ* (noise/trouble), he washed his hands of the decision, explaining, "I wanted to do something easy, that would take me five days." But three children later, he doesn't hesitate to voice his regrets. "I had a very traditional marriage," he lamented, "like Baba Abdullah, like poor Abdullah." Baba Abdullah was the poor, blind storyteller at whose house I first met him. A widower in middle age, he had married a poor, partly hobbled, black-skinned woman regarded as more a curse than a fitting wife. Mohammed continues:

It's difficult, very difficult, very difficult. If somebody wants to get married, he should marry someone he knows. He should know her character. As soon as she moves, he should know what she wants, even if you only move the eyelashes like this, you must be able to tell. For example, if Zahara only moved her eyes, I knew what was in her brain. If she looked at things a certain way, I knew what she was saying. On the other hand, this one [Mohammed's wife] is far away from you, and you're far away from her: you don't know her character, and she doesn't know your character. (Story 57)

He still thinks of Zahara: "Sometimes when I'd pray, she would appear to me." Even after his wife gave birth to a son, he says,

What came back to my brain was Zahara. . . . I wanted to go to Rabat and change my way of life. But I said to myself, it's not Aisha's fault. I was the one who searched for her. She didn't come to me and ask me to marry her. Therefore, if I turn her out, I'll be the criminal, because I'm the one who messed up with her life. She's not the one to blame for all this. So, what am I going to do?

After a while, I made a decision to stay with her. After all, we're only here in this life for a short period, so there's no point in making problems. Everything will pass and then we'll die, so there's no point in making problems and troubles. And so we stayed together, and now, *raḥ*, I have three children and my wife is pregnant. There is no place for me to go now. (Story 58)

Mohammed's account of his marriage thus shows the familiar cycles of entrapment, rebellion, and flight that appear throughout his narrative. At an earlier time in his life, he fled in pursuit of what he now sees as the devil's whisperings, but Mohammed the *fqih* puts himself into God's hands, turning to the grand framework of cosmological time ("We are only here in this life for a short period, and therefore there is no point in making problems") and to practices of purification and Quranic recitation to disintegrate the entrapment-rebellion-flight constellation before it can coalesce into a persona. He chooses to weave his character into a seamless whole, centered in the *home* he has found in God, in the home he has found in loyalty to his father and family, and in the practices of worship that restore his purity and link him to his mother. This identity consolidates an affective-relational constellation that forms the core of a "true self," embodying caring and compassion rather than deprivation, attachment rather than entrapment, loyalty rather than rebellion, and self-control rather than impulsiveness.

Still, the seams continually fray: his discontents (that he resembles "poor Baba Abdullah"), his longing for intimacy of the sort he felt with Zahara, and his dream of leading a larger, more heroic life still leave him feeling a lack and evoke impulses to flee. The whole character Mohammed would achieve turns out also to be but a subself permanently in dialogue with another: the domination of *fqih* (religious devotee) over *jahel* (wild/rabid) proves to be more a Manichean struggle than a vanquishing of darkness by daylight.

A Dream Renewed

I interviewed Mohammed for the last time six weeks after he told me about his marriage. He had spent three weeks on vacation with his brother, who had moved to Rabat, and began by telling me he was again thinking of moving there:

> Maybe, I said to myself, one would find a little cleaner/better living there, among the civilized, and the kids would grow up in civilized surroundings. It could help them to do whatever they eventually want to do, and there are a lot more things there in the city than here in the country, where things are quite limited. (Story 59)

He could learn computer programming, he said, or work in his brother's clothing business. "He told me to come there and we'd help each other," Mohammed said, "and I've started considering it. . . . But I haven't talked to anybody. All this is only brewing up here [pointing to his head]." Surprised by this news, I asked him how he saw his life in Skoura after returning from Rabat, and his answers covered familiar themes:

> Well [pause], what can I tell you? When I returned from Rabat, it was very hard here. It was like being here by force. I couldn't wait to go back to Rabat. . . . I became different and I came back with new ideas.
>
> Their life has become more organized, their children have become well bred. . . . But we have stayed over here doing nothing. What are we doing in Skoura? Nothing. In the morning we go to our jobs, and then back to the house and so on and so forth everyday. If I stay this way, like my father—he came back twenty-five years ago and stayed the same way in Skoura until now. He didn't change his situation, he just stayed the way he was before—I thought, if I stay like this, I'll be the same person and stay in the same situation. (Story 60)

Suddenly he feels trapped, "by force," and the imagery by which he defines himself reverses. He can't stand "doing nothing," just following in his father's footsteps, and life in Rabat looks "more organized," his relatives' children "well bred." Before his recent trip, he says, "I was thinking good things of the *bled* (countryside). Can you see the contradiction?" I assured him with a chuckle that I had my own contradictions, and he continued:

> I liked the countryside very much. I thought . . . one can lead a good life here. But when I went to Rabat, I changed my mind and asked

myself what was best for me to do: to stay here and maybe start raising some livestock, or to go and study computer programming.
(Story 60)

Now, he says:

> I see my future here as an obscure one: it's *ghamed* (dim/foggy), un-
> known, you can't foresee/anticipate anything. I can't look forward
> to anything because it's impossible to fulfill/achieve anything here
> in Skoura. . . . Moreover, I have children, and the most important
> thing for me is the kids. I must help them make their way in life. They
> can't do anything here. They only go to school and come back home,
> they can't do anything. They keep walking round and round in the
> street and outside . . . I can't see any future for them now. (Story 60)

Actually, he has an even grander dream that he first sketches as an ambition
for his father. When I asked if his father has been happy living out his life in
the village, Mohammed says they see things differently:

> Indeed so, according to him. He's content with his job. But accord-
> ing to me, it's not that simple. We've discussed the matter many
> times, and I've told him that he needs to change his job instead of
> doing the same thing all the time. At your age, *rah*, you should get
> out of the shop and move to another field that concerns religion.
> You should direct a large Quranic school and become a counselor,
> one of the senior counselors. But he doesn't think about this; he likes
> going to his shop and talking with everyone. (Story 60)

A few minutes later, in response to no particular question, Mohammed voices
this dream as his own. "My head is telling me to devote myself to the Quran":

> I want to get out of here and go to Rabat and contact people who
> study the Quran and give myself over to the art of reciting the Quran,
> and to study the *hadith* (sayings of the Prophet), *safi*. I've not talked
> to anybody about this, it's only my head. But this is the goal I want
> to fulfill.
>
> I've met some of those people who are in radio broadcasts and
> teach how you should read the Quran and the art of reciting. Like
> the one who reads the Quran during Ramadan, I met him before he
> was on that program. They've sent him to several Islamic countries:
> he went to Pakistan, to India and Afghanistan. . . . I think about the
> same thing. That's what I think about. (Story 61)

So now as Mohammed sees his life following his father's, he feels stuck "by
force," in Skoura, doing "nothing"—"In the morning we go to the Centre,
from the Centre to the house, and so on and so forth everyday"—and his
children just "walk round and round in the street and outside," and all face

obscure, cloudy futures. The anxious state of directionless, trapped movement and sense of deprivation returns and inverts the order of his life: the simple pious life of the countryside now looks dirty, disorganized, and imprisoning. His yearning for a bolder, grander, more heroic life returns and beckons him: to recite at great mosques, on the radio, perhaps in distant Muslim lands. Mohammed indeed has a beautiful voice and a local reputation as a powerful and skilled reciter. To step onto national and international stages would bring him as close as he could come to the Prophet's mission.

Personality and Identity ❀

Mohammed can experience his life in Skoura as one of order, control, cleanliness, nurturance, piety, and brotherly comradeship with his father. As *fqih*, he is recognized as deeply devout, a beautiful reciter of the Quran, a professional, a father of sons, and a maturing pillar of the community. But in the blink of an eye, this experience can reverse, and his life turns into one of boredom, confinement, frustration, obscurity, and endless repetition of meaningless patterns. He follows his father's now-little footsteps, purifies away the anger his father's authority repeatedly evokes, and tolerates a traditional marriage as Zahara's image still haunts him. His life then feels dirty and disordered; it angers him and makes him want to flee, and he regularly turns to God, to purification, and to prayer to restore himself as a loyal son, father, teacher, and Muslim.

Order, confinement, flight; loyalty, oppression, rebellion—these cycles give his narrative its emotional rhythm. They suggest, as I noted earlier, that an obsessive-compulsive tension between holding on and letting go styles of emotional expression is a central feature of his genotypic or core-level personality organization. His oscillation between these contrasting styles gives distinctive shape to two interpersonal tensions that appear equally central. One entails a powerful ambivalence in his relationships with male authorities: he quite consciously seeks a powerful "model" to emulate and follow, someone who will both guide his maturation and accept him as a man among men. But he also quickly perceives, resents, and rebels against confining or "despotic" authority. The other tension concerns a more maternal form of nurturance and interdependence that resembles the *amae* or "indulged dependence" that Takeo Doi believes to be central to Japanese culture.[10] He feels the loss of his mother as having left a hole in his life, and he repeatedly feels an acute lack of sustenance and compassion, which he repeatedly blames for his failure to achieve his potential in life. He looks to strong men (his father, the "heroes" who led him into delinquency, the Prophet) to fill this lack and finds the compassionate guidance he seeks most reliably provided by his extended family and in the "home" God provides to orphans. Loyalty thus appeals to him, not just as a kind of defensive identification with the aggressor, but as a form of attachment to sources of nurturance. Rebellion and flight similarly do not just represent reactions to restricting, demanding authorities, but even more important, they appear as responses to feelings of deprivation and neglect. Indeed, it appears to be feelings of deprivation and abandonment that shift his experience of authorities from empowering to constrictive, and that fuel his rage at the world.

In character as the young man his friends and relatives call *fqih*, Mohammed appears to have achieved a culturally approved alignment of identificatory loyalties to paternal and religious authorities and embedded these within the region's rhetoric of masculine honor, on the one hand, and within the highly ritualized self-care practices prescribed by Islam, on the other. He leavens the synthesis with a quick and hearty sense of humor that yields a symbolic framework that enables him to marshal and publicly project a good deal of personal power. He comes across, not as timid and constricted, but as a man who uses his loyalties and practices to harness a formidable wellspring of potentially dangerous aggression, that once given free rein, turned him *jahel* (wild/rabid). But as *fqih*, his ready humor, flashing smile, and deep, sonorous voice counterpoise and soften his confrontational, hostile side and sublate these into a not-inconsiderable measure of charisma. It takes vigilant hard work, however, to transform his feelings of deprivation, to pacify his quickly evoked anger, and to sustain his loyalties in the face of wishes to rebel and flee. And he suffers from wrought-up, churning, hostile anxieties that often show in muscular and facial tensions and that find release in dramatic gestures and laughter. His struggle to contain this hostile anxiety may well have contributed to his intensifying abdominal pain and to his second surgery.

Biography and Identity

Let us look more closely at the self-representational system Mohammed employs to narrate his biography and at the discourse that configures these prominent core personality tensions into an ideal alignment. Specifically, let us focus on the symbolic organization of his personality—his use of cultural symbols to differentiate the affects that mingle and merge at the core level into a contrasting pair of selves: an ideal *niḍam* (orderly/responsible) or *fqih* (devoutly religious) self he labors to fashion and maintain and a *jahel* (wild/rabid) antiself he works to keep in his immature past.

In its most rudimentary outline, Mohammed's life story is a familiar, even stereotypic one: a good boy deprived of his mother and then left unsupervised in adolescence starts running with the wrong crowd and goes bad, but after a stint in the army, he finds the religion of his youth, straightens himself out, and comes back to the fold. This account reduces his life to a perhaps universally intelligible dimension, but it is an outsider's distillation that excludes precisely the events and meanings he feels give it structure: the betrayals he suffered along with his mother's death, his raging hunger on the Night of Destiny, the delinquencies he committed in hatred of humankind, his defiance of an officer and facing down of death in the military's interrogation chamber, his rebirth in the mountains, and his persistence on the straight path in the face of recurring discontents. Mohammed's recounting of these incidents indeed outlines a universal plot structure—that of a heroic quest—but it also employs story schemas that give it a distinctively Muslim, Middle Eastern, and North African character.

Numerous attempts have been made to identify a general structure of hero narratives, most by analyzing European, Mediterranean, and Near Eastern materials. Rank[11] and Campbell[12] sought to identify hero patterns in terms of underlying psychological processes, Rank focusing on the heroic struggles in the first half of life, culminating in marriage and career, and Campbell focusing primarily on the process of individuation that Jung[13] believed unfolds in the second half of life. Both are intriguing because they offer plausible explanations of seemingly bizarre and paradoxical features found in many epics, but they have not proven especially suitable to accounting for the overall structure of single tales or of the genre. By contrast, Raglan[14] and Propp[15] sought to delineate characteristic sequences of episodes or *functions* (Propp's term), and although these do not account for "the moral of the story," they have proven useful for identifying the heroic genre and analyzing the structure of individual narratives.[16] These two schemes differ in that Raglan analyzed epics and legends that dealt with the hero's fate until and, in some cases, after his death, whereas Propp focused on folktales that usually end with the hero's marriage and return home or assumption of power. The first 13 of Raglan's 22 incidents and 11 of the major functions in Propp's scheme of 31 appear in Table 3–1.

Neither Raglan nor Propp holds that a hero narrative must include all of these points or that it must be limited to them. Addition and repetition of episodes and subplots provide much of their richness, and the omission of a few constitutes a legitimate means of creative variation rather than a departure from the genre. Differences in the collections these investigators studied probably account for some of the divergence of the elements they list, especially the first five or six on Raglan's list, which are summarily covered by Propp's "initial situation." Both incorporate the threat to the hero, his departure, his finding of a protector/empowerer figure (Raglan's foster parents; Propp's donor), and his struggle, victory, marriage, and ascent to formal power. Raglan appears to view the hero as *seizing* power (though "magical" powers are given in many of the legends he analyzes, which include the biblical Joseph and Moses), whereas Propp appears to view power as *bestowed* and then demonstrated and confirmed in battle. Propp's lack → departure → donor (testing/attack) → magical agent → struggle sequence brings his schema closer to the psychological stages of the hero's development into manhood—which is definitive of the genre.

Table 3-1 Hero narrative structure

Raglan	Propp
1. The hero's mother is a royal virgin;	Initial Situation
2. his father is a king, and	*Lack*: One member of a family lacks or desires something.
3. often a near relative of his mother, but	
4. the circumstances of his conception are unusual, and	*Departure*: The hero leaves home.
	Donor: The hero is tested, interrogated, attacked, etc. . . .*
5. he is also reputed to be the son of a god.	
6. At birth an attempt is made, usually by his father or maternal grandfather, to kill him, but	*Magical agent*: The hero acquires the use of a magical agent.
	Struggle: The hero and villain join in direct combat.
7. he is spirited away, and	
8. reared by foster-parents in a far country.	*Victory*: The villain is defeated.
9. We are told nothing of his childhood, but	*Redress/Attainment*: The initial misfortune or lack is liquidated.**
10. on reaching manhood he returns or goes to his future kingdom.	*Return*: The hero returns.
	Pursuit/Chase: The hero is pursued.
11. After a victory over the king and/or a giant, dragon, or wild beast,	*Rescue*: Rescue of the hero from pursuit.
	Wedding: The hero is married and ascends the throne.
12. he marries a princess, often the daughter of his predecessor, and	
13. becomes king.	

*It is typically at this point that the "donor" character, who will confer magical powers on the hero, enters the story, and it is usually the donor who tests the hero.
**"Redress/attainment" is my title, as Propp does not define this function.

The major episodes of Mohammed's biography parallel those identified by Propp, though with greater development of his struggle with inner as well as external forces. His life begins in plenitude: his description of his birth and his earliest memory both convey an aura of completeness, bounty, and specialness. His ensuing early childhood memories place him in a more troubled world, where his well-intentioned but less-than-competent attempts to act as a man among men leave him with injuries and humiliations. Yet these memories convey a sense of admirable innocence rather than gravity or harm; he tells them as funny stories, retrospectively enjoying his immature efforts to be adult, and he ends most on positive notes with relationships restored. Gravity descends with his mother's death, which introduces the lack and deprivation—of succor and compassion—that he ultimately feels subverted his attempts to realize his potential. In the aftermath of her loss, however, he shoulders adult responsibility for his siblings and becomes serious about his religious studies, acquiring the donor figure (in the person of the Prophet) who later will empower him.

He next tells of a series of departures, struggles, and small victories (over his nemesis in Skoura, over the relatives who entrap him in Rabat) and then of the departure that leads to his *jahel* (wild/ignorant) period in Ouarzazate. His return home proves premature when his father falls ill, and he departs again, this time to become an *ᶜskeri* (soldier). Beyond the borders of civilized society, he again struggles with hostile forces and wins his freedom by offering to die at his inquisitor's hand. His victory returns him home but to a liminal state in which he finds himself again tormented by boredom and what he figuratively terms *shiatan* (demons/devils). Then, in a kind of solitary mountain refuge, he undergoes a rebirth, names and conquers the forces that repeatedly led him astray, and returns home to marry, begin a family, and await his ascension to family patriarch.

This plot structure annuls the lack—God takes in the orphan and provides him a home, as then does his father—and constructs him as a heroic character: as *fqih* (religious teacher) in contrast to an alternative sort of hero, the soldier, and in opposition to the antiheroes or Satans he followed into delinquency. The first contrast reflects the prototypic ideals of honorable manhood in rural Moroccan, North African, and Middle Eastern societies: the fighter and the man of religion—the *rajel kabir* (big man) or *ᶜskeri* (soldier) versus the *fqih* or religious sheikh. These ideals merge in the person of the Prophet, but in many regions—including rural Morocco—they stand in a complementary opposition as belligerent and peacemaker. This contrast was literally woven into southern Morocco's tribal geography, with *zawiya*s of important saintly lineages located on the borders of frequently hostile tribal groups and with tombs of important saints providing peaceful sanctuaries for weekly markets. The contrast of fighter and holy man also is woven into the hagiographies of Morocco's most prominent saints, many of whom prove their *baraka* (divine blessedness) in mystical combat with strong men and despots. And it is deeply woven into everyday life, where the realpolitik principles of familial interests often clash with religious principles, and *fqih*s and imams are frequently called into households to loosen the interpersonal knots that aspiring big men have tied.

Mohammed's life narrative can thus be seen as documenting a struggle for contrasting ideals of honorable manhood: one belligerent, intimidating, and associated with his individual prowess and repute; the other restrained, pacific, devoutly religious, and associated with the community of believers. This contrast weaves through his narrative (his "big man" great-grandfather versus his father's saintly foster father; the child in the *zawiya* versus the child who attacked his father; the "well-bred" child versus the kid who "got to like fighting"; the *fqih* versus the *ᶜskeri*), appearing both in the feelings and relationship he attributes to himself and in the character types he brings on stage with him. These personas appear as subselves that have crystallized from the linkage of distinctive cultural prototypes with contrasting sides of the core ambivalences animating his core personality. The *fqih* uses religious principles and practices to hold on to anger and sustain familial loyalties, whereas the tough guy/soldier projects a belligerent attitude that serves as a hair trigger for letting go aggression and egoistic assertion. We can say either that Mohammed has *internalized* a pair of cultural personas or social selves or that he has *differentiated* his personality or self along the lines of this cultural contrast.

Mohammed's *fqih* self-representation thus derives crucial features of its meaning from its contrast to ᶜ*skeri* (soldier), which sets out an alternative construction of honorable manhood. But it acquires even more salient features of meaning from its opposition to his *jahel* (wild/ignorant) self-representation, which defines a veritable antiself. Mohammed presents his descent into delinquency as arising from the confluence of two processes: (1) a desire to cultivate a sense of manhood based on physical prowess, daring, and rebellion —fully consonant with his and his culture's heroic *rajel kabir* (big man) persona and (2) an increasingly distressing feeling of deprivation, which, reaching its crescendo of hunger on the Night of Destiny, triggers a misanthropic rage. Here a different cluster of core-level affects coalesces to form a subself: feelings of deprivation and confinement, unleavened by loyalty to a nurturing authority, trigger a generalized hatred of humanity that takes shape as a rebellious search for indulgences and destructive troublemaking. These form an out-of-control, dishonorable subself, which at least in retrospect, he represents primarily in religious terms: Mohammed says he was led "off the straight path" into "ignorance" or "wildness" by "devils" and that he "sullied/dirtied" his once-pure, innocent self. These representations construe his tough-guy, hatred-of-humanity persona as an abomination, as a crossing of the boundary out of the community of believers and into animality and pollution. His use of these antiself representations after his rebirth reflects his attempt to prevent the feelings of deprivation, anger, entrapment, and rebellion, which he clearly continues to feel, from again coalescing and demanding their due.

The heroic plot structure thus constructs Mohammed's identity as a configuration of three self-representations, each of which organizes a subself or voice: *fqih* names the devoutly religious ideal he seeks to live as his true and authentic self, as Mohammed, named for the Prophet; ᶜ*skeri* (soldier) names an alternative, now past and rejected self that faced down death for honor; and *jahel* (wild/ignorant) names a rejected dishonorable antiself. Each of these discourses defines *an identity*, but *his identity* consists of the configuration of the three. This is because (1) ᶜ*skeri* and *jahel* are essential to defining *fqih*, and (2) ᶜ*skeri* and *jahel* embody affective states that are his but that Mohammed as *fqih* strives and often claims not to experience. *His identity* thus appears organized as a tripartite *differentiation* by which the fluid affective tensions comprising his core-level personality are crystallized as distinctive outlooks on life and as culturally archetypal social persons.

As *fqih*, Mohammed stands close to God, created by him, nurtured by his compassion, and sheltered in his divine home. In the earthly world, he, like the Prophet whose name he bears, cleaves to the *triq l-mustaqim* (straight/ pious path), maintaining his purity, beautifully reciting his message, and spreading his beneficence. This is the ideal he wills to be his "true self," and the act of willing sets it against a "false self," the sullied, misanthropic, clamoring after the "devils" sinner he terms *jahel*. That is, *fqih* versus *jahel* legislates a moral imperative and weaves it through the entirety of his character —endowing the affective tensions that continually come over him with ontological, ethical, and soteriological meanings.

Erik Erikson often spoke of identity as a configuration of subself-like "elements," perhaps most explicitly in his biography of Martin Luther, whom he described as shifting between being son, rebel, and father.[17] More recently, Hermans and Kempen have drawn on Bakhtin's theory of the "polyphonic" novel to develop a model of self as a dialogical play of voices.[18] So it is with Mohammed: his narrative proceeds as a dialogue among and about these three subselves. They achieve integration not only by virtue of the hero-narrative story line that places them in a temporal order and touts the *fqih*'s triumph over *jahel* and *ᶜskeri* but also in the structure of dialogue. In addition, the system of self-representation he sets out in the interviews shows a third integrative structure that employs key symbols in a manner analogous to that by which tonal music uses the notes of a scale.

Chambers and Homes

Mohammed describes many of the most important moments and turning points of his life as having occurred in chambers with distinctive qualities of light. These form a thread of motifs or type scenes that runs through his narrative and links disparate events of pivotal import, many of which entail nonordinary forces or at least "religious" significance. The terms *motif* (a recurring phrase, figure, or image) and *type scene* (a prototypic event, like "departures for sea" in Homer and "meetings at wells" in the Old Testament) come from studies of oral epic and ancient scripture,[19] in which they serve as important structural features. They help sustain a sense of continuity for audiences, but more important, they provide the performer or reciter with mnemonic and organizational devices. Like a jazz musician, the performer can master general story lines, type scenes, and motifs and gain the freedom to improvise the specifics of setting, action, and dialogue as she or he performs on any particular occasion. In Mohammed's narrative, chamber images also appear to serve as what Suzanne Langer terms *life symbols*—images that "present the basic facts of human existence, the forces of generation and achievement and death"[20]—and what Sherry Ortner terms *key symbols*, which combine and intensify ultimate meanings.[21] Most of them entail a struggle with or for light in a kind of ambient darkness and form a sequence that marks out the steps of loss, descent, and rebirth that his life history portrays him as traversing.

As background, however, I must offer an aesthetic observation: the pre-Saharan rhythm of daylight gives the area's traditional yellowish-beigy-reddish rammed-earth buildings a distinctive range of interior atmospheres. Bathed in streaming or filtered sunlight, they can take on a warm yellow-golden hue that easily evokes a sense of plenitude and repose. But darkened by dusk or nightfall, they can take on a mysterious, frightening quality that is only enhanced by the flickering light of a charcoal brazier or butane lamp that dances shadows into abysslike corners and corridors. These effects result not from the light alone, of course, but from comforting meals and siesta retreats from the midday desert sun, from beliefs about the jinn spirits' residence under thresholds and their emergence at sunset, from folktales told only after dark about ogres and giants and ghouls, and from purifications performed and prayers recited at midday, dusk, bedtime, and sunrise. These rhythms and tones echo those of ancient Arabia and add to the poetic power of the Quran. Their power may be intensified by Islam's prominent use of light imagery—a divine luminosity—to represent the Prophet and his message, which Sufi and folk Islam especially emphasize.[22] They thus comprise a facet of the culture's aesthetic and symbolic lexicon that individuals can draw on to articulate more idiosyncratic personal meanings.

Mohammed's earliest memory of curiously studying a yellow cat in the *zawiya* encodes a quality of fascination with specialness in an ambience of plenitude. It preserves, I suggested, an archetypal image of well-being: his curiosity in an enchanted world, anchored or nested in familial harmony. His second memory of his parents' nighttime quarrel rudely breaks the spell, though his impulsively heroic action restores the harmony. His visits to his dying mother appear to have taken place in a chamberlike setting, and he strongly associates the period of deprivation after her death with his practice of rising alone in the chill before dawn and lighting a fire in the hearth for his siblings. His memory of the terrible beating, tying, and threat of being smoked at his father's hands represents a real and serious injury, especially as Mohammed believes it caused his appendicitis and surgery. His troubled stay with the wrong relatives in Rabat reached its climax when they deprived him of electric light to study, and he found himself up late in his room alone, hunched over books by candlelight. This appears as a kind of prelude to the hunger and possession-like "fall" he suffered on the Night of Destiny, which turned him against humanity and eventually into a soldier on the edge of the war. Narratively, this incident marks his descent into an underworld, where his travels take him to a land of "nothing but death" in the Sahara and eventually bring him face-to-face with sacrificial death in the army's dark but floodlit interrogation chamber. There, he stares down death, survives, and finally takes control of his life, beginning his return journey toward home. Home, however, is not a physical place but a spiritual one, and he initially remains something of an outsider in his father's dwelling. Finally, in the darkness of his solitary mountain retreat, he, like the Prophet, is reborn and given a home with God—a home he characterizes as bathed in the beneficent light of daybreak.

These chamber images organize his life history and identity like notes forming a scale, the saint's tomb of his earliest memory and the *home in God* of his reconversion standing in a kind of "octave" relation that defines its key. They form the "tonic" anchor points in relation to which he experiences all of the others as degrees of "departure from" and "return toward." The encounters with pain, rage, and death that animate his *jahel* (wild/rabid) and *cskeri* (soldier) selves—the beating that caused his appendicitis, his hunger-induced fainting on the Night of Destiny, his offer to be killed in the army interrogation chamber—sound as the tones of greatest "departure from" the octave end points. Extended playing of these distant-from-home tones brings about something akin to key change, into a "key of honor," anchored by his second earliest memory (attacking his father in his mother's defense) and his fight with the bully in his neighborhood. But the resolution to be reached as a *rajel kabir* (big man) is never achieved, as his feelings of neglect enrage him and lead him into delinquency rather than valor and distinction. As he narrates his life, Mohammed uses this key of honor to evoke his *cskeri* (soldier) and *jahel* (wild/rabid) subselves, sketching the ground that frames and foregrounds what he seeks to perform as his authentic melody, which we might entitle "variations on the theme of *niḍam* (orderly/responsible) and *fqih* (devoutly religious)." The sacred space of the mosque, designed to represent God's dwelling on earth with a domed interior lit by divinely ambient light, organizes the rhythms of his daily and weekly life into a melody of such departures and returns, as does the purification ritual by which he prepares for prayer and recitation. Perhaps like the place-and-action images Bakhtin termed *chronotopes*, they serve as paradigm-defining exemplars that establish a sacred space-time-causality system and give him a home near its center.

Culture, Personality, and Self

What does Mohammed's life narrative teach us about the cultural shaping of personality or self? Perhaps most important, it shows that this question is better posed about three levels of organization: (1) core-level personality, described as a set of recurring affective and relational tensions; (2) three subselves, each appearing as a configuration of core-level affects, integrated as culturally constructed orientations (honor via piety, honor via masculine prowess, and delinquent dishonor), and (3) an identity that configures the three subselves as an ideal self (*niḍam* or *fqih*, responsible and devout), an alternative past self (*cskeri*, soldier), and a rejected antiself (*jahel*, wild/delinquent). His personality encompasses all three of these levels, each of which appears subject to different kinds of cultural influence.

It is impossible to determine the extent to which Mohammed's culture (be it that of the Middle East, of the circum-Mediterranean, of pre-Saharan

North Africa, or of Skoura) has shaped his core-level personality. It is plausible that the paradigm of distant, demanding, fearful paternal authority, which he so well describes, has fashioned his ambivalent rebelliousness and search for authorities to follow and emulate. And it is likely that his mother's death deprived him of the intense maternal interdependence many observers believe to be characteristic of North African men. But an adult's life narrative can never establish the *causes* of his or her development, and it is plausible that these affective-relational tensions are at least as rooted in his inherited temperament as in his familial experiences.

It is at the second level that he appears to have deeply internalized his culture. And "his" culture appears to be circum-Mediterranean, perhaps with pre-Saharan colorings, for the three subselves closely follow the contours of the region's most prominently defined masculine orientations. This observation has an especially important consequence: although the constitution of these three orientations fundamentally makes him a member of his culture, it does not integrate him smoothly into it. Rather, it puts him disturbingly in question: it poses the question of what person to truly become, and this is the question that an identity must then answer. Mohammed feels he answered this question once and for all when he turned to the Prophet as his guide and found a "home in God," but his narrative suggests that he must reanswer it continually with vigilance and will.

What, then, of the cultural shaping of identity? With regard to *which* of the three orientations he has elaborated into his ideal or authentic self-representation, it would appear that forces *within* his culture—rather than "culture"—have influenced him to become *fqih* rather than ᶜ*skeri* or *jahel*. Other men become tough guys, big men, or soldiers and enact piety only for its social expedience. Still others, including some of his neighbors, have become delinquent and even *meskhot* (accursed) and disowned sons. And many men fashion identities of very different subself components. This is a simple point but one often lost in recent discussions of the "cultural construction of self," which emphasize shared meanings and psychological characteristics at the expense of the great range of individual variation to be found within every society.

At the same time, Mohammed's identity is *thoroughly* culturally constructed in that his culture provides him with the symbolic lexicon and integrative templates by which he defines and organizes the three subself orientations. He is *fqih* rather than priest or preacher or monk because he is North African rather than Italian, American, or Japanese.[23] It is the specific character of his *fqih*ness—elaborated in terms of the Islamic cosmology, in his *inḍibat* (self-control/restraint), in his *teqowa* (fear of God), in his purificatory practices, in his Quranic recitations, in the imagery of the sura morning hours, in its opposition to ᶜ*skeri* and *jahel*, and in the scale of chambered darkness and light—that makes him appear most alien to a Western interviewer and most distinctively a pre-Saharan Moroccan Muslim.

Theoretically, then, culture has not constituted Mohammed's self but provided the materials from which he has fashioned an identity that integrates three subselves. A world of difference separates these two views of the culture-self relationship. Other than the discourse of identity that fashions an overall integration, we will scour Mohammed's life narrative in vain for an overarching "sense of self," "concept of person," or "self." At the same time, we do not find only the hundreds of linguistically constructed speaker "positions" taken up in the course of our conversations. A kind of overarching identity does appear, consisting of the *dialogue* among three subself voices—the *jahel* (wild/ignorant one) with the *ᶜskeri* (soldier) and with the *fqih* (religious devotee), of the heroic biography that resolves the dialogue in favor of the *fqih,* and the set of chamber images like a musical scale by which he orchestrates his life history and self-representation.

CHAPTER 4

Hussein

Soon after I began my research, I asked a neighbor in Ouarzazate if he had acquaintances I might interview in Agdez, his small hometown to the south. He immediately thought of Hussein, who had failed his second-year exams at the university in Agadir and come home two years ago to live with his family. He often rode the bus to Ouarzazate to run errands, apply for jobs, and see his friends, so he might have time free to talk with me. Two weeks later, we met over tea at my neighbor's house. Hussein appeared as a thin, slightly frail young man with finely chiseled features, fastidious in his Western-style dress, and deferential and almost fidgety in his demeanor. I described my research and told him I would begin with some psychological tests and then ask him to describe his present life, his childhood, and his view of the future. Hussein seemed both curious and apprehensive and said he would be happy to help me out. Our conversations stretched over a year and grew to eighteen hours, during which time I also visited him in his home and accompanied him to social and community events. His narrative is more extensive and complex than Mohammed's, and the interpretive questions it raises provide further opportunities to discuss theories of the region's honor code and gender constructions, as well as of identity.

My initial self-presentation probably shaped Hussein's role as "interviewee" in two important ways. First, I asked him to teach me about Moroccan culture, and throughout the interviews I occasionally addressed him appreciatively as my 'ustad, or "teacher." I suspect this encouraged him to adopt a more intellectual tone than he might have, but I also think it built rapport by giving him a way to see our exchanges as a collaboration. Given what he repeatedly described as the consuming fact of his life—that he was sitting at home with no work, little self-respect, and darkening pessimism about his future—our conversations provided him with an opportunity to feel his hard-won education still had value. Second, by stating my interest in his view of Moroccan culture in contrast to the traditions of more remote areas, I probably encouraged him to emphasize rural versus urban differences, which emerged as a central dimension of his identity. I am convinced, however, that this theme was not *only* a product of our conversation. Not only did he draw the tradition-modernity contrast in terms used spontaneously by most of those I interviewed but also he brought me a prize-winning essay from high school in which he had developed these same themes.

To the extent that Hussein narrates his life as an example of something,[1] it is of the *chomeur*—the French term used in Moroccan Arabic for "unemployed." He is one of tens of thousands of young men in Morocco with good educations and no work, men who often appear to outsiders—and sometimes to themselves—to be stranded between tradition and modernity. He reads popular books and magazines like *Jeunne Afrique*, and he keeps up with world affairs on TV, but his father now presses him to irrigate their ancestral fields and do other manual labor he thought he had risen above. He spends much of his time resisting temptations to join other students-turned-*chomeurs* in their smoking, drinking, gambling, and womanizing. And in spite of the fact that he never felt much enthusiasm for religious observance, he has begun listening to taped sermons by the Egyptian "Islamist" sheikh Kishk and focusing his anger on "the bourgeoisie," official corruption, and leaders who have strayed from the egalitarian principles of true Islam. Here, too, he presents himself as representing a group, and I believe that in listening to him we can learn something about the dilemmas faced by all those who have fallen into the *chomeur* category. In the first interview, he described his future as *ghamed* (cloudly/murky) and cited a proverb that conveys his sense that childhood incidents have crippled him: "If the reed is bent when it sprouts, it will stay bent forever." When I asked him about this proverb in the last interview, he underscored the uncertainty of his future by commenting on the reed: "It may grow big, but bent. It may reach the sky, but bent. If you try to straighten it, you might break it."

At the age of twenty-four, then, Hussein is a no longer very young man who has been unable to consolidate a position within his family or outside of it, and who—largely because of this—has not consolidated an identity. As he describes his struggles to build an adult life that will keep him "innocent before God," he shifts among contrary self-representations and views of Moroccan society. Over the course of the interviews, these shifts trace three contrasting identities—each set out as a *discourse* about who he is and what his world is like. Each discourse offers interpretations of his fears and weaknesses and shows by exemplars how these might be transformed into strengths. Each casts him into an array of disempowering and empowering forces, with its own set of moral temptations and imperatives. Yet as different and often contradictory as the three identities are, a familiar set of affective tensions, relational schema, and representations appear at the core of each, giving his life narrative the character of variations on a theme.

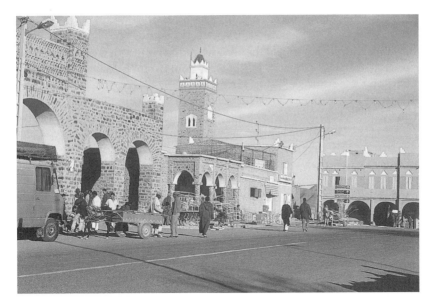

Agdez: town center

Agdez: carpet shops and café in the town center

Above all, Hussein has sought the knowledge and culture that would give him a modern, urbane, "civilized" way of life in contrast to the "tribal" world that begins on the outskirts of Agdez. His father grew up in a small village a few kilometers upstream but raised his children to work with their minds rather than their hands. Hussein sees him as an embodiment of tradition, and quarrels over Hussein's modern ideas and ambitions have strained their relationship nearly to the breaking point. Yet even while he was working so hard to become one of the few who passed the baccalaureate exam, Hussein himself harbored doubts about the promises of modernity. These themes appear in many of the stories he composed to Thematic Apperception Test (TAT) cards in the first interview, so evocatively that he had to break away and tell me about his real-life conflict with his father.

The first card shows a boy sitting at a table, chin resting on palms before a violin, his expression ambiguous but clearly not joyful. Hussein examined it for a moment and then said it depicts a naive boy "from the countryside" who has been given a violin by an urban relative. The boy feels taken aback because he does not know what to do with it—"*kaysteghreb* (he's stunned/surprised): how is it used?"—and sits anxiously, hoping the gift-giver will return and help him out of his *ḏlam* (darkness/confusion). He has the relative come back to teach the boy, who then goes on to become "a pretty good artist" and benefit from the deeper "culturing" effects of music. He clearly identifies with the boy, and his later account of his first encounter with the urban culture of Casablanca parallels this shock-to-mastery story. Indeed, this picture appears to have served as a mirror in which Hussein outlined his own life project: to overcome backwardness, triumph over modernity's shocks, and acquire the education that will turn him into a cultured adult.

But the boy's predicament also allegorically describes the awkward situation in which Hussein found himself as my respondent: left alone with an instrument he doesn't know how to use, the boy feels "amazed/surprised" and thrown into "confusion/darkness." He has the boy reject an angry urge to get rid of it—"Why did you bring it to me? Do I hit the wall with it?"—and then looks for help from its provider in the hope that it will eventually have a salutary, perhaps culturing effect on him. The story thus rather transparently reflects the discomfort Hussein feels at being "tested" (I had termed the TAT an *ikhtibar*, a test or exam) but also his hope that I might bring him empowering aspects of modern culture he sought to acquire at the university.

His response to a card I had redrawn to depict a traditionally dressed older man leaning over the shoulder of a younger one in a suit initially develops the same theme: a modern son needs to go his own way and rejects his traditional father's advice. But the son then arrives at *shi mawqif harij* (a halt/stoppage) at an embarrassing point and comes to recognize his father's wisdom. "Times change but the ideas stay the same," he says. "If you don't follow them, there will come a time when *twqef qedamek* (you stop in front of yourself) and you regret it: Why didn't you take his advice?" Hussein can't imagine a decision the fictional son might have made, other than his own decision to reject his father's plans for him to become a low-level *functionnaire* and instead enroll at the university. This forces him to "leave the picture" and talk about himself: "My father told me, 'If you go to the university, I won't give you any money. You'll be on your own.' I told him I'm going, and I went." When he failed, his father welcomed him home angrily:

> What did we tell you? It's you who left and now you have to solve your problem. If you had gone to the training school, you'd be living like the others now. But now you're sitting unemployed, you've found *la khadma la redma* (no work or anything).

He then concludes that a son oughtn't "cut" his ties to his father:

> Whatever the son's ideas were, they mustn't be different from the ideas of the father, they must always be *mertabet binathoum* (tied together). If one comes to cut the *silat* (chain/links) of ideas or the chain of tradition or customs, you can't live. Even if you're in the middle of a big city, you can't live. There isn't anyone who can live without his traditions and customs.

Throughout the interviews, Hussein forcefully voices aspirations to "become modern,"[2] to master the shocks modernity holds for boys from places like Agdez, to educate and culture himself, to strike out on his own, and finally to fashion an "urbane" way of life. But he also often reverses himself, as he does here, embracing a traditionalist ethic of filial loyalty.

The term *waqef* proves critical to the emotional tensions underlying these projects and ultimately to his self-representation throughout the narrative. Words built from the *w * q * f* root, whose core meaning is "to stop," also include "to stand up" physically, "to take a stand" to defend one's honor or a principle, and to become "erect."[3] Slightly different forms mean "to hesitate," "to block," and to be "halted," and the forms *teqef* and *meteqef* sometimes are used to refer to sexual impotence, especially that caused by sorcery. So Hussein's entirely ordinary and appropriate uses of *w * q * f*-based terms here (the boy "arrives at *shi mawqif harij*, a halt/stoppage at an embarrassing point"; "there will come a time when *twqef qedamek*, you stop in front of yourself") connotes an opposition between the bold, manly assertion of will against "the" father and an ensuing collapse into anxious immobility and powerlessness. His terms *mertabet* (tied) and *silat* (links) both mean "relationship" and commonly are used to refer to close relations cemented by kinship and love, so in coming to a halt, his courageous decision to separate turns into abandonment. "It's you who left," his father threatens, "and now you have to solve your problem." These TAT stories thus show an emotional tension that appears in a multitude of contexts: a desire to achieve and assert competence, strength, and autonomy, often against or for powerful male figures, and a liability to feel threatened, brought to a halt, or disempowered, often under the threatening gaze of powerful male figures. This tension emerges as a central feature of Hussein's core-level personality, and we will see that his modernist, traditionalist, and religious identities promise alternative routes to empowerment and security.

Father, Son, and Mother ❀

Two weeks later we met for a second interview, and Hussein quickly elaborated on his conflicts with his father. He moved back and forth between recounting their ongoing disputes and tracing the roots of their estrangement to a series of childhood incidents he says permanently "marked" or "scarred" him and "wrecked" his life by leaving a crippling residue of "fear." These events also led him to "prefer" his mother, who shelters him from his father's threats as she always has.

I Live with a Scar

Hussein traces their troubles to the time his father beat his mother:

> kanⁱish waḥed te'tir (I live with an effect/scar), with a worry/anxiety I can't get rid of. That effect/scar is from when I was small, six or seven, and I was present once when he hit my mother. . . . There was a quarrel between them. We'd just had breakfast and I'd gone outside until I heard my mother's voice and came in and found him beating her. If I'd had the mind I do now and the strength I have now, I would have thrown him out the window—I wouldn't have hesitated for a moment [said angrily, boldly]. That effect/scar has remained, and that's what has caused me to not love my father much. I prefer my mother. (Story 15)

Hussein in fact watched helplessly: "I was a little kid. There wasn't anything I could do. I cried and waited until he went out and sat next to my mother and cried with her. I hated him!" This turns out to be his earliest memory, and he presents it as *the* formative moment in his development; it was "inscribed" so "deeply inside" that "it stays with me every day . . . it stays in front of my eyes." He says he accepts ḥaq l-'ab (the father's right/authority) and accords him due respect so that "nothing shows." "But deep inside," he emphasizes, "he and I aren't very close. From that point, he's taken that path and I've taken this one."

This story segment, like several of those that follow it, actually develops three larger story lines: one describes his current troubles with his father, another chronicles his father's mistreatment of his mother, and a third

---

sketches his father's biography and rehabilitates him as an honorable if tough character. Orphaned at an early age, he explains, his father grew up in his sister's husband's household, herding their sheep and often going hungry. "He had a life of hardship," he says, as he "went into life having to take care of himself." As a teen, he ran away to Fes, where a French colonist hired him, came to trust him, and helped him get a government job that enabled him to transfer back to Agdez with a steady salary. There he built a modern-style house in the "new" town center and bought enough fields in his ancestral hamlet to become a major landowner—vindicating himself against his relatives' charges that he had shirked his responsibilities. Hussein neither takes back his words nor lets his father off the hook but tells his story in admiring tones. He portrays his father as a complex character with whom he has a troubled but many-sided relationship, and he accepts his ambivalent feelings to a greater degree than did many of the Americans I interviewed.

As he moves among story lines, he makes important shifts in tones of voice, points of view, and emotional "stances." He begins speaking hesitantly about the distance between himself and his father, but when he describes the beating, he becomes angry and speaks forcefully. He rather proudly recounts his father's life story but then returns to a tone of hesitant complaint to explain how his father feels that sons *should* experience hardship. He cites an example that seems trivial—his father denies him money to go to the cinema—and his voice shifts to an almost pleading tone as he meekly asks for money ("give me some money to go to the *cinema*") and argues his own case ("to see a film is to develop one's ideas"). This stance of supplication is a familiar, culturally scripted appeal of juniors to elders, and as my English adjectives convey, laden with a resentment-tinged sense of dependence. Hussein then rises out of this supplicant's stance by reevoking "that incident with my mother" and angrily describes again how "it" has remained f l-^{c}umq (deep inside). He then reestablishes his father as a man of honor who sometimes behaves dishonorably and ends by angrily challenging him: "I don't want him to be saying things like that. I want him to be a man!"

Hussein here moves among three stances vis-à-vis his father: at some points, he feels little, intimidated, weak, and defeated and acts like a supplicant in need of protection; at others, he feels strong enough to stand up to his father and challenge him, especially in defense of his mother; at still others, he admires and identifies with his father as someone who overcame deprivation and hardship to prove himself an honorable man. I term these relational positions *defeat*, *challenge*, and *identification*, respectively. They appear in a great many story segments—including those in which Hussein tells about the other figures who make up his world—and they provide narrative and psychological schemas that organize many characters' feelings and actions. In this story, he repeatedly shifts out of the squirmingly uncomfortable "Defeat" stance by recalling the inscribed beating incident, which arouses his anger and repositions him in the "Challenge" stance as his mother's protector. But when this threatens to cut his relationship with his father, he shifts to the biographical story line, preserving through the "Identification" stance the possibility that he will ultimately acquire his father's strength and honor.[4] These cycles do not trace a regular pattern, as he can shift among them as the intrapsychic and interpersonal demands of the moment pull him. But each stance defines a different *kind of man*, and so together they map a moral realm in which each figure embodies a set of moral sentiments or imperatives.

These movements recur in the ensuing story segments. He begins to describe a dispute with his father about whether he had smoked a cigarette but then shifts to tell of an incident in which his father wrongly accused his mother (who keeps *ḥajba*, secluded) of leaving the house. He "witnesses and swears"[5] in her defense and returns to the pitch of anger he reached in the beating incident, boldly proclaiming that "if he continues with that violence, I'll get up and do something terrible that everyone will hear about" (Story 16). Then he recalls a dispute over his brother's future that replicates his own: his father wants him to take an entry-level job in his bureau, but Hussein argues he should study law because the family needs to build connections in many ministries. In the end, his father again cuts him down to size: "You just want to send him off so he'll become . . . a *chomeur* [Fr., unemployed] like you" (Story 17), and he backs down: "If I see that he's getting angry, I break off the dispute and shut up" (Story 18). He then returns to his father's biography, this time using nearly the whole vocabulary of honor: abandoned and mistreated, his father "wanted to hold his head high/proudly" and persevered through hardship by his *nefs* (here: spirit/pride) and his *l-ᶜned* (determination) to return home and vindicate himself. He matured into a man who "measures/focuses each word"—the poetic quintessence of a man of honor (Story 19).

He Wrecked My Life

Hussein moves on to another series of incidents that further estranged him, in which his tyrannical second-grade teacher repeatedly beat him and then his father beat him for running away from school. He says these beatings instilled a pervasive fear that *kherj liya ᶜla ḥayati* (wrecked my life) (Story 20): "He [the teacher] left a mark on me, a mark of fear, and it's still with me today. I'm still preoccupied by that fear. . . . He's the cause of the fear I have in my life" (Story 23). He finally got some relief when a relative talked his teacher into easing up and his father began giving him small money rewards (and later on, soccer equipment) for staying in school and bringing home good grades. He recalls that his mother comforted and protected him: she "covered for me," he says, because "the mother is always *ḥanouna* (empathic/compassionate)" which he explains by saying that a mother needs her son "to sit at her side," worries that he might encounter animosity or violence if he parts from her, and easily cries at his misfortunes (Story 20). These were the very qualities his teacher lacked: "There was no *raḥma* (compassion), no *ḥanen* (empathy/compassion)" (Story 23). He again shifts between weak stances in which he feels threatened and defeated by authorities and strong ones in which he challenges them. He describes his abusers in a raised, angry, dramatic voice, first imitating his father's commands and then characterizing him as "like *cntar*," a legendary warrior/giant figure, and as "despotic." His teacher, he says over and over, was "like a lion . . . like a lion."

As if to restore a semblance of symmetry, he then tells how he recently tried to get his sister's teacher to stop beating her (Story 24) and eloquently articulates his opposition to using violence and fear to educate children (Story 25), arguing that parents and teachers need to use *l-ctef* (caring/compassion). Then he again shifts to portray his father in a compassionate light, fondly recalling being told that as a child he was often unable to fall asleep until he could rest his hand on his father's knee (Story 26). He also remembers waiting eagerly for his father to return with fruit from their ancestral fields, both to receive them as special gifts and to help him distribute them as presents to their poorer neighbors—which he cites as his happiest childhood memory. This sketches a very different relationship: one of special intimacy with his father that his siblings do not share, leading to a joyous identification with him in his role as a generous patron. But he ends by again blaming his "fear" on the beatings he suffered. "That fear entered, and it's still with me today," he says, and he elaborates by describing his disconcerting timidity in his father's house (Story 27). Hussein views his fear as a kind of illness and even considers having a traditional healer treat it by cauterizing the "vein" said to carry it along his spine.

Months later, Hussein talked again about family quarrels and again shifts among these stances. His father once threatened to beat his mother for attending a soccer game, and she fled to the safety of her sister's home with Hussein and the other children (Story 83). Initially a bystander, he soon became ensnared in their dispute, alternately protecting her and being consoled by her after his father snubbed him. In the next story, his father hears some malicious gossip and impulsively casts false accusations at his mother and then at him (Story 84). Hussein describes challenging his father at three points, twice in language that implies standing up and physically confronting him (*kanḍour fih*, I would get into it, and *kannoḍ lih*, I get up at him), but he ends up defeated or withdrawn in each case, seeking his mother's solace. He then criticizes his father's failures to appreciate his mother's labors, challenging him in defense of her against his *menker* (false accusations/betrayal) (Story 85). Then he shifts abruptly to rectify this portrait, emphasizing that his father has always been a good provider to his family and a man of *mcqol* (honesty) (Story 86). And at the end of this segment, almost as if to describe his own shifting stances and opinions, Hussein cites a pair of puns that give us a good laugh and pick up his spirits. The first plays on the similarity of *'insan* (person/human) and *nesian* (forgetful), and the second on the similarity of *qelb* (heart) and *qleb* (turn/flip), so both attest to the fickleness of human character: "people wouldn't be named '*insan* if they weren't forgetful," and "the heart wouldn't be named *qelb* if it didn't turn/flip." These jests show a rather remarkable capacity to accept and chuckle at his father's and his own inconsistencies.

It hardly needs to be said that Hussein feels "ambivalent" about his father, as do many young men in many societies. But Morocco's economic underdevelopment, especially acute in areas like Agdez, probably influences its character and intensity. As in most traditional societies, young men remain long dependent on their fathers, who control marriage and economic resources, and they must work psychologically to renounce, defer, or divert their strivings for independence. In modern societies, by contrast, most fathers cannot provide their sons with a livelihood and a bride, and so separating and achieving "autonomy" becomes a key psychological task. Hussein's father recognized early on that his children's futures lay in the modern sector rather than in subsistence agriculture, and so he sent them to school and pushed them hard to succeed. But modern opportunities have proven to be disappointingly few, so like many of his generation, purely practical considerations prevent Hussein from committing himself to the difficult psychological work either of separating or of remaining dependent. This cannot help but amplify his ambivalence, so he finds himself vacillating between rebellion and loyalty, making but provisional efforts at both.

The Mother

Hussein "prefers" his mother, but she appears mainly as a third character in father-son dramas and as a more stereotypically idealized figure to whom he feels intensely, "interdependently" attached. When I first ask about their relationship, he says, "It's good. It's good! Good 100 percent!" and he describes how she comforts and sustains him:

> She has compassion and worries about me. She gets money, for example, from my uncle and gives me some. And when they all go off to school, she'll make me some hot breakfast [and say:] "There's no reason to get upset. God wants good things for you, and until you have work there's no reason to get angry or lose sleep or cry." She'll wake me and I'll eat a little. She'll smooth things over. I don't know quite how to explain: she knows the problems I'm living and she tries to help. (Story 29)

He volunteers an insightful sociological account of the preference he perceives boys to have for their mothers, and girls for their fathers. In most families, he says, the same-sexed parent acts as disciplinarian, so the children seek out the other one, who more freely expresses "fondness": "he [the father] grabs him and beats him and his mother gives him compassion/kindness—that's the reason" (Story 36). Asked for childhood memories, he says, "*walida ḥanina* (my mother was compassionate)" (Story 73) and gives more examples of how she tried to protect him from his father. In the last interview, I asked again about maternal compassion, and he says:

> That's *ḥanan dyal 'um* (mother's compassion/caring). Khalil Gibran, an Egyptian writer, wrote about the mother, and he says the mother is everything in life. He who has a mother has everything in life. The mother is the greatest thing/everything sweet in life. "It's beautiful to be called/summoned by one's mother" [classical quotation]. The sun is the mother of all existence, she covers all with her warmth, and like the moon gives light at night. And there's a writer who says, "He who loses his mother, loses one *ṣder* (chest/bosom)." If one has a mother's bosom/understanding, he can return to it when in need. (Story 170)

Hussein's mother thus emerges as a near-sacred being whose warmth radiates throughout life and who provides a compassionate refuge from life's bitterness. His attachment to her appears at the heart of his ambivalent feelings about leaving home and living on his own. When he left for the university, he first recalls wanting "to be independent, to take care of myself. I wanted space from their problems. . . . Even though they sent letters, I didn't read them" (Story 28). But he soon began to worry about his mother's welfare and felt compelled to make regular visits to make sure she was all right. He goes on to describe his great longings for her and recalls sitting sadly alone during Ramadan, wishing he had an automobile so he could take her for drives, as he saw other grown (and prosperous) sons doing:

> I said to myself, if only I had a *tomobile* (car) I would take my mother out with my friends. She doesn't go out. She sits in the house and takes care of her children and does housework, and that's it. She isn't relaxed/contented. She has a lot of children, and the kids make it hard on her. You know our fathers, they didn't do anything back then: every year or two another kid. So she's stuck in the house taking care of all those kids. She needs some relaxation, she needs to get out. I'd sit out at the corner of the *appartement* [Fr.] and watch those people and I would cry: why can't I tomorrow or the next day get her with a car, and take her out of the house?
>
> And him [Hussein's father], I don't think of him, truthfully. I even wrote and told her, "If only you could come out with me, get out of the *ṣeda*ᶜ (trouble) of the house." And that continues to bother me. My father was annoyed/hurt, and he told her, "He isn't just your son. He doesn't even acknowledge me!"—and still today that continues to bother him. But I don't deny that feeling. I'm telling you truthfully. (Story 29)

Hussein's ambivalence about separating deepens when I ask whether he plans to live at home, and he imagines himself playing out the script he narrated as his father's biography (Story 30): his father accuses him of being poised to flee as soon as he finds work, but he insists, "I'm going to show him the opposite, so he'll know he was wrong!" by continuing to support the household. Then he tries to endorse living away from his family but caustically imagines how they would "really" love him when he is gone but sending money. He finally resolves his mixed feelings by imagining he would take his mother away to live with him: he could free her from seclusion and "show her another life" and also regularly "find her in the house, so she will be waiting for me there."

These stories coalesce around familiar stances: he challenges his father in defense of his mother; his father defeats or belittles him; he turns to his mother for comfort. He rarely describes dyadic interactions with his mother but repeatedly brings his father into the picture, fashioning triangular constellations that contrast maternal compassion and paternal threat. Many North African social scientists have described this pattern as typical of families in the region and observed that because women ultimately depend economically on their sons rather than on their husbands, they often seek to cultivate lifelong bonds of nurturance and interdependence with them. In a world in which most marriages continue to be arranged, many men report a trust and intimacy with their mothers that they find with no one else. So the sentiments Hussein expresses in these stories appear to be fully in character with the interdependent relationship it is believed a son should have with his mother.

The Burdens of Patriarchy

My question about Hussein's responsibilities as the eldest son evoked the scenario he dreads: stepping into his father's shoes as head of the household. "I have to remain in the house," he says, "and take responsibility for the *mwalin dar* (people/women of the household)" (Story 31). This brings him to a pitch of rage and resentment unique in his narrative: "I think about it and say *la merd f-bledi* [Fr. & Arabic: shit on my land] and in life." His father has brought him nothing but "hardship" and "suffering," he says, on three accounts: having brought him into the world, having spent his days on earth with him, and "the suffering he is probably going to leave me, when he dies." He resents that his father has failed to empower him and sooner or later will bequeath to him a challenge he fears and detests: "policing" the women of the house. "The problem that affects me deeply," he says, "is that I have girls, four girls—they're a problem, the girls!" He goes on to rail against women: "You know women, praise be to God, he created in them some *ghera'iz mokhalfa* (instinct of quarrelsomeness/ill will)." He ends in bitter resignation, imagining that no one he might marry could find happiness in his household of quarreling women, and so "I'll live with my family and won't marry. I'll live a narrow/weak kind of life until I die, and *ṣafi*."

This image of women as creatures of ill will and disorder strongly echoes Fatima Mernissi's analysis of the culture's misogyny as rooted in the notion that women embody powerful forces of *fitna* (chaos/disorder).[6] It appears as the backdrop to his idealization of "the mother" as a deep well of compassion. His often-voiced antichauvinist attitudes appear quite sincere, and he invokes the women-as-*fitna* image on only a few occasions, but it is this image that emerges into the foreground as he pictures himself filling the patriarch's shoes.

Triangular Relationships

Most of these story segments are built around a triangular structure of characters and relationships: a tyrant or harsh authority figure, a victim figure, and a challenger/defender figure. Within these triangles, Hussein shifts between positioning himself as a victim in need of protection and as a challenger defending a victim—and flies into rage and despair when he contemplates inheriting the tyrant's role. Throughout his narrative, he casts other people and characters as well as himself in similar triangles, creating a world in which forces of threat, challenge, protection, and defeat operate everywhere. In his account of the "inscribed" beating incident, this relational triangle can be diagrammed as in Figure 4-1.

In other incidents, he appears in the victim's role, and his mother acts as his defender. In others, his cousin comes to school with him to protect him from his "lionlike" teacher; Hussein acts as his sister's protector by challenging her abusive teacher; his orphaned father is abused by his adoptive father but protected by his sister; and so on. The defender's role also changes according to context: it sometimes requires "standing up to" the authority figure on behalf of the victim, sometimes protecting or comforting the victim, sometimes promoting the vulnerable junior's interests. Thus his father flees his abusive foster father to Fes, where he finds a French colonist who becomes his patron and empowers him to return home and vindicate himself. I think it likely that Hussein perceived me as this sort of patron/empowerer figure who might help him get over the fear he feels keeps him timidly under his

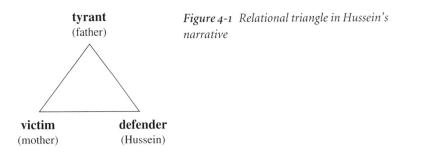

tyrant
(father)

Figure 4-1 Relational triangle in Hussein's narrative

victim
(mother)

defender
(Hussein)

father's thumb. His stories thus show a pair of relational triangles, as diagrammed in Figure 4-2. In its most ideal form, the defender acts as a patron to a vulnerable junior and empowers him to "stand up" to threats—the role Hussein wishes his father would play in his life. In its most nightmarish forms, he finds himself abandoned in defeat or cast to play the tyrant himself.

Whether we look at the characters and actions that typically comprise them or at the rhetoric and moral sentiments they express, the relational triangles construct a socioemotional world according to what many ethnographers of the region have termed the *honor code*. Hussein appears to feel recurrently vulnerable and faced with the psychological task of "standing up" and acquitting himself: of turning threatened disempowerment into triumph or accusation into vindication. The relational triangle fundamentally puts in question the hero figure's "honorable" manhood (when viewed culturally) or "phallic" strength (when viewed psychologically), but it also shows how honorable strength might be achieved.

Honor-based schemas take a different form in this narrative than they do in Mohammed's, and Hussein does not always cast himself and his world in triangular relations. But he does so automatically and pervasively enough that the schema clearly plays an important role in his personality organization, construing a range of emotions and social interactions as matters of honor. This observation takes us to the heart of culture-personality relationships: What is the "honor code"? In what way does it organize or integrate personality?

Honor and Personality ❀

This triangular schema appears throughout Hussein's narrative. It shapes discussions of his romantic adventures, his "addiction" to soccer, his views on societal modernization, his practice of Islam, his enjoyment of folk tales and novels, and the profession he chose but now cannot pursue. It organizes his world and his "sense of self" as an actor in it. It does not provide a single

Figure 4-2 Variants of relational triangle in Hussein's narrative

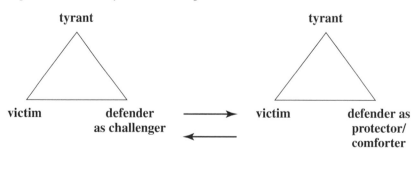

sense of self, however, but two diametrically opposed senses or *subselves*—vulnerable victim and powerful challenger—and a third that appears as a kind of necessary foil or *antiself*, the patriarch/tyrant. The relational triangle *integrates* these three subselves by defining each in relation to the other two and setting them in drama, dialogue, and counterpoint. It appears in his narrative as at once a personality pattern he has developed from idiosyncratic experiences and as a widely shared cultural pattern he has assimilated. So what should we term it? *National character* or *basic personality? Self, self-concept,* or *identity?* Is it "core"-level personality or an identity? An answer can be found in the convergence of ethnographic accounts of the region's honor code with psychological accounts of masculinity developed by several North African scholars.

The Honor Code

Classic ethnographic discussions treat honor as a system of values or code of conduct. Ahmed Abou Zeid, for example, explains how a Bedouin group's honor rests on the "nobility" of its genealogy, its dominance over client groups, the heroic acts of its ancestors and senior men, the generosity of its stronger members, the protection of its women from outsiders' aggressions, and the compliance of its women with the rules of self-concealment and chastity. It enjoins ongoing aggression, with "raids on large hostile camps . . . still regarded as the most daring action of chivalry and heroism which enhances the prestige of the young man and his group."[7] And it enjoins a sacralization of the group's women:

> In Bedouin usage, the word *beit* covers both the tent and its occupants who always form one family. . . . It is often referred to as the *haram* (sanctuary) and is regarded in this sense as a sacred thing. It is also *haram* (taboo) and thus strangers are forbidden to come near it without the permission of its members. For the *beit* is, in the first place, the abode of the *harem* (womenfolk) . . . [who are] always regarded as something sacred and to be protected from desecration. In fact, much of the honour of the *beit* and the lineage depends on observing this sanctity. . . .[8]

Unfortunately, the notion of honor has been used in blatantly ethnocentric ways, with both scholarly and popular writers attributing the Middle East's economic and political problems to its purported psychological preoccupation with honor and shame.[9] More important, many scholars who study honor now reject accounts that treat it as "a solid body of values which control the patterns of behavior,"[10] as does Abou Zeid. More recent ethnographies show great regional variation in the rules and vocabularies of honor and in the acts and personal qualities held to be honorable. These portray social life not as governed by a code of honor but rather as unfolding through everyday exercises of authority, resistance, and struggle carried on as a *debate* about the nature of honor. Michael Herzfeld has been the most sustained critic of the honor code rubric, arguing that "'honor' and 'shame' are inefficient glosses on a wide variety of indigenous terminological systems."[11] He also takes an important step away from treating it as a code to emphasizing its rhetorical character: "There is less focus on 'being a good man' than on 'being *good at* being a man'—a stance that stresses *performative excellence*, the ability to foreground manhood by means of deeds that strikingly 'speak for themselves.'"[12]

The "Rhetoric" of Manhood and Modesty

Pierre Bourdieu provides one of the more insightful treatments of honor, focusing on the "game of challenge and riposte"[13] that takes place between individual men of Algeria's Kabyle region as they jockey for power and repute:

> ... this stake [*nif*, point of honor] for the Kabyle is worth more than life itself. *Nif* is also the desire to overcome one's rival in man-to-man struggle; it is that "jealous emulation," that struggle for glory of which Hume spoke with reference to Greek cities. . . . [14]

Bourdieu separates the two core dimensions of honor, which the Kabyle distinguish linguistically as *nif* (point of honor), entailing an assertion and defense of one's public image, and *hurma* (honor), enjoining defense of one's home and women. Threats to *nif* set in motion the "dialectic of challenge and riposte," whereas threats to *hurma* invoke the more deadly "logic of outrage and vengeance."[15]

Bourdieu's struggle to theorize about honor proves especially instructive. In addition to *oppositions*, *postulates*, and *values*, he uses a wide range of terms to refer to the honor system, including *game*, *logic*, *rhetoric*, *ethos*, and *sentiment*. Each of these implies a rather different theory of culture, and he never makes clear quite which he intends. He ends with a psychological view that emphasizes "ethos" and "sentiment," suggesting that the "values of honor" may serve as "unconscious models of behavior":

> In practice, the system of the values of honour is lived rather than clearly conceived. Thus, when they spontaneously believe that such and such a mode of conduct is dishonouring or ridiculous, the Kabyles are like someone who picks out an error of language without being in command of the syntactical order which it infringes.[16]

Bourdieu's mixed terminology grasps something important: that these components are widely, deeply, and nonconsciously internalized and, above all, *felt* to cohere, even if they more often generate dispute than consensus. He struggles with terminology partly because he sees how the syntaxlike rules allow for reversible interpretations. As even Abou Zeid observes, "It is diffi-

---

cult to say where exactly lies the line at which honourable deeds may find their sense reversed and become a source of disgrace. . . ."[17]

Lila Abu-Lughod's *Veiled Sentiments* adds another crucial dimension: the honor that derives from displays of modesty, especially for women.[18] Among the Awled 'Ali Bedouin of Egypt, she writes, male honor rests on strength and autonomy:

> One man explained, "A real man stands alone and fears nothing. He is like a falcon (*shahin*). A falcon flies alone. If there are two in the same territory, one must kill the other." Freedom and fearlessness are coupled in another word for falcon, "free bird" (*ter hurr*). The courage of the warrior ethic applies not just to matters of war or fighting . . . but to the interactions of everyday life.[19]

This notion of honor entails an egalitarian ideology that contradicts the hierarchical relationships organizing society. The Awled 'Ali resolve the contradiction, she says, by representing relationships of subordination—and gestures of deference to seniors—in terms of the "natural" hierarchy of family relationships. Thus the weak and dependent not only do not shame themselves when they voluntarily show deference but also accrue honor. They *tahasham*, which in these contexts does not imply "shame" but "modesty." The honor system thus generates not only shame as its dishonorable antithesis but also modesty as its honorable complement: "The general rule is that persons *tahashsham* from those who deserve respect—those responsible for them and/or those who display the virtues of honor."[20] This formulation fundamentally changes our understanding of honor, as it moves away from the honor-shame dichotomy and beyond the male game of "challenge and riposte" to incorporate the range of stylized male-female, senior-junior, and patron-client interactions and the crucial role that deference and modesty play in building an honorable persona. Henceforth, I will refer not to an honor code, but to an honor-modesty system.

The Ecology of Honor

Jane Schneider helped catalyze the last two decades' discussions of the Mediterranean as a "cultural area" by providing a historical and ecological context for understanding the evolution of the honor-modesty system. She argues that it defines the region's "cultural unity," which has developed "from a particular set of ecological forces."[21] Tracing the interaction of agriculture, pastoralism, and state institutions, she shows that Mediterranean societies long have been characterized by struggles for scarce resources (land, water, and women) among distinctively small, "fragmented," patrikin-based groups, often linked in fragile and shifting alliances. Exacerbated by inheritance rules that divide rather than conserve parental property and aggravated in some areas by endogamous marriage preferences that encapsulate rather than link patrilineages, the forces of fission repeatedly tear at even the smallest units, including extended and nuclear families. Schneider argues that the deeply cherished values of family and patrilineage loyalty found throughout the region represent often unsuccessful ideological attempts to mask and counter a resilient underlying "individualism." This nexus of forces patterns familial relationships:

> It is typical of the Mediterranean that the father-son relationship is somewhat strained and potentially competitive; that brothers are not emotionally close after they marry; that the most enduring and solidary bonds are those uniting a mother and her children. . . . In other words, the conditions which have fragmented the economic and political structure into its minimal, nuclear family components, have also fragmented the family.[22]

Here lies honor's primary ideological function: "Honor as ideology helps shore up the identity of a group (a family or a lineage) and commit to it the loyalties of otherwise doubtful members."[23] Control of women's fertility emerges as a practical strategy for building and sustaining patrilineages, so women emerge as key symbols in the ideological system:

> Women are for them [men] a convenient focus, the most likely symbol around which to organize solidary groups, in spite of powerful tendencies towards fragmentation. . . . The sanctity of virgins plays a critical role in holding together the few corporate groups of males which occur in many traditional Mediterranean societies.[24]

Eric Wolf's analysis of the informal social networks that often adopt "a kinship dogma of organization" points the way toward theorizing about this enlarged view of the honor-modesty system. Many ethnographers have described the prominent role played by face-to-face patron-client networks in circum-Mediterranean societies, as do Clifford Geertz, Dale Eickelman, and Lawrence Rosen for Morocco. Hildred Geertz's study of a large Moroccan household details how this negotiation of kinship works, and she appropriately calls the resulting network not a "family" or a "patrilineage" but a "patronymic association."[25] Eickelman writes that he came to believe:

> that Morocco's social structure was best conceived with *persons* as its fundamental units, rather than their attributes or status as members of groups. Moreover, persons are not arranged in layerlike strata or classes but are linked in *dyadic bonds of subordination and domination* [emphasis added] which are characteristically dissolved and reformed.[26]

Eric Wolf discusses the culturally distinctive interpersonal etiquettes that pattern the negotiation of patron-client relations in most complex societies and ends by pondering their psychological importance. He points out that Ruth

Benedict, Margaret Mead, and other culture-and-personality theorists often took data "on the etiquettes and social idioms" governing familial and patron-client relations as their primary ethnographic facts, misinterpreting them as expressions of "national character." He does believe, however, that such stylized "patterns of interpersonal etiquettes" are central to the cultural integration of complex societies and that they "indicate the way in which the parallelogram of social forces in one society differs from that of another."[27] Wolf here suggests that if we refrain from regarding cultural etiquettes as expressions of an underlying "basic personality," we nonetheless can recognize their psychological importance—though neither his "parallelogram of social forces" nor Bourdieu's "habitus" clearly captures it.

All of these investigators struggle with how to describe a cultural pattern that becomes a psychological one. They perceive the honor-modesty system to be nonconsciously internalized, such that it operates simultaneously as a relational framework, within which selves are crafted, and as a moral grammar, by which acts and relationships are debated. We certainly must reject the notion that this forms a "national character," a "basic personality," an "Arab mind," or a "self." It defines not a single model of personhood but a matrix of prototypic characters in relationship. And it does not provide the *only* system within which selves can be constructed and actions evaluated. As many Mediterranean ethnographers have pointed out, religion often provides a framework that people set against that of honor, and as Abu-Lughod elegantly shows, women of the Awled 'Ali turn to poetry and song as a counterdiscourse to communicate feelings that the honor-modesty system requires them to conceal. We need to describe the honor-modesty system's role in organizing personality but without describing it as forming *a* personality.

Social Personality

The relational triangle appears in Hussein's narrative as an internalized variant of the honor-modesty system, generating a world in which honorable manhood is continually challenged and tested. It provides him with a system of culturally constituted interpretations of affective tensions he chronically experiences—especially his ambivalent attachment to his father, strivings for autonomy versus interdependence, and feelings of "phallic" vulnerability versus strength. It organizes these tensions by locating and emplotting them in a configuration (e.g., tyrant, victim, defender) that renders them matters of masculine honor, modesty, and dishonor. It thereby integrates his personality in accordance with a cultural "value system" or "code" or "logic" or "ethos," at a level above that of core-level personality. It defines the set of roles he can play or the personas he can assume, but it does not determine *which* of these he will take up on any particular occasion. It makes him solidly a member of his culture but in so doing challenges him to claim an identity and prove himself worthy of it—setting the developmental task he faces as achieving honorable manhood. It thus coalesces as a middle level of personality organization, to some extent *between* the core level and identity.

What can we term this level of organization? As a dynamic multiplicity, it is not *national character* or *basic personality*, nor is it a Moroccan *concept of person* or *sense of self*. Erich Fromm's notion of "social character" appears more appropriate, in that he holds that multiple social characters arise from positions in a social structure and from the interactional styles that enmesh people in hierarchical relationships. In their much criticized *Social Character in a Mexican Village*, however, Fromm and Maccoby struggle to define the concept, vacillating between viewing it as a "character matrix," which fits the present case, and as a "syndrome of character traits," which does not—and they ultimately fall back on the latter.[28]

G. H. Mead's notion of "social self" consists precisely of such a matrix of social positions,[29] and his theory provides perhaps the best account we have of the relational triangle as an internalization of the honor-modesty system. Mead believed that as children play at social roles, they learn not only how to enact the requisite behaviors but also to take the perspective of other players in the "game," which constructs a representation of "Me." They take on progressively more complex roles as they grow into adulthood, and broaden the context until they consolidate an encompassing social self by viewing themselves from the perspective of the "generalized other"—essentially a map of the social structure and its interactional rules (or perhaps *etiquettes* in Wolf's terms). The relational triangle appears in Hussein's narrative precisely as such a Meadian social self constructed as an internalization of the generalized other—in this case, the circum-Mediterranean honor-modesty system. To use Sartrean terminology, which more closely approaches Mead's view than most investigators of "self" have recognized,[30] Hussein often experiences himself as "thrown" into this world, as "fixed" by the "gaze" of others into a particular position or persona, and forced to choose what he will stand for—in his own words, whether he will *waqef* (stand) or *tweqqef* (be brought to a halt).

But at the same time that Mead's model helps us understand Hussein, Hussein's narrative shows features of self for which Mead does not adequately account. Most important, the generalized other does not complete Hussein's self or confer an identity. Rather, it puts him in question, challenging him to stake a claim to an identity and prove himself worthy. I will use the terms *social personality* or *social persona* to describe this middle level of organization. This term still evokes some of the negative connotations of *national character* and *basic personality*, so it is important to emphasize two crucial points. First, social personality does *not* consist of modal or ideal personality traits but a matrix of stances or character types defined by their relational orientations to each other—that may coalesce within an individual as a set of subselves or senses of self. Second, a society can be expected to fashion not *a* social personality but many (often a set of social personas), and individuals can be expected to differ not only in *which one* they internalize but also in *what combination* of them—as a comparison of Mohammed's and Hussein's narratives makes clear.

In the Kingdom of the Mothers

We have seen that many ethnographers treat the honor-modesty system as a *cultural* pattern that *psychologically* organizes individuals' thoughts, feelings, and values and shapes their selves or identities. Several North African scholars have undertaken psychological analyses of this pattern of gender constructions. Sociologist Abdelwaheb Bouhdiba employs terms I prefer to avoid, viewing the "Arab male personality" as grounded in a culturally distinct variant of the universal Oedipal complex, but his description of this personality echoes throughout Hussein's narrative (though not through all of the narratives I elicited from men). He emphasizes the many ways in which economic, kinship, and legal systems converge to give emotional priority to the mother-child relationship over that between husband and wife. "The wife is devalued," he writes, "but by stressing the child-bearing role of women, one valorizes the mother. In fact misogyny represses woman into her maternal role and by that very fact sets up a veritable 'kingdom of the mothers.'"[31] He believes this "cult of the mother" to be a key to Arab "basic personality." "The physical mother/child relationship is transformed into an extended psycho-sociological unity," he writes, symbolized by the *ṣilat raḥim* (tie to the womb):

> In an Arabo-Muslim setting the mother appears even more as a font of affection, all the more precious in that it is a restful oasis in the arid social desert. How pleasant her water is to drink under the hot midday sun! And these private bonds between mother and child are reinforced by the fact that the fathers hand out so parsimoniously the external marks of their own affection. . . .[32]

At the center of the family, the society, and the psyche, however, stands "the terrible image of the father: *Ab*. This all-powerful, all-serious colossus cannot but represent an impenetrable wall between the child and his father." Autonomy tends not to be granted as long as a young man's father remains alive, and concentric circles of authority relations radiate beyond the family:

> The authority relationship has deep roots in our traditional society. It binds not only man to woman and parents to children but also teacher to pupil, master to disciple, employer to employee, ruler to ruled, the dead to the living and God to man. It is not only the father who is castrating; society as a whole emasculates.[33]

It is in this threatening, patriarchal context that the maternal bond assumes its significance:

The mother often plays the role of buffer between the father and his children . . . by the pity that she inspires and by the love that she unstintingly gives, the mother appears as an effective, unconscious recourse against the castrating intentions of the environment.[34]

Psychiatrist Assia Msefer develops a complementary analysis,[35] suggesting that the North African practice of sudden and often traumatic weaning thwarts the infant's gradual separation from its mother, throwing him or her back into a symbiotic dependence that becomes the basis of the sort of sacralized uterine bond Bouhdiba describes. Sociologist Fatima Mernissi has explored Arab-Muslim stereotypes of women in a remarkable series of books, arguing that these center on a fear of unsequestered female sexuality, equated with the forces of *fitna* (chaos/disorder), which means chaos, disorder, insurrection. She, too, sees men's sustained interdependence with their mothers as the critical element in the patriarchal configuration:

> The close link between mother and son is probably the key factor in the dynamics of Muslim marriage. Sons too involved with their mothers are particularly anxious about their masculinity and wary of femininity. In Muslim societies, not only is the marital bond actually weakened and love for the wife discouraged, but his mother is the only woman a man is allowed to love at all, and this love is encouraged to take the form of life-long gratitude.[36]

Bouhdiba and Mernissi emphasize the Oedipal character of the typical relationship between a dependent son, a threatening father, and a sheltering mother. These features appear prominently in Hussein's narrative: he "hates" and curses his father, tyrannical authorities of often mythic proportions loom everywhere, and he repeatedly describes his struggles to *waqef* (stand up) in this world. Conversely, he "prefers" his mother, whom he idealizes as "everything sweet in life," and imagines taking her away to live with him. It appears plausible to interpret this as an Oedipal structure, but I do not believe the narrative fully warrants this interpretation, nor do I believe the use of this term adds to understanding it. Without the Oedipal label, Bouhdiba's, Mernissi's, and Msefer's analyses prove even more helpful in recognizing the relational triangle as Hussein's idiosyncratic internalization of the region's honor-modesty system—especially because they emphasize the psychological dynamics of interdependence rather than sexuality.

At the level of *social personality*, then, the honor-modesty system provides an integrative schema for more amorphous core-level affective tensions and configures them into a culturally familiar set of stances and figures. Hussein's interdependent attachment to his mother, his ambivalent struggles with authorities, and his paralyzing fear all gain moral significance by animating a set of cultural dramas: they become matters of masculine honor, dishonor, and modesty. This organizes a *repertoire* of personas and prototypic relationships—which I am terming *social personality*—establishing the foundation for an identity but not a specific identity. He must still acquire a set of social roles and meanings through which he can enact some subset of the dramas that are potentially his.

Adolescence ❀

North Africa lacks the formal rites of passage into adulthood found in many sub-Saharan societies but requires adolescents to master religious practices—including the month-long Ramadan fast, formal prayer, and techniques of self-care that manage states of pollution and purity—that signal maturity. And for much of Hussein's generation, public education has created something of a modern "liminal" adolescence, during which school achievement, sports, and romances also provide boys with fields for taking steps toward adulthood.[37] Hussein never gives an account of his teenage years per se, but he touches on them in story segments throughout his narrative. I have assembled these to describe three key themes: his mastery of traditional self-care practices, his "addiction" to soccer, and his nostalgia for romances lost. When I asked directly about this period, he offered a rather conventional view, according to which he gave up childish feelings and acquired the ʿqel (reason/social maturity) needed to become a member of the adult community. But his spontaneous recollections sketch a different story line, one filled with lament over uncompensated renunciations and losses.

Pollution, Chills, and Blessedness

During his teenage years, Hussein mastered the rudiments of three overlapping systems of self-monitoring and care that have their origins in both religious and folk health practices. One entails managing cycles of pollution and purification. Orthodox and folk belief hold that any bodily excretion—including urine, feces, spit, sweat, and tears—bring a minor increment of pollution that builds over the course of a day, rendering one vulnerable to the whisperings of Satan, to attacks by jinn spirits, and to damaging glances of the evil eye. The ritualized ablution and prayer that observant Muslims practice five times a day restore a protective state of purity. The washings most Moroccans do on waking, after meals, and before sleeping follow the style of ablutions and can purify even in the absence of formal prayer. In addition, traditional dream theory holds that sleep makes one vulnerable to chthonic ("supernatural") forces but also opens one to receive omenlike communications from divine messengers or actual visits by saints, prophets, or the Prophet. Many people therefore try to protect themselves from nightmares and sinful dreams by going to sleep in a state of purity, which may also help them receive "true" messages or beneficial visits. This regimen encourages continuous self-monitoring and provides a set of minirituals for managing one's emotional states. From a Western psychological perspective, it forms a sophisticated security system[38] by which vague worries and fears can be externalized: experienced as pollution, interpreted as vulnerability to chthonic forces, and countered by purification and prayer.

A second system of self-care entails maintaining a balance of heat and cold by following a set of folk principles for adjusting clothing and ventilation. It also provides a culinary aesthetic because many foods, spices, and medicinal herbs are thought to heat or cool the body. Meals are designed to maintain a healthful balance, and their ingredients adjusted for the seasons, the weather, and prevailing family stresses. As Bernard Greenwood shows, a range of degenerative and wasting-away ailments associated with aging tend to be attributed to the cumulative effects of coldness that penetrates deep within the body, and so heating substances are prescribed as treatments.[39] This system also encourages externalized interpretations of one's fluctuating energy levels and feelings of well- and ill-being.

A third system involves strengthening or restoring one's health by ingesting substances rich in *baraka*, which can be translated simply as "divine blessedness" but proves to be a much subtler concept. *Baraka* is regarded as a kind of all-purpose healthful substance that emanates from God and flows into the world through various material and spiritual conduits. In humans, it appears as saintly charisma, and the Agdez area has not only dozens of prominent saints' tombs but also several living descendants of saints said to "have *baraka*"—one a near-neighbor of Hussein's family. Many neighborhoods hold celebrations that involve the sacrifice of a ram or bull at a saint's tomb, followed by distribution of its *baraka*-saturated meat to all of the households. And cuisine is based not only on the heating and cooling properties of ingredients but also on their *baraka* content.

This became especially important to Hussein during his recovery from the emergency appendectomy he had at the age of twelve or thirteen—which effectively began puberty with another "inscribed" incident of terror. When he first complained about stomach pains, his father accused him of malingering to avoid school and forced him to go, even though he was doubled up and collapsed on the path. That afternoon, his father hired a car and took him to the hospital in Ouarzazate, and when appendicitis was diagnosed, he promised to stay by Hussein's side until he was under the anesthetic. But Hussein recalls him leaving once he was on a gurney: "He lied to me. He said 'I'm going to get a little water and come back,' but he never returned." He then remembers being wheeled alone in terror into the operating room and placed beside frightening instruments and beneath brilliant flickering lights, and he reflects that it may have been this incident that caused his deep-seated fear (Story 104). When he came home, his father sacrificed a ram to speed his recovery with its *baraka*-rich meat, and Hussein seems to feel this rehabilitated their relationship. His account also uncannily echoes the Abrahamic sacrifice (in which Abraham prepared to take a knife to his son but then sacrificed a ram in his place) as it might be experienced from the son's perspective, hinting that he may have structured his memory of these events by its schema of fidelity, terror, and redemption.[40]

Hussein learned the rudiments of all three self-care systems as an adolescent. He says he easily mastered the Ramadan fast, learned to purify at the public bath after nocturnal ejaculations and intercourse, and began attending the mosque for Friday services. He never has performed the five daily prayers or conscientiously purified minor forms of pollution. He jokingly explains that nocturnal ejaculations are termed being "hit by Satan," but nothing suggests he feels troublingly "polluted" or securely "purified," as do many others. He does not know quite what to make of Satan and jinn spirits. He has been troubled by many nonnatural experiences but commits himself to neither scientific denial nor religious affirmation of their existence. Like Mohammed, he sometimes turns to purification to control his anger—as he did in response to a TAT card depicting a woman holding a man who has turned away from her. He quickly saw violated honor: someone has broken into the man's home and assaulted his wife, and the picture shows her restraining him from rushing out to attack the intruder: "He's determined to go out and fight, or even be called by obligation to kill him, and the authorities will get involved and he'll be taken to court and sent to jail" (Story 3). Imagining imprisonment, he recalls a *ḥadith* (saying of the Prophet) that prescribes the purification ritual to cool dangerous anger: "He said to you, the thing which angers you comes from Satan, and Satan was created from fire . . . and what puts out that fire? It's water." This shifts the moral framework from honor to religion, and he turns to the rule of law rather than vengeance.

He pays more careful attention to maintaining *tawazoun skhounia* (the balance of warmth). He suspects that coldness contributes to his tired, lethargic feelings, and he turns to purging-style purifications provided by the public baths and by medicinal herbs that warm the body and restore energy (Story 98). He reports getting over apparently depressive bouts of feeling rundown by breakfasting on honey, which, with his mother's help, he has stolen from his father's supply (Story 101). Also like his father, he sometimes drinks ambergris tea for its heating and purging effects. He does not explain, but certainly knows, that ambergris is mainly used by older men to increase or restore sexual potency.[41] He does point out that mint tea has the opposite effect: "It decreases that *force dyal sexualité* [Fr. & Arabic, sexual desire], so you don't begin to think of sex—it's cooling, unlike almonds or peanuts, which heat one up in the area of sexuality" (Story 98). These accounts indicate that Hussein's primary concern is to manage feelings of weakness and malaise and perhaps the intensity of his sexual desire by using his father's *baraka*-rich and heating substances. This appears consistent with the anxiety he so often expresses about masculine strength and with many passages indicating a liability to depressive moods.

Hussein's responses to the TAT, Rorschach, and sentence completion tests provide further evidence about the affective tensions he seeks to manage with these traditional self-care systems. Ambivalence over masculine strength versus weakness and familial attachment versus separation appear prominently in all of them, as do feelings he terms *lonely, sad, weak, tired, disappointed,* and *pessimistic,* which clearly seem depressive. These emerge even more poignantly in his sentence completion responses, where to fourteen of the fifty stems he voices feelings like:

> "*Larbi's defeat made him* . . . give up. . . . Like me now. . . ."
> "*Nothing makes me feel disappointed like* . . . now."
> "*My lot in life* . . . is a piece of earth [a grave]."
> "*Most of the time he considers himself* . . . weak/wasting away, just moving through life."

The protocols also prominently show a free-floating, hypervigilant anxiety. He was especially attracted to shading and chiaroscuro features of the Rorschach blots, which he often perceived as clouds billowing or smoke swirling, with tension building in fearful apprehension of danger (flame, a snake, a powerful leader figure) or in excited anticipation of a beneficent release (rain, a cool flowing spring). He volunteered after the test that he especially liked the sense of *ḥaraka ᶜshwa'iya* (random/haphazard motion) these blots conveyed, suggesting that shadowy imagery evokes an anxious arousal that can either intensify to terror or "counterphobically" turn into excitement. Shadow or chiaroscuro imagery, in fact, forms a thread that runs through his narrative, representing this volatile state of anxious apprehension-anticipation and enabling him to narratize it in multiple story lines. I will refer to this imagery as forming a *chiaroscuro motif,* and it serves, along with the $w * q * f$ motif, as a key self-representational symbol.

A Future in Soccer

Hussein says soccer got him through all the years of imprisonment in classrooms and paternal oppression. Throughout elementary school, he says his father beat him and forbade him to play soccer whenever his grades slipped but rewarded him with new balls and equipment when he did well. As he narratively flees his memories of "despotism" for the excitement and triumphs of soccer, so he portrays the rhythm of his childhood: he carried his ball to school and played before class, deflated it and tucked it into his satchel for the day, and then inflated it after school and played until his father made him go home and study. When his father left to pray, he recalls his mother standing watch while he inflated his ball and played in the house with his sisters. When she announced his approach, he would deflate it, tuck it away, and get back to his homework (Story 73). He also recalled a soccer triumph as the childhood incident that made him most proud:

I scored three or four times, and when we finished the soccer coach for the big kids called me over and I was happy, happy, I was proud of myself, really proud. . . . One day the sheikh of the neighborhood told my father, "Hey, your son has become a good soccer player," and my father still tells about that. (Story 82)

But this recollection leads him on to nostalgically imagine "what might have been" had he kept playing. As he got older and saw a player deliberately break an opponent's leg, he became "frightened for myself" and gave it up. Still, he recently played in a neighborhood "old timers'" game and scored several goals, and another player told him he could have "a future in soccer." "Sometimes I still think about returning to soccer," he says wistfully, but as he imagines trying to do it alone, he adds, "but I would need *li waqef b-jenbi* (someone to stand up beside me) and support me." Lacking a mentor or patron, he says depressively, "it's better not bothering. . . . Now there's just *khemoul ou n^cas* (apathy and sleep)" (Story 82).

At first, then, soccer provides an empowering—modern—escape from threatening traditional authorities. Supported by his father, he displays his prowess to the admiration of peers, authorities, and women. But with the threat of injury, his fear of being "broken," immobilized, and abandoned returns, provoking a debate about strength, threat, and honor: "Why should one break/injure someone? It's soccer, that's all. Today I win and maybe to-morrow you win . . . people should stay *b-khir ou ^cla khier* (good with each other)" (Story 82). Like some of the American autoworkers I interviewed who experienced their greatest triumphs on high school sports teams, Hussein can't easily renounce his "glory days." But the thought of returning to the field reevokes a sense of physical vulnerability and again leads him to feel the need for a defender-patron to stand up with him, in whose absence he tumbles toward depression. In the end, this story, too, comes to be structured in tri-angular form, and Hussein signs off, resentfully surrendering to "apathy and sleep."

Puberty's Problems

No sooner does childhood pass, Hussein observes, than "one enters *morahaqa* (puberty) with its problems, and then comes the age of *shebab* (youth), that brings its problems. God gives us problems, plenty of problems!" About puberty he explains, "You know the age: you feel you've got *wahed jins akhor* (another sex/person) at your side, *li twaqef m^cah* (that stands up with him)." It is not clear whether his ambiguous words refer cleverly to his own sexual responsiveness or to discovering the "other sex," but he goes on to talk about his crushes on girls at school and the love letters he used to write to them.[42] In his teenage years, he says he became "addicted" to chasing girls, but with innocent, romantic objectives. Now, he says, "It's another matter."

There's an enormous difference. . . . The goal of relationships today is just instinct, the sexual instinct. It's no longer like in puberty when *ya Allah* you just yearn to sit with a girl or joke around or talk a little. . . . That's all changed now. If you meet someone you say, "Come with me to my house," and if she comes and you have a good time maybe you'll feel pushed by the impulse to have sex with her. (Story 59)

When he was sixteen or seventeen, he convinced a cousin to go with him to a prostitute for the first time:

I led the way, and I was frightened. I talked to her, I told her there were two of us, and she said, come in, come in. I was frightened someone might see me, someone who knew me . . . and *tnoḍ l-foḍa* (some trouble/commotion would start) and people would gather and see me, or the police would come knock and take me away. (Story 67)

The experience left him feeling guilty, and he recalls apologizing to her, "I felt like she didn't want me, and I said, 'You did that just to satisfy me, but I didn't feel satisfied. Good-bye. I'm sorry, I've wronged you. I'm sorry, I'm very sorry.'" Like many bachelors, Hussein now visits a prostitute "every three or four months," but he still feels frightened of both trouble and *les maladies* (diseases). Another frightening adventure occurred when he began seeing a high school classmate who had been betrothed against her will to a soldier. One night they ran into her fiancé and some buddies, who chased them around the outskirts of town in their jeep. He grabbed her as Hussein fled and took her to a friend's shop, probably intending to rape her. Hussein ran to find a tough ex-soldier he knew, who rushed to the shop, fought with the soldier, and took the girl home. He ends his account:

I was frightened, if someone wasted her or abused her, or maybe someone might even kill her, and the neighbors knew I went out with her. I was frightened my father might find out, I was frightened of other people. That was the most difficult night I've ever experienced. I slept under the bed and I felt myself seized by shivers of cold [whispered intensely]. I couldn't awaken my mother to tell her what had happened. I never slept. (Story 78)

This story shows familiar features: Hussein's preeminent concern with his "honor," the relational triangles that organize the action both on the streets and back at home, and the frightening-exciting atmosphere built with descriptions of dark, shadowy scenes around Agdez's outskirts. It also shows why sexuality and romance so easily feel dangerous: nearly every liaison has this clandestine quality, putting reputations on the line and risking violence.

In spite of these obstacles, Hussein fell in love during his last year in high school, and he describes this relationship with none of the fear that pervades his other romances. Fadila was a friend of his sister who often came to visit in his home, and their families approved of their courtship. "We weren't doing things behind the scenes," he says. "We were relaxed/tranquil here, the two of us together. . . . She was the first girl I really cared for" (Story 61). The year he began college, a suitor asked her to marry, and when her parents left the decision to her, she asked Hussein whether he wanted her to wait for him. He agonized but finally told her too many years would pass before he could support her:

> I answered her truthfully, "You know I'm still at the university and I haven't guaranteed my future. . . . I'd like you to wait for me, but I can't tell you it'll be a year or two years or even five years. Your parents would pressure you, and time would part us: it wouldn't be up to you and I, it's time that would part us."
>
> She saw that and told me I was right and we separated. She got married and has a couple of children now. . . . I had a good life with her. She was the only girl I've had a good relationship with, and I regretted it. In truth I came to regret it. . . . But it's gone. (Story 61)

A moment later, he says he no longer looks for romance:

> There are girls I go with, one who comes over to the house, but I don't feel anything for her. There's no one like the one who left. I doubt any more that I'll find anyone like her, *ṣafi* (it's over). It no longer concerns me to look. (Story 63)

Romance Displaced

Hussein's pessimism deepened when I asked about marriage: "I try not to think of it. Marriage is a stage of big responsibility, and one must become a creature of duty. Anyone who enters marriage, enters a prison by his own feet . . ." (Story 64). And in spite of so often contrasting himself to the backward people living in Agdez's hinterlands, he speaks wistfully of the tribal life in which he believes sons were married in their early teens and didn't struggle with a "stage of puberty" (Story 60). He also imagines flight. "In truth," he says at one point, "I think of a *Europiya* (European woman), to marry a *Fransiya* (French woman)." He explains, "At this stage in which I don't have work, I beg/hope for a *Fransiya* who works as a *functionnaire*, a manager in a company or the government—so I can get my papers and go live with her there" (Story 62). More than a few young Moroccans share this dream, and everyone knows a friend of a friend for whom it has come true. But Hussein also wants the sort of egalitarian, trusting relationship he imagines the French have: "Maybe they have a kind of reciprocal trust. You can let her go off traveling, and there's trust, she won't be attracted by anyone. And she's not materialistic like Moroccan women." Moroccan parents make economic demands in their daughters' marriage contracts, he explains, and wives' thirst "for gold and fashionable things" grows from there. "You're trapped," he says. "You've got to take her a gift today and tomorrow something else, and the day after something else, until *ṭiḥlik l-yid* (your hand falls) from exhaustion." By contrast, "If you go to a foreigner, you put your hand in her hand, the minister/priest reads some things, and they go to their house married. And maybe, from what I've read and heard about France, they have trust, reciprocal trust."

These images may not quite match French views of French marriage, but they preserve Hussein's wish for a relationship based on equality and consent. Yet his evocative image of a hand held out to another in trust versus one dropped in exhaustion entangles both neocolonial and gender stereotypes, with his fantasy of being rescued by an accomplished, free, trustworthy *Fransiya* sustaining a fear of Moroccan women as embodying the forces of *fitna* (chaos/disorder): as dependent yet demanding and incapable of controlling her sexual desires without "policing." If Hussein now sees romance out of reach across the Mediterranean, he also finds it in the distant past—in pre-Islamic poetry, which he loves for the inspired intensity he feels modern poets have lost (Story 55). He recalls the tale of Qays and Layla, a love-doomed-by-family-quarrel story that brings together the central themes of his discussions of romance into an explicitly triangular configuration (Qays, Layla, and her tyrant-father) and elevates the dream of romantic love in its destruction by the paternal authority. He appears especially drawn to Qays's wasting away to self-destruction, in which he vicariously feels not just "depressive affect" but sublime tragedy (Story 184).

Hussein's scattered accounts of his teenage years thus show continued use of the tyrant-victim-defender relational triangles that organize many of his childhood memories. And in addition to documenting his perseverance, accomplishments, and capacity for empathy and self-reflection, they provide further evidence that he chronically experiences emotional tensions related to masculine empowerment, interdependence, sometimes paralyzing fear, and depressive lethargy. His "official" story line of these years tells of his maturation: of mastering the methods of self-care and self-restraint his community mandates for adults; of giving up immature crushes, teasing on the street, and dangerous adventures for acceptable adult sexual outlets; of putting *ᶜqel* (reason/social maturity) in charge of *nefs* (desire) and the *fitna* (chaos/disorder) it threatens to set loose. But when he gets down to specific incidents and relationships, he tells a tragic story of so far uncompensated renunciation: he has lost his "future in soccer," his "inspiration," and the woman he loved and has come to settle for liaisons that satisfy "just instinct," dreading the arranged marriage that will put him in "prison." And in spite of the fact that he often describes pre- and non-Muslim worlds as places where immorality reigns, he also "displaces" romance across these boundaries, representing the *jahiliya* (pre-Islamic period) and the West as repositories of love, inspiration, and rebellion that he otherwise struggles to renounce as "merely adolescent."

Identity ❀

I have so far discussed two levels of psychological organization, core-level and social personality. To summarize, Hussein's narrative shows him to experience a cluster of affective tensions so intensely and pervasively as to regard them as core-level characteristics: (1) free-floating, hypervigilant anxiety, that he describes as an often crippling fear; (2) ambivalent wishes for familial attachment and secure interdependence, on the one hand, and for separation and autonomy on the other; (3) shifting senses of masculine prowess and disempowerment that he repeatedly describes as "standing up" versus "being brought to a halt"; (4) feelings of excitement and exhilaration that perhaps counterphobically transform anxiety into a love of adventure; and (5) feelings of depressive lethargy and hopelessness that lead him to hold a "pessimistic outlook on life." These appear in association with many different images, figures, and story lines, and Hussein chronically faces the task of representing and interpreting them. I also identified a schema of triangular relations that structure the characters and action of many story segments, integrating two opposed senses of self—as a vulnerable, weak junior and as an honorable, strong man—and casting these in dialogue with threatening patriarch figures. I argued that this reflects his internalization of the circum-Mediterranean honor-modesty system and comprises a social personality—organizing core-level affective tensions by providing a culturally distinctive configuration that interprets and emplots them. In so doing the Generalized Other (as per G. H. Mead) or the "gaze" of the social other (as per Sartre) interrogates him as to his essence and mettle, challenging him to formulate an identity and stand up for it.

The following sections describe the three primary discourses he has fashioned to answer this interrogation: a *modernist* discourse that sets him on an empowering route of achievement that leads toward high culture and urbanity; a *traditionalist* discourse that inverts the modernist with often stunning symmetry, sending him imaginatively back toward his rural "tribal" roots in search of natural sources of strength; and an *Islamic* discourse that casts him into a world of threatening chthonic (invisible or "supernatural") forces and empowering prophets. All of these chart transformations of his vulnerable, weak sense of self into honorable manhood, but by dramatically different routes, such that each symbolically organizes his core affective tensions into a different configuration, each embracing a set of feelings as ego-syntonically *Me* and rejecting another set as ego-dystonically *not-Me*.

To weld these diverging linkages of affect and cognition, we will see that Hussein employs a unifying set of *structurally ambiguous* representations—

images, symbols, and scripts that can articulate opposed meanings, depending on the narrative context in which they are embedded. I will term the most diffuse but prevalent of these a *chiaroscuro motif*: the shadowy or flickering light-dark imagery that evokes a mixture of anxiety, fear, suspense, and anticipation (or, as Hussein says, of *ḥaraka ʿshwa'iya*, random/haphazard motion) and therefore can portend either threat or empowerment. A second consists of derivatives of the *w * q * f* root meaning "stand," "stand up for," "stop," and "be halted" and so define distinctly masculine forms of empowerment and disempowerment—which I will term a *w*q*f motif*. In addition, three type scenes appear prominently in these discourses: a *judicial type scene* in which Hussein or the central figure is arrested, imprisoned, or falsely accused of a crime; a *chthonic type scene* in which Satan, a jinn, or some other chthonic being threatens or injures someone; and a *prophet type scene* in which a saint, prophet, or God appears to save, heal, or bestow power on someone. Each of these casts triangular challenges to prowess in culturally familiar episode types but leaves open who will play the roles and what the outcomes will be. These representational devices provide something akin to a unifying musical scale and set of themes with which Hussein orchestrates diverging identities.

Identity I: Becoming Modern

Recall that Hussein's very first TAT story concerned "a boy from the countryside" who had never experienced "the *teṭewour* (progress) of city life" and is thrown into a state of *ḍlam* (darkness/confusion) by the violin he has been given, which represents the "*ḥaḍara* (civilization/high culture) of the city." He strongly identifies with the boy's initial bewilderment and eventual mastery of the instrument, and he describes his own encounters with urban culture as similarly producing dismay and then gradual mastery. These and many other passages clearly set out Hussein's ambition to "become modern," as Inkeles and Smith describe in their classic study of the psychological dimensions of economic development.[43] In his daily life, Hussein seems to wholeheartedly embrace modernity, and his dress, etiquette, and bearing convey a conservatively urbane style. He prefers the modern shower in his home to the public bath, modern clothes from upscale "display window" stores to traditional djellabas, and his full Arabic name to its various Berber shortenings. His modernist identity encompasses two contrasting senses of self: it casts him as having begun life as a vulnerable traditional youth, whose educational achievement set him en route to empowerment as a modern, professional man.

When Hussein first visited Casablanca as a teenager, "I found myself like I knew nothing. . . . The youth, *fin weselou* (where they had gone/what they had achieved)! They were open." Home always thereafter looked different: "That child returns to the land of his birth cursing his environment. . . . I found everyone the way I had left them: their ideas are limited . . ." (Story

176). Generational conflict ensues: "When the son is worldly and school-educated or cultured or has developed himself," he says, "there will be disputes with his father. . . . He comes back and *kayṭewour* (develops) beyond that family" (Story 35). In his view, a child first knows only ideas based on his father's "power and authority," but each level of schooling broadens his horizons. He contrasts the "open minds" and "cultivated knowledge" of the educated to the "limited" outlook of country folk, "just living" out their days. The traditional way of life "buries" one's youth, he says angrily, while modernity promises an exhilarating personal transformation—"Come and see!" —bringing "progress" and freedom to choose one's mate (Story 109).

Paternal authority becomes especially grating, he says, when a boy reaches the "age of manhood" and naturally wants "a little freedom for himself," to *kellef b-rasu* (take care of himself) and "to cut that relationship [in which] he is like a child" (Story 176). When he left for the university, "I said I was going to cut them off, leave them with their problems and live a little of my own life . . ." (Story 28). He contrasts his backward, distrustful father with a sophisticated neighbor he admires, who gladly fulfills his son's request to buy him a book with a naked woman pictured on the cover (Story 159). In another segment, he explains that a boy first tries to imitate his father because he wishes to have his father's *sayṭara* (authority) and *qowa* (power/strength), but then some man appears on the scene who outshines his father—arriving in a car, wearing a suit and tie, and projecting an aura of *anaqa* (elegance)— and the boy shifts his admiration to him.

A charismatic man of this sort appeared in Hussein's life as the professor who taught his first law class at the university and crystallized his decision to become a defense attorney:

> He'd act in class like he acted in the courtroom: he'd pound the desk and say, "I swear by God . . . the court is never on the side of the accused. The defendant is presumed to be guilty, and even if he's innocent, the court is against him." . . . He'd tell us a lot of examples like that, and that's why I really liked him. (Story 33)
>
> He'd tell us, "When someone stands before the court, it's always opposed to him, even if he's innocent. Its objective is to send him to jail." He [the defendant] comes and stands, and even though I scream I'm innocent [Hussein speaks in first person, as if he were the defendant], the prosecutor always asks for the maximum punishment. . . . He [his professor] had *nefs* (courage/self-respect), *iḥsas* (passion). (Story 173)

All the core themes in Hussein's life narrative coalesce in his description of the occupation and identity he chose for himself:

> I decided to become a lawyer, to *waqef* (stand up) for *nas doᶜafa* (poor/weak people)! It wasn't for money; I really wanted to help

people. If a family was *medlouma* (accused/under suspicion), even if they had no money, I'd work with them. My main goal is to give their rights back to them. And to have a *bari'* (innocent/good) relationship between myself and God—when you do good with people, you do good with God. I don't care whether people know what I do, but that God recognize the good I do—that's my main objective. (Story 33)

As a defense attorney dedicated to vindicating the innocent against false accusations, he fashions a life's work around his ideal position in the relational triangle.

Hussein often sets up triangular relations in explicitly judicial terms by describing the hero figure as falsely accused, imprisoned, or in danger of committing a crime and being arrested. This serves as a *type scene* throughout his narrative: the characters and actions differ, but they emplot familiar types of figures (victims, police, defendants, judges) and themes (guilt and innocence, tyranny and justice, self-control and delinquency). Fully a third of the story segments contain at least elements of the judicial type scene, which, together with the prominence of fear and often unidentifiable threat, creates an atmosphere reminiscent of Kafka's *The Trial.* Like Kafka's Herr K, Hussein seems to feel always accused, always braced for a new indictment from unknown accusers. And in the absence of civil rights and a free press, the largely unchecked operation of police agencies and informers in fact creates a pervasive sense of surveillance, threat, and vulnerability. Hussein characterizes this world by saying:

The government *kayloumouk* (suspects you). They don't teach you the law, and then they come and they don't know you, *ma kayreḥemouksh* (they have no mercy on you). They say you committed an offense—where are people supposed to know of it? (Story 33)

He also feels his traditional small-town world observes and suspects him. Recalling the time he was chased by his date's fiancé, he cites a proverb that explicitly evokes the chiaroscuro motif: "a rial's worth of incense can *bekher* (scent) all of Agdez" (Story 131). That is, gossip spreads, intrudes, and surrounds like smoke—which leads him to imagine that some gossip about him might reach his father and result in an accusation. "I'm afraid, not of death, but of people," he says. "I'm frightened people will say something and the news reach my father, and he'll say: 'What's this you've done?' How many problems have happened like that!" (Story 131).

But Hussein also feels frightened that he might lose self-control and commit a crime that will bring ruin upon himself—parricide, rape, or simply a drunken blunder—were he to indulge in the delinquencies enjoyed by other young men he knows. At bottom, he is not so sure of his innocence. He appears beset by guilt, and each night, he says, he lies awake reviewing and passing judgment on all his acts of the day. Guilt and fear seem to slide easily into one another, and in this respect, too, he resembles Herr K: a man accused by hidden dystopian authorities; uncertain of his accusers, his judge, or the charges lodged against him; uncertain of his guilt or innocence; unable to defend himself and unable to find the right connections through which he might influence the court.

So in this world—created by the "fit" of Morocco's political culture and Hussein's personality—he decides to make a profession of taking up the defender-challenger position and standing up for the unjustly accused. He wants nothing to do with the authority's role—recall how he contemplates replacing his father as family patriarch with a sense of near-panic at the thought of "policing" the household's women. The lawyer role positions him in the thick of the action but safely out of the line of fire, enabling him to combine the honor system's core virtues—strength, courage, protection—into a distinctly modern, *ḥaḍara* (urbane/cultured) form of *anaqa* (elegance). This identity integrates the components of Hussein's personality with stunning parsimony and symmetry, and it is significant that he articulates his vision in explicitly moral terms: it represents not just an exciting but safe stance vis-à-vis the dual threats of crime and prosecution but an activist life lived for an ethical ideal, the restoration of deprived persons' rights. This is one of a very few places Hussein conjoins secular and sacred concerns, enthusiastically embracing God as his judge and also as his empowerer as he confronts corrupt secular power in the name of the innocent. These passages thus define an *ego identity* in precisely the sense that Erikson used the term to refer to an encompassing moral, political, spiritual ideology that integrates the emotional forces animating his inner world, and these with the forces animating his historical epoch. Structuring the persecutory forces that saturate Hussein's reality within judicial type scenes, he can engage them heroically and stand up as a man among men and before God.

The interweaving of sacred and secular concerns confers upon this identity formulation a profoundly modern character: the quality Weber termed a sense of "calling." [44] Yet this is not the modernity of Goethe's novel *Wilhelm Meister*—the first statement of the distinctly psychological view of individual development as an organic unfolding sustained by engagement with archetypal images. And he narrates his life neither in the "pop psych" rhetoric of self-cultivation nor in reference to TV and movie characters, as do many Americans. Rather, his modernist discourse more closely resembles the early Protestant notion of living one's earthly life as a single good work witnessed by God and rewarded in the afterlife. By elevating life as a "unified system" of good works as *the* route to salvation, Weber believed the Protestant ethic facilitates the progressive rationalization and "disenchantment" of the social world. This closely parallels Hussein's view of reason and faith: if one follows the dictates of reason, he believes, one automatically conforms to the highest ethical principles of Islam and will be judged accordingly. A life lived by reason, dedicated to the restoration of secular rights, glorifies and pleases God. This is life imagined as a calling.

Then he failed.

Identity II: Becoming Traditional

Recall that moments after Hussein composed the story about the rural boy who civilizes himself by learning to play the violin, he perceived another card to depict a modern son rejecting his traditional father's advice, only to be "brought to a halt," and he turned 180 degrees:

> Whatever the son's ideas were, they mustn't be different from the ideas of the father, they must always be *mertabet binathoum* (tied together). If one comes to cut the *silat* (chain) of ideas or the chain of traditions or customs, you can't live, even if you live in the middle of a big city." (Story 5)

This reversal forms part of a second point of view Hussein takes on the process of modernization, one that sees it as a disempowering process of alienation that renders him vulnerable to threats from cold bureaucracies and corrupt authorities. From this perspective, he sees the disappearing tribal world as offering a simpler and more certain path to personal strength, vigor, and security. He in fact articulates a *traditionalist discourse* as an almost point-by-point inversion of the modernist and sets out an alternative identity that depicts him rejecting the modern world for the traditional. It encompasses the same two senses of self or subselves but associates the vulnerable one with distinctively modern threats and the empowered one with distinctively traditional sources of strength. Many story segments trace seemingly contradictory oscillations between modern and traditional worlds, which make sense when seen as shifting between these discourses.

COUNTRY AND CITY

Hussein often makes symbolic use of urban-rural contrasts, as he does in responding to a TAT card that depicts a schoolgirl in a traditional farm setting. He says the girl is a "daughter of the city" and portrays her parents as mired in the blissful ignorance of the countryside. She has left the tension-inducing noise, pollution, and smoke of the city for a peaceful, fresh-aired place to study for her exams. No sooner does she arrive, however, than he says she feels beset by the anxious boredom of "empty time" and has to flee back to the city where, as a "daughter of the city," she belongs (Story 4). He also uses the country-city contrast to develop a story about a card depicting a woman slumped against a couch. He first describes an urban scene in which she has been used and abandoned by her philandering husband but then abruptly places it in the countryside and offers a lengthy explanation of why rural traditions would prevent a man from straying. In several other stories, he says that the urban-based "progressive" life of his generation brings sexual delinquency, prostitution, and family disintegration, whereas the rural-based traditional life of his father's generation brings fidelity, procreative sexuality, and family continuity. He even attributes syphilis to modern sexual delinquency, insisting the disease was unknown in rural, traditional areas (Story 109).

His turn from modernity becomes most pronounced when he takes up traditional views of health and healing. Just moments after praising urbanity, he shifts to tell how the natural, rural world of tradition empowers a growing child, producing fear-free, healthy, long-lived adults (Story 179). Today children start their lives off badly with chemicalized mother's milk, and modern medical treatments further weaken them. Then comes school: "when we reach seven they give us a satchel to carry *al hemm* (worries/troubles) on our backs." Beatings add fear to worry, "and he begins to age, so by the time he's twenty, you'll find him old and *ᶜyan* (tired/weak)." The children of modernity die young, while those who follow traditional, natural ways live into their eighties or beyond. Where his modernist discourse credits school with opening minds and empowering backward children, here he blames it for decline. Modernity enfeebles because of *al hemm* (worry): "A person enters the stage of ideas, the stage of learning, the stage of fear, the stage of work."

THE ASSAULT ON NATURE

Hussein often represents the city as a world of masculine qualities and ambitions, and the countryside as a more feminine place, and his depictions of nature typically follow the generative analogy Sherry Ortner believes to be universal—Nature : Culture :: Woman : Man[45]—a schema many ethnographers have seen at the core of Arab-Muslim cultures. He employs this analogy in his modernist discourse to represent urbanity as masculinizing but also in his traditionalist discourse to mark out a masculine stance in defense of nature. This analogy explicitly animates an award-winning essay he wrote in high school, which, after blaming school for afflicting children with worry, he recalled and subsequently brought to me. Written before he passed the baccalaureate exam, rebelled against his father's plans for him, lost the woman he loved, and flunked out of college, it shows that the major affective and representational patterns evident in my interviews with him were in place much earlier.

The essay begins by pointing out that man is "tied" to nature and by linking *teṭewour* (progress/development) to cities and "the continuation of generations" to nature (Story 179). He foreshadows the gender analogy by insisting on the importance of "conserving . . . its [nature's] creative, beautiful distinguishing aspects" and "protecting the *bikr* (virgin/untouched) parts of nature." He then contrasts life aimed at "money and fame" with the "true enjoyment" to be found in "the feeling of beauty/romance in life and what we find in it from magic." It is progress, he writes, that corrupts:

Nature has changed from what it was. The progress/development of human efforts . . . to extract wealth/resources from a reluctant/forbidding nature . . . has led to the air pollution that makes us *mhaij* (aroused/enraged), that damages people's health and weakens the body's resistance to diseases. . . . Even modern medical science can't replace the effects of open, clean nature on a person's psychological health.

Then he introduces an explicit nature-as-woman analogy:

Today nature appears as an ʿ*jouz* (old woman/crone), bent over herself, and nothing appears but the weak body and white unkempt, dirty hair thrown on her bent back. Her shabby clothes have lost their color, and time has taken its toll on her original beauty. Her eyes speak with silence, red from great bitterness: she laments her lost youth that *gheseb menha* (was raped/stolen from her).

Her dirty/ugly face is blackened from the dust and smoke of scientific progress. She is pained/saddened by the happiness of people who she lost, who had lit a flame/glow in her, which she has lost forever. . . . Now she is slowly committing suicide. How sad it is when humans *medlouma* (are accused/wronged) and have no one to support/defend them—that is an execution!

The conflict of modernity and nature receives a representation here that is remarkably homologous with the honor-modesty system: as the essay's author, Hussein manfully stands up (presents his "*mewaqif* (position/stance)," he writes) to defend the virgin from assault. But in the end, virgin nature has "no one to support/defend" her, is "raped," and declines in suicidal bitterness toward a lonely death:

She is remembering youth, lamenting the birds that have no home, feeling pain for the life that used to sing songs of dawn and dusk to her—for the waters that now flow in artificial containers, running without sound, while their riverbeds have become ruins without poets. She knows that the universe became her enemy, and that humans take from her what is left of her old age. . . . She mourns the painful present, and goes on her way until taken by the unknown.

Hussein appears to have constructed this crone/nature figure as a negated self-representation: the flame that enlivened her youth has been extinguished, as he reports his romantic inspiration (represented in a love letter he recalls with a candle burning below a heart) has been extinguished; her once proud stature has wilted, as he is a "reed bent"; she has been wronged and left with no one to support/defend her, as so often has he. The essay describes a process of corrosive decline that he often feels happening to himself, but by embodying it in the figure of a woman who represents nature, he not only distinguishes himself from the depressive affect but also positions himself in the familiar defender/challenger role.[46] It also links aging and modernization through the chiaroscuro motif: it moves from the dust and smoke that have blackened nature's face to the *niran* (flame/glow)[47] that once signified her vitality and then back to a term for wronged that also means "darkened." He ends by deepening the sense of gloom with T. S. Eliot-like "here is no water but only rock" imagery. Perhaps most remarkably, his essay coordinates a series of truly traditional honor-modesty themes into a truly modern, environmentalist, "Green" critique of modernity, in which the heroic challenger/defender takes up his pen as a protest essayist.

THREE PRISONS

We have seen Hussein give voice to despair in many contexts: feeling he is *iswa zero* (Fr. & Arabic: worth nothing) (Story 141), saying, "I always feel myself *diya*ᶜ (weak/wasting). I just go ahead through life, I eat and I drink" (Story 162), cursing his father for bequeathing him nothing but suffering, and professing a pessimistic view of life: "We just shouldn't come into this life. We'll come and we'll go, and we just shouldn't come/exist at all" (Story 131). Depressive feelings also appear in a range of sad, lonely, and tragic characters with whom he strongly identifies, from the boy sitting alone with a violin in the first TAT card, to nature the crone, to Qays, who wastes away to death when he cannot marry Layla. After lamenting that humans would be better off unborn, he recalls a story that illustrates life's futility: a young girl considers putting her terminally ill father out of his misery as he had done with their prize stallion who could no longer *waqef* (get up):

> Their stallion got sick, and it no longer could *waqef* (stand up). He was ᶜ*yan* (weak/helpless), and there was nothing more her father could do. He couldn't *waqef* (stand up). He just slept, he didn't eat and was *ḏᶜif* (weak). So the father decided to kill him. The girl asked, "How could you kill him?" And he said, "It's better he die than suffer in life." (Story 132)

Hussein's traditionalist identity begins to take an especially depressive form in his avid identification with Abu l-'Ala' al-Ma'arri, a celebrated tenth-century poet (whom he mistakenly places in the *jahiliya*, the pre-Islamic period). al-Ma'arri comes to Hussein's mind after he observes, "I have something of a pessimistic outlook: I sometimes prefer death over life":

> He also has a pessimistic philosophy about life. He became blind before he was six, and he also had some illness that made him ugly. People couldn't stand to see him. He became a pessimist about life, and his poems were nearly all of them full of pessimism. He taught students in his house, but he never went out. And in one of my, er,

of his poems, "Imprisoned in My Room," he wrote: "I just need my room, I don't go out, I just sit in the house, like a prison."

In his opinion, there are three prisons. He kept his *nefs* (psyche/desire) hidden, he even *qeteʿ* (cut off) his desire for sex with women. He lived by himself, in the prison of his house, and in the prison of *ḍlam* (darkness/gloom), for he was blind, and in the prison of having no intimacy with women. (Story 133)

al-Ma'arri indeed is renowned for his images of darkness, shadows, and gloom, regarded procreation as a sin, and asked that his grave bear the inscription: "This wrong was by my father done to me, but never by me to anyone."[48] Hussein quotes from memory several verses of a poem expressing life's futility:

Tread lightly, for a thousand hearts unseen
Might now be beating in this misty green;
Here are the herbs that once were pretty cheeks,
Here the remains of those that once have been.[49]

The world al-Ma'arri evokes with his images of darkness, imprisonment, and wasting away clearly resonate with that Hussein inhabits when he slides—or finds himself pushed—into pessimism. It portrays an important sense of self and the possibility that Hussein's life could turn out to be one of defeat and deprivation. Yet even here he does not simply collapse into depression but turns to the poet to give voice, form, and beauty to his depressive sense of defeat. Indeed, he knows of al-Ma'arri because of his esteemed place in the canon taught in Moroccan schools, and reciting his poetry—like authoring the essay on nature—affirms his intellectual accomplishments. For Hussein, al-Ma'arri charts the route to a poetic transformation of depression, a "raising" of pessimism to a form of art, a transformation of the deformed, world-renouncer into a great philosopher-poet. It is this romantic element, the making of poetry from corrosive forces, that shows the traditional world's capacity to transform despair into art and, for Hussein as author (Story 131) and reciter (Story 132), to define a traditionalist identity that gives meaning to some of his most distressing feelings. And to restore his vigor, he takes solitary walks through the ancient fields along the Drʿa River and ingests substances traditionally believed rich in "heat" and *baraka* (blessedness).

THE RHETORIC OF DEVELOPMENT

Hussein represents himself as always in motion: either en route from the disempowering rural/traditional world to the empowering urban/modern one or in retreat from the disempowering urban/modern world toward an empowering rural/traditional setting. He reverses direction by shifting between his "official" modernist discourse and its traditionalist inversion. Each discourse thus separates and realigns features that are thoroughly mixed in

Moroccan social reality. In Hussein's narrative, features of tradition and modernity are arrayed as if in a figure-ground reversible illusion, so that at turning points the exhilarating vista of urban modernity can suddenly morph into a dystopian landscape of pollution, delinquency, and bureaucratic labyrinths, and the healthful atmosphere of rural tradition similarly can turn into a barren terrain of poverty, Sisyphean work, and oppressive patriarchy, as Figure 4-3 illustrates.

These narrative reversals appear motivated by emotional tensions, but they follow a pattern of social role and language adjustments he makes in his daily life. In the modern world of schools, bureaus, and media, for example, he speaks French and high-register Arabic; in many of his personal relationships he speaks slangy Arabic and Tashelhait Berber. In addition, he and his siblings speak Arabic with their father (who sought to prepare them for the wider Arabic-speaking world) and Tashelhait with their mother—a contrast intensified by visits to his father's relatives in Casablanca and to his mother's in her native village outside Agdez. These shifts may partially account for the gendered character of his modernist and traditionalist movements.

His oscillations thus reflect an internalization of the cultural divide that crystallized under colonial domination and has intensified since Independence, leading observers like Aziz Krichen to term this an "era of dualism."[50] It was the construction of identities from symbols of French versus Arab ways of life that struck Minor and DeVos in their study of Algerians, and the creation of "modern" schooling has meant that now "ten times more Francophones are plunging into Western philosophy than during the French colonial period."[51] This dualism and its vocabulary—which I will term the *rhetoric of modernity*—has become so pervasive as to define the new culture of North Africa.

Figure 4-3 Hussein's modernist and traditionalist identities

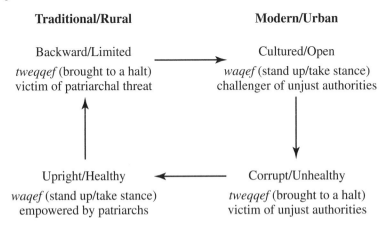

Traditional/Rural	Modern/Urban
Backward/Limited	Cultured/Open
tweqqef (brought to a halt)	*waqef* (stand up/take stance)
victim of patriarchal threat	challenger of unjust authorities
Upright/Healthy	Corrupt/Unhealthy
waqef (stand up/take stance)	*tweqqef* (brought to a halt)
empowered by patriarchs	victim of unjust authorities

These two discourses also parallel the opposed social identities studied by Sawsan el-Messiri in Egypt: *ibn al-balad,* or "son of the homeland," versus *ibn al-zawat,* which translates roughly as "son of the upper class."[52] These emerged in the eighteenth century to identify the long-time inhabitants of Cairo in opposition to what became a series of foreign ruling elites and their educated Egyptian bureaucrats, many of whom adopted elements of the foreigners' style. The Western suit and the traditional djellaba quickly came to symbolize these two social identities. The educated, urbane, suit-wearing *ibn al-zawat* regards the rural *ibn al-balad* as low-class, backward, and uncultured, and the uneducated but clever and virile *ibn al-balad* "conceives of the *ibn al-zawat* as a cowardly, weak, loose person who will not stand up and fight. He is pampered and soft . . . coquettish and effeminate in his manners . . . the source of corruption and immortality in Egyptian society."[53] Hussein's reversible discourses even parallel those Raymond Williams describes as prevalent in English literature during the early modern period, when some writers portrayed the city as a center "of learning, communication, light" and others as a "hostile" place "of noise, worldliness and ambition." Writers correspondingly depicted the countryside as home to "a natural way of life—of peace, innocence, and simple virtue" or "as a place of backwardness, ignorance, limitation."[54]

Hussein's reversible discourses most closely resemble the formulation of Ibn Khaldun, the great fourteenth-century philosopher who theorized that North Africa's political culture manifests an underlying dialectic between opposed social-psychological principles: the *ḥaḍara* (high culture/civilization) that animates settled urban life and the *ᶜasabiya* (solidarity) that characterizes nomadic Bedouin society.[55] *ᶜAsabiya,* often translated as "group feeling" or "group solidarity," also means "tough" and "strong," and as a conjunction of virile strength, familial compassion, and ascetic endurance, it describes the traditional archetype of honor. Although the Bedouin are "closer to being good," Ibn Khaldun noted, they hardly feel contented with their difficult lives, and so seek the comforts and luxuries of civilization, which their military prowess enables them to conquer and then assimilate. *ᶜAsabiya* (rural solidarity) thus inherently aims to become *ḥaḍara* (urban civilization), which Ibn Khaldun praises as the highest form of human society, embodying "elegance." But elegance leads to decadence and corruption, dissipating an urban-based dynasty's *ᶜasabiya* so that it collapses from within, just as a newly risen Bedouin challenge appears on the steppe. Ibn Khaldun even emphasizes that Bedouin strength derives from blood ties (which Hussein emphasizes as "maintaining the ties of tradition"), from eating simple natural foods (which Hussein emphasizes in his involution view of progress and his use of traditional remedies), and from breathing the countryside's clean, invigorating air. Elegance, by contrast, opens the door to decline, as unrelated groups intermarry, and adultery and homosexuality follow (as Hussein associates modern/urban life with both the freedom to choose one's mate and sexual delinquency that leads to venereal disease).[56]

Interestingly, Ibn Khaldun repeatedly links his theory of the body politic to images of the body anatomical, especially to the individual life course. He represents the lean, mean, hard, hungry body of young adulthood as Bedouin ᶜasabiya (toughness, solidarity) in contrast to flabby urban corruption and the soft, elegantly adorned, sated body of mature adulthood as urban ḥaḍara (culturedness) in contrast to muscled Bedouin bestiality. Hussein similarly traces cycles in which he strives for an adult virility he depicts in images of urbane elegance, only to have the corrosive forces of modernity lead to delinquency and sickliness and send him fleeing back into the rural natural world for revitalizing doses of honey, ambergris, and maternal compassion, only to find himself unable to bear patriarchal authority and "time that kills" and renew his striving for ḥaḍara (high culture). In moments of dread and pessimism, he feels prematurely old and demasculinized and imaginally shifts himself into a youthful defender-challenger stance by representing his sense of oppression and decay with female figures like nature-turned-crone or Lalla Hallou the cancer victim (related later), whose plight he manfully champions. Selectively drawing on his culture's history and its partially modernizing, partially underdeveloping political economy, Hussein articulates modernist and traditionalist discourses as movements along a Khaldunian gradient of ḥaḍara versus ᶜasabiya, supplemented by gender contrasts, that demarcate reversible *Me* versus *not-Me* identities.

Identity III: An Islamic Discourse

In addition to these two discourses, Hussein also draws on his religious heritage to fashion a Muslim identity. We saw that his modernist lawyer identity incorporates religious concerns, but this is one of the few places he brings his projects of "becoming modern" and "becoming a mature Muslim" into alignment. His discussions of religion generally chart a different terrain than do those of modernity and tradition, though his recent interest in Islamism suggests he may be seeking a more comprehensive and perhaps "totalistic" identity.

Hussein appears lax about many beliefs and practices that other Muslims follow with rigor. He does not perform the five daily prayers, and he attends Friday mosque services mainly to show his membership in the adult community. He keeps the Ramadan fast for much the same reason and knows surprisingly little about Islam's early history or Quranic texts. He does, however, take special interest in Satan, jinn spirits, and saints—neither quite believing nor disbelieving in their reality—and in the lives of the prophets and the Prophet. Here Islam comes alive for him, delineating a more mystical, Sufi-ist identity than the carefully orthodox, antisuperstition version adopted by many young Moroccans (like Mohammed and Rachida).

Hussein knowledgeably describes traditional beliefs about jinn spirits, voicing his curiosity about their habit of awakening from their homes beneath the earth at dusk and returning underground to sleep at dawn, and his amazement about the time "something" seized his aunt's hand and held it in her cooking fire until it was permanently disfigured. He feels similarly uncertain about Satan, who he says is commonly held to act in the mental sphere, especially in dreams. He offers his own hybrid theory of mind to explain humans' struggle with temptation, drawing on both Islam and modern science's discovery of the unconscious to propound a rationalist or natural law conception of religion. The Quran implores humans to reason, he says, and a person who follows the dictates of reason will automatically conform to religious laws, "even if we don't believe in the existence of God" (Story 112). He again cites his fear that should he lose self-control, he might get drunk, commit a crime, be thrown in jail, and live out his days in poverty. Wayward impulses come from *la sha*^c*or* (the unconscious), he begins to say, but then he recalls that "the Quran says that Satan exists" and explains that "it is Satan who works the unconscious." He stops just short of endorsing Satan's existence and ends with a playfully ambiguous comment: "But if the unconscious triumphs, you'll go to *l-hawiya* (limbo/confusion)." Hussein wants badly to believe in the power of his own reason to direct him through a moral life. But when he tries to trace irrational impulses to the "unconscious" he reaches a dead end and turns to religious explanations—and to purification and prayer as practical means for maintaining self-control.

He often has disturbing dreams, for which he turns exclusively to religious explanations. After he mentioned that nocturnal ejaculations are termed being "hit by Satan," I asked if Satan causes other dreams, and he recalled one in which he was chased by an enormous snake that he wrestled and hit until it "exploded" into a bloody mess (Story 114). He remembers turning on the light to show the blood to "the people of the house" and then being surprised when he awakened to find none. Because he had gone to sleep in a state of purity, he regards this as a "true" dream that conveys a message about his real life rather than mere mischief caused by Satan. He asked his mother for an interpretation, as is customary, and later visited one of the itinerant *fqih*s in Marrakech's *jame^c l-fna* (Square of the Dead). They both offered the conventional explanation that a snake represents an envious person, and Hussein felt pleased his dream meant he would triumph over the unknown rival.

The dream raises intriguingly thorny problems of interpretation. The fact that he recalls it in the course of discussing sexual dreams caused by Satan certainly suggests that the snake might be a phallic symbol, so from the perspective of Freudian theory it is likely to concern masturbation, an Oedipal conquest, or perhaps defense against a projected homosexual wish. But Hussein has his own interpretation based on Moroccan dream theory, and because snakes are widely known to represent envious rivals, he may have used this knowledge to construct the dream in the first place. How might we decide between a Freudian interpretation and his? First, we must admit that we cannot ascertain the dream's true latent referents. But whether or not it has sexual meanings, it clearly concerns attack, defense, and conquest. It traverses a sequence of scenes—fleeing in terror; getting up, taking a stand and fighting; an explosive victory; showing off the blood (to his family in the dream, to his mother in real life as he tells her the dream)—that concern the absence, establishment, and exhibition of masculine strength. Even as he tells the dream, he expresses a sense of confidence and pride in his victory, and his wish to display the blood echoes the public display of a bride's bloody underwear as the culminating moment of traditional marriage ceremonies—which confirms the groom's virility as well as the bride's virginity. Second, we can recognize that a social environment in which a man continually expects challenges from rivals, confrontations with intimidating authorities, envious glances, and concealed machinations makes it somewhat "natural" to experience the everyday probing of vulnerabilities as simultaneously "envy" and "masculine threat." Third, the dream may have depicted him vanquishing the "effects" of the childhood experiences he had been recalling to me, or the threat I posed to him as interviewer. These points suggest a confluence rather than a conflict of interpretations: that envy crystallizes in the dream as a challenge to masculine prowess.

Hussein has had other nightmares, especially of a type called *bou gheṭaṭ*, which literally means "the covering thing." Typically, the dreamer experiences waking up to find a beast sitting on his chest, paralyzing, strangling, or smothering him. These probably have physiological causes: a small proportion of individuals in all cultures have sleep apnea, in which the reticular activating system begins to awaken the perceptual system before the motor regions, and the individual tries to move but cannot. Panic follows from the sense of paralysis, and dreamlike images emerge to account for the sensations. Our term *nightmare* originated from the medieval sleep apnea–induced hallucination that a mare sat atop the sleeping person. Hussein cites these dreams as additional incidents of the fear that riddles his life, and although he says the "bird" that sometimes seizes him is not a jinn, he thinks a *fqih* (religious specialist) could help get rid of it (Story 120). He responds to a TAT card of a ghoulish character in a Christian graveyard with similar themes: after a long pause, he says it depicts someone dreaming of himself in a cemetery, "seized/grabbed by fear that something will come out and eat him" (Story 8). Rather than seeing the figure as the threat, he identifies with him as the victim: "he's waiting in fear, *kaywaqef* (he is stopped/standing still), waiting to see what will come out upon him, and what he'll be facing." The semantic ambiguity of *w * q * f* here perfectly fits the emotional tension: as "stopped," it implies a posture of weakness; as "standing," it implies a stance of readiness and perhaps even strength.

Hussein shifts repeatedly between chthonic threats and manifestations of divine powers, subsequently telling about a pious elderly relative who frequently sees the Prophet in his sleep (Story 118). The appearance of divine messengers in sleep has a long history and a controversial status in Arab and Islamic culture. It was the angel Gabriel who brought the Quran to the Prophet in his sleep, and nocturnal visits by saints signal to many men that they should join the religious brotherhood that follows his teachings, and to many women that they are "tied" to the saint and should employ him as an intermediary to the Prophet and God. Hussein believes that the Prophet may visit or send messages to a pious believer who has gone to sleep in a state of purity[57] (Story 118), and he avidly describes a questionably orthodox dream technique for obtaining omens that allegedly comes from a keeper of secret books within the palace of the king (who was widely believed to have miraculous powers, including the ability to make assassins' bullets curve around him). Hussein has not tried this method, nor has he been visited by the Prophet, but he tells at length about the miraculous cure of a cancer-stricken Casablanca housewife named Lalla Hallou, whose testimonial he recently had read:

> She was near death. For two days she slept in her bed and didn't even recall who she was. On the third night, after purifying even though she couldn't get up, she dreamed that the Prophet came to her. He touched/caressed her head and gave her the health/strength he had in his arms. He grabbed her, and she shivered/shuddered in fear. When the fear finally left, she stood up and turned on the light . . . and told her husband the story of how the Prophet visited her. Her hair returned, her appearance was restored, and she's still living, without cancer. She put her address in the book! (Story 121)

In remarkably similar terms, he recalled a terrifying incident that occurred when he was about twelve, in which "something" or "someone" he suspects might have been a saint or ghost buried beneath his family's house appeared in his room in bright flashing light just as he was drifting off to sleep. "I was seized by shudders of fear," he says. "I never saw sleep, as I was shaking with fear" (Story 90). He even speculates that this incident may have been *the* cause of his crippling fear, which he previously attributed to witnessing his father beat his mother or to being beaten himself. The sudden, frightening appearance of saint-prophet figures or jinn-Satan figures have the character of narrative type scenes and play prominent roles in organizing his religious discourse, similar to the role played by judicial type scenes in his modernist discourse. I will refer to them as *prophet* and *chthonic* type scenes.

PROPHETS

The topic of dreams leads Hussein to recall the Quranic story of Youssef (the biblical Joseph), which he says often moves him to tears, and then to recall the lives and miracles of other prophets. His version (Story 115) unfolds through three episodes: (1) Youssef's dream reveals that he has been chosen above his brothers, his father's open favoritism provokes his brothers' envy, and his brothers throw him into a well; (2) the "sultan" takes him in, he resists his adoptive mother's seduction but is thrown into prison anyway, and his interpretation of the sultan's dream leads to his vindication and appointment as head of the treasury; (3) Youssef's brothers arrive to ask for food, he forces them to admit their crime, and the family recognizes his greatness and reunites in forgiveness. Together, these tell of a boy wronged, tested, falsely imprisoned, and vindicated—exiled from his family but empowered by a foreign sultan—who finally assumes his destined place at the head of his family. It begins and ends with a cosmically powerful sense of *baraka* (blessedness), presaged by Youssef's dream of bowing planets in the first episode, revealed in his irresistible sensual beauty (associated with *nur*, divine luminescence) in the second episode, demonstrated by his dream interpretation in the third, and finally consolidated in the vast wealth and populace he commands. These triangular configurations and judicial themes bring the sura (verse) to life for him: Youssef's expulsion from his family, his empowerment in an alien land, and his triumphant reunion in "the sweet revenge of forgiveness" parallels Hussein's biography of his father, several other stories he tells about prophets, and the script he imagines his own life might have.

Hussein then tells of the defeat and conversion to Islam of a pagan ruler named Kisra (Story 116). The story unfolds as a battle of dreams: Kisra's of riding triumphantly atop an elephant, which "his people" interpret to mean he will defeat the Muslim army. That night, in the Muslim camp, "One of the Muslims dreamed that *wqef ᶜlih rasul* (the Prophet stood over him/came to him) and told him *tenoḍ* (to get up) at dawn and wash/purify yourself, because Kisra is going to send for you, and you will go explain the dream to him." He tells Kisra that his dream of triumph portends defeat, because impure dreams foretell their opposites. Hussein loses his way in the story's details but concludes with the "king of China's" testimony that Muslims have the *irada qawiya* (great strength) to move mountains, which induces Kisra to convert peacefully. The relational triangle crystallizes again, with the $w * q * f$ motif and prophetic type scene at its core: a tyrant threatens to force the believer to bow to him, but then the Prophet *waqef ᶜlih* (visits/stands over him), and orders/enables him *tenoḍ* (to get up) and challenge the tyrant.

Hussein repeatedly emphasizes that the Prophet "was all forgiveness" (Story 124) and elaborates the contrast of tyrannical and beneficent authority portrayed in the story of Kisra. He contrasts unbelievers, who would seize, imprison, and beat Muslims to make them renounce their religion, to the all-forgiving Prophet, who rejected beating and torture for kinder methods. To the many people who would take their enemies to court and "look for some trick/ruse . . . to send him to jail," the Prophet taught forgiveness. He illustrates the Prophet's gentle methods by recounting how he cleverly brought a convert to adopt Islamic practices by relying on the man's own sense of *ḥashem* (shame/modesty) as he lived in the Muslim community. And he ends by condemning those who would be *ᶜasabi* (tough/obstinate/harsh) or *anani* (selfish). The terms in which he opposes these principles—equality, forgiveness, and sociability versus brute strength and aggressive individualism—imply the broader Islamic critique of the tribal-based honor-modesty code, which Eric Wolf sees in the Prophet's founding of the first Islamic state in Mecca.[58]

Hussein then recounts a series of incidents from the Prophet's life, highlighting his plight as a mistreated orphan, the Night of Destiny when Gabriel commanded him to recite, and two incidents in which he was miraculously saved from assassins. This approximates a biography, but a highly selective one, in that he neglects to mention many events others emphasize. And nearly two thirds of the segments in his account employ the chiaroscuro motif and the type scenes described earlier. He especially emphasizes the terror he experienced at the first command to "read/recite!"

> Gabriel came down to him and told him to write. He said, "I don't know how to read/recite." Gabriel said, "Read/recite," and seized him between his hands and squeezed him and let him go and ordered him to "read/recite . . . in the name of the Lord of Creation." Then the verses came down to him. He was afraid. (Story 126)

Commentators note that the Prophet's wife reported that this revelation came "like the break of day," as an "abrupt rending asunder of the darkness,"[59] and that he at first wondered whether he had been visited by "an unclean spirit or a figment of his imagination."[60] The fear, trembling, doubt, and light-shadow imagery are as widely known among Muslims as the nativity scene among Christians—and for Hussein this emerges as the pivotal incident in the Prophet's life, echoing the fear of unknown attack he says plagues him in his own life. The central passages also repeatedly set up the attacker-victim-patron/protector triangle, and Hussein says even the Prophet's family was out to kill him (a view at odds with most accounts).

He then brings up the story of Moussa (the biblical Moses) and covers three familiar episodes: his terrifying but ultimately empowering confrontation with God's manifestation in the burning bush, his battle of magic with the tyrannical pharaoh, and his flight through the parted seas that destroy the pharaoh and his army (Story 127). The key symbol in all of these is Moussa's staff—which changes into a snake and back to a staff twice, echoing the $w * q * f$ nexus of terms and Hussein's "bent reed" proverb. God bestows Moussa power in this staff, and with it he defeats the tyrant's magicians and parts the ocean waters. Emotionally, the story again is driven by Hussein's "fear in general" that threatens to crystallize into a sudden confrontation with a disempowering tyrant figure. All three episodes then traverse cycles of disempowerment and empowerment to transform fear into triumph. The transparently phallic symbolism casts his account as another sacred quest for manhood, with the opposition of God and pharaoh defining the archetypal figures that might emerge upon him. Here we see the core psychological moral of all these stories: to semiotically differentiate the disempowering-rejecting from the protecting-empowering features of patriarchal power that come confusingly intertwined in real, this-worldly patriarchs, into an ideal, sacred opposition. Youssef's, Mohammed's, and Moussa's life trajectories map a route to achieved manhood that begins in rejection and disempowerment, ascends with a bestowal of divine *baraka*, and confirms the hero's masculine prowess in miraculous battles with beasts and tyrants.

LIGHT AND SHADOW

The chiaroscuro motif plays a pivotal role in Hussein's religious discourse, linking the idiosyncratic affective tensions he associates with shadowy/flickering images with a rich theme of light symbolism developed by more mystical and popular strains of Islam. The most prominent Quranic source is the famous "Light Verse,"[61] which begins:

> Allah is the Light
> Of the heavens and the earth.
> The parable of his Light
> Is as if there were a Niche
> And within a Lamp:
> The Lamp enclosed in Glass;
> The glass as it were
> A brilliant star. . . .[62]

It describes unbelievers as submerged in deep-layered billowing darkness. Their state

> Is like the depths of darkness
> In a vast deep ocean,
> Overwhelmed with billow
> Topped by billow
> Topped by (dark) clouds:
> Depths of darkness, one
> Above another. . . .[63]

Yet God brings day from night and rain from these clouds.

Many religions employ light imagery, but it assumes special importance in Islam, as it poetically celebrates the light as a manifestation of *nur Mohammed* (the divine radiance of Mohammed). Annemarie Schimmel writes that the Prophet's luminosity "has colored every literary expression of mystical Islam, and was also featured widely in folk Islam, from early days to our own century."[64] She notes that poets have used what I would term the *structured ambiguity* of light imagery in a technique of "feigned ignorance," as in as-Sarari's thirteenth-century praise of the Prophet: "Is it your face or the morning light that dawns?"[65] The unorthodox notion that the Prophet was created as an emanation from God's divine light has had great power and appeal, setting out what may be one of the central octavelike oppositions in the Islamic cosmology: *nur* (divine, eternal light) versus *nar* (earthly fire), of which Satan is made, in which sinners burn in hell. Ontologically opposed, an identity is established between them by their verbal and visual similarity: initially, a person may not know whether one confronts *nur* or *nar*—as when Moses stands before the burning bush or Hussein awakens to flashing light. Serving as a key symbol in Hussein's narrative, the chiaroscuro motif links his recurring states of hypervigilant anxiety and anticipatory excitement to these religious representations. In other words, it enables him to embed these feelings in religious cosmology of a distinctly Sufi-ist stripe that interprets, structures, and transforms them—constructing him as a Muslim in the process.

A HEROIC IDENTITY

As a Muslim, Hussein expands the temporal and spatial boundaries of his everyday world an order of magnitude and adds a dimension through which chthonic threat and divine *baraka* (blessedness) flow. He becomes subject to these forces, a subject who can follow the exemplary lives of the prophets to avoid the dangerous forces and tap into the empowering ones. The stories of the prophets—as he selectively tells them—follow the sort of hero epic structure described in the previous chapter, as does his father's biography and many of the episodes he tells from his own life. The religious stories set out two systems of symbolic opposition: one defining an opposition of malicious and beneficent seniors and the other a process of transformation by which a weak, vulnerable junior acquires power and proves himself a man. They thus set out two prototypes of senior-junior relationships: a prophet-believer type and a tyrant-victim type. In the first, initial terror is transformed into awe, protection, and then empowerment, revealing the senior's essential gentleness and turning the junior into a senior with juniors of his own to defend and protect. In the second, terror builds and victimizes as the senior attacks, imprisons, and oppresses the junior. Figures 4-4, 4-5, and 4-6 (over-)simplify this structure, showing how it differentiates (a) affective-relational, (b) conceptual, and (c) symbolic ambiguities into clearly defined alternatives.

These oppositions distinguish as ideals what appear mixed and muddy in social reality, resolving shades of gray (such as "gentlemen" fathers who "forget" their honorable bearing with frightening ease) into *nur* and *nar*, prophets and tyrants. The center row shows the chiaroscuro motif, representing an ambiguously free-floating state of anxiety-fear-excitement, which Hussein conceptually associates with the immanence of power and the proximity of authority. The arrows then indicate the prototypic forms of development and arrest that he perceives to occur in his world. His discourse draws on light imagery associated with prophetic power and chthonic threat to narratively disambiguate this fluid constellation, often via chthonic or prophet

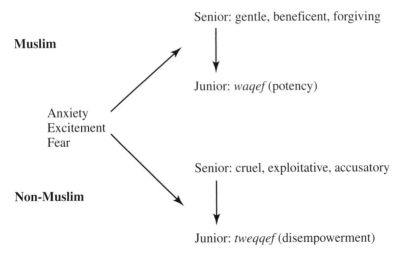

Figure 4-4 Affective and relational oppositions in Hussein's religious identity

type scenes: the *ḥaraka ᶜshwa'iya* (random/haphazard movement) of chiar-oscuro imagery thus gives way to the actions of *tweqqef* (being brought to a halt) and *waqef* (standing up). All of the actions he performs as a Muslim evoke and place him in the *dar al islam* (House of Islam) and thereby bring him closer to protection, vindication, and the bestowal of *baraka* (blessed-ness/prowess).

Figure 4-5 Conceptual oppositions in Hussein's religious identity

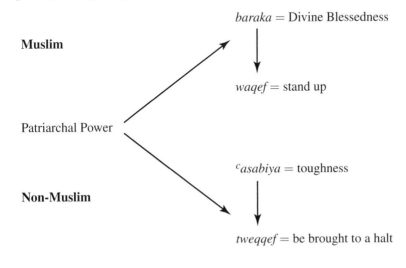

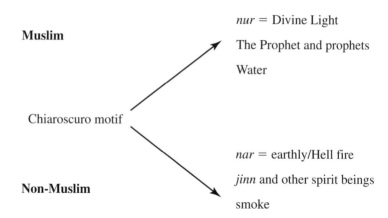

Figure 4-6 *Symbolic oppositions in Hussein's religious identity*

For the most part, Hussein's religious identity charts an inclusive path that offers gentle encouragement for doubters and forgiveness for sinners and blends readily with his modernist commitment to reason. But as months of unemployment have grown into years, he has begun to take interest in more political strains of Islam. We never discussed political matters, but when he cited Sheikh Kishk as his source of religious information, I knew he was listening to taped sermons by the popular Egyptian Islamist. He had learned of the Muslim victory over the tyrant Kisra from one of these, and he stated its political moral clearly: Islam holds that rulers must be "equal to the ordinary people" and "those jails . . . shouldn't exist, that ta^{c}a (obedience/subservience) to the king shouldn't exist" (Story 16). Islamist rhetoric often incorporates a sharp critique of inequality and the ruling elite that can resemble liberation theology, which offers Hussein a revitalization of the heroic dimension of his faith. One of its major themes—identifying the ruler as *pharaoh*—powerfully taps into the specific images of tyranny at the heart of his religious discourse. This imagery would place Hussein in his ideal position: empowered by God, a prophet, or a charismatic teacher figure to challenge the pharaoh in defense of the weak and oppressed.

Here, too, he borrows selectively, resisting depictions of God as a harsh judge and the notion that religious law should be imposed on those reluctant to obey it. He appears motivated by empathy with the oppressed rather than identification with conventional authorities. On occasion, however, he singles out women who adopt bourgeois Western ways. The moral of Lalla Hallou's testimonial is an Islamist one: she was afflicted with cancer because of her bourgeois lifestyle (exposing herself while sunbathing), she sought medical treatments in France that would have mutilated and poisoned her, and the Prophet's cure returned her to propriety, which has kept her healthy. This story centers on the same psychological structure as his essay on nature in that it represents his sense of vulnerability in the form of a female body decaying under modernizing influences, but it shifts the moral from a Green critique of industrialization to a religious critique of Western-style freedoms. At other points, he condemns haughty bourgeois Moroccan girls who speak French to "show off at others' expense" and "imitate an elite level that isn't ours." "That's empty!" he says. "I'm *contre* (Fr., against) that!" (Story 181). He generally advocates modernist positions on the status of women, but he appears to be of two minds about their progress: no positive image of an educated Moroccan or Muslim woman appears in his narrative.

Islamist themes resonate for Hussein but also evoke an equally deep ambivalence. He followed his fantasy of marrying a *Fransiya* by recalling one of Kishk's sermons, and in other passages he followed lessons he had learned from Kishk by fondly talking about deviance. In one passage, he recalled parts of a Kishk sermon and then, without breaking stride, smilingly recalled some of his favorite verses about "the gazelles, the pretty girls" that convey a rather different sensibility:

"I kissed her and she said:
Don't go too far, it's Ramadan.
[And I said:] You're like the moon,
And kissing you is worthier than fasting. (Story 183)

As he experiments with gathering Islamist themes toward an identity, his ambivalence appears to drive him through the kind of oscillating movements that characterize his modernist and traditionalist discourses: disempowering encounters with the Frenchified elite draw him toward the Islamist critique; but then threatening voices of religious authorities drive him back toward images of freedom and romance he perceives to flourish in Europe and in the pre-Islamic epoch.

Islamism can be pursued either as a widening of one's empathy and commitment or as a narrowing of "I" and "we" to the ultradevout. Its critique of modernity's corrupting effects on women may give Hussein courage to combat injustice in one sphere but at the cost of perpetuating it in another. Ashis Nandy has cogently argued that one of empire's costs to Britain was the hypermasculinizing of manhood and that India's pre-Gandhian anticolonial movements sought to respond in kind, fashioning a hypermasculine ideology from elements of Kshatriya militarist tradition.[66] Arab feminist scholars like Evelyn Accad[67] have similarly traced the way militant nationalists have drawn power from metaphorizing oppression in gendered terms that evoke sentiments of honor—ultimately reproducing and entrenching them. We have seen that Hussein regards his achievement of ᶜ*qel* (social maturity) as coming at the cost of renouncing romance, and it would come as no surprise if he were to turn increasingly against the sort of "Westernized" woman he now, more than ever, cannot hope to have. But we also do not know how narrow a religious path he can bear to tread.

Identity IV: Characters in Search of an Author

Hussein presents himself as a well-educated young man who has been "brought to a halt," whose once bright future now looks dim and cloudy, and who waits out too many days "with neither work nor rest." The formative incidents of his childhood show a pervasive and often automatic structure of triangular conflict, which organizes core-level affective tensions in accordance with his culture's honor-modesty system. His accounts of his adolescence also repeatedly construe him within triangular relationships and show him ambivalently constructing a narrative of steadily increasing social maturity in the face of so far uncompensated renunciations and losses. All three of his self-representational discourses are built around the relational triangle and chiaroscuro and $w * q * f$ motifs, and these serve to "carry" core affective tensions into each of the three worlds his discourses map. The religious discourse employs chthonic and prophet visitation type scenes, and the modernist and traditionalist discourses make frequent use of judicial type scenes to generate and integrate plot episodes. In the modernist discourse, the junior figure flees an ignorant and tyrannical rural patriarch by educating and culturing himself, with the aid of a senior urban man of knowledge and elegance. In the traditionalist inversion, the junior flees threatening representatives of bureaucratic or state authority by nostalgically returning to a world of rural tradition, where a wise, beneficent senior patriarch bestows empowerment upon a loyal son. Alternatively, the junior figure may flee threats from either traditional or modern tyrant figures into the Islamic discourse, where a senior saintly figure bestows empowerment. Within any of these frameworks, Hussein or the identificatory hero challenges a tyrant and often also comforts or defends a vulnerable junior or woman.

These discourses not only map Hussein's social world in alternative, mutually exclusive ways but also provide three distinct systems of internal affective differentiation, among which he shifts. As representations of honorable manhood, each defines an identity by affirming some of his core-level affective states and motives as "Me," by rejecting others as "not-Me," and by situating him in a characteristic nexus of interpersonal relationships. In brief, this works as follows:

- The "modernist" identity affirms Hussein's sometimes rebellious strivings for separation, autonomy, achievement, romantic sexuality, exhilaration, and "standing up" displays of prowess. It denies his yearnings for dependence, passive indulgence, and security as confining and imprisoning and represents his feelings of anxiety, weakness, defeat, and depression in not-Me images of backward tribal tradition. It explicitly associates school with opening, freedom, and prowess, and he embraces a rational, scientific conception of intellect in contrast to tribal/traditional ignorance and superstition, so rural nature looms on his horizon as a milieu of deprivation and boredom. Young women appear as potential lovers and liberating equals, sharing his aspirations for achievement and urbane elegance. Mothers represent the long-suffering imprisonment of juniors under the tyrannical rule of traditional patriarchs.

- In a nearly direct reversal, the traditionalist identity affirms his yearnings for interdependence, security, and passive indulgence,[68] with these rendered as positive elements of the tribal honor-modesty system, within a context emphasizing loyalty to family and gradual assimilation of patriarchal authority. It represents feelings of anxiety, weakness, defeat, and depression in images of abandonment before the cold or hostile forces of urban bureaucrats or state functionaries, and rural nature appears as a beautiful and bounty-giving, maternal/feminine milieu. It explicitly associates *l-hemm* (worry) with the prison-house of school and rejects sterile scientific thinking in favor of the wisdom that comes with age and of *wahiy* (intuition/inspiration). Mothers appear as sacred icons, but younger women as quarrelsome *fitna* (insurrection/chaos)-prone embodiments of rejected rebelliousness and acquisitiveness, and so in need of "policing."

- His religious identity defines an altogether different organization, setting out a Muslim path to empowerment in contrast to pre- and non-Muslim states of weakness, anxiety, vulnerability, and ignorance. It combines masculine empowerment with more actively ascetic forms of self-control (performing purifications and prayers, controlling sexuality, fasting, etc.) and emphasizes passive receptions of empowerment even more prominently than the achieving or winning of power. It affirms loyalty, security, and sometimes rebellion on behalf of a community, but it rejects personal autonomy, romantic sexuality, acquisitiveness, and display of achieved status. Weakness, anxiety, and depression often appear associated with states of pollution and threats from jinn spirits or Satan. It embraces knowledge in the form of memorized and recited holy texts, and of social maturity acquired by learning to regulate one's bodily functions and social conduct in accordance with religious guidelines, rejecting displays of modern forms of knowledge (especially French) as sacrilegious, bourgeois elitism. It especially employs women as "not-Me" representations of his potentially wayward sexuality, his ambitions for possessions and status, and his depressive sense of decline.

These provide Hussein with three quite well-defined self-representational frameworks, but they do not comprise a consolidated identity. The modernist comes close to serving as a "primary discourse" in the sense that he presents himself as living it most of the time—with the traditionalist providing an imaginal escape and relief and the religious appearing ambivalently as a complement and critique. But he positions himself within each one only tentatively, and he experiences an often intense confusion as he shifts from configuration to configuration, unable to hold onto an empowered position in any of them. He clearly is experiencing a crisis of identity but not the sort of identity crisis that Erikson believes arises as a developmental task in late adolescence—especially because it comes in the aftermath of the defeat of his just-consolidated lawyer identity by a higher educational system that weeds out the majority of its underclass students. Nor is it more pathological "identity diffusion," in which fragmented relationships and representations cannot be consolidated into a coherent whole. He lacks not symbolic or narrative integration but access to the resources he needs to live these identities within a life structure.

As Erikson, Marcia,[69] Levinson,[70] and others have spoken of a premature closure of the identity task, in Hussein's case we can speak of its prolongation. What Western psychologists regard as an acute developmental task has become a chronic labor, as all of his commitments retain a provisional character. A kind of involution has occurred in his development: "brought to a halt" in front of himself, he has been thrown back into a developmental task he has intellectually and emotionally outgrown. He has been suspended in this crisis long enough to present his life to me as representative of the many young men suffering similar plights. To view Hussein—and others of his generation—as experiencing a developmental involution in early adulthood runs the risks of drawing on too distant an analogy, but it captures his (and perhaps our) sense that modernization has left him suspended in a liminal, neither modern nor traditional existence, in which he can elaborate both discourses but become neither. The notion of involution also encourages us to view his narrative not simply as a testimony to arrested development but as displaying a different developmental task than we associate with either traditional or modern life courses.

FEAR AND THE FANTASTIC

If Morocco's underdevelopment bears much of the blame for Hussein's predicament, he nonetheless feels himself crippled by a fear that he sees as a psychological "complex." His narrative and projective tests indeed indicate that he chronically experiences a free-floating, hypervigilant anxiety that his identities are organized to anticipate, avoid, and manage. How did this fear originate? At one point, he thinks it was the "inscribed" incident in which his father beat his mother; at another, he confidently asserts that it was the beatings he suffered at the hands of his lionlike second-grade teacher and his despotic, ʿntar (giant)-like father; at another, he suspects it may have been the terror he felt as he was being wheeled alone into an operating room for an appendectomy; later, he suspects it was the apparition that came into his room as he slept. In the end, its origin remains unclear. It even may be that these memories mask an injury or assault that left his fearfulness as a post-traumatic symptom.

It is equally possible that he experienced no trauma but grew up and lives in an environment saturated by threat. Studies of child rearing in Arab-Muslim countries have repeatedly reported considerable reliance on threats (of chthonic beings, as well of physical punishment), mixed with relatively frequent, spontaneously given blows that many researchers have seen as "inconsistency." But another observation by many of these same researchers—that parents often cite fear as a key to controlling and socializing children—suggests that there may be a more coherent message to this parental style: that a man must be braced for threat, a master of his fear, and skilled at reading which threats require riposte and which deference. Bouhdiba sees children growing up in a "castrating" environment, created as an extension of the public world of male adulthood, where despotic authority often demands gestures of submission and where challenges and defenses of virility are continually enacted. Mohammed has mastered his fear, risked his father's wrath to fight the neighborhood bully, brawled in Rabat, held off soldiers at gunpoint, and stared down his would-be torturer in a military interrogation cell. Hussein has not mastered his, and it remains a generalized, diffuse threat.

The chiaroscuro and $w * q * f$ motifs and all three type scenes appear to provide devices for representing fear, for making it available to thought and interpretation, and for narratively transforming it into a sense of prowess. But these representations also crystallize in ways that amplify his distress, bring him to a halt, and render him unable to stand. Hussein appears to have deeply internalized the first stage of his culture's traditional anxiety-management system, by which he diffusely externalizes anxiety and hypervigilantly scans the shadowy environment for threatening authorities or chthonic beings. But his modern education and personal relationships have led him to not internalize the traditional system's second stage: defining the threats as jealous cousins, the evil eye, Satan, or jinns and seeking security in religiously based self-care practices. He therefore often finds himself in the realm of what the literary critic Tzvetan Todorov terms the *fantastic*, in which nonnormal events take place and suspense reigns as to their nature. "The fantastic occupies the duration of this uncertainty," he writes, and once nonnormal events have been revealed to be the work of illusion, imagination, or real supernatural forces, "we leave the fantastic for a neighboring genre, the uncanny or the marvelous. . . . 'I nearly reached the point of believing': that is the formula which sums up the spirit of the fantastic . . . it is hesitation which sustains its life."[71]

Hussein repeatedly has disturbing experiences that raise the possibility that unseen chthonic beings or faceless agents of the state may be endangering him, and these pull him into a fantastic realm, for the present resolvable neither into the space-time-causality coordinates of traditional Islam nor into those of modern science or liberal democracy.

As a number of ethnographers have recently observed, state surveillance and violence in a society lacking civil rights and a free press can readily generate fear that merges with fear of supernatural forces to create the sort of magical realist atmosphere evoked in the novels of Marquez, Allende, Rushdie, and others. And this may help account for why resistance to undemocratic regimes so often takes religious form. Indeed, Islamism offers young Moroccans an appealing way out of the fantastic, proclaiming jihad against both the pharaoh who threatens from afar and the *nefs* (desire) that threatens from within. One of Hussein's great strengths is his tolerance for ambiguity, and so far he has accumulated his many nonnormal experiences only as disturbing curiosities. But the reader of his narrative can only wonder how soon he may reach the "point of believing" and intensify his religious practices and Islamist outlook.

IN SEARCH OF AN AUTHOR

Hussein's three self-representational discourses show an often stunning degree of representational integration, in that each is built from a core set of motifs, type scenes, and themes that can be rearranged to differentiate a common core of affective tensions into contrasting configurations. He thus remains fundamentally the same person even as he changes personas and senses of self so dramatically. He has succeeded marvelously at differentiating the affective flux he lives into distinct sides of his character and integrating them within a symbolic scaffolding that allows him great fluidity of movement. He has done the work of identity consolidation, and there is no representational reason that he could not move among these discourses as enriching complements. Yet his narrative shows him often moving in distress, confusion, and flight and taking up each identity only as a provisional one that may not hold.

It is in this sense that the confusion we see in Hussein's life narrative resembles that of Pirandello's *Six Characters in Search of an Author*, in which a set of characters, "created by an author who did not afterward care to make a drama of his own creations,"[72] push their way into a theater during a rehearsal, seeking a director to script them into a play. The characters have histories with each other, secrets to conceal, and scores to settle, but no way to put themselves in order or bring themselves to life, and so no way to surpass their frozen relationships and fixed personas. Pirandello uses the dialogue between the characters and the theater's director to draw his audience into a philosophical inquiry about the self. At a critical point in the third act, the "Father" confronts the director ("Manager") with the characters' reality:

The Manager:	Excellent! Then you'll be saying next that you, with this comedy of yours that you brought here to act, are truer and more real than I am.
The Father:	But of course; without doubt! . . .
The Manager:	More real than I?
The Father:	If your reality can change from one day to another. . . .
The Manager:	But everyone knows it can change. It is always changing, the same as anyone else's.
The Father:	No, sir, not ours! Look here! That is the very difference! Our reality doesn't change; it can't change! It can't be other than what it is, because it is already fixed forever. It's terrible. Ours in an immutable reality which should make you shudder when you approach us if you are really conscious of the fact that your reality is a mere transitory and fleeting illusion, taking this form today and that tomorrow, according to the conditions, according to your will, your sentiments, which in turn are controlled by an intellect that shows them to you today in one manner and tomorrow . . . who knows how?

Identities are thus real only insofar as they have a Platonic formlike permanence. Individuals do not have a single "true self," as The Father insists midway through the first act:

> . . . we have this illusion of being one person for all, of having a personality that is unique in all of our acts. But it isn't true. We perceive this when, tragically perhaps, in something we do, we are as it were, suspended, caught up in the air on a kind of hook. Then we perceive that all of us was not in that act, and that it would be an atrocious injustice to judge us by that action alone. . . .[73]

Hussein finds himself on stage as a cast of three well-defined characters but with no play to perform, and this makes him distressingly aware of his own insubstantiality. His richly elaborated and eloquently voiced identities fail to make him the author of his life, and "sitting . . . with neither work nor rest," he has no way to develop. He experiences his insubstantiality not only as a glimpse into the existential plight he shares with all humans but also as a chronic sense of vulnerability and impotence before his angry, impatient, quick-to-accuse traditional father, on the one side, and a cold, corrupt, quick-to-accuse modern bureaucracy on the other—and in this he resembles Kafka's Herr K. Perhaps some degree of psychological conflict amplifies these feelings, and perhaps psychotherapy could help alleviate them.[74] Perhaps a bolder, more resourceful, less fearful young man might more quickly find a job and get his life moving again. But Hussein's failure at the university and his current malaise must be viewed in its political-economic context. His educational achievement puts him in about the ninety-ninth percentile of his cohort of young men from pre-Saharan villages and signals no small amount of talent, drive, and perseverance in the face of tough competition and disappointments. His sense of insubstantiality, of being a set of characters without a play to set them in motion, reflects a social construction of early adulthood I believe he shares with many of his generation, whose quests for identity have become chronic, often Sisyphean labors.

5

Rachida

One afternoon in an Agdez café, I asked Hussein and a friend of his whether they thought I might be able to interview some women for my study. The friend mentioned his cousin Rachida, who he said was *moḥafiḍa* (conservative) and *mutadiyina* (devoutly religious) but also a primary school teacher and interested in child development. He offered to talk with her about my project, and when she expressed interest, he set up a meeting at her family's home. Rachida met me alone in the guest room, dressed conservatively in a traditional djellaba and headscarf. She expressed enthusiasm for participating in the project in a formal, professional manner—interacting with me as I imagined she would with her male colleagues at a teachers' meeting. I was used to having modern conversations like this in traditional settings with men, but it felt strange to do so with young woman, especially one who adopted such a conservative style.

I explained my research, and she said she would find it "worthwhile" to tell her life story, adding that she would be happy to help me with my project. She struck me as understatedly proud of her accomplishments and perhaps eager to narrate how she had attained a position in which she could act as an important person in the house, entertaining a high-status foreign guest while other women (to whom I was not introduced) brought tea and dates. We agreed to begin the following week, and all of the interviews took place in her family's guest room, in the same manner.

Rachida lives with her parents and five siblings in a Drᶜa River hamlet that has become a neighborhood of Agdez. Her grandfather had been a religious leader of their community during the colonial era's years of hardship, and a decade after his death they continue to be known as his family. A few years after Independence, her father was hired as a clerk in the post office, and his modest but steady salary enabled them to live comfortably, turn their fields over to sharecroppers, and send their children to school. Many of their neighbors are poor, but their traditional rammed-earth home is a spacious, well-appointed one, with a cooling, carefully attended garden in the courtyard.

A Life of Piety ❀

"All of my hopes have come true," she said matter-of-factly in the first interview, "my life is good, and I feel *b-sa*ᶜ*ada* (happy)." For a woman from an undercaste black family in a rural village to pass the baccalaureate exam and become a teacher can be regarded only as a remarkable achievement, and it did not come easily. Rachida was a good student but often ill, and unlike her brothers, she had to add homework to a burden of household chores. She failed her first attempts at the baccalaureate exam but then passed a few years later after studying on her own, which opens more doors to advancement. She says her parents encouraged her in school, but she mainly credits her grandfather for her success. Venerated by some as a local saint, he sent her to Quranic school, recognized her intelligence, and insisted she be enrolled in public school. He became her mentor, sometimes nurturing, sometimes scolding, always checking her progress. He bequeathed her his Quran, which she treasures and studies daily.

Rachida keeps herself virtually *ḥajba* (secluded) except for trips to school and to the mosque and for summer vacations that seem a bit out of character: she and a friend had recently gone to Italy and delighted in strolling the streets unchaperoned. She has forced her parents to decline several marriage proposals, the first when she was thirteen, and at twenty-seven, she now may not find a suitable husband. She views marriage as a religious duty but still wants no part of it: marriage would remove her from her family, perhaps end her career, and probably bring her children, which she dreads. Because her brothers have not done well and her job provides nearly half the family's income, her parents seem to have made an uneasy peace with her prospective spinsterhood, and they allow her freedoms few other women in the region enjoy.

Rachida strives to blend a belief in modern science with her passionate faith, a worldly sophistication with traditional family loyalties, and a commitment to women's rights with conservative standards of modesty. The synthesis often approaches a strand of Islamic "fundamentalism," but she disdains politics and distrusts movements. Her values more prominently echo Weber's account of the Protestant ethic—as do Hussein's—in which religiously inspired self-sacrifice and hard work achieve a "calling" that her intellectual gifts and her family's good reputation conferred upon her, and in which she experiences her success as divinely bestowed *baraka* (blessedness). Her synthesis also appears quite ascetic and perhaps psychologically "rigid." She continually reads about and discusses questions of proper comportment with her devout friends, disentangling practices rooted merely in cultural traditions from those issuing from core Islamic sources and sorting out how they should apply religious principles to socially ambiguous situations. She repeatedly extols the virtues of order and discipline, roundly condemns those who stray "off the straight path," and rarely paints human affairs in shades of gray—unlike Hussein, who often thrives on ambiguity. She maintains constant vigilance of herself, not only to avoid sin but also to avoid leaving even the slightest impression of impropriety. At points, she leavens her tough language by chuckling at herself about her conservative views, noting that no one can be so holy as to never sin. But she has no doubt that everyone should at least be committed to the straight path, and she insists that force may sometimes be needed to keep people on it.

Teacher

After she asserted that her life consists of teaching, studying, and prayer, I asked first about teaching. She responded with an almost technical lecture on pedagogy but then talked about the responsibility of a caring teacher:

> Teaching is an honored but difficult profession, because the teacher carries a responsibility for the development of the children. . . . He must always watch over the student in the classroom, and try to know about his life, about the problems he lives with at home. . . . (Story 2)

A teacher's responsibility begins with instilling "Islamic culture," by which she means forms of politeness and proper address, cleanliness, respect, orderly sitting, and "love for the teacher":

> For example, eating: like how to wash their hands before eating, and after that to say *bismillah* (In the name of God), and to eat with the right hand, and after they finish to say *al-ḥamdallah* (Blessings to God)—we give that kind of lesson. The teacher gives them a story about a polite person, for example, how he sits, how he eats and finishes a meal, and after that they copy the lesson, and when they go to their houses, they practice it. (Story 2)

Many students already know these things:

> Some have learned these practices at home, like *naḍafa* (cleanliness) . . , like sitting *b-niḍam* (in an orderly/proper manner), like *'iḥteram* (respect), respect for the teacher, like *moḥaba* (love/friendship), so he will love his teacher, because the teacher is considered to be in the same position as the parents. . . . It's the family that takes care of his upbringing; the mother who tells him to sit still in his place, to not make trouble for others, to not bother people, that he mustn't make a mess of things, not to make *l-foḍa* (a mess/racket) in the middle of the room.

But some arrive unmannered, and she has to work tirelessly to teach them proper comportment:

> There are those who come *mamerbinsh* (unmannered), and the teacher must do the best he can to teach them the habits that will work to their benefit in their studies. How can one explain the lesson if there's a *foḍa* (mess/disruption) in the middle of the classroom?

Some pupils prove so difficult that her best efforts fail, however, and they're destined to end up "in the street":

> Some don't go to the mosque or the preschool, and you find they have some psychological complexes. . . . At first they fear school: when they hear the word *medrassa* (school), they know that there's a responsibility associated with it, that they're going to be within the four walls, that they're going to be beaten with the stick, and so they're not ready, they aren't open to school. . . . One finds them difficult/reticent. And however much the teacher tires to bring them up to the level, they won't reach it. *Natija dyalhoum shariᶜ* (their outcome will be the street). (Story 2)

She goes on to describe her own difficult first two years as a teacher, when the school lacked books and materials, and she had to teach ten subjects each day and prepare lessons, visual aids, and assignments from scratch. She also was "frightened" to take charge of a class on her own and had trouble building the kind of relationship she wanted with her students: "The first time I took a class, there wasn't a certain *indimaj* (interweaving/rapport) in the classroom, there was a distance" (Story 4). But she gradually developed a style that works, one that sounds rigid and authoritarian by American standards but eschews physical punishment and so appears permissive by Moroccan standards. Her evaluations by the ministry "inspectors" have been good, and she has received the equivalent of tenure.

In addition to conveying her pride at succeeding in an honored profession and her frustration at finding herself unable to reach reticent students, her accounts show a structure of conceptual oppositions and emotional tensions that prove to organize her world and personality. The contrast of orderly and ultimately "productive" or "successful" Islamic culture versus unmannered disorder that leads to "failure," "distance," and "dissolution" recurs throughout her narrative, defining the religious contours of her identity, on the one hand, and its most salient antiself or not-Me representation on the other. Table 5-1 shows the three oppositions she repeatedly employs to organize accounts of what is at stake in her life and world, as the positive and negative outcomes of human action. Although she certainly experiences the range of human emotions and subtle textures of joy and sadness, these terms appear to describe characteristic states of well-being and distress: bounty, plenitude, and relaxation versus deprivation, emptiness, and frustration.

Table 5-1 *Conceptual and emotional oppositions in Rachida's narrative*

Positive		Negative
natija = positive outcome or yield*	vs.	*b-doun natija* = without yield
		or
		feshel = failure
koulshi metwafer = everything available	vs.	*matwafersh* = nothing available
or		or
moujoud = bounty		*makayn walou* = emptiness, deprivation
lebi 'ajemi't reghbat = satisfy/comply with all one's desires	vs.	*khaser l-khaṭr* = deny or refuse one's wishes

Natija means "yield" of crops and livestock, as well as human outcomes.

She feels lucky, for example, to be living in a time of progress, when "everything's available," rather than in the sort of deprivation her grandparents experienced. When she was a child, Agdez was "just a small village, where the things you see here now *ma-twaferetsh* (weren't available). There were just country folks." But like Hussein, she feels that modernity's bounty has also had a corrosive effect on culture and character. Back when she was a student, she recalls:

> The teachers were really strict with us, they *kayziyerou 'lina mezian* (really squeezed/pressured us). . . . If you ran into a teacher on the street, he'd ask you what you were doing, and you'd better have a good reason, or there was the stick. And you couldn't lie, because they'd beat you. . . . The teachers were strict, but *kayna natija* (it got results), not like now. Students feared the teachers and respected them, any place they met them. . . . (Story 16)
>
> Everything was *mziyr* (strict) then. If you didn't memorize your lesson, the teacher beat you. You couldn't leave the classroom until you'd learned it. But look at those students: they're doctors, engineers, teachers. . . . But now, no. Now it's *kif walou* (like nothing). (Story 18)

She believes radio and television have all but "destroyed" the generation she teaches. "They say it's progress," she comments, "but I don't know, myself. Now *koulshi moujoud* (everything's available), *koulshi metwafer* (everything's provided), and today's kids learn so many things that the teacher doesn't teach them. That's the problem" (Story 17).

At other points, however, she insists that children need understanding and *ḥanan* (compassion) rather than commands and beatings. Children introduced to a "world of beating" just come to hate their parents and develop "complexes" that keep them from succeeding. Grandparents are especially important because they "*kaylebi reghba* (they satisfy the desires) of the children and *makaykhaser li-houmsh l-khaṭr* (don't break/disappoint their wishes)." Some of her neighbors have relied more on punishment than compassion, but *b-doun natija* (without results), as they have produced *mamerbinsh* (unmannered/troublesome) children (Story 116). She sees her own childhood as combining the best of discipline and indulgence. Her parents have told her that as a baby she suffered terribly from the summer heat, and "*kaylebouli reghebat* (they gave me whatever I wanted) because they didn't want the heat to be so hard on me" (Story 38). She recalls them as demanding responsibility yet willing to "satisfy all her desires" or as wanting to not "disappoint her wishes."

By using these oppositions to frame nearly all of the topics we discussed, she constructs a world resembling that evoked in Fadhma Amrouche's *My Life Story*,[1] with its stark contrast of almost paradisical bounty and hellish deprivation. Rachida, however, does not follow Amrouche in representing these as simply given by God but casts bounty as the divine reward for ceaseless hard work, sacrifice, and self-control and deprivation as divine punishment for disorderliness and indulgence.

A Feminist Voice

Rachida says she fought for the ambitions her grandfather helped nourish, even against her parents, who planned for her to get married rather than pursue a career. She was shocked one night—she was only thirteen—to overhear her parents planning a marriage for her with an eighteen-year-old cousin. She cried through the night and then confronted them, *dafeᶜt ᶜla rasi* (defended myself), and "that was that." She says:

> When I was in school, I always thought I'd work. I never thought that I might waste my education. When I was little, my family thought that I would go and make my own house [meaning: get married], but me, I don't know, *ᶜandi l-ᶜqel bezaf* (I'm really independent/stubborn), and I always try to defend myself. I'd cry. I'd try any means. I'd run away. They'd follow me and I'd say, "Do whatever you want, you won't *ḥakmou ᶜliya* (rule me)."
>
> Every time I advanced in my studies, my ambitions increased: I'd read books and see the ideas of the other girls who were with me— they gave me how many ideas! . . . It was always *kelma dyali* (the force of my word) that defended me. I would come and say to them [her family] look at this, look at that, and they'd accept it. (Story 59)

This changed her relationship with her parents, and "from that time until now, anything they want to do, they consult with me about it. Even if it's just some small matter, if I'm not there, they won't do it. Now they say thank God that I have good/correct ideas" (Story 209). Girls' resistance to their parents' marriage plans is hardly rare, even in traditional village communities, but these passages show her use of the typically masculine idiom of honor, culminating in her remarkable claim that her parents won't act in ways that affect her without consulting her first. Her boastful claim that it was her "word" that defended her emphasizes a quality traditionally associated with powerful men: *klem*, which literally means "word," carries the connotation of possessing a forceful, authoritative *voice*.

Now she contrasts her life with that of her sisters who left school and married: "For me, now, everything's in my hands. I can do whatever I want. I've got freedom. I can travel wherever I want, and they can't: they're under the control of their husbands. . . . Me, no. Now if I tell my father I want to do something, he tells me there's no problem at all." She explains that her grandmother chose one of her younger sisters to give up school and help run the household, and when I ask why that role didn't fall to her, Rachida characterizes herself in remarkably individualistic terms:

> I don't know, I'm strange, [we laugh] I'm difficult. Everyone follows one's path and *ṣafi* (that's that). That was always my idea. [How's that?] I had to study and *ṣafi*. . . . Everyone chooses his own life. There's a proverb that says: *ḥayatek men ṣenᶜat yidik* (Your life is your own creation)—that is, you fashion your own life. It's not other people who make your life for you, it's you who fashion it. (Story 22)

A few minutes later, she says her mother gave her the freedom she needed, but only in response to her insistence: "She can't tell me, 'You *have* to do something!' I think with my own head. I have to decide things for myself—it's not they who decide" (Story 29). And she does not just defend her personal rights but those of women. She spoke at length about *The Liberation of Women* and *The New Woman*, two writings of the nineteenth-century Egyptian philosopher Qassem Amin, which she had studied in high school:

> He says women must become equal with men; that women have to get out of that oppression of the past; she mustn't be *ḥajba* (secluded)—she must get rid of the veil. She must go out to work, you understand, to work like men, and not be under control of men, to not just do what her husband tells her to do. And she has something to say. . . . A woman has to see to her own life: a woman's objective isn't just to raise children and take care of housework. She too must see to her life, however she wants. (Story 58)

The Muslim world has changed for women, especially for women of her generation:

> If the equality he spoke of hadn't been brought about, you would find most women staying in the house, just taking care of the house and raising their children and cooking. Now they're all working. Women share work with men at the hospitals, in elementary schools,

in high schools, there are women engineers, anything. Women have the right *tehḍer* (to talk/speak up). (Story 58)

"It was the force of my word," "She has something to say," "Women have the right to speak"—the issue of *voice* emerges as the critical concept in the feminism of this devout Muslim who has not read Western treatises on the cultural politics of silencing and finding a voice.

In an interview two months later, she returns to this topic, having prepared two pages of notes from an essay on women whose title and author she had forgotten, but emphasizes that the ideas "are in my brain, like it states my opinion exactly." She refers to the views held by some Muslim leaders that men are fundamentally stronger and more rational than women and that therefore women should be restricted to taking care of affairs in the home except when some extraordinary duty requires her to leave it. She, along with the essay, criticizes this view:

> A woman can go outside for the sake of war, a woman can partici-
> pate in battle, and she can participate in medicine or helping others;
> women participated in the raids of the Prophet, and in commerce,
> and farming, and crafts. And she has responsibility for future gen-
> erations, it's she who prepares them to bring about something in the
> future. . . . So it's not possible for us to prohibit the woman from
> going out. It says here that it's impossible for the woman to live just
> inside the house. (Story 150)

In a tone of rising indignation, she ridicules the oft-cited Quranic line *arijalou qawamouna ᶜla a-nisa'* (the man is the ruler of the woman), that "she doesn't have the right to speak; she must just carry out what he tells her" (Story 151). She then mentions a collection of offensive Egyptian proverbs about women, which, "if you heard them, you would think that a woman is some, some, some, something worthless, that the man can do anything he wants with her." Angrily, she insists:

> But she, too, has her rights, and she must defend herself. It's said
> that he has ᶜ*qel* (reason/maturity), and she doesn't, that she must be
> always remain ignorant. That guy says this one [m.] has a mind, and
> that one [f.] is ignorant—that's impossible! (Story 151)

She appeals to what she sees as the true core of Islam:

> Islam gave women the right and calls her to exert all her efforts in
> religion and in this world. Understand? She must always try her
> hardest in religion and in this world! . . . God the Exalted and
> Magnificent says that the world was created for the marriage of be-
> ings, as animals were all created in pairs, and God made men and
> women equal in their humanity. Is the woman an animal? She isn't
> an animal, and so she isn't different: they are both humans!

She eloquently presses home her case:

> God gave everyone an intellect, and a heart, and a mind, and emotions and desires, and everyone has need of the development/culturing of their psyche/desires, and the education of their intellect—hopefully to guide one along the proper path, to follow a path of *slah* (propriety/benefit), not to sabotage propriety, *mashi fesad had shi* (not to corrupt it). I endorse those ideas *nit* (precisely). (Story 151)

A Duality of Views

These statements would seem to leave no doubt about the strength and consistency of Rachida's views. But in other passages, she expresses sentiments that flatly contradict them. After she first spoke of Qassem Amin's writings, I tried to find out if she had come to her views through a kind of "consciousness-raising" period, and so I asked her, "Was there a time, even when you were young, when you thought men had the right to control/rule women?" Without hesitation, she said, "Yeah, now, the man rules, even though you see women working, it's necessary for men to *hakim ʿla l-mra* (govern/rule over women)." Not sure I had understood her or that she had understood me, I repeated, "a time when you agreed with the right of men to control women?" She stood firm in the face of my dismay: "I agree with the governance of men over women. Even though I defend my own freedom, the authority of men is good/beneficial" (Story 60). When I pressed her about why, she said that it's "the idea of God" that "men's intelligence grows to be greater" and, what proves to be the crucial reason for her, that without the rule of men, "it will always be a failed family":

> The rule of men is good because now, right here, if my family wasn't around, if there wasn't the word of men, what would everyone do? Yes, there's freedom. But one needs the word of a man, the advice of a man—even if it's just my brother, or my cousin, or my father or my uncle—if they talk to me, *rah*, I have to act by their word.
>
> [Why? What's the difference?] There always has to be word of a man. Even though there's the word of the woman, his word is above her word. [Why?] That's the idea of God. [laughing tensely] I don't know. [pause] Because we've seen it: we're an old family—why have we gone along without any problems? . . . [And if there isn't the control or word of a man?] It will always be an *ʿaʾila fashla* (a failed family), there won't be any *natija* (results/things won't work). (Story 60)

She reverses herself in a similarly stunning manner after criticizing the "Islamic leadership" and defending women's humanity, when I ask her again about the saying "The man is the ruler of the woman":

My opinion? [short pause] Maybe I support this saying. [softly, hesitantly] I support it sometimes, because the *kelma* (word) of the man or his decisions, gets results. If there weren't men, there would be *l-foḍa* (conflict/chaos) and things like that. If a woman doesn't have someone [m.] who is responsible *ᶜliha* (for/over) her, she'll do whatever she wants, go out and do whatever. If there isn't that *ᶜirtifaᶜ* (elevation/superiority), if the man and woman are equal, each one responsible for himself, there won't be agreement. (Story 155)

My questions clearly elicit a measure of distress, but when Rachida picks up the theme of women's unreliability and quarrelsomeness, she minces few words in her support of men's authority. "If one sees a *marʾa ḥashumiya* (modest/proper woman)," she says, "you'll probably find that her husband *rghem ᶜliha* (forces/compels her) to be a modest/proper woman. His word and his decisions *jaᶜlet* (make/bring) that woman to *ḥashem* (be modest/proper)." In conversations with other teachers at school, she says, "I always defend the man, because if you consider the reality of women, *fiha ghir l-hdour* (it's just a lot of words/talk)" (Story 155). In a remarkable reversal of her feminist insistence that women's voices must be heard, this last comment dismisses their speech as "just a lot of words." She elaborates:

Women just keep talking—that's why it's necessary that there be a man there, to *isiyrhoum* (control them); if he isn't, *ṣedaᶜ* (noise/trouble/squabbling) will develop, understand? [speaking angrily] Once we were discussing women, women this and women that, and someone said to me, what's your opinion, and I said, "If you consider it, the woman is always in need of a man. It's not possible for a woman to *tsiyr rasha* (to control/govern herself), with regard to anything."

[Do your friends agree with you about that?] No, they said, "Shame on you!" I said to them I'm a girl (i.e., virgin), and I'll become a woman in the future, but I know women, because I see them, I have intimate companionship with them, and their ideas are always *sefer* (zero/worthless). (Story 155)

How might we understand this duality of views? It is not just that her religion inculcates patriarchal views, as she has plenty of textual support for anchoring her egalitarian views in "true Islam." More important for her—as for the Pakistani graduate student interviewed by Katherine Ewing[2]—may be her desire to combine the independence and autonomy of a modern professional woman with the propriety of a daughter in a traditional household. Given her need to maneuver in both of these worlds, she needs not so much to work out a golden mean as to be firmly modern in some circumstances and firmly traditional in others. But other portions of her narrative make it clear that beyond her need for contrasting styles of self-presentation lie contrasting senses of herself as a woman. It is in this context that her distrust of women as inherently prone to irresponsibility, disorder, and rebelliousness— the *fitna* (chaos/disorder) Fatima Mernissi sees at the core of Muslim stereotypes of women—emerges as the psychological key to her duality of views.[3]

The Sufferings of Women ❀

Rachida's life of piety, order, and modesty has been threatened by "sicknesses," many of which she associates with "the sufferings of women." Since she was fourteen, she has experienced a variety of symptoms—including paralyses, fainting spells, and slurred speech—that could have a neurological basis but more likely are psychosomatic or "hysterical" in character. She says the summer heat causes a host of other weakening ailments, and she feels plagued by nightmares in which "horrible things" happen. Friends and relatives suggest these troubles are caused by jinn spirits and *shitan* (the devil), and she regularly purifies, prays, and recites passages from the Quran, partly to protect against them. But she prefers to see modern doctors and piece together medical explanations. Even more serious are her phobic reactions to pregnancy and childbirth and the distress she experiences before and during her periods. I was surprised that Rachida discussed these with me, but she suspected they were psychological in origin and probably hoped that an American psychologist might help her with them.

Fainting

Rachida says she was unable to pray throughout her teen years because she got dizzy and felt like fainting whenever she bent forward for the prostrations. She attributes this to a sickness that sometimes still comes upon her, caused by falling from a high bar in her school physical education class when she was fourteen:

> I was trying to flip, and I fell, and *dakht* (I got dizzy/fainted), and fell on my head. It hurt my forehead, and these front teeth. I went to the doctor up in Ouarzazate, and they gave me some medicines, but *natija kif walou* (with no results). One time, my speech got strange, and I went to be examined at a hospital in Marrakech. Again they gave me some medicine, but the illness stayed the same. My eyes get red when I feel ill, and I can't see. I just have to sit down.
>
> One year, a few years ago, half of me became all ill: I couldn't move my hand/arm and I couldn't stand up much. After a half hour, I fell/fainted in the classroom. When I saw that my head was really tired/weak, I thought that I was going to die right then. So I went to a doctor in Casablanca, and he took some x-rays of my chest, and my head, and my back. (Story 31)

I asked what her doctors told her, and her response suggests they suspected her problems were psychological:

> They kept questioning me like this now. They wanted to find out if I sit by myself, do I have friends with me? Someone from my family told them that wherever she goes, she has her friends with her. The doctors said if someone sits alone, they get sick. They told me, "You ruminate over things too much. Even when you sleep, although you're lying comfortably, the motor of your head keeps working." I couldn't get to sleep. They took my blood pressure and it was normal. All they could do was an operation on my head to see if there was a cut.

She continues:

> I have some other illnesses, and whenever I get sick, it's not something normal, like I get diarrhea. They gave me some medicine, and told me to try to *forget*, that I have to always talk, to always laugh, to never be alone. *Ṣafi*, that's what I did. They told me not to drink Coke or tea—only mint and sugar—and don't eat lentils or beans or peppers.
>
> I haven't eaten or drunk those for five years now. But when I get really happy or really nervous, it returns. I have to get happy just a little. If I get really happy, I always get sick: the blood leaves my face, I get yellow. Before I went to Casablanca, I didn't know what was happening. My eye would fill with blood, and these teeth wanted to fall out. Everything was hot. I always slept on my left side. This has been a problem in my life, from that accident until a few years ago I was always sick. . . .
>
> My uncle always told me it's maybe *shi ḥaja* (something), like *ḥmeq* (crazy), *shi waḥed ḥmeq* (someone crazy) or something. But when I learned the cause, he relaxed. They'd always find me sick, and tell me to go see the doctor. But when they saw result of that treatment, they said *al-ḥamdulillah* (thanks to God).

One of the most important themes in this account remains largely implicit: Rachida worries her unusual symptoms might be caused by jinn spirits. Three times she uses the word *ṭiḥ* (fall) to mean "pass out," the term often used to describe the seizurelike attacks caused by jinns. And her uncle clearly suspects that jinns might be at play.[4] She also reports that her Casablanca doctors questioned her about whether she sits or goes out alone, behavior that in folk belief renders one vulnerable to jinn attack. It is doubtful her doctors suspected jinns, especially because most doctors are quick to dismiss jinn-attack symptoms as "*la hysterie.*" Her doctors indeed appear to have suspected some sort of emotional distress, as she says they told her she thinks about things too much and should try to talk, laugh, and "forget" her troubles. But they also appear not to have ruled out a brain lesion that they had no means other than surgery to detect. Their advice that she avoid Coke, tea, lentils, and peppers makes no obvious sense, but she has seized on these as the cause of her sickness and keeps them out of her diet, which is not easily done.

Rachida may suffer from a lesion or seizure disorder. Or her symptoms may have a "hysterical" character: her emotional life may be constricted within such narrow moral standards that affective excitation tends to evoke "incompatible ideas" she avoids by dissociating (feeling dizzy or faint) or by surrendering her speech or bodily movement to hypnoidlike control. As Alan Krohn argues, cultures that silence or emotionally straitjacket segments of their populations produce hysterogenic environments, and a strong case can be made that this applies to young women in most North African milieus.[5] Indeed, Rachida's concern with "speech," "voice," and "mere words" can be seen as a commentary on her culture's traditional silencing of women. And her symptoms may represent distorted efforts to give voice to thoughts and feelings she turns against in her efforts to embody propriety and piety.

Nightmares

Rachida also says her health deteriorates in the summer, because of the Saharan heat. Her family has told her that she suffered inconsolably from the heat as an infant, and she continues to feel enervated and unable eat or sleep well (Story 38). The heat brings *bou gheṭaṭ* ("covering/wrapping thing") nightmares of the sort Hussein reports, though where they keep him from "getting up," they keep her from speaking: "It completely closes your mouth: some times you want to scream, or you feel yourself screaming, but there isn't anyone to come rescue you" (Story 163). Like Hussein, she believes the beings are real: "It's not a dream, you feel it *nit* (for real). . . . I don't know what it is, I doubt it's a jinn. But it has killed how many people! . . . They do some really bad/evil things." Also like Hussein, she refrains from attributing them either to jinns or to mere "imagination." "Maybe, it's something real, that is alive, that exists/comes only at night," she says, but then ends, "I don't know. Only God knows."

Rachida has other nightmares and tells of a horrible recent dream of a man murdering and dismembering his mother. She dreamed she was at a wedding and went off to use a bathroom:

> I looked in one room, and I found a man, a man killing his mother. He killed her and took off her head, he took off her arms, and he took off her legs. And that room, there was blood all over the place. . . . I found him holding a knife. The woman, pieces of her body were spread about and there was blood flowing. . . . I wanted to scream . . . I felt *waḥed l-irtibak* (muddled/confused), and I was really frightened. . . . All I saw was blood [breaks off]. I was saying to myself,

"That criminal! Where's *l-ḥanan dyal ʿum* (his compassion for the mother)?" (Story 163)

When she awakened, she immediately told her mother the dream, and it frightened her: "She said *ya laṭif, ya laṭif* (may God protect us from calamity), your dream is *khayb* (a bad one)."

Like Hussein's dream of wrestling a snake, Rachida's matricidal dream presents a challenge of interpretation. She suggests that it may have been related to her sister's anticipated delivery (and she did give birth, without calamity, a few days later). She concurs with my suggestion that it might echo her memory of witnessing her mother's miscarriage, which she had described in an earlier interview. Indeed, psychodynamic theory would view it as an intrusive reexperiencing of the traumatic miscarriage imagery, triggered by her sister's approaching delivery and her discussions of sexuality and reproduction in the interviews. Its setting at a wedding raises the possibility that it also represents a defloration scene, because in traditional marriages, the groom, wearing a sheathed dagger at his waist, takes his bride's virginity and then passes her bloody bloomers to her relatives to display from the rooftop. And it depicts hostility toward a mother, perhaps toward mothers in general, which emerges as a prominent theme in other portions of her narrative. Although we cannot settle on a precise interpretation, it certainly depicts her strong association of female sexual and reproductive powers with terror of bodily violation and disintegration.

Childbirth

An important set of Rachida's childhood memories concern the "shock" she experienced, at the age of seven, when she witnessed her mother miscarry:

> My mother lost one, but not after it was born, that is, it didn't finish. That's when I learned women *kaytkerfsou* (suffer) in childbirth . . . I'd always thought it's just something ordinary. When I saw that scene I got sick. I saw a lot of blood and all that, and my head got a little, *mḥemaqt* (I almost went crazy).
>
> [Do you remember how you felt?] *Ṣafi, kantkereh men l-wlad* (I felt repulsed by babies). I can't stand them when they're first born. That's really an important incident. [You said you got sick?] A little sick, I didn't fall [faint]. I saw that, and *rasi bgha yḥmaq* (I wanted to go crazy). I'd pictured to myself that birth was something simple, but when I saw that scene, and I saw so much blood and all that, from that time an illness entered me, like, if that's what childbirth is like, *ṣafi*, I no longer [want it]. In my heart I felt that thing is *khayb* (horrid/ugly) and I was frightened.
>
> [Did you throw up?] I went to sleep, immediately. My grandmother . . . was frightened, as she saw me *skheft* (faint). [You fainted?]

Umm [yes]. Even now, if I see something like that, I faint. . . . And of course, my mind always imagines that day. I couldn't forget it. (Story 95)

She later describes the miscarried fetus as looking "like some jinn (demon/spirit)," and says that in its burial shroud it looked "like some kind of insect" (Story 124). When I ask about having a child herself, she says she still feels revulsion:

I'm frightened *nit* (really!) of having a child. . . . When I hear women talking about what happens, I always flee/stay away. [What do they say?] They say that childbirth is very hard, that it involves suffering, that a person is between life and death. It strikes me as *f-shi shkel* (odd/weird). I really can't stand little children, I can't stand them. Now that's the problem I worry about. (Story 124)

Talking with other women doesn't help: "I run/stay away. I don't know why. I see a group of women sitting around and talking, I know that *hdra dyalhoum kif walou* (their talk is nothing/worthless)." Women were always putting babies in her lap, she says, "but I'd throw them off like a ball, I wouldn't touch them. Mothers are afraid to give me their babies." To this day, she says, "*makanḥmelsh drari sgher* (I can't stand babies)," using the verb for "can't stand" that is built from the *h* * *m* * *l* root, which means both "carry" and "pregnant." She avoided her mother after her later births for the whole forty-day lying-in period because "I'm afraid of that that's in her." Rachida sees this as a serious psychological complex:

I don't think I want to get married, because they suffer, they get sick and all that—that's all I see. If I just see the women sitting together, I feel like I'm actually going to throw up. I don't know how I can change. I don't know if this is going to continue for my whole life, or [breaks off] I wonder if it's not something psychological, *men dat dyali* (from inside my self).

It's not just being *shiki* (Fr. & Arabic: fashionable/selfish). I try to face reality, but inside I'm odd/weird: if I even just smell an odor of the food they cooked [for a postpartum woman] my stomach turns. If I go to a house where a woman has delivered, it's as if *glest ᶜla rasi* (I was sitting on my head), *kantqelleq* (I become upset/anxious), and all I can think about is going back to the house right away. Have you ever heard about a phenomenon like this?

I reassured her that everyone fears childbirth, but she continues, "I try to get over this, but I can't. It's been nearly twenty-three years that I haven't been able to stand it. I don't know how. . . ."

I was taken aback to be having this conversation with Rachida, in part because it so dramatically broke the distanced, "never any strife" story lines of so many of her childhood recollections, and in part because she revealed such intimate experiences and feelings to a male outsider. She spoke openly and passionately about these matters, without approaching either panic or tears, and maintained a remarkable measure of control without becoming rigid or defensive. In retrospect, I realized that my status as an outsider may have made it easier for her to discuss them, and the fact that I am a psychologist (though not a therapist, I had carefully explained) may have given her hope that I could help. I tried to help by empathizing with the horror she felt, encouraging her to express her feelings about it, and reassuring her that most women feel fears about pregnancy and childbirth—and overcome them. But I was careful not to join the chorus of voices telling her she would get over her revulsion, and so I added that a growing number of American women are choosing not to have children and finding they still can lead satisfying lives. I believe this was the first time Rachida had "talked out" her feelings in this manner. I perceived at the end of the interviews that she had felt some cathartic relief, but I doubt that it brought her any long-term therapeutic benefit.

Pollution

Rachida talked about another facet of her "complex" in the following interview. In the course of discussing her later childhood, I asked about her first period, and she matter-of-factly explained that although she "had no idea what to do," she quickly came to feel it was "something ordinary" and to accept her more responsible status: "it's said that from that time a girl's period comes, I was considered as an adult." In recent years, however, her period has become "very difficult," and she surprised me again by describing her distress:

> I get really sick before I get my period—everything hurts me, and *kantqelleq bezaf* (I get really upset/mad). *kattla' li ras* (I get uptight) and just have to pick a fight with someone. [Really?] Yeah, just someone in my family, my mother or my sister. If not, I just talk to myself. Or if I see something, anything, that doesn't please me—just some food or someone's face, even though it's handsome/nice—I tell him that your face is dirty. I just talk like I'm crazy. Now it really hurts me, and I don't know why. (Story 128)

She became increasingly animated as she talked:

> [Were you frightened of the bleeding?] I was frightened! Because at that time there was so much blood. . . . I really hated it. I took a really bad view of women. I'd told myself that maybe a girl doesn't get her period until she marries. . . . My mother got married when she was very young, before she got her period, so she couldn't teach us any-

thing. . . . I didn't know what to wear or what to do. When I went to school, I'd always check if I have blood spots on my clothes or something; I didn't know the methods.

So when my period came it was weird, because I was very shy/modest and I couldn't tell anybody. Even today I can't even tell my sister, because I'm shy/modest. Eventually I came to understood that it was something ordinary/natural. But then I started to get sick, and now it doesn't begin until I've suffered . . . my back hurts me, I feel pain everywhere, and I have to sleep. I can't wake up in the morning, and I can't have people talking to me. I'm afraid, I wonder if it's some problem or something.

She shares the local women's understanding:

People say that the blood/period is something *darra* (noxious/harmful), *shi wesekh* (something dirty), and if it stays in a person's stomach, it will always cause a disease, some illness in one's stomach. It's better for it to get out.

I asked directly if she felt frightened of the blood as she does of the bleeding of childbirth, and she said, "Yes, I can't stand it":

When I have my period I can't stand myself—understand? You know, the smell of it and the *tkerfes* (pain/difficulty). One feels that one is dirty. I always try to stay away from myself/keep from touching myself. I say/think to myself that even if one is *nqi* (clean) and has a pretty smell, in my view I feel dirty, *kif walou* (like I'm nothing/worthless).

For at least the last five years, then, her menstruation regularly has brought on a cluster of physical and emotional symptoms, causing her to lose control of her temper and speech, which we have seen to be so important to her as the vehicle for convincing others of her ᶜ*qel* (reason/maturity). Most poignantly, she says she can't stand herself, feeling "dirty" and "worthless." In addition, these "sufferings/hardships" have caused her to take "a really bad view of women" because their very gender condemns them to pollution and unconcealable shame:

Women always have problems. I have a point of view on women: I think they're *mkerfsin* (in a bad position/hardship), and they still talk too much—it's odd/weird. They suffer during their period, and when they marry, and then when they have children, and when they're raising their children. In everything, the woman suffers, and the man is *nqi* (clean), always *mezian* (OK/good). It's odd/weird. And the woman always shows [her state]—like in Ramadan when a woman doesn't fast everybody knows why [that she is having her period]. (Story 129)

Rachida thus reports a cluster of bodily and emotional difficulties she has not been able to understand or overcome, and she regards herself as having serious psychological "problems" about menstruation, pregnancy, and childbirth. She describes a sense of self—as sick, uptight, out of control, dirty, and worthless—that differs markedly from that of the accomplished woman who fights for her rights and feels "all my dreams have come true, and I'm happy." The duality in her views of women appears rooted in these two "senses of self."

Core-Level Personality ❀

These senses of self, in turn, appear to coalesce from affective states and tensions that characterize the genotypic or core level of her personality, especially those related to attachment versus loss, bounty versus deprivation, and order versus chaos—polarities we saw her use to organize her account of herself as a teacher. Her early memories and projective test responses contain disturbing depictions of deprivation and disintegrating social bonds; prominent feelings of frustration, anger, and depression; and images of hungry, devouring creatures set in barren niches. Surprisingly few portray joy or contentment, and most initially good scenes somehow turn bad, in much the same manner as her pride in her honored profession degenerated into feelings of "distance" and frustration as difficult students end up "in the street."

A House Divided

Rachida's childhood memories generally portray her relationships with her parents and others as distant and formal. When I asked about her earliest memory of her mother, she told instead about the relative who carried her while her mother worked and tried—often in vain—to comfort her when the summer heat "did me in" (Story 84). When I asked again for her first memory of her mother, she recalled, "I always saw her working," and then she told how her mother taught her and her sisters household chores (Story 85). My question about her earliest memory of her father brought a similar response: "I would always find him working," and she then went on to describe how he took interest in the children by regularly checking on their progress in school (Story 86). When I asked if she recalled her father being "playful" with them, she said, yes, "he would ask us to recite something from the Quran or to see some schoolwork, and when he saw a good grade, he would give us some money" (Story 90). She describes all of these familial relationships as "good" but volunteers emphatic and sometimes extended denials of strife: she "didn't hate" the woman who carried her (Story 84), and she recalls family meetings to discuss "problems" but insists "there never occurred any discord among us" (Story 87).

Her most positive recollections tend to be of family unity, her grandfather's honored status, the pride they took in helping the poor, and the celebrations marking births of new members. These frame two clusters of distressing memories of the times her household divided when senior brothers separated. Early in the third interview, Rachida explained what it means to carry the legacy of her ancestors:

> It's a *moḥafiḍa* (conservative) family We follow religion, we follow a single path, so we have to always be good and keep our original state/status . . . like of my grandfather, because he was good in his day, and we have to follow in his footsteps. We don't want people to say, "See how they were then and how they've become now." We've got a good reputation, and we've got to always keep it. (Story 72)

When I asked about her grandparents' household, which once had more than thirty members, she immediately focused on its division. Rachida was in junior high school when her father's brothers decided to move to their own houses, leaving her grandparents and her family in the main house. She denies that there had been conflict in emphatic terms: "There weren't any problems or anything. We lived in an organized/orderly atmosphere. . . . We didn't divide because of some problems or something" (Story 66). She even casts them as dividing for the sake of younger members' maturation:

> My grandparents were the *l-mes'ouline* (authorities), but when we divided, everyone tried to take responsibility for himself. If the younger ones stay dependent on the seniors, they won't learn what life is, and they'll go *ghalṭin* (wrong)—that's why. It was for them to have the freedom to act according to their own *ᶜqel* (mind/maturity). (Story 69)

When she returns to this period a few minutes later, however, she says she worried a good deal about the division:

> I always said it's not possible for us to split up. . . . The important thing is that the relationship hasn't changed. [But at that time, did you want to divide?] No, I didn't, and for nearly a month we were *mqelqin* (upset/ worried). [How's that? How'd you feel?] It was *f-shi shkel* (strange/weird). [pause] I'd say to myself that I didn't want it to happen. (Story 79)

Emotionally, this division may echo the earlier one that occurred when she was three, when her grandfather moved his branch of the family away from his brothers and built the house in which they now live. Her earliest pair of memories are of this move and prove to be the richest she narrates in detail and feeling. Her earliest runs as follows:

> I remember when they were just building the house, and my grandmother or mother would bring me to see the workers. Every place

they went, they'd take me. I remember when they had just begun it and they were dividing/partitioning the rooms. We had just the lower part, and they were making a garden there, and we'd come water it. We still hadn't moved, but we'd come over and bring the tea service and drink some tea. (Story 81)

Drinking tea by a watered garden appears as one of the classical representations of plenitude and bounty in arid North Africa and throughout the Middle East, and this memory of grandmother, mother, and daughter—"Every place they went they'd take me"—evocatively links bounty, familial unity, and generational continuity. It preserves an archetypal vision of well-being against the background anxiety of familial division and a barren landscape. She later recalls another memory from roughly the same period: waking to find her grandmother preparing breakfast for the household, bringing fodder from their fields, milking her cow, and making buttermilk—archetypal representations of *baraka* (blessedness/bounty) in the rural pre-Sahara. "I really liked helping her," she says, "because it was traditional, not like now. Their work was *mufriḥa* (joyous), *nashṭa* (happy); it didn't have that *taᶜab* (drudgery)" (Story 70).

Her second earliest memory sketches the breakup and move as having been terribly distressing for her:

After we moved in, we began to look for things to 'iḥesnou (fix it up), because there was just adobe in the rooms. . . . When our family members first began to move, they were reluctant to leave our old house and come here. Everyone cried because we'd left. But then people began to come visit there to welcome us to the new house. . . .

We didn't really settle in here immediately: we went there and they came here, until some time passed. We left some things there, we left the livestock there in order to go back, that is, so we wouldn't forget our past. (Story 82)

Rachida felt especially distressed:

Even though I was happy, I *tqelaqt* (became upset/anxious) a little. I was attached to the little kids there, and we needed a long time to get used to it here. . . . We'd stay here for a while, and then we'd have to go see the other house and stay there a little, and then here a little. With time . . . we started getting accustomed to it.

[When you say you became a little anxious/upset, what do you mean?] I wouldn't just stay in the house, I had to play with other kids, and there wasn't anyone to play with here. It made me cry, and my grandmother or mother would take me back to the other house, and I'd stay there a while, in order to try to forget a little. Then at night I'd come here. (Story 82)

She recalls the new house as at first barren, with only adobe walls, and herself crying for her relative-playmates. She also recalls it as isolated, the first in a stretch of rocky land between the road and the river:

> Everything was empty . . . there were no houses or people or anything, just dogs. . . . People would imagine there were wild animals in the hills that would attack them, and they'd run away. Always one would be frightened there. . . . But now *koulshi kayn* (everything's there), and the whole atmosphere has changed. There's no longer that fear. (Story 41)

As an origin myth, her two earliest memories preserve both her dread of separation, isolation, and barrenness and her yearning for belonging, for '*indimaj* (interweaving). They appear to show just the kind of anxieties about fissioning relationships that the household life cycle characteristic of this region easily generates: brothers typically try to maintain joint households after their father's death but ultimately divide their shares of inheritance and separate, often with acrimony. This and other memories also show her constructing a familial world that provides protection and security from the hostile world that lies beyond her doorstep: her teachers threatened to beat her if they saw her "on the street" (Story 16), neighborhood boys harassed her and tried to "break" her reputation (Story 132), neighbor girls fought with her and scarred her face (Story 98), wild animals lurked in the empty areas (Story 41), and she even told of a recent incident in which she cut her leg while riding to school on the back of her brother's moped and suspected the accident had been caused by a glance of the evil eye cast by an unknown neighbor (Story 112). For much of her childhood, Rachida stayed inside the house, so much that her parents began to worry that "maybe I had some kind of psychological illness" (Story 38).

Her fear of separation and threat crystallize in the folk tale she recalled when I asked about traditional stories her elders told:

> There are a lot of them about *ghoula* (ogres). Like a ewe would take her children outside to the fields to eat, and then she'd bring them back to a special place to spend the night. There was an ogre always on the watch to see how she talked to her children. One day it watched until she left to get them some food, and it went and knocked on their door like she did and imitated her voice, in order to eat them.
>
> But the children knew their mother's voice too well to open the door, and when their mother came back, they told her the story. She told them you have to do the same thing if it comes again, or it'll eat you. When their mother left again, he came and spoke to them like their mother. This time they opened the door, thinking it was their

mother, and it ate them. When their mother returned from the fields, she found them gone. They didn't listen, they didn't listen to their mother's *hdera* (words/talk).[6] (Story 114)

This tale not only shows the outside world to be a dangerous place but also conveys a core uncertainly about whether even a mother's voice will portend protection or a predator in disguise. And it holds the victims responsible for their misfortune, as Rachida so often does.

Fears of Fragmentation

Themes of deprivation, neglect, or depression appear in ten of the thirteen stories Rachida composed to TAT cards. Three end in success or well-being, three have ambiguous resolutions, and seven end in failure or fragmented relationships. Ten develop themes of separation: six in which the main character wishes to separate and four in which the protagonist is threatened with loss or separation. She describes a total of eleven families: five of these fragment, two remain intact in ideal forms, and four remain together at the cost of inner deprivation or broken dreams for a son or daughter. But beyond providing additional evidence of these relational tensions, her TAT stories show how she may try to master them by transforming anxieties about attachment and rejection into matters of moral rectitude and then placing herself on the side of virtue. Female characters get treated especially harshly: mothers die in four stories, and women get blamed for six of the seven instances of failure or fragmentation.

For example, in response to a TAT card depicting a woman holding a man who perhaps is pulling away, she focused on the upset and rejection she perceived in the man's "eyes and expression" and imagined him leaving his wife for another woman. She describes the woman as "begging him [to stay], but without success," but then she goes on to compose a story that blames the woman: he has "satisfied all her needs," but she has "failed to fulfill all his desires," and so the family will *tfekek* (unravel) or fragment, and "she will wake up and find herself a failed woman." In response to a card depicting a man and woman standing, he partly turned away from her, she begins by commenting that the woman is about to cry and then searches for a theme that would explain what has "wrecked" the family's reputation and is driving him to leave. To explain the family's *tshetet* (disintegration), she invents a daughter who has "left the path" and been thrown in jail. The mother didn't want to deprive her of the freedoms that other well-off girls enjoyed, but "as soon as her daughter found a little freedom, she forgot everything. Anything repugnant or shameful, *ghadi nemshiliha, temshiliha.*" In the last phrase, she slips and initially says, "I'll go to/after it," and then corrects herself, "She'll go to/after it." And in response to a card depicting a woman lying in bed and a man standing, an arm across his eyes, she begins to construct a story about a male intruder but shifts abruptly to the thought that "Maybe this woman isn't good." She constructs a story in which the woman seduced this respectable man "because she wants to destroy his honor. . . . When she saw that he was good, she wanted to cause him some problems." Again, his family will be destroyed, and "everything will be wasted or ruined." The woman grew up in a strict, conservative family, Rachida comments, but got fed up and ran away from their *sayṭara* (authority/control), and her corruption followed naturally. She commented:

> I can't stand this picture. . . . She's got to try to reform herself, or even in my opinion, they must kill her. Because if she stays in that state she'll attract a lot of girls . . . she will try to break the reputations of everyone. . . . The government must try to remedy this, put them in prison and *tkerfes ᶜlihoum mezian* (really make them suffer). Because if they leave one or a second or a third, everyone, the majority will follow them. (Story 146)

These stories show her to be primed to perceive impending abandonment and disintegration, in response to which she constructs narratives of virtue and sin, which both explain the abandonment and protect her from it by placing her on the side of virtue. She thereby keeps to the straight path, her eyes set on the bounties of heaven and the torments of hell, in order not to slip away from the authority that prevents her from sinning.

Rachida's Rorschach protocol shows continual use of her substantial intellectual skills and suggests that her emotional reactions are quite "constricted."[7] Nearly two thirds of her responses are of animals, many with body parts she says aren't visible or that she describes as wounded, deformed, or dismembered. They also show an emphasis on themes of hunger and devouring, which appear in half of her responses and in at least one response to each card. In seven of her thirty responses, she perceives figures at play, but five of these then turn into images of hunger, devouring, or rage. She also feels a sense of tranquility from two cards in which she perceives religious archetypes: one a statue of an honored, bearded old man set atop a mountain, the other of two people praying beneath a tree at sunset. She similarly tells a story of relief and tranquility in response to a TAT card depicting an old man praying. Her Rorschach responses thus sketch a world in which males hunt, fight, and sometimes play; in which females appear as both prey and predators and mothers are often absent; in which little and baby animals appear hungry and vulnerable to attack—and in the midst of all this distress, two images of older, male religious figures provide islands of sheltering calm.

Her sentence completion protocol yielded two sets of responses that cohere with her core values: a group of nine items expressing positive striving and achievement and seven items stating admired moral virtues. In contrast to the achievement items, a group of five express failure, disappointment, and loss of hope; in contrast to the morality cluster, five items express immorality and six items quarreling and strife. Fragmentation also emerges as a key concern: she completes ten stems with desires to separate from or reject others, and seven stems with rejection by others. Her responses again show her strong commitment to achievement and moral orderliness set against forces of disruption and disorder. Gender again differentiates her answers, as she describes good and bad men but only bad women. Perhaps most revealing may be her completion of stem "My lot in life" with "is loneliness/solitude," which conveys how isolated she sometimes can feel in the midst of her densely sociocentric network of relationships.

Rachida's projective protocols thus suggest that she is a person of strong intellectual abilities and self-control who constricts or suppresses her emotional experience. She appears beset by intense anxieties about fragmenting social relationships, linked with powerful feelings of deprivation, defeat, and rage. These anxieties extend to bodily integrity and to the coherence of what Kohut, Stern, and others have termed a *core self*. Her depictions of women seem especially harsh: mothers often abandon or fail their children, wives fail their husbands and cause families to disintegrate, and daughters lack the judgment to resist the lure of sin. Taken together, her life history and projective tests suggest that she chronically struggles with disturbing feelings of deprivation, fragmentation, and self-disgust. Her phobic reactions to childbirth probably are posttraumatic symptoms, and some of her somatic symptoms may be conversion responses to incompatible ideas. She experiences these symptoms as unpredictable intrusions of chaos and disorder that threaten her sense of self-control. And she responds with a rigid style of emotional control—by comparison to the richer imaginative and interpersonal worlds of the other Moroccans I interviewed.[8]

Many of the feelings and sicknesses she describes put her at odds with her culture's ideals, but they also may have been created or intensified by cultural influences. The pediatric style of infant care[9] facilitates the development of strongly interdependent familial bonds (as we have seen in Mohammed's and Hussein's narratives), but at the same time, the periodic division of extended households may exacerbate attachment anxieties. Rachida's memories of divisions also might "screen" a stressful weaning experience, as a number of North African psychologists have criticized abrupt weaning practices as damaging to infants' sense of security and strivings for autonomy. She might even have been sent to another household "to forget her mother's milk," which is a common practice, and her sister's child was staying in Rachida's household for this very reason. At the same time, Abdelatif Chaouite has pointed out that other family members typically rally around a weaned infant to provide a broadened circle of attachments and lay the groundwork for the household to become a kind of "group self"[10]—as it has for her.

It is especially important not to underestimate the "constricting" pressures her culture and conservative milieu bring to bear, creating the kind of emotional straitjacketing that makes the conversion hysteria studied by Janet and Freud commonplace among women. These pressures also constrain her from exploring aspects of her character and styles of relationship other than those to which she has confined herself in order to remain scrupulously proper. These constraints are likely to make her feel and appear more disturbed than she might in other milieus, and she mentions how much she relaxes and enjoys herself when she travels to big cities and Europe. But she does continually experience distress, and her religious identity appears ingeniously fashioned to interpret it and transform it into feelings of order, control, and bounty.

Social Personality ❀

When Rachida teaches, studies, brings home a paycheck, receives an American researcher in her family's guest room, and above all prays and reads/recites the Quran, she feels strong of ᶜqel (intellect/maturity) and klem (voice/word) and at once autonomous and enmeshed in her family's honor. But when she menstruates or pictures pregnancy or childbirth, nature turns her into what her first story about teaching and her religious identity set out as her core antiself figure: dirty, foul-smelling, worthless, unmannered, and lacking in self-control. Here is the deep cultural construction of gender Mernissi describes in Beyond the Veil: Rachida's womb, her sexual/reproductive femaleness, embeds a shameful font of pollution and fitna (chaos/disorder) in the core of her being. This renders her vulnerable to losses of control: pain, lethargy, anger, and "crazy" behavior during her period and possibly even to straying off the straight path if freed from male authorities. Here is the flaw, the lack that betrays itself under the harsh light of interrogation by patriarchal culture. It is this "dirty," "worthless," "crazy," "odd/weird," vulnerable-to-fragmentation sense of self that turns the klem (voice/word) with which she defends herself into shi hdera (just empty words), that leads her to doubt her ᶜqel (intellect/maturity) and self-control, and that makes her feel the need for male authority to stay on the straight path of striving and propriety. She is of two minds about women's autonomy and equality, not only because she strategically aims to pass for both traditional and modern but also because she is of two diametrically opposed senses of self.

Here the honor-modesty system and Islam appear to play organizing roles in her personality analogous to those we saw in Mohammed's and Hussein's narratives: they reconfigure idiosyncratically personal anxieties and strengths in congruence with a set of cultural prototypes and moral sentiments. As Hussein typically experiences anxiety, masculine vulnerability, and wishes for empowerment as "automatically" configured within relational triangles, so Rachida tends to "automatically" experience herself enmeshed within the group self of her extended family house, suffused with the baraka (blessedness/bounty) associated with her grandfather. Conversely, she "automatically" experiences intimations of rejection and fragmentation as matters of temptation and sin, and her menstrual distress as a matter of pollution and loss of self-control. Two subselves or senses of self are at least partially integrated in this process, in which core-level affective tensions—over which she experiences little control—are transformed into matters of honor-modesty-dishonor and purity-pollution that she feels she *can* control. Several of her TAT stories are particularly telling on this point, as they show her first perceiving rejection, abandonment, or assault and then fashioning morality tales that ultimately place her, as narrator and commentator on immoral and failed characters, on the side of the righteous.

Like Mohammed and Hussein, she has internalized the interrogating gaze of the honor-modesty system as a Generalized Other that positions her in a world of distinctive social personas, interactional etiquettes, and moral sentiments. But unlike Mohammed and Hussein, this fixes her as distinctively female, loosely consolidating her distresses in accordance with the *fitna* (disorder)-prone stereotype of woman. Enragingly for Rachida, her gender unfairly imposes suffering and demands concealment at the same time that it forces exposure. This gaze—backed throughout her life by very real threats of beatings and rejection—puts her in question as to what destiny she will fulfill with her reproductive powers, her intellect, and her voice. She responds in an intriguingly androgynous manner, rigorously embracing the etiquette of modesty and then claiming traditionally male rights to pursue the profession of her choosing. By no means does Rachida always automatically construe her feelings and sense of herself within the schemas of honor-modesty and Islam, nor does she readily experience herself as self-controlled and blessed with bounty rather than sick or crazy and fated to deprivation. The psychological integration created at this level of social personality is but partial and assigns only elements of an identity. Especially because she has so many experiences that do not cohere with the culture's ideals for women, these elements challenge her to assemble and elaborate them into an identity.

Identity ❀

Rachida's religious identity seeks to encompass and represent both of these senses of self or subselves. It provides a conceptual/symbolic system by which she can transform *fitna* (chaos/disorder) into *mᶜaqel* (rational/mature) comportment, *mamerbinsh* (unmannered) impulses into *mḥashuma* (modest/proper) behavior, and a *wesekh* (dirty/polluted) self into a *nqi* (clean/pure) one. As she reads the Quran and lives by religious principles, she transforms fragmentation to unity, isolation to belonging, anxiety to tranquility, deprivation into bounty, and disgust to pride. As I described before, the first stage in this process takes place at the level of social personality, where intimations of rejection, fragmentation, and self-disgust are transformed into sentiments of shame that attach to rules of propriety and into feelings of dirtiness that attach to rules of pollution-purification. But if Rachida has internalized this patriarchal gaze, she also has stared it down. With the mentoring of a wise grandfather, the culturing of a modern education, and the power of a monthly paycheck, she has used the traditionally male powers of *ᶜqel* (intellect/maturity), *klem* (voice/word), and *qiraᶜa* (recitation) to defeat the patriarchy's most noxious demand that she become only what her reproductive powers would make of her. And she has strengthened her resistance by fashioning a *moḥafiḍa* (conservative) persona that appears ultralegitimate in the light of interrogation and surveillance.

The Straight Path

Rachida portrays herself as having a natural affinity for religion, but it still has not been easy for her to achieve the piety she now practices. She has always studied the Quran and lived by religious principles, but she has observed the daily prayer cycle only since she was twenty-two:

> I learned everything about prayer in school, but *l-ᶜqel mazal maka-melsh* (my mind wasn't yet finished then), my mind was still small. One has to wait until one's mind has matured . . . to know that one believes and that one is going to live by it. (Story 31)

Soon after she began teaching, a couple of devout women teachers convinced her to pray:

> It was some six or seven years ago, during Ramadan. We began talking about prayer, and they said, "What's wrong with you? You don't pray, shame on you!" And I told them that if I began to pray, I couldn't stop doing it, because it's a sin, that it's a bad thing if someone just plays around with religion. So from that time, I decided to *always* pray. . . . I said to myself I've got to become like them. They showed me how, and I began to pray, and since then, I haven't stopped. If I don't pray, I become *mqelqa* (anxious/worried).
>
> We studied about religion together and we just became intertwined through those conversations, and we agreed to pray. We'd meet and talk over how we'd done: had you come to think correctly? Because if one has a *triq meziana* (good/correct path), one never encounters difficulty. Praise be to God. (Story 31)

She had no religious reconversion, like Mohammed, and does not go to the mosque to show her participation in the adult community, as does Hussein. Religious principles guide her public comportment, but her faith is also intensely private, as she prays, recites the Quran, and studies religious commentaries largely on her own.

As if foreshadowing her love of Quranic recitation, she twice tells how her family members say that as a very young child she used to find "relaxation/tranquility" by singing alone:

> They tell me that I was always *nashṭa* (happy), and that I always liked to sing. . . . I'd sing, just by myself I'd memorize some song that I heard and I'd keep singing it. (Story 80) [They said:] "If you didn't find anything to do, you'd go some place where there wasn't anyone, and sit singing, in a loud voice." And they'd say, *raḥ*, now she's relaxed/tranquil with herself, leave her alone. (Story 107)

And she repeatedly recalls excelling at Quranic school while the "lazy" students were getting beaten. She also recited at home:

> When I was in elementary school, I used to come home and read/recite the Quran in the house, not just with the voice used for memorizing, but with a really loud voice, and people passing in the street would laugh and say she likes that really a lot. (Story 16)

The beauty of Quranic recitation is a major force in the lives of both Mohammed and Rachida, though she does not perform in public. Recitation sounds to an outsider like a cross between singing and chanting but is regarded as a use of the voice distinct from either. The Quran itself has a deeply poetic quality. It tells stories and gives laws, but these recede in importance during recitation to imagery, exhortation, and emotional resonances that provide a glimpse of divinity in this life. Touching the Quran requires one be in a state of purity, and recitation requires a purity of concentration that goes far beyond ritual purification. Like prayer, recitation requires *niya*, a kind of focused sincerity that comes with and brings tranquility, but which Rachida finds sometimes difficult to form:

> If one wants to pray, his intention must be on prayer; and not, for example, for his body to be present but his mind living in some other place, for his intention to not be present. When I pray, I should pray and nothing else should be in my mind. One needs *niya l-ḥasana* (proper/good intention), it means I must follow precisely this path—and not take two paths or three paths. If a person doesn't have *niya* (intention), it's worthless.
>
> [But what if your mind gets full of problems? How do you get rid of them?] I say, "May God give me refuge from Satan the accursed one." [What's that?] Sometimes Satan, he's the enemy of humans, and if a person wants to do something, Satan comes and tells him no, don't do it. And he fills his mind with some *khorafat* (myths/heresies), and even though he wants to do something, Satan won't let him do it, Satan fills his mind and doesn't let him follow the path of prayer. Sometimes that sort of thing happens to me, sometimes

if I'm really upset/angry I won't pray. . . . It's better to wait until I'm relaxed/tranquil, until my mind is *mertabet b-Allah* (tied/linked to God). (Story 191)

She explains recitation:

The Quran has its own special voice/recitation style. There are some who read it as if they are reading a story or a book, but the Quran must be read with a voice that *kaynabet men l-qelb* (grows/sprouts from the heart). (Story 189)

When she recites:

I must have a disposition/liking for it from my heart. My mind faces the sura (verse), and as I read/recite it and understand the Quran's words, I feel my/its whole body moving/shaking,[11] that is, I really get caught up in what the Quran says. You see me sometimes almost stop, not from my own volition but without perceiving myself. I have an intense attachment to the Quran.

If I hear the Quran anywhere, on television or the radio or if someone is reciting, I try to listen and understand what's being said. Its words have an objective, and sometimes they take me off until I begin crying. [Really!] Because a person makes mistakes in his life, but if one just listens to the Quran and understands its words, *raḥ*, I must really live religion. (Story 189)

Al Raḥman

By really living her religion, Rachida creates herself as her ideal. Her religious discourse embraces her antiself—like a pearl embraces the grain of sand at its core—and transforms it by purification, recitation, and prayer into divine and worldly blessedness. Stunningly, the primary route of transformation winds through the sura *al raḥman*, the sura she says she reveres and that often brings her to tears as she reads/recites it. It follows rich metaphorical extensions of "womb": *al raḥman* means the Merciful (or the Beneficient) and *al raḥim* the Compassionate, and these are the most prominent of the ninety-nine names of God, recited at the beginning of every sura and prayer and uttered by devout Muslims (*bismillah al raḥman al raḥim*, In the name of God, the Merciful, the Compassionate) at the beginning of every undertaking. Both names are derived from the root $r * ḥ * m$, which means "womb." Popular and orthodox Islam rhetorically make much of these derivations to represent a God who appears to outsiders as the consummate patriarch as in fact possessing profoundly feminine, maternal qualities. As mentioned in chapter 3, one of the sermons recorded by Antoun in a Lebanese village eloquently used terms built of the $r * ḥ * m$ root to set out the Muslim life course as one in which the individual is sundered from the womb (*rahim*) by the cutting of the umbilical cord, sustained through earthly life by bonds with uterine kin (*rahem*), and finally returned to the source of being (*al rahman*, the Merciful, *al rahim*, the Compassionate) at death.[12]

Early in the first interview, Rachida talked about how her grandfather encouraged her memorization in Quranic school, and when I asked if she has favorite suras, she immediately replied *al rahman*:

> The *sura al rahman*, it's the best/most beautiful, I like it so much. [What's in it?] It has one sentence in it that it repeats again and again. It has a pretty/beautiful pronunciation, and if one reads it, one feels that tears are going to fall, because it speaks of God. . . . It says in it that *al rahman* is God, it's a name from the names of God, *as rahman* is the name/sign of the Quran, of *khelq l-'insan* (the creation of humankind), it's a name/sign, the meaning of which is precisely the Quran. It speaks about the sun and the moon; it speaks about all existence; it speaks about *nar* (hellfire); it speaks about *jenna* (heaven), and what the reward is for the *mwalin nar* (people of fire/hell) and what the reward is for the *mwalin jenna* (the people who go to heaven). (Story 15)

This is the ultimate point of every Quranic sura, she points out, to contrast the bounties of heaven and the torments of hell as the *natija* (yield/consequences) of one's life:

> Just from the reading of it, if you read it, you understand it. Every sura in the Quran differentiates between heaven and *nar* (fire/hell), and that's that: this is *zwina* (good/beautiful), and that is *khayba* (bad/ugly). That's that: *natija hia hadik* (these are what the consequences are). (Story 15)

In our next-to-last meeting, Rachida brought her grandfather's Quran, explaining that "he knew I'd come home and read/recite the Quran in the house in a really loud voice, and when he died, he told my grandmother to give me his book—that's this book, this is the one he read/recited from." She then read/recited the *sura al rahman* to me:

> In the name of Allah, the Compassionate, the Merciful.
> It is the Merciful who has taught the Koran.
> He created man and taught him articulate speech. The sun and moon
>   pursue their ordered course. The plants and the trees bow down
>   in adoration.
> He raised the heaven on high and set the balance of all things, that
>   you might not transgress that balance. Give just weight and full
>   measure.

He laid the earth for His creatures, with all its fruits and blossom-bearing palm, chaff-covered grain and scented herbs. Which of your Lord's blessings would you deny?

He created man from potter's clay and the jinn from smokeless fire. Which of your Lord's blessings would you deny?

The Lord of the two easts is He, and the Lord of the two wests. Which of your Lord's blessings would you deny?

He has let loose the two oceans: they meet one another. Yet between them stands a barrier which they cannot overrun. Which of your Lord's blessings would you deny?

Pearls and corals come from both. Which of your Lord's blessings would you deny?

His are the ships that sail like mountains upon the ocean. Which of your Lord's blessings would you deny?

All that lives on earth is doomed to die. But the face of your Lord will abide forever, in all its majesty and glory. Which of your Lord's blessings would you deny?

All who dwell in heaven and earth entreat Him. Each day some mighty task engages Him. Which of your Lord's blessings would you deny?

Mankind and jinn, We shall surely find the time to judge you! Which of your Lord's blessings would you deny?

Mankind and jinn, if you have power to penetrate the confines of heaven and earth, then penetrate them! But this you shall not do except with Our own authority. Which of your Lord's blessings would you deny?

Flames of fire shall be lashed at you, and molten brass. There shall be none to help you. Which of your Lord's blessings would you deny?

When the sky splits asunder and reddens like a rose or stained leather (which of your Lord's blessings would you deny?), on that day neither man nor jinee shall be asked about his sins. Which of your Lord's blessings would you deny?

The wrongdoers shall be known by their looks; they shall be seized by their forelocks and their feet. Which of your Lord's blessings would you deny?

That is the Hell which the sinners deny. They shall wander between fire and water fiercely seething. Which of your Lord's blessings would you deny?

But for those that fear the majesty of their Lord there are two gardens (which of your Lord's blessings would you deny?) planted with shady trees. Which of your Lord's blessings would you deny?

Each is watered by a flowing spring. Which of your Lord's blessings would you deny?

Each bears every kind of fruit in pairs. Which of your Lord's blessings would you deny?

They shall recline on couches lined with thick brocade and within their reach will hang the fruits of both gardens. Which of your Lord's blessings would you deny?

Therein are bashful virgins whom neither man nor jinee will have touched before. Which of your Lord's blessings would you deny?

Virgins as fair as corals and rubies. Which of your Lord's blessings would you deny?

Shall the reward of goodness be anything but good? Which of your Lord's blessings would you deny?

And beside these there shall be two other gardens (which of your Lord's blessings would you deny?) of darkest green. Which of your Lord's blessings would you deny?

A gushing fountain shall flow in each. Which of your Lord's blessings would you deny?

Each planted with fruit trees, the palm and the pomegranate. Which of your Lord's blessings would you deny?

In each there shall be virgins chaste and fair. Which of your Lord's blessings would you deny?

Dark-eyed virgins sheltered in their tents (which of your Lord's blessings would you deny?) whom neither man nor jinee will have touched before. Which of your Lord's blessings would you deny?

They shall recline on green cushions and rich carpets. Which of your Lord's blessings would you deny?

Blessed be the name of your Lord, the Lord of majesty and glory![13]

Though Rachida believes, as do many, that the Quran can be grasped only in classical Arabic, she tried to explain it to me in Moroccan dialect. She says she especially loves the refrain, repeated thirty-one times, "And which of your Lord's blessings would you deny?" because it silences doubts "that anything that exists on the earth comes from the hand of God." She sums up *al raḥman* as establishing God as the creator of all and then showing the judgment and punishment that await those who would deny the Lord's blessings and the bounty that awaits those who cleave to the straight path.

Although many suras sketch images of heaven and hell, it is *al raḥman* that presents the most elaborate and sustained contrast. On Judgment Day, the sky will split open, reddening "like a rose or stained leather," and the sinners will be seized by their forelocks and feet and pitched into the abyss, forever to wander between flames and scalding water. But the righteous will ascend to heaven, where they will find gardens watered by flowing springs and gushing fountains, and shaded trees laden with pomegranates and dates. There, Rachida explains, female kin will be reunited as "virgins chaste and fair . . . as fair as corals and rubies . . . shall recline on green cushions and rich carpets . . . on couches lined with thick brocade and within their reach will hang the fruits of both gardens." The imagery of *al raḥman* thus parallels her earliest memories—of her mother and grandmother taking her to their new house and then the distress of division—in contrasting the bounty and sweet delight of the garden to scenes of barrenness, deprivation, and abandonment and visually depicting the continuity of *arḥam* (uterine kin): daughter, mother, and grandmother together in the garden site and tea-drinking ritual that are recognized to be foretastes of heaven.

Rachida's exegesis thus presents heaven not as a masculinist sexual utopia in which virgin houris endlessly satisfy the men but as a chaste harem: the reunited women dwell together in their own elegantly brocaded realms, with angels gratifying all their wishes. The reparation to virginal femaleness appears complete, but she adds an additional element: heaven restores racial purity. "The women who are in heaven are like gems," she says, "like pearls: they are white. When they enter heaven they appear, they aren't like those who have committed sins and have black faces and blue eyes. These are really beautiful, they are white" (Story 186). Explaining the sura in colloquial Arabic, she actually misinterprets the obscure word *medehemetan*, used in *al raḥman*, some commentators say, to mean "dark green."[14] She translates it as *l-khelin* (the black ones), one of the more polite terms for her traditionally low-caste group of African ancestry, whose skin color the pre-Saharan cosmology construes as a sign of divine disfavor. Rachida's dark skin appears to expose her to the same sort of shame as does her menstrual bleeding, which God promises to annul in the afterlife. She concludes: "those beauties, those women who have entered heaven, it says that their whiteness, that there's nothing comparable to them in this world."

The structurally ambiguous set of $r * ḥ * m$ derivatives thus unifies the beginning and end of Rachida's life in a manner that parallels the sermon on *arham*, with heaven restoring the purity, innocence, harmony, bounty, and compassion of uterine bonds she represents as spoiled by the division of her extended household, her mother's horrifying miscarriage, and her own menstrual distress. It establishes an octavelike relation that distinguishes the polluting, chaos-radiating physical womb from the purifying, redeeming radiance of God, the Merciful, the Compassionate. This essentially legislates a moral imperative at the core of her identity: to check, purify, and conceal her body's dirtying fecundity and stay on the straight path that leads back to the Creator. She thus oscillates, at least on a monthly basis, between being the Me and the not-Me figures fashioned by her discourse of identity. By her rationality, spirituality, hard work, and strong voice, she creates herself as a modern and honorable Muslim whose essence is defined by her intellect, piety, and recitation rather than by her gender. But nature inexorably transforms her into the traditional stereotype of woman: impure, irrational, quarrelsome, and *fitna*-prone. She hates and fears the woman nature makes her and also hates and fears women who give in to nature and stray "off the path"—so much so that in some passages she would have the government "really make them suffer." At the same time, she celebrates the woman—rational, self-controlled, pure—she perceives God calls her to be and will make of her as heavenly reward for a life of piety. And also at the same time, though in a different breath, she supports the right of all women to equality with men and to live the lives they choose.

Conclusion ❀

Rachida's life narrative shows a number of important features of personality development in the North African context, as she experiences it in the small town of Agdez. First, like Hussein, she fashions what may be termed a "Muslim ethicist" identity, in which she represents this-worldly achievement as a divine calling and views the rewards accruing to her ascetic self-control and dedication to her profession as divinely bestowed blessings. Like many Moroccans of her generation, Rachida has linked traditional sentiments of honor to success within the educational system and in their modern careers.

Second, in spite of the fact that this is generally considered to be a collectivist, sociocentric culture, Rachida's narrative—like Mohammed's and Hussein's—shows a prominent mixture of collectivist and individualist strivings. Rachida presents herself as interdependently attached to her household's unity and reputation in a way rarely seen among Americans, and her sense of self can even be said to fuse with her sense of family. Stretching back generations and including people who no longer live in it, her household serves as what Winnicott termed a *self-object*. But these sociocentric self-representations coexist alongside powerfully egocentric representations and individualist strivings that pit her against her parents, her sisters, her brothers, and even her household as a supra-individual unit. She, in fact, uses her individualism to resist marriage and preserve her sociocentric attachment to her household. Her self simply cannot be said to be either sociocentric or egocentric, as she so clearly articulates both types of representations and interpersonal strategies.

Third, Rachida's personality organization differs in fundamental ways from Mohammed's and Hussein's because she is female, and these differences appear most pronounced at the level of social personality. At the level of core personality organization, Rachida appears no more different from Mohammed and Hussein (or from Khadija) than they do from each other. And at the level of identity, her "authentic" discourse resembles Mohammed's in their adoption of "straight path" Islam, in the importance of Quranic recitation, and in their use of the imagery of $r * \d{h} * m$. It differs most dramatically from that of Khadija (chapter 6), whose way of life Rachida would condemn as an abomination. But while Mohammed, Hussein, and Rachida all have internalized their culture's honor-modesty schema to organize social personas, the two men seek to build honor by bodily, phallic projection of themselves into agonistic public arenas, whereas Rachida seeks to fashion honor from modesty, which mandates concealment and confinement. These are matters of relative emphasis, as Islam enjoins both men and women to observe rules of modesty. But where Mohammed feels "dirty" because of his behaviors in public (lying, stealing, smoking, drinking, and fighting), Rachida feels "dirty" because of menstruating and stays modest by keeping her head and arms covered whenever she leaves the house.

Yet her narrative all but lacks the positive representations of female fecundity and nurturance that abound in the culture and that other ethnographers have seen as the core of women's identities.[15] Only her memory of her grandmother rising early, bringing fodder from the fields, milking the cow, and making buttermilk—work she says was *mufriha* (free/easy) and unlike today's *ta^cab* (drudgery)—begins to convey this traditional view of women. The Sudanese women Boddy studied repeatedly told her *nihna bhaym* ("we are cattle"), the very phrase we often heard from women in traditional households in pre-Saharan villages, and Boddy correctly understands this to have two opposed meanings that together convey the character of women's lives: (1) we are but beasts of burden for our men; (2) we are the prized, life-giving, life-sustaining beings whom our men protect and honor.[15] Rachida's menstrual distress and phobia of infants paradoxically help free her from being any man's beast of burden but deprive her of the redeeming, "sacred" qualities traditionally associated with reproduction.

Although Rachida frequently defends her claims to run her own life in a male idiom, her narrative does not appear to have the sort of hero epic structure that Mohammed's and Hussein's do. She neither casts her own life in terms of this schema (as does Mohammed) nor identifies with heroic lives of family members or religious or historical figures (as does Hussein). A few features do fit: her earliest memory conveys a sense of blessedness amid deprivation, she certainly has been tested and proven that she can persevere in the face of adversity, and her grandfather perhaps served as a "donor" figure. But she portrays her troubles as disruptions rather than as episodes in the plotline of her life. She does not depart from home or quest for power or knowledge but suffers and perseveres to lead a *mohafida* (conservative) life, not a grand or adventuresome one.

Fourth, Rachida's narrative also shows an organization at the level I have termed *social personality* or *social persona*, which reconfigures core-level affective tensions within a framework of honor-modesty-shame and purity-pollution. This integration appears to coalesce in the view of the Generalized Other—or in the "gaze" of Sartre's anonymous "they"—as she feels merged with her household's honorable group self but also as she perceives her menstruating body to dirty her, to cause her intellect to give way to "craziness," and to turn her forceful voice into "just words."

Fifth, Rachida's life narrative, like Mohammed's and Hussein's, shows that identity takes shape as a dialogue among contradictory self-representations or, to phrase this differently, that personality develops by differentiation into subselves, that identity then integrates in dialogue. Rachida's dialogue takes shape as a rather rigid and one-sided one, as she aims punitive hostility toward figures representing antiself qualities—especially women, whom she often stereotypes and denigrates in patriarchal terms. The sura *al raḥman* epitomizes this quality in the tone of its repeating threat, "And which of your Lord's blessings would you deny?" which she finds so meaningful and moving. Religion thus defines one of the major semiotic axes by which she differentiates *Me* from *not-Me*, and age demarcates another, as she looks to the elders of her household to "advise" juniors on matters of propriety and as she teaches "Islamic culture" to children who still lack "reason/maturity" and arrive at school "unmannered." Gender delineates a third important axis, as she shifts between claiming equality with men in a largely masculine idiom and justifying patriarchal authority with stereotypic indictments of women. A fourth line of differentiation, race, may have remained unspoken until it appeared in her exegesis of *al raḥman*. Historically, pre-Saharan Morocco was a race-based society, with slaves and sharecroppers from sub-Saharan Africa often living in residentially segregated communities (including the hamlet in which Rachida grew up), their dark skin regarded as a sign of divine disfavor. Her vision that women's skin will become a beautiful pearly white in heaven suggests that she may have internalized damaging features of the region's white supremacy in the same manner as she has its patriarchy.

Sixth, Rachida's narrative sets out the simultaneous identity and opposition of womb and *al raḥman* as a structurally ambiguous key symbol that anchors her identity by linking her despised and ideal senses of self as lower (corporeal, polluting) and higher (spiritual, pure) versions of each other—as fonts of creation, nurturance, and belonging. Her earliest memory of her grandmother and mother taking her to water the garden and drink tea in their family's new home and her vision of women kin reunited as beautiful virgins in the bountiful, brocaded quarters of heaven score the beginning and end of her life on its tonic tone. This establishes the scale within which she can experience life's tensions and disharmonies—which unavoidably occur because families separate, bodies pollute, mothers miscarry, and immature characters stray off the path—as departures from the tonic tone that promise a return at the conclusion. This octavelike relation orchestrates her life, enabling her to play classical compositions (prayer and Quranic recitation) and improvisations (teaching and conversations) that give meaning to her worries, frustrations, and womb-based sufferings as departures that ultimately lead to the power, beauty, and tranquility of *al raḥman*.

Finally, this representational system, charting both self and world, provides Rachida with a culturally sanctioned route of individuation. Devout Muslims recognize that there is one God but as many paths as there are humans, and Rachida certainly has personalized her religious heritage, selecting features she finds "most beautiful" and tailoring their meanings so that they speak directly to her as she hears, reads, and recites them. In this personalized form, they simultaneously enable her to share "true" Islam with other devout Muslims, give meaning to many personal experiences she does not understand, and calm at least some of the idiosyncratic forms of distress she feels. Even if her version of the straight path seems especially narrow, it is one she can travel within the real developmental constraints of her life in Agdez.

CHAPTER *6*

Khadija

Khadija's life hardly could differ more from Rachida's. She wears her hair short and uncovered, dresses in European styles, smokes, drinks, swears, dances in discos at local tourist hotels, and has what she calls "love affairs." She is attractive, independent, and sometimes flirtatious and has a "bad" reputation to show for it. She is just the sort of woman Rachida would have jailed and "really made to suffer." I met her through my spouse, who sometimes worked with her father, a water-pump technician with the Agriculture Ministry. We visited her family several times at their home in Taznakht, a small town an hour east of Ouarzazate famous for its carpets. We also occasionally had coffee with Khadija and her siblings in Ouarzazate, where they shared a small apartment on the edge of town. When I asked if she would like to record her life story as part of my research, she enthusiastically said yes, and a week later she arrived at our apartment with a story to tell. "I've been writing all my life," she said near the end of the first interview, and I'll begin by letting her tell the mostly chronological story she told in those first two hours.[1]

Khadija's History ❁

First I'm going to talk about my parents. *Bon.* My father and my mother are *Berbers* [Fr.]. My father comes from Boulmalne, and my mother from Taznakht, but she didn't grow up there. She went to school in Casablanca because her *parents* [Fr.] moved there. She went as far as primary school, graduated, and became a teacher.

My father never went to school, *jamais* (Fr.: never). His father and mother died when he was seven years old—that's what he told me— and he went into the army and went to *Indo-Chine* (Fr.: Indochina). He worked as a mechanic. *Voilà*, when he came back, the government assigned him a job working on water pumps in Taznakht.

Ouarzazate: market square in a traditional neighborhood

My mother was in Casa then, and she was married to another man with whom she had Farid and Fadila. When she got married, her husband brought her back to Taznakht and made her quit. He didn't want to marry a working woman, [he said:] "A woman mustn't work!" Things were like that at the time. Then they got divorced, but Farid and Fadila stayed with her. My father was also married when he was in the army. His brothers found him a wife, but then they separated, or maybe she died. Then he married my mother, and Ahmad was born and then I was born. My father got transferred all over the place, but we finally came back to Taznakht, and I grew up there. (Story 1)

We Had Nothing, Really

We always lived in government houses near the offices, but then after my youngest sister was born we moved into a house in the country-side, an old adobe house with trees that had been left by some an-cestors. We didn't have any running water then, any electricity, any refrigerator, any music. We didn't have anything at all. We rode a donkey to get water from a fountain, we used a gas lamp, and we cooked over a wood fire stove. We had a few goats and hens, and each year we'd pick almonds and apples and olives. I mean life was a bit hard.

Ouarzazate: modern neighborhood under construction

[Why was life hard?] Life wasn't as it should have been. We spent all our time working and never had the chance to know what was going on elsewhere. It was a routine life, we didn't have a radio or cassettes, and the newspapers hardly reached there. We had nothing, really.

On days we didn't have school, we were forced to help my mother with her weaving. I didn't like that at all. We'd have to get up early and spend the whole day weaving, and if we didn't want to do it, she'd beat us. She was a very hard woman. But my father was *gentil* (Fr.: gentle/kind), and he still is. [She'd beat you?] She was *nerveux* (Fr.: anxious), hot-tempered, and got worked up very easily. I liked my father very much, he never beat me. But my mother used to beat us for nothing. When I was in elementary school, I couldn't bring my friends to the house with me, and I couldn't go outdoors and play with the kids. She used to beat me often. (Story 2)

It was *surtout* (Fr.: mainly) because of her first divorce. A girl must learn how to cook, how to make bread—that was my mother's idea. I think all that ᶜ*qedni* (gave me a complex). She'd say, "When you grow older and get married, you'll see." She sets you a limit/constrains you, and then you grow older, and something you've been brought up with stays with you and constantly bothers/frightens you. This is the matter I want to tell you about. She'd say, "When you get married, the man who takes you will bring you back. He won't keep you because you don't know how to cook or wash or look after his house properly." From the age of seven or eight, we used to hear that kind of talk. "You mustn't get friendly with boys"—that kind of stuff, you see? "You should have nothing to do with young men." "If you aren't afraid to stay outdoors at night [you'll get in trouble]"—that was her talk. You were imprisoned. . . . (Story 3)

She went to school and became a teacher and could have gone beyond all that. She could have worked and not gotten married, but she couldn't do that herself. She worked one year and then quit. So she stayed like that, and our life carried on like that, and nothing changed or improved. We didn't know what life was—we didn't know things like the beach, the train, or planes.

Life carried on like that, until the fifth grade of elementary school. I repeated the elementary graduation test three times, and the problem was that my mother became sick. She got sick because she and my father used to fight all the time. Life was like that from the beginning: they never got along, they were always quarreling and fighting, and this was really a big problem. We'd be gathered all to-gether laughing and playing with each other, and all of a sudden *kaynoḍ l-ᶜks* (a conflict would erupt), and my mother would pack up her things and say she was going to Casablanca.

So, that year I was in the fifth grade, my mother beat me, and they fought between themselves. She used to have a problem with her bladder, so she went to Casablanca with Farid and Fadila for three months, and we stayed with my father. All the kids were young, and I used to do everything: I had to make bread, take it to the oven, and when I came back home from school at 11:30, I'd cook lunch. Things stayed like that all year, and I repeated my class. The next year she came back. I repeated my class again, and the fights carried on be-tween them, and things went on like that until I passed the fifth-year exams. We both passed, Ahmad and I, but there was no secondary school in Taznakht at the time, and we had to go to Ouarzazate. (Story 4)

A Crush, "la Crise," and Psychotherapy?

Khadija tells a series of tales about living arrangements that didn't work out and distracted them from their studies. First, her father's niece threw them out: "I used to wear only pants and she found this weird, and she told every-body that I was a bad girl because I dressed like boys and talked to the boys." They moved into a room owned by a poor single mother: "It was sickening. How was I supposed to study? The white wall was black with cockroaches, there was no *W.C.* (Fr.: bathroom), and we had to go outside in the dark to relieve ourselves." (Story 5) Finally her mother convinced her older half-brother Farid to take a job in Ouarzazate, and the family rented a cheap apartment in a poor part of town for the three of them. (Story 6) Khadija moved on to high school, and one at a time, her younger siblings joined them. In the equivalent of American ninth grade, however, she again failed and repeated the year.

I confess I had a problem, a romantic problem, a serious one. I had awful complexes since the ninth grade. I was *complexée* (Fr.: troubled), *tⁱeqedt mezian* (I had a serious complex). I didn't have any friends. I had never had any relationships, and I was afraid. I could hardly speak with a boy, for fear that something might happen to me. [Why were you afraid?] Because from when I was a child, my mother used to tell me that a girl shouldn't talk to a boy because she would become a woman, not a girl any more. Do you know what I mean? I couldn't even say hello to a boy because I had in mind what my mother told me and feared that something might happen to me, losing my virginity or getting pregnant. I was really afraid and always shy around boys.

So that year I had a problem and it was a big problem. I had a teacher, a biology teacher, and he used to *ikereblia* (approach/befriend me). He tried to be nice to me. I was always sitting alone at the back of the classroom, absentminded, and he'd ask me to stay behind after the students had gone out to talk to me. He would ask me why I was always sitting by myself, always *isolé* (Fr.: isolated), always *la solitude* (Fr.: lonely), if I had any problems. So the first day passed, the second day, and I'd wait for him to ask me to stay and tell him what was the matter. You know, he tried to approach/ befriend me.

Then after a while he became everything to me. I really had a crush on him and thought the world of him. He was only trying to be nice to me, to help me, but I thought something else was happening. I fell in love with him. I felt miserable if I couldn't see him, but I was never able to tell him what I felt for him. Had I been wiser, I wouldn't have had any problem. I used to love him so much. Any time I met him, my heart would beat so hard, I'd tremble and go pale.

This went on for a while, but then he started shunning me, for he noticed that *kanketer* (I was getting carried away). If I waited to see him, he'd try to avoid me. I still don't know what was in his mind. I used to enter the classroom with my heart beating, beating so hard, until I'd faint and see the teacher spinning around me, and then I'd start throwing up. [Really!] I wouldn't realize what had happened until I opened my eyes in the hospital room with the *serum* (Fr.: IV fluid) and all that hospital stuff. It happened to me two times, as if I was in a trance. I started trembling and my heart beating and I ended up crying. . . . I was afraid, really afraid, and kept crying, I'd keep crying all the time. [What were you afraid of?] I didn't have the slightest idea what I was afraid of, but I knew I needed something, that *naqsni shi ḥaja* (I lacked something), but I didn't know what was wrong with me. (Story 7)

I had been like that for quite some time, and then I quit school. They made me quit school in March and go into a hospital. They did some *analyses* (Fr.: tests) and found nothing. I came out of the hospital feeling quite well. . . . I went back to school for a week, but as soon as I saw him, everything came back again. I hated him because he didn't change a bit and kept running away from me. So I couldn't stand him anymore. I hated him and hated the school, too. As soon as I saw him, everything came back again: I'd start throwing up, I'd faint and then find myself in the hospital again. Farid always had to take me to the hospital. But this time things worsened. I started losing my hair and eyelashes. My skin peeled and I was losing weight. (Story 8)

Her account of her treatment grows even more confusing:

I was in the hospital again, and they told me I had *goitre* (Fr.: goiter),[2] and because of a nervous breakdown, when I got depressed, it starts swelling. They said I needed an operation, that the goiter weakened me and caused all that to happen. I left the hospital and told them I didn't want an operation.

Farid and my sister took me to a hospital in Casablanca. I had a temperature of 40 degrees, so they told them she has typhoid. They put me in the hospital with people who have typhoid. I nearly caught typhoid. I didn't really have typhoid. Then Fadila told them she knew a doctor in Rabat, so they took me to Rabat. I had a radiograph made of my heart and all that stuff.

A doctor came to see me and asked me questions to find out what I was suffering from. Never had any doctor asked me such questions before. I stayed in the hospital, and that doctor was the only one to take care of me. I'll never forget him: he would ask everybody to get out of my room, and he'd ask me to tell him how things started, how I felt, and all that. I'd tell him everything. At the beginning, I didn't want to tell him anything, but afterwards I told him everything from A to Z. He asked me to forget and started bringing me books, a tape recorder, pictures, and always kept telling me that if I could forget what happened to me, that then I'd get over it. Things started getting better little by little, and I got out of the hospital. (Story 8)

Marriage

Khadija came back to Ouarzazate, but the principal at first refused to let her reenroll in school, even with all of the medical *certificats* [Fr.] she produced:

> They said Khadija had been three months pregnant, and her family took her to Casablanca to get rid of the baby. [Who said that?] Everyone did. The whole town was spreading this rumor. It was the principal who said that: "I threw her out because she was pregnant." When I'd greet somebody, they'd touch my belly like this to see if I was still pregnant. I got so sick of all that. I kept hearing that talk, and I couldn't even go outdoors, I couldn't talk to anybody. I became afraid of people and the way they looked at me and kept saying she was pregnant. They still do, I still hear that. It was hard to accept, but now I just don't care. (Story 9)
>
> So I repeated the year, and passed to the tenth grade year and then to the eleventh grade, and I failed again and quit school, and went to the vocational training center . . . and studied to become a secretary, but I only stayed six months. I didn't like that either, and two years seemed too long. So I quit and kept thinking about things. But then there was another problem to be solved. Do you know the Kabiris, that big merchant family in Taliouine? Their daughter was a friend of mine in school, and they have a son who works in their store now. When I visited them, their mother would tell her daughter that Khadija is a nice and pretty girl, we have to marry her to my son Hassan. He didn't know I existed at that time. I met him once at his sister's marriage. So when I went back to school, he went to see his mother and told her that he wanted to marry that girl, and *ṣafi.*
>
> But there was another problem. There was a soldier who was studying engineering at the school, who'd come up to us and talk to me. They lived next door, and we'd walk together to school. One day somebody went to see Farid and told him that your sister is having an affair. Farid told my mother, and my father came and told me that if I wanted to study, I could study. If I didn't want to study, I should stay at home. "We allowed you to go to school, but not to go with that soldier," and this and that. Things went too far, and they made a big deal of it. I was so upset, ready to explode, and I didn't know what to do. Then Kabiri's son came and told me, "We'll get married, but you'll stay on at school until you graduate." So we agreed on that.
>
> I didn't like him, we didn't have any relationship, we'd never seen each other. I agreed because I had a problem. I didn't think it over. I had a problem, and I wanted to get away from my family. I thought by marrying him, we'd find a solution. During the school

break in March, the Kabiris came to Taznakht and made out the marriage contract. When the holiday was over, I told him that I had to go back to school. . . . He told his mother he didn't want me to study, he didn't want any wedding celebration at all. He just wanted me to take my belongings and join him. So his mother came to see my mother and told her they didn't want to celebrate the wedding, that they just wanted me with them. My mother told her everything was up to me. So I packed all my belongings and went to Taliouine.

I settled in there like a woman who'd been married for a long time. For the first week they were nice to me. Then everyone *ban ᶜla ḥaqiqtu* (showed his real self), and I became aware of their tricks, one by one. His mother was *khayba bezaf gaᶜ* (really, really wicked). It was a big household, and there was a lot of work to do. She'd come into the kitchen and look over my shoulder and say that's not a good job, or she'd knock over everything and make us start all over again. She was even worse than my mother. She also said horrible things. She really gave me a hard time. (Story 10)

Divorce

Once I was visiting my family in Taznakht, and I went to a celebration at the youth center with my brothers Farid and Ahmad. But some of their friends went to see Hassan and told him I was with two guys. That day he was supposed to get me, but he didn't. I finally heard from him two weeks later when my father went to see them. They said, "How could she go with guys at night while she was married?" But Ahmad was there! My father told me to go back to Taliouine in spite of all this.

She went back, but her mother-in-law "treated me like a housemaid" and forced her to do long days of "really hard work." She went to her family and announced she wanted a divorce, she but got no sympathy:

Nobody helped me. My father told me if I got a divorce, I should go to some other place on my own. My mother told me to *ṣber* (be patient/endure it). She said her life wasn't any better: "It had been the same with your father, but I was patient, so you have to be patient, too. Life is not what you might think." This is very important. I cried my head off. I had a good cry and went back with him to Taliouine and put up with everything.

One day when she stayed in bed ill, her mother-in-law got fed up and told her, "There's something between you, you have to separate. You've gone too far. This is too much for us." Khadija didn't answer and went back to sleep. Hassan withdrew: "he stopped talking to me. When we went to bed, he would stay away from me, and *ma wṣelnish* (he wouldn't have sex with me).³ When I talked to him, he'd only give a nod; he wouldn't answer me at all." He took her home for "two or three days" to "sort out the problems," but when he dropped her off, he told her he had finalized their divorce three days earlier.

> I didn't know what happened to me after that. I went out of my mind. It was a good thing, but I couldn't accept it. I found the whole thing weird: I'd been divorced for three days and I didn't know it. I stayed like that. Fadila would come to me and try to calm me down and comfort me. They sent me the rest of my belongings. I didn't see him anymore.
>
> [Had you ever talked about your lives together?] We didn't think about that. We only talked about the marriage and the marriage certificate. That was all we talked about. I never, ever thought or saw how my life would be with him. The day we got married, I regretted it. When I signed the marriage certificate, I started crying because I'd never thought about getting married before, never, ever. Then I found myself married. I wanted to run away from school. I was fed up with it, and all the talk at home, too. I didn't know where to go. (Story 11)

To Casablanca

A week after her divorce, Khadija took flight again. She moved in with relatives in Casablanca and enrolled in a secretarial school. She was twenty.

> I got away from all the quarrels, but other problems sprang up in Casa, especially with my uncle, who was a fundamentalist. It was that veil again. He had a long beard, and I wasn't allowed to greet a man. I wasn't allowed to wear pants or show my hair. My uncle and his wife, they were all like that. When a man knocked at the door, a man had to open the door for him, and you had to hide to let him in. I did all that, but I was only acting. I didn't believe in it. I'd wear a djellaba and put on two veils. [Really!] I swear by God. And I wore stockings and said *salem ᶜlikoum* (may peace be upon you) rather than *ṣbaḥ l-khir* (good morning).⁴ I was only pretending, it was a lie.
>
> I didn't believe in that. I respect myself: I don't lie, I don't steal, I don't speak ill of other people. I respect myself. I can't say I'm without any faults, I just don't believe in that. But I had to put up with it. Then I'd go over to my other uncle's, and things were softer there. I'd put on trousers. . . . I had two years of hard times until I graduated and came back here and got a job at the Club Med. (Story 12)
>
> I had other problems at the Club Med, but I could handle them. The people there had no respect. All of them were *comique* (Fr.: ridiculous). It was a problem just to ask somebody something at work,

because he'd try to date me, and I couldn't get rid of him: "You could come to my place, I live alone." I was patient/endured, but then the boss came on to me, too, the *directeur general* [Fr.]. That's the big problem I've been having in my life. That's why I don't like it here. It's *pire* (Fr.: worse) for a girl.

You always have to be on your guard. A girl can't defend herself. Even if you go to the grocery store, people harass/shout at you. But what's important to me are my principles and *'akhlaq* (moral character). Everybody has his own principles, and that's something I respect, I have regard for respectable people, but you can't have that respect. [She cites a proverb:] "If they can't approach you, they'll speak ill of you." This is a big problem.

After I divorced, I wanted to have another relationship with some other man, but I couldn't do that. You can't have a relationship *choisir* (Fr.: of your choosing). It's very difficult. Everybody has the right to have a relationship for *échange* (Fr.: companionship), but that's a problem here. I'm talking about affection. [You're looking for love.] *Voilà*. I haven't been able to find someone who will be as nice to me as I am nice to him. Maybe I don't make the right choices, but it's very hard to make any choice in Ouarzazate. This is getting very difficult: I'm twenty-four and still without a man.

[It's hard to be alone.] That's what I really miss, and sometimes I feel lonely. I read books, but I get bored and I don't know what to do. I smoke, but that's not a solution. But the first day you meet somebody in Ouarzazate, even if it's an innocent relationship, he invites you home. You can tell what he's up to. He doesn't care to know you. They don't care if you're nice or bad.

I had a relationship in Casablanca, but I didn't stay there very long. We kept in touch, phoned, and wrote letters, but then we broke up. In Casa, things were easier than here. You can meet someone and have a drink in a café and talk to him. You're not afraid. If you talk to somebody here, everybody knows it immediately. You don't know what'll become of you. You're always afraid. (Story 13)

I've Never Had What I Wanted

Sensing that Khadija had brought her life up to date, I asked how she sees her future:

I want my life to be different. I don't want to live *superlux* (Fr.: wealthy), but *quand même* (Fr.: then again), why not? [laughing] I want a great change, to *nqi* (clean/purify) my life, because my life hasn't been as I wished since childhood. We're a big family, and nobody gets a good salary. You want to live a *moderne* [Fr.] life, and dress *moderne* [Fr.], eat with a fork and sit around a table, but you can't do those things. I think all about this, but I can't fulfill it in my parents' home, not unless I get away from them. I haven't had any good time so far, even when I was a kid. I've never had what I wanted.

When I was a little girl I never played with *jouet* (Fr.: toys) like the other kids; we didn't have any. . . . I couldn't go to a park like all the kids, or see anything, *jamais* (Fr.: never)! *Surtout* (Fr.: above all), my mother limited me, ⁽qdetni (she gave me a complex), she didn't allow us to go and play outside. If she caught us playing with other kids, she would beat you. If we'd just [breaks off] I grew up *timide* (Fr.: timid/introverted), but now I'm less *timide* [Fr.] than before. I couldn't look at another person's eyes. You weren't free.

They didn't stimulate us, they didn't encourage you in your life, to be happy, or to be *qafez* (someone who is capable) and gets along well, who knows a lot of things. They wear you out. They start stifling/suppressing you when you're a child. My father and my mother would fight once, twice, three times, and swear at each other like children. You'd wonder what's going on. You'd watch them with shock. It's given me a terrible complex. They'd fight over nothing, because others would say that my father keeps going with girls and with other women. This gossip would come from the women of the neighborhood: *voila*, Brahim did this, Brahim did that. Then they'd start fighting, and she'd pack up her things and go to Casablanca. Do you think this is a life? But they kept having children, eight kids, one following the other, *l-ḥamdulillah* (blessings be to God). And he was only a technician and didn't have a good salary. (Story 14)

Her father drank too much, she says, but he never abused her:

Jamais (Fr.: never). He never beat anybody. He was OK. When my mother beat me, he'd come and tell her to stop, and he'd start calming her down. He'd buy me something or he'd give me some money—that's it. He used to like me a lot more than he liked my brothers and sisters. He'd buy me things and give them to me secretly. He loved me very much. He still loves me very much. He used to be like a friend to us. Even if he didn't understand things, he wouldn't argue with you, like about the way you should live. Still, he's so limited intellectually, he doesn't think about things deeply; he'd play and laugh with you, and that's it. According to them, you were born to eat and to sleep, just *le necessaire* (Fr.: the basics). If you happen to think beyond that, they'd tell you: "What do you want? You eat, you drink, and you sleep, what else do you want?" They don't realize you have other things you think about. They didn't live the way we live today.

My mother was very harsh on us. She beat everybody. Once I had a *cicatrice* (Fr.: scar) because she hit me with a *brochette* (Fr.:

skewer). Can you imagine? It entered here, and blood started to fly from my leg, and I ended up in the hospital. She did the same thing to Farid and he still has a *cicatrice* [Fr.]. She hit him on the head with a pan, and he had to have stitches. She'd beat you and leave you crying on the floor. She'd beat you and bite you and do anything to you. She'd swear at you and use foul language. When I come to think of that language now, I wouldn't dare repeat it. I hated it all! I still hate it! I don't want this; I don't want my life to be like this; I want to have a *differente* [Fr.] life from my mother—from them all! So, if you want to have a different life, you need to get away from them. (Story 15)

I asked if she recalled feeling frightened, angry, or *timide* when her mother beat her:

I was afraid of her. I wouldn't do anything. When I was twelve or thirteen, I'd think about running away. If somebody had come and wanted to take me with him, I would have run away with him. I thought very much about that. I thought about death or suicide. I thought about something to enable me to get away from them. [Really!] I thought about committing suicide several times. I thought about killing myself several times, not once, not twice. You needed something to get you away from them. I still have this idea in my mind that I want to get away from them.

Khadija says her older sister and brother have resigned themselves and no longer flee or resist. I ask what makes her different, and she angrily explains that her modern Casablanca relatives had shown her a different life:

I saw how my uncle's children were living. He had a good position in a company, and his wife had a good position, too. They had a car. They had a comfortable life, and they had only three children. Look: if your father is a technician and your mother's unemployed and you have eight kids and you live in the countryside! When we go and stay with them, you see how their kids play. Their parents take them to the beach and show them around the *parc* [Fr.]. You see how they eat, you see their bedrooms: everything is OK. But you have nothing! I don't know what to tell you. We had one blanket, we slept one next to the other and used the same blanket for all of us. But they have their own bedrooms. And all this made me think about us, about the way we lived when we came back to Taznakht. [speaking angrily] (Story 15)

[What did you try to do at home to get away from the beatings and quarrels?] I wouldn't do anything. She'd beat you, but I couldn't do anything. [Did you think of anything?] I'd picture myself in some place without my mother and my father. I'd dream about living with a family I'd found, with a man and a woman who raised me, and I had become well off. I'd get a good education and I'd have everything I wanted—that's what I would think about. . . . But that was all a dream. (Story 16)

[What about when you went to school?] I didn't like school. I was afraid of being beaten. I was afraid to not know how to read. When I learned how to write, I liked school. I did well until the fifth grade, when I repeated. And I did well again until the fourth grade, and then I became lazy. [They beat you at school?] Yes, they did. I used to get beaten a lot at school. The teachers were ancient and very strict. Yeah, I got beaten a lot. I went by force. I didn't like it. I cried sometimes. I was afraid to go back home and tell them I didn't want to go to school. It was better to go to school than to stay at home. It was worse at home, as my mother would beat me. I'd rather stay overnight at school than go back home and face my mother's shouting. My classmates had different lives with their mothers, and I'd tell them they were lucky. If I could have exchanged my mother for another, we would have.

[Did your mother encourage you to go to school?] Yeah, she did. She was educated. She used to teach us the letters of the alphabet with a stick. [With a stick?] She always taught us with a stick. I was afraid when she'd ask me to bring my books and sit beside her. [Really!] I was really afraid. Even if she was like that, she wanted us to be educated. But she was a problem; she was so harsh on us. (Story 17)

Ravings and Seizures

I asked Khadija if she ever recalled her mother happy:

Sometimes she was happy, but it wouldn't last long enough. A half hour of happiness would mean that the two hours that followed would be *le contraire* (Fr.). She'd start shouting and tearing off her clothes until she became sick. We'd put cold water on her, and blood would come flying from her mouth until she woke up again with a terrible headache. If I had a fight with my sister, she'd start shouting, "Why are they doing this to me?" She'd pull at her hair and tear off her clothes.

[What did they say about her fits?] I don't know. [Was it something to do with her brain?] It may have been her brain. When she screamed, she'd pull at her hair and rip off her clothes. She'd bite her tongue and bleed afterward. She'd become strained, and she'd fall down and start trembling for quite a long time. [Was it maybe something to do with *jnoun* (spirits)?] Maybe *jnoun*, or they would say *mselmin* (submission to spirits). [What was your mother's idea about it?] She would think she had a *crise* (Fr.: fit). She knew what was going on, but she was skeptical, she didn't believe in superstitious practices. But when they'd tell her that my father had gone out with other women, I recall that she'd throw some sorcery on him. [Did she ever take medicine?] She never took anything. She didn't even go see a doctor. We'd only use incense or pour cold water on her. She'd wriggle and then could stop. [Who would help her?] We helped her. We'd try to bring her under control, but she'd be lifted up, she'd become a stranger at that moment. . . .

She tried to educate us, to raise us well so we'd be better than the children in our neighborhood. We were *étrangers* (Fr.: strangers) to them. My mother was envious, and she wanted to be better off and to have a lot more things than those people. She'd do all she could to get whatever she wanted. But she was wrong in her doings. She couldn't get anything positive from us the way she used to treat us. She didn't understand that she had to be more lenient than she was. She'd beat you whether you were wrong or not! She'd beat me, and I'd keep quiet. But when I grew older and became aware that I didn't do anything to get beaten, I started hating her, really! I didn't want to put up with that any more. (Story 18)

As a child, she says, she sang love songs to take her mind off her troubles:

When I was young, I liked Abd El Hakim and Andalusian music. I used to sing his songs whenever I was washing the clothes or the dishes, I was always singing Abd el Hakim's songs with him. [What did he sing about?] *l-ᶜṭifa* (love/passion), *dima l-ᶜṭifa* (always love/passion). He was very emotional/romantic. . . . When I'd sing my mother would remind me, "You're going to get married." I used to think, "I'm going to get married and become like my mother." I was ten or eleven at that time, and I'd think of marriage, that I'm going to become like my mother. I was waiting for that youth, a handsome/dashing young man who sweeps one away. When will he come? When will he appear? I was always waiting for him to turn up instead of looking for him. I'd always dream about some nice, tall, handsome youth who'd show up. But that was just a dream that never came true. So I'd keep singing to get over it.

Then she turned to writing:

I kept singing until the fifth grade, and then I started writing. [What did you write?] I've spent all my life writing. I kept a diary full of things from the fifth grade on. I wrote everything, good or bad. I'd jot down anything, any idea I had in mind. Once my mother found my diary, and she read it and burned it up. She thought I'd written bad things about her. It was all true. I didn't lie about anything I was writing. She asked me why I was keeping a diary, and she beat me. But I wasn't discouraged, and I started all over again. If she beat me, I'd immediately take a pen and write down everything I'd been through. I'd cry, but I liked to take my pen and write down everything as if I were talking to someone, to unburden my heart. It was a way to escape it all. (Story 19)

Two Khadijas

A few days later, Khadija arrived for the second interview saying, "I couldn't wait to see you. I was thinking about what I'd say, and what I didn't say." She began:

I want to talk about another aspect I didn't mention before: *dima sekta* (I'm always a very quiet person). I don't like getting involved in anything, *comme on dit, la solitude* (Fr.: as one says, solitude/loneliness). [Do you like being alone?] Yes, I like being alone very much. I don't like talking to people. I like being alone. I've tried to get rid of this matter/problem. I'm trying to get more involved with other people. I haven't liked to mix with other girls, or anybody else. Even at school I had this problem—I'd never participate in the classroom. I'd write about everything I couldn't talk about. Even if I was at a wedding or something, I'd go some place and sit alone and keep quiet. I can't tolerate the noise and bustle. [How do you feel then?] It makes me dizzy. I get all confused, and I can't figure out what people are telling me about. All I want is to get away from that noise. I feel more relaxed when I'm alone.

[What do you think of when you're alone?] Even when I'm alone, I still feel like I'm in the middle of a *groupe* [Fr.] of people, and like I'm not in a quiet place at all. At that moment, I get involved in a *ḥiwar* (dialogue/dispute) with myself. I keep asking and answering myself, like what are we doing now? It's like I separate myself in two parts, I become like two personalities, like there are two Khadijas. I question myself about any subject and get angry with myself. (Story 21)

For instance, if I go out and meet somebody, somebody who's not nice and I shouldn't talk to him because he's not on my level, but I talk to him and laugh with him. I don't feel anything at that moment, but when I get back home, I concentrate on things and I start *kanʿateb* (blaming/scolding) myself and I *ʿitab* (insult) myself. And I swear at him and tell him off *au même temps* (Fr.: at the same time). *Kannaqeḍ* (I contradict myself). I say, "That person isn't proper, I shouldn't talk to him. So then why did I talk to him?" I keep swearing at myself, and I regret that I did it. Whatever I do, afterward there'll be an argument between the two Khadijas. The two of them speak, *deux personnes* (Fr.: two people), one answering the other. *Donc* (Fr.: so), if I hadn't talked to him, people wouldn't say anything. But I keep saying to myself that there's nothing wrong with talking to a person. This is what happens inside me. I ought to talk to somebody else about it, but I don't. If I don't write about all this, I keep thinking about it all the time.

[How would you describe these two personalities?] *Voilà*, the two personalities are different. One is *qwia zyada* (much stronger) than the other, and it's that personality which insults, which blames, which tells off. So there's one personality that is the quiet and *dˤifa* (weak) Khadija, and the other one's the *qwia* (strong/powerful) Khadija. The strongest Khadija knows how to handle the problems and understands everything. But there is the other Khadija who is the opposite. If I fail an exam, that Khadija who is weak keeps quiet, but the stronger one comes up and tells the other one: if you had studied hard, you wouldn't have failed, and it keeps *katˤayer* (insulting/abusing her). Then the other one keeps quiet.

[Does the weaker Khadija argue with the other one?] She has nothing to say, actually. She does say something, but the other one doesn't trust her, because she always does right and the other one always makes mistakes. So the other one doesn't say anything— understand?—because the lonely personality does wrong but doesn't realize it until she sits alone and thinks about it: I made a mistake and this and that, and it becomes a dialogue, then there are two personalities. (Story 22)

I asked when she first recalled having inner dialogues, and she said, "I've always been talking to myself," at least since she began elementary school:

From elementary school on, I was having that matter/problem. . . . From the first day, I remember I'd always be in some corner, leaning against the wall, watching the other girls, especially the daughters of the important families who were so well dressed and formed a kind of *clique* [Fr.]. I couldn't go play with anyone, those girls. Or even if I was sitting alone, it's like I'm not really alone, I'd keep thinking about those girls, I'd wonder how is it that they, *donc* (Fr.: therefore), maybe they're more intelligent, I don't know, *gaˤ* (at all), how is it that they're different from me? And *kanḥger* (I'd belittle myself). I'd belittle myself and fall from my level—as if I didn't have any *mustawa* (level/standing), any *ḍamir* (conscience), and I'd just stay like that. I'd try to encourage myself to go and get to know those girls, to feel free and play with them.

[The stronger personality would say that?] Yes. The weaker one always, *raḥ*, stays always sitting quietly/still, it's always *khasra* (a failure), and she doesn't know anything. I'd say, no, I must go and play with them, I'd really try to go talk to them, but I couldn't. I'd always find them above me, like they don't care about me the way I do for them, like it's not reciprocal. [How did they treat you?] Like I'm invisible to them, *ga^c* (completely). Like I'm someone *zayda naqṣa* (totally lacking), like I'm invisible to them. From that problem—I was seven or eight or nine—it was from that *age* [Fr.] that I've been alone/lonely. (Story 23)

She often knew answers to her teachers' questions before her classmates, but couldn't bring herself to say them: "I was frightened. I was like I wasn't certain about the answer, and I'd hesitate. I'd have the answer, exactly, but when he'd call on me, *ṣafi*, I wouldn't know what to say. I'd get all confused" (Story 24). It was her ninth-grade biology teacher who noted the discrepancy between her written work and her silence in class and began "experimenting"—testing her orally and then in writing on the same material—and encouraging her to speak. Other teachers just told her she was *kasoula* (stupid/dunce) because she couldn't answer them. "They wouldn't try to understand *nefsia* (my personality)," she said. "I felt that *naqeṣ* (lack/inadequacy) a lot."

Apocalypse

Just a week ago, she says, an incident occurred that threw her into inner argument:

My uncle's daughter came from Casablanca, and *une groupe* [Fr.] of us went to the Club Med's discotheque. Everyone was dancing, and I got up, too, and danced a little, and then all of a sudden, I felt like someone had grabbed me, understand? I felt like dizziness had grabbed me, and I went to a corner and sat down, and did like this [putting her head in her hands], and kept watching them.

My cousin and some of the others came over to me and asked me to get up, but I no longer wanted to get up. *tqelleb ^cndi l-jow* (My mood flipped/changed), I was no longer in the mood to dance. I got a headache and I went to the *toilet* [Fr.] and washed my face and held my head like this, and just asked, when are we going to leave? *Ṣafi*, I no longer liked that scene at all, and I stayed in the corner by myself until we left.

[What do you think happened to you?] Like someone told me I no longer wanted to dance, and quickly everything changed/flipped over. I was having fun, and then dancing seemed to have no meaning. [Did you feel like you were doing something shameful or improper?] It's like I regretted what I was doing. I regretted it. I didn't understand it at all. I didn't understand those *les choses* (Fr.: those things). I was dancing and laughing with them, that is, it was *normale* [Fr.], I danced, just for *une demi heur* (Fr.: a half hour), and suddenly I felt tired and light-headed, and suddenly it was all ugly, all that in front of me was ugly, it no longer appeared *zwin* (cool/appealing). It all looked ugly—so why are you dancing?

At first, I saw *la danse* [Fr.], *ou bien* the music, *ou bien,* the movement, *comme une sorte du drogue* (Fr.: like a kind of drug), something that *katherbek* (helps you escape), that *katbeʿdek* (gets you away from) [trails off]. I was *se defoulée* (Fr.: enjoying myself), *voilà, kanconcentra* (Fr. and Arabic: I was trying hard) to change the *l-jow* (mood/atmosphere). You may try to get away from something, but *au même temps* (Fr.: at the same time) in the middle of all that, I saw that those problems, that mood/atmosphere that I was in, *raḥ,* would come back again, that after *une demi heur* (Fr.: a half hour), or *une heur* [Fr.], or *deux heures* [Fr.], or that *journée* (Fr.: day), that thing [the enjoyment] will pass. You can't stay in it forever. After all, it's something superficial, it's like I was lying to myself, and I had to go back to the reality that I was in *justement, voilà* (Fr.: that I was *really* in). I never know when it [her problems] will come back to me; then I keep thinking, *voilà,* therefore I have to confront all these problems. I have to face a lot of things.

I keep debating this with myself: my job isn't good; life—what's life? *ca veut dire quoi l-ḥayat* (Fr. and Arabic: what's the meaning of life)? And in addition, life is limited: I'm waiting for the day of death, *voilà, comme ça* (Fr.: here, like this), you'll die. So I shouldn't laugh/enjoy myself because I'm going to die—that's the way I think. I eat food, that is, *la nouriture* [Fr.], I eat in order to please/satisfy *la stomach* [Fr.], *c'est tout* (Fr.: that's all). I don't eat because the food has any taste. I eat, *parfois* (Fr.: sometimes) I eat only because I'm hungry and for *la corps* (Fr.: the body) to stand up and move—and I don't really enjoy it. And I keep thinking of the end, there is an end, and *on ne sait jamais* (Fr.: one never knows when): right now, who knows, I may die—and that *film* [Fr.] keeps passing/playing in front of my eyes.

[What did you think about when you were sitting alone at the disco?] The idea that fell on my mind, I kept holding my head and looking around at the lights and all that, and I pictured all of it crashing down, everything, that's what I thought, *comme un tremblement de terre* (Fr.: like an earthquake), you know? That's what I thought, *donc,* like that, *un tremblement de terre* (Fr.: an earthquake), that everything would blow up but nothing would happen to me: I'd stay like that, I'd watch it all and see how people would die, and how all the lights would fall down and shatter. Everybody would die, and the mood/atmosphere would be different. People who were laughing and happy would be suddenly crying! And after a little while *les pompiers* (Fr.: the firemen) would come and the police—that's what I thought of. I said this one will be lying here and that one lying there, the bottles of liquor will be there. That is, what's this all about? Why don't people think about that matter, and sit lamenting?

I got angry and regretted that I'd danced. It didn't mean anything to dance, that's what I thought of at that time. When I sat alone, I watched people jumping up and down and I thought *koulshi msṭi, koulshi ḥmeq* (they were all crazy). . . . Why didn't they think of anything better to do than dance? Why don't they think of things like I do? They should be sorry instead of dancing. Why dancing? It doesn't mean anything (i.e., it has no value). They should be thinking about people who are starving, instead, or about *civilisation* [Fr.], what people have achieved. But they were only dancing and getting drunk and falling one upon the other. They should think of reality first and analyze things before dancing. I think things are related to each other, there's nothing *apart* [Fr.].

And that dancing, for me it was gross/ugly, an error—they're making an error, and that's why they got what they deserved. Like if all that crashed down upon them, and it was I who stayed from them in safety. Nothing happened to me, I only watched them. (Story 25)

Sometimes other cataclysmic scenes come suddenly upon her:

I picture a lot of things, for example, the flood. The flood would come and *kaygad denya* (demolish/level/set right the whole world). I always think of that. I'd also think about war. I'd always be afraid, and always when I sleep, I'd dream of a war, and I'd scream and see soldiers and I'd hear gunfire—everything would run past my eyes. I'd sometimes daydream those things while I'd walk along the street, and I'd be very scared. If I'm alone in my bedroom and think about that, I get frightened.

Sometimes when I'm busy cleaning up or washing the clothes, all of a sudden I'll recall somebody told me a story about *jnoun* (devils/spirits) or some woman who was *sheduha jnoun* (seized by spirits) because she threw hot water in the sink. So whenever I throw hot water in the sink, I get scared because of what I've been told. I'll be anxious the whole day, waiting for the *jnoun* to come out, or for something else to happen to me, like somebody following me with a knife in his hand. But that's all imaginary. I'm always frightened. I guess I live more in an imaginary world than in a real one?

[How so?] For example, if something doesn't work out well, I keep replaying the *cassette* [Fr.]. Then I try to go several years back, and I picture myself still young and we've become well off. I have my own bedroom, and we've traveled abroad by plane. I'd say all this to myself as if it's true. I enjoy this because it makes me feel a little happier. If I'm *mqelqa* (anxious/depressed), it gives me a kind of *'infijar* (relief/release; *f* * *j* * *r* is also the root of "flood" and "explosion"). [What do you mean, *'infijar*?] It's like pouring water every day into a glass, and when it's full, it overflows—that's *'infijar*. If you beat me with a stick every day, I'll end up killing myself or running away—therefore, that's *'infijar*.

Instead, I dream about having a *nqia* (cleaner/better) life. If I see a girl in a magazine I'm reading, or if some girl comes over and she lives a better life, or if I see a movie or television show or if I go to the cinema and I see a girl about my age who is better off, therefore I keep thinking about her. I think that girl is me, that girl is Khadija. So I go back to my imagination, that's what we call a kind of *'infijar* (release/relief) because I can't live that way. I can't afford a car or a moped, but at least I can in my imagination. Therefore, I *nfijer* and give my imagination free rein. I picture myself driving a car or going back to my *villa* [Fr.] and receiving my servant. I live all this for a while, maybe two or three hours.

Each time it's something different, and each time I have a different personality. Sometimes I don't live in Morocco any longer: I'm in Europe, for example, I live in Europe with the Europeans and I speak French; even the language I speak is different, I won't speak Arabic anymore. I'd also dream in French, no more Arabic. I'd be alone, living the way I always wanted, like a European. I'd come back to my *apartement* [Fr.] and I'd cook whatever I wanted in a European style. I'd forget I'm Moroccan, and that I'm Muslim. *Voilà*, this is one point. So when I have this fantasy, I see myself like a European, living alone and smoking in the street. I don't have to fear anybody like I do here when I smoke—I'm afraid somebody will see me—so I smoke without fearing anybody. I dress the way I want. I receive my friends. *Voilà*, that's it.

When this happens to me, I'll regret it at the same time, because it's all imaginary: I shouldn't have thought that. I'll say, "I'm Khadija. I'm Moroccan." I'll come back to Islam, to the Quran and what it says. I'll come back to that talk: they tell you that death is real, that God exists, and that God will punish you. Therefore, I'll say I must have nothing to do with all that. Why should I think about it? *Kansare* (I'd struggle/quarrel) with myself. I don't know the good from the bad: shall I pray and fast and worship God? But if I pray and fast, I mustn't live alone—this is what Islam says. I mustn't greet men. So I try to strike all that [her imaginary world], to get it out of my mind, and again, I'd live like a Muslim. This is the struggle I've been through up until now with myself. [long pause]

I've been living a *sare nefsi* (struggle with myself). The matter is between Islam and not Islam. I think I should live life in my own way, or in a way that gives me tranquility/relief, and when I have that dream, it's like I've been through it in reality and I feel a kind of relief/

tranquility. But, *au même temps* (Fr.: at the same time), I also regret within myself, because of Islam. I think about the Quran, and death, and God, *voilà*. God says this and that and other things, and when I come to think of it all, I find it the opposite of that, of my dream/fantasy that gives me some relief/tranquility.

When I put my head down to go to sleep at night, I put down a European one; I put down a Muslim one and a *nasraniya* (Christian one). I try to choose between the two: this one says this, the other one says that, but I end up in the middle, not knowing which side to follow. (Story 26)

Contrasts of tradition versus modernity shape the identities of all the young Moroccans I interviewed and often take on the character of French versus Moroccan or Western versus Muslim. But Khadija was the most extreme in explicitly describing herself as living in a state of war between "two selves," one European and one Moroccan. By her own account, she experiences both as having an intrusive quality: whichever "personality" she seeks to live, the other forces itself on her. When she has tried to live by proper and modest Moroccan standards, she has found herself unable to check her attraction to men and her cravings for "relationships." Yet when she tries to exercise her right to European-style independence and love affairs, she finds herself suddenly terrified by images of apocalypse and sickened by modernity's seeming insignificance when cast against ultimate questions of death and divine judgment. One can see admirable strength in her struggle to claim her freedom and rights, but once the inner dialogue gets underway, she feels the European Khadija to be the weaker, *timide*, easily silenced one and the accusing, insulting Muslim Khadija to be the stronger one. And perhaps it is: in a later interview she explains that in spite of knowing "many means" to give and receive sexual pleasure, she remains a virgin. She has tried to perform intercourse, she says, but tension, pain, and thoughts of sin have rendered her unable to complete the act, even during her brief marriage—and she reiterates that she is afflicted with a serious "complex" about sex. She makes it clear that she regards the European Khadija as her truer, more authentic self, but she also leaves no doubt that neither the "Arab" men in her milieu, nor her family, nor the Moroccan Khadija seated deep within her psyche will grant her the freedom to live as she wishes.

To explore Khadija's personalities, I first examine how she portrays her world and her family and then turn to a set of emotional themes that suggest that the core level of her personality entails oscillating states characteristic of "trauma-related syndromes." Then I discuss her struggle with exposure versus concealment, which appears as an internalization of the region's honor-modesty system, shaping the social persona level of her personality organization. Finally, I return to the discourses by which she gives voice to Moroccan and European identities.

Men

Khadija says she seeks "an honorable relationship" in a world of pervasive harassment, intimidation, gossip, and betrayal. Her girlhood attractions to boys stayed in bounds until her ninth grade crush on a teacher that brought on *la crise* and ended her dream of studying at the university. Her "relationship" with the soldier while in secretarial school, her quick divorce amid rumors that she had flirted with other men, and her job at the Club Med all amplified her reputation as a young woman of loose morals. At the Club Med, she says, male employees immediately came on to her, and when she couldn't get the *directeur* to stop making advances or interfering with her work, she quit. Now she regrets her decision, as harassment at the bank where she works has become even worse. The director tried flattery and then bribes to get her to become his *maîtresse*, and he bumps or brushes her whenever he passes. The chief accountant tried flattery and then blackmail, claiming he had snapshots of her naked he would share around town, until she called his bluff (Stories 71 and 114).

> So what are you going to do to him? I just lowered my head and shut up. I knew what he was up to, because I'd closed the door on him. There's a saying: "When the cat doesn't find any meat, he'll say it's rotten." It can't get to the meat, so it starts saying it's rotten, it stinks. . . . Arabs! I swear to God, if I could have some other nationality, I'd do it. How can I live with these animals, with this dog? (Story 74)

Whenever she walks into the street, she weathers more harassment:

> That's the most onerous, repugnant thing that I have to deal with. Everyone has something to say: one calls/courts you with some flattery, someone else with something *khayba* (dirty/ugly). When I go by a café and it's full of the servants of God, I need cotton balls for my ears! I don't know what to do! . . . Someone will tell you some ugly words: *bint zenqa* (streetwalker), or something like that that cuts/wounds you, that touches your feelings. *Alors*, do you go fight with him? Do you go insult him? What are you going to do with him? You have nothing you can do with him. They're just street dogs, street dogs. (Story 115)

Sometimes Khadija talks back; usually she keeps silent and tries to walk by. As she says, it can be dangerous to fight:

> I fight, with a lot of them: *kaṇḍor fih* (I'll get up at him) and keep insulting/cursing him. And he'll grab you and let you go, he'll to do something to you, or spit on you, or stab you. *Alors*, this matter is

especially bad in Casablanca, it's very dangerous. You'll find girls who've been cut with a knife. The guys will tell you some *ḥḍera* (words/talk), and you turn your head like this, lower your head, and keep going. What words I've heard, and lowered my head and gone by. (Story 115)

Rachida avoids this world of men. She stays in her house, covers herself conservatively when she has to go out, and her piety and propriety protect her at school. Khadija claims public freedoms and rarely finds herself free from hisses, words, touches, and threats.

Family

Khadija goes home to a small apartment she shares with a changing assortment of siblings. Her older brother Farid heads this branch of the family, which means he has responsibility for guarding her honor—and he has threatened men she sees. She contemptuously describes him:

> He's really *taysh* (spacey/up in the air); he doesn't really think about things. *Voilà*, that's Farid. He's got in him *waḥed ghariza* (instinct/vice)—*l-jins* (sex), that's all Farid knows, he only knows sex, *c'est tout* (Fr.: that's all). I can't ask any of my girlfriends over to the house, because I know Farid too well: the minute he sees a girl, even if he doesn't know her, *ṣafi*, he has to see how he can come on to her. And in addition to that, *raḥ*, he's married! He has a wife and a son living in Taznakht, and he's over here fooling around. Every night you find him bringing home a new girl, always. We've always got problems between us.
>
> My parents got him married because of that. They said he'd settle down, but he just got worse. . . . Everything revolves around sex for him. It's a girl every day. *Je suis sûr* (Fr.: I'm certain) he will always stay like that: *ghayb* (absent/empty-headed). I think all Arabs are like that. . . . But if he sees me with somebody, he doesn't want that. He says he has the right to go with girls, but that a girl doesn't. . . . I know where he stands, my brother Farid. (Story 44)

Khadija paints her father in more complex hues. Rumored to be a drinker, hash smoker, and womanizer, she says he and Farid are cut from the same cloth:

> I think if my father were still young, he would do *le même chose, enfin* (Fr.: the same thing) as Farid. I overhear people who come over and tell my mother that *baba* (father) still does all that, too, but, you know, I've never seen him with my own eyes. I still hear that he goes with women in Taznakht. Farid knows what *baba* does, and he laughs at it and accepts it. They're both the same type. (Story 44)

But her father also takes a keen interest in his work and serves the rural villagers with dedication. He never struck her, and he often tried to comfort her with presents after her mother beat her. He grew up in a French-run orphanage, told her the "Christians" treated him better than "Arabs" ever had, and behind her mother's back encouraged her interest in Western styles and her desire to live independently. But he, too, gets upset by her bad reputation and helped push her into her hasty marriage.

When I asked for an early memory of him, she again recalled that he favored her:

> *Baba*, I think good things about him, always. When I was little, he would always buy me some pants or buy me a dress, he would bring them to me. He'd call me first and say, "Here, choose what you want, you're first," and I'd always take the nice one, and then he would give the rest to the others. . . .
>
> Always *baba* was patient/tolerant with us. My mother always screams/shouts. He didn't beat us, he didn't shout/scream at us. *Baba* used to comb my hair, how many times, he would put my school bag on me and take me to school, and at school he'd straighten/arrange my clothes; he'd do a lot of things for me. My mother, no. My mother appeared to me like someone *moqedasa* (sacred) or something, I don't know. But *baba*, on the contrary, I'm fond of him. *Baba* is lovable. My mother isn't. (Story 53)

At the same time, she sees him as lacking sophistication: "He's so limited intellectually. He doesn't think about things deeply: he'd play and laugh with you and that's it." And she often feared he would abandon her and her siblings. She recently wrote about him in her diary, blaming him for her childhood of hardship:

> He'd go away and leave you [pl.], *raḥ, baba* was always removed from my problems. He never caused me any problems, but at the end I said, *donc* (Fr.: therefore), he's the cause of the problems, because he didn't think about things. He just had a lot of children and he couldn't afford it. (Story 69)

Khadija has an older sister, Fadila, who she says was bright, inquisitive, and ambitious until her parents forced her to marry a stranger at the age of fourteen: "He had a good job and a house and a car—my parents agreed out of self-interest/greed. She'd never seen him, she'd never gone out with him, she'd never known him" (Story 42). When Fadila came home from Ouarzazate for a school holiday, they told her the marriage contract had been signed and the date set. Fadila ran away and tried to kill herself by drinking bleach. Her father found her and dragged her back: "*Baba* beat her and brought her back home by force." Her husband treated her well but then got fed up with quarreling and divorced her. Unhappily back home with her daughter, she has turned to religion and berates Khadija for her loose morals. Khadija looks at Fadila's life with dread. She was eight when she watched her beaten into marriage: "I kept crying with her. I'd look at her and cry. It was as if that might be done to me: I, too, would grow up a little, and they'd do that to me too" (Story 42).

Khadija looks at many traditional women's lives with dread, as examples of what might happen to her. Describing how her mother frightened her about sex, she told of an acquaintance's recent wedding in Ouarzazate:

> Picture this: the day when the bride was brought to the groom's house and had entered the room where, you know, she will become a *femme* (Fr.: woman). . . . Are you familiar with the traditions and what people do with the bride's underwear when there is blood on it? [I have heard about it.] So when the bride and groom went into the room, all the girls started singing and playing the drums—as if to say come on do it fast and show us the pants. He never opened the door to them. They both stayed in there until the morning. When his mother walked into the room, she found him sitting in a corner holding one of his fingers. His bride was lying down on the bed and crying. He told his mother that his bride wasn't a virgin. He'd cut his finger and smeared the blood on her pants.
>
> Once he told them that, they all said that she had to go back to her house, that she wasn't worth anything, that she was a bitch. So, they chased her. Could you imagine that? I felt so bad. When she was first brought to his house, she was wearing all white. But when his family kicked her out, they made her wear a black djellaba, black sandals, a black scarf. The poor woman was ushered out by her mother, and the kids were yelling at her. It was a horrible scene. At the end, they took a black earthenware pot and put it on top of the house. It was a horrible scene. (Story 97)

Beatings, Butterflies, Butchers ❧

We cannot treat a life narrative as a historical record, and so we cannot know where and when Khadija accurately describes "real" events. Many of her accounts raise more questions than they answer—especially those about her high school crush and illness, her marriage and divorce, and her troubled "love affairs." Yet it does matter that she sketches a fairly accurate portrait of the forces brought to bear on her in her family milieu and larger social world. We came to know her parents and most of her siblings and do not doubt that her mother verbally and physically abused Khadija and her siblings. Her older brother Ahmad confirmed this to us, and her father also consulted us about his granddaughter's nightmares and bedwetting, which he thought might be due to beatings by Khadija's mother. In this section, I examine a set of emotional themes that weave through Khadija's narrative and suggest that her "complex" indeed resembles a "trauma-related syndrome,"[5] especially in its oscillations of dissociative flight and reexperienced terror. At the same time, these themes show that her flights of imagination—encouraged by her father and fed by modern media—have enabled her to develop a sense of herself as attractive, strong, loving, and potentially loved.

Quarrels and Beatings

When I asked Khadija for her earliest memory, she recalled feelings of "sadness/despair," a "lack of freedom," and that "I was deprived of so many things" (Story 48). I asked for a specific memory, but she still recalled only diffuse feelings: of "intense fear, always drawn/painted in front of me," and of awakening from sleep to the frightening "noise" of her parents' quarreling (Story 49). I pressed her again for a specific incident, and she recalled a terrible fight over her father's affair that ended with both of her parents leaving the house and the children alone. Khadija remembers she had not yet started school:

> We were sleeping all together, and it was winter and rain was falling. . . . He came in about 10 o'clock, and she told him to go back to wherever he had been. I don't know what she was holding in her hand, but she threw it. I jumped out of bed, and we all got up and we were crying—we were all little. She was fighting with my father, and he pushed her and she fell down. We went over to her and tried to console her. She kept shouting and tearing off her clothes and all that, and he turned to her and cursed her and spat on her and left. *Baba* left and we followed him to the door. It was raining so hard you can't imagine it.
>
> That was an incident I'll never forget. We kept crying the whole night, and she kept shouting. She packed her things and went to Casablanca. I don't know who covered us or how we slept. I remember the next day we didn't have any breakfast, we didn't eat at all, because there wasn't anyone there to cook for us. . . . My father finally came back in the afternoon with some food, and a neighbor came over and cooked it for us. When she'd leave at night, we'd go to sleep, and all night long I'd do like this [huddling and shuddering] and keep ahold of my sister. My heart would keep beating, beating, beating, beating, beating—I'd die of fear! And I'd keep waiting for the dawn to break, for the sun to rise. . . .
>
> We didn't know whether we still had a mother and a father, or who was going to take care of us. From that time on, I started taking the responsibility. Even though I was still small and still needed

someone to *igheṭini* (cover/care for me), I had to care for the children. (Story 50)

Then she recalled another incident, of being beaten for knocking over a bowl of olive oil her mother had worked all day to press:

> That's something that made me hate my mother! You understand why I hated her? She scratched/scraped me with her fingernails, and she beat me with a stick. I still have a *cicatrice* (Fr.: scar). I ran away, but she ran after me, hitting me with rocks, and I kept running and running and running. My mother swung the stick and the point went in here, and it was black with rot.
>
> Some women grabbed me and tried to get it out, but they couldn't, and she kept on beating me and scratching/scraping me from here all along, and she bit me and pinched me. I became black all over. She bounced me up and down and up and down until those women grabbed me away. She nearly killed me with the stick. I had to treat that wound for a long time. That's my second memory. . . . I didn't quiet down for the whole day, I kept crying. Finally she came to me and put some medicine on me, but even though she was doing that, she kept on insulting/cursing me. (Story 51)

Her third memory was of her mother hurling a chipped bowl at her older brother Farid:

> He went out into the courtyard, into the mud and dirt, and fell down, and his blood was running down with the rain. He had to have stitches at the hospital. You can still see the scar from here to here. [How did you feel?] I was crying. I can't stand thinking about childhood—it's all been *khayba* (bad/ugly). [I'm sorry.] On the contrary! I've never been able to discuss it with anybody, you understand? . . . We've been through such horrible things! (Story 52)

Khadija actually portrays her estrangement from her mother as going back even further: "I never nursed at the breast. She said she'd give me her breast, and I'd scream and refuse to take it. I always took the *biberon* (Fr.: bottle)" (Story 59).

She repeatedly describes herself as an easily frightened, skittish child, who awakened each day in fear. She recalls feeling terrified by her mother's whispering of the dawn prayer: "It'd be four in the morning and still dark, and I didn't know what was going on. I was so frightened. You start to imagine it's somebody or some demon standing over your head" (Story 90). In response to the sentence completion stem "When she was little," she wrote, "*kathashem bezaf* (she was really shy/modest) and frightened" (Story 118), which she explained:

> I was *timide* [Fr.], I couldn't start a conversation with anyone. I'd be afraid of anything, if someone just spoke loudly, I'd do like this

[shows startle and ducking response]. I'd jump, I'd be afraid. I'd hear thunder, and I'd be afraid. I couldn't stay by myself in the room, I'd always have to run and sit with someone. If someone was passing by and said something loudly, I'd die *ga*ᶜ. I wouldn't know what to do, I'd fall and faint. I had really a lot of those fears that followed me when I was little. I couldn't sleep in a room by myself: I'd just fall asleep, and then I'd wake up and *nari* (oh, my goodness), my face, *nari*, my face would appear to me, like if someone had turned a light on me or someone was holding a knife to me. Things like that would keep coming into my imagination—always something. (Story 118)

A diffuse fear of unpredictable violence, intimations of impending chaos, and dread of abandonment recur throughout Khadija's narrative, adding up to a "hypervigilant arousal" characteristic of trauma-related syndromes.

Sadness

Khadija says she often withdraws into silenced *solitude* [Fr.], which she describes as a fearful, angry, self-reproachful state, in which she sometimes ponders suicide. Since elementary school, she has turned her solitude into pages of journal entries, short stories, and poems. She says her poems come from "meditations" on sadness: the sadness that comes from grinding poverty, from the loss of her freedom, and from her own failures to make the kind of life she wants. Some of her images evoke feelings of depression:

> My life is wasting its leaves, its flowers
> its leaves are falling, fading/withering
> its leaves are falling, and my blood is wearing out
> to the last drop
> the last drops circulating in my body
> are passing like the seasons,
> like the time passing away because I'm dying.

Other images convey a tone of agitated frustration and sometimes chaotic rage. In a rather strange but important poem—difficult to follow as she reads in classical Arabic and intersperses comments in Moroccan Arabic and French —she writes:

> Sadness is like a *ţfel semer* (dark/black child), a dark little boy who breaks up whatever he finds in his way. He turns over a table and breaks it, knocks over a glass and breaks it, he knocks over and breaks up whatever he can, he throws and breaks whatever he finds in his way. He makes me drunk. . . . Sadness is like a child who makes you tired, like a child who doesn't let you sleep, like a child who cries, or screams, or misbehaves. Sadness is an unbearable child who stays up when everyone else falls asleep. . . . A child with tears who can't

be consoled. I can't bear the sight of a child with tears. I can't bear those tears any more.

Sadness is a dark child. He breaks up everything breakable, he makes me drunk and gets drunk himself. He visits when it rains, and plays upon my feelings. He plays upon my sheets of paper, and I endure him. Sadness is an annoying child who stays up while everyone sleeps, a child with tears that I can no longer bear. (Story 136)

The poem charts the tension she chronically experiences between enduring sadness and being overwhelmed by it. Sadness as an unruly "dark child"— certainly herself as "a child with tears who can't be consoled"—alternately flees into drunkenness and enrages, destroys, and brings visions of apocalypse.[6] The alternation produces a questionable poetic effect but follows the dialectic of trauma: jarring oscillations of dissociative numbing and intrusive reexperiencing.[7]

Flight

Khadija flees fear and sadness into daydreams that often turn explicitly erotic. As she said in the first interview:

If I'm *mqelqa* (anxious/depressed), it gives me a kind of *'infijar* (relief/release). . . . I get some relief/release by giving my imagination free rein. I picture myself driving a car or going back to my villa and receiving my servant. I'll live all this for a while, for two or three hours.

Almost as early as she can remember, she sought refuge in romantic daydreams. Unlike her younger sister, who fought and talked back when her mother beat her, Khadija says she fell silent. Then she would dream of escape, often imagining a different family for herself, a family like that she glimpsed in the home of her more Westernized relatives in Casablanca, or imagining herself in an orphanage "being raised by Europeans." It was in elementary school, she recalls, that her craving for someone to understand her turned erotic.

I *premierement* (Fr.: first) started to imagine/dream of sex was when I was at school. I had *un ami* (Fr.: a friend) who used to bring me books and pens and things. . . . Once he brought me a necklace, and I've never forgotten that, *jamais* (Fr.: never). I still think about him. When the other kids teased me, I'd turn red and become afraid, and he'd come shout at them. He'd say the things that I couldn't say myself. He'd tell those girls off, and say she's better than that. It was like he'd rescue me from things I couldn't defend myself against on my own.

I never did anything [sexual] with him—maybe he was just like me. We were both young, but I always dreamed of him. I'd imagine the two of us in school, and I'd wish if we could only hold his hand or embrace. I'd wish if he could only sit next to me in class. However, it was something that I could neither ask for nor do, and if he'd tried to do something to me, I'd have screamed or cried.

Still, I wanted to nourish it in my imagination. I used to imagine that *une bise* (Fr.: a kiss) alone would make something happen in the universe. I found that kind of imagining *il me console* (Fr.: it consoled me), that it would lighten things a little bit. It actually helped a lot. I started to make things I could not do/have . . . happen in my imagination. In imagination, you have no witness over your back. Neither your father nor your mother are there to watch over what you're doing. Nothing would scare you. You can act in total freedom. (Stories 66 and 93)

[You don't recall an experience with sex yourself when you were little?] When I grew up a little bit, when I was in bed at night, I'd always think to myself that I was with somebody doing that, and it'd be really good! When I'd wake up, back then, I'd wish that the dream would come true: if only that boy would show up now! I'd do exactly that with him! Really! I used to give sex a great importance. Just kissing a young man, for example, I don't know how I used to picture it, as something *ghriba* (strange), strange, strange. I didn't know what would happen to me if someday somebody kissed me. (Story 64)

When she was about twelve, she developed a crush on a cousin, a slightly older son of her progressive uncle in Casablanca:

When he came to visit us, I'd feel he was trying to get near me, and I felt drawn to him. But, at the same time, I didn't know why or how I had wanted him. Whenever he was around me, I had no thoughts [about sex], and I wouldn't want him to touch/come near me. But as soon as I'd go to sleep, I'd feel *une envie* (Fr.: a craving), I'd long for him in my dream. I'd picture myself naked with him and that we'd be doing things—to the point that when I'd get up, I'd still think it was real, and I'd feel scared. I'd have the thought that I had bled, that I'd lost *ma virginité* [Fr.]. It felt like I did all of that with him, as if you'd had *un rapport* (Fr.: intercourse). (Story 92)

As Fatima Mernissi eloquently describes in her autobiography, romantic dreams of flight have traditionally played an important role in the lives of secluded North African women.[8] And the culture generally does not condemn lustful thoughts as sinful but only prohibits illicit sexual liaisons and the exchanges of glances, words, or touches that are believed to so easily dissolve men's and women's self-control. Khadija is not necessarily unusual for "nourishing" erotic fantasies, though she may be for the intensity with which they carry her away and provide relief from the fearful tension she says characterizes so much of her waking life. Her imaginings express a craving for a love that will annul her fear of abandonment and vulnerability and confirm her otherwise damaged worth in the eyes, touch, and loyalty of a man who desires her. Nurtured in daydreams and glimpsed in her love affairs, the erotic rush associated with falling in love appears as the prototypic positive emotion and source of meaning for her.

Beauty

As Khadija takes flight from fear into romantic daydreams, she repeatedly shows an impulse to beautify the ugly, disarm dangers, and turn sources of anxiety into attractions. This may be *the* main story line of her narrative, but it also appears as a script—if not a "type scene"—in many of her Rorschach, TAT, and sentence completion responses. She perceived dangers lurking in several Rorschach blots, for example, but gave elaborate, enthusiastic responses to three in which she "beautified" the scenes. She saw a dangerous cave in Card II and suggests a spring could be hidden inside and carvings of lions added to the sides of its entrance—both to "beautify the scene" and to make it "something touristic":

> It's like we want to add some prettiness, some beauty to those lions in order to give us a nice scene, in order to attract people, *voilà*, something that's going to attract their attention. To keep them looking, we added some *décor* [Fr.], and some water, a spring, or a waterfall.[9] (Story 130)

She gives a similar response to Card VII, imagining a *maᶜbed* (place of worship) of an "unknown desert people," with carved symbols at the entrance that show their power and fearsomeness. She looks closely and elaborates on the carvings—"made of marble in order to add *waḥed décor* (Fr. and Arabic: some decoration), that is, *shi teHsin* (some enhancement) and some beauty" —that she makes out to be standing elephants, which are "powerful" but "never assaults or kills or does anything unless you ill-treat/provoke it." "I like the scene very much," she adds, both because "it's got a lot of symbols" and because of its *décor* [Fr.]: "it's precisely balanced with respect to its *architecture* [Fr.]." Her wish to beautify and her ambivalent senses of bodily femaleness appear most clearly in the "bat" and "butterfly" responses she gives to the very first card. These are common responses, but she then points out features that make it a female and perhaps a mother bat ("Here's its mouth, its face, and the place between its wings where it carries its babies when it gives birth") and says:

I don't like it, because it's got an ugly appearance, I don't like it. And they say that if a bat goes into a house, there will be a lot of problems or some ṣedaᶜ (trouble/quarreling) will happen. I especially don't like its face. I don't know what form it has, but I don't like it because it's like meat, it hasn't got hair or bodily hair. And even though you want to hold/grasp it in your hand, *cela me derange* (Fr.: it would bother me) to catch/hold it in my hand like this. It comes out always at night, never in the day. (Story 129)

As a butterfly, however:

It's open, but butterflies aren't usually fat in the middle like this. . . . I like it. It's the only insect I like very much. *Alors*, it's got *les ailes* (Fr.: wings), both of them. It has *des couleurs* (Fr.: colors), it has a lot of *les couleurs* [Fr.], and they're pretty. *Alors*, when you look at it, it's something beautiful because it reminds you of spring, or it reminds you of flowers. It doesn't bite/sting, it doesn't do anything. It adds beauty to anything she lights upon. It gives a pretty and beautiful scene as it flies above the flowers or trees or plants. . . . It doesn't fly at night, it doesn't fly in the dark. When we see a lot of butterflies outside, we know that it's the opening of spring, the prettiest season of the year. (Story 129)

She hardly could draw this contrast of an ugly, night-hovering maternal figure and a beautiful, *multicouleur*, open, flowerlike girl figure more starkly. She feels disgust as she imagines catching/holding the bat but shifts to convey an expansive sense of joy as she imagines the butterflies beautifying a spring scene. It is not clear what it means that she imagines *bghiti tshedu* (you want/go to catch/hold it) the bat, which she describes as having a hairless, "meatlike" body. But the fact that she explicitly points out the center section as "where it carries its babies when it gives birth" and comments that a butterfly wouldn't be "fat" there indicates that her feelings of both disgust and joy concern the body's femaleness. In addition, it appears likely that she perceives the butterfly at least partly in response to having first perceived the bat. The ugly bat clutches its babies to her as her mother imprisoned her, but the butterfly opens and shows off its beauty, as she defiantly yearns to do in her life. Her dual responses to this card appear to depict the core imperative that animates her life: to break free of her mother's dark, ominous hovering and to beautify and expose to the world the lithe, *multicouleur* body her mother taught her to conceal.

She indeed uses a butterfly to symbolize herself as a "butterfly of spring" in a poem she wrote, which, following a familiar sequence, depicts her sadness, solitude, and then yearning for reparative romance. She sketches her feelings of invisibility by addressing a "you" she leaves at first undefined:

Like you'd picked up a butterfly of spring and put it in the desert
with no water, no flowers, no place to alight
so it settles on rocks or mountains or sand.
I was born with you in life, like a lost butterfly
which loses its way, and everyone ignores it. . . .

After developing these images, the poem takes a sudden romantic turn:

You're always with me, in my eyes
I see your body in front of me
and hear the voice of a man in my heart. . . .

which she explains: "*je tombe amoureuse de quelqu'un* (Fr.: I fall in love with someone). It's a man I'm addressing." And she continues:

Who can come to my rescue?
I'm talking to you and you're listening to me
and you can save me. . . . (Story 137)

We see Khadija at work here as she creates figures from the inkblots and endows them with meaning—playful and creative work. She initially "automatically" perceives dangers, but then she decorates and beautifies, annulling the danger and fashioning scenes that attract admiring crowds, and perhaps the lover who will save her.[10] This creative work may have something of a "hysterical" character to it, to the extent that beautification and display are driven by needs to defuse fear, overcome *la solitude*, and quiet the "dark child" of sadness. But it also testifies to her strength to make beauty, nurture a sense of worth, and sustain hope in the aftermath of abuse and in the midst of harassment.

Eros and Thanatos

Eros, however, often proves dangerous, and Khadija's sexuality appears fraught with mistrust and vulnerability. Sometimes this appears as the kind of suspicion her mother tried to instill in her:

They'll tell you that *shitan* (the devil) sometimes appears in the guise of a man, a handsome and kind/nice man. He'll stop you on the street/path and talk to you, as if he was a real human being. All of that would appear to me in my dreams, and I always was afraid of it. (Story 61)

In some passages, she paints the modern world in almost paranoid hues, describing most young women as manipulatively out for money, high-fashion commodities, and men with good looks (Story 45). She sees traditional women as envious of her freedoms and progressive ones as contemptuous of her low status and bad reputation. Men, she says, are manipulatively out for sex, ready to betray one woman for another, and ultimately looking to marry a girl for her family's status:

> They all think about sex, always—they'll love you for sex. . . . When he wants to get married . . . his eyes go for the daughter of the *Commissaire* [Fr.] or the daughter of a *docteur* [Fr.]. (Story 46)

She describes the love affairs she has had since her divorce as beginning in trust but eroded by suspicion and betrayal. As one relationship grew serious, she brought an attractive girlfriend on a visit to her boyfriend's apartment to "test" his loyalty and broke up with him when he failed (Story 36).

She organizes several TAT stories around themes of mistrust and betrayal. To a card depicting a man turned away from a woman who holds him, she says that if she interprets it from a Moroccan woman's point of view, "It's the Arab man who always runs away from the woman . . . while the woman sticks with him like glue." She continues:

> He's an Arab man: he always makes a distinction between himself and the woman, but she's always the one in need of him. . . . She could trust him, but he still looks at other people and stays distant. . . . That's because here we believe that the man is something that we worship, something sacred, something greatly esteemed. Women are always below and men always above—they're seen as higher. There's always a difference, and women aren't recognized. (Story 77)

She zeros in on the woman's haircut, nails, and posture, which show she is *metᶜelma* (an educated/sophisticated) and liberated woman: "She knows how to deal with a man, it shows that she is *ṭayba* (a mature woman). . . . If we met, we could get along." A Moroccan man, she points out, would only suspect and accuse her:

> She's holding him in a *position* [Fr.] that he couldn't imagine in his mind. It would start looking to him as if she was a *khayba* (bad) person, someone *à la portée de toute le monde* (Fr.: who could be in everyone's hands). *Voilà*, like *a trottoir* (Fr.: streetwalker), someone who is experienced, who has done that with a lot of men.

She goes on to comment that many Moroccan girls "know how to have sex" but will *katsmeh f-plaisir* (Arabic and Fr.: give up their own pleasure) and act passively with their husbands for fear they will suspect them of having lovers:

> So, *bon*, she leaves her body *hak hak* (to him) [said with angry resignation], in front of him, and he plays with her as he wants, in any way he wants, for *plaisir dyalu* (Fr. & Arabic: his pleasure). [pause] Here again the power/strength of the man and the weakness of the woman appear. The woman is always weak. (Story 77)

In response to a card depicting a woman partially uncovered in bed and a man standing with his arm across his face, she perceives the woman's vulnerability to the man's sexual aggression and angrily complains that men "in backward society" view women as meals to sate their hungers.[11] If Eros provokes mistrust, its dangers reach their peak in those moments in which women find themselves served as "meals" to men, in which lovers turn into predators, and in which fantasies are broken by apocalyptic visions. Her earliest dream/daydream of having sex with her cousin became so real, she says, that suddenly "I'd feel scared. I'd have the thought that I had bled, that I'd lost *ma virginité* [Fr.] (Story 92). She feared the devil's ability to "appear in the guise of a handsome and kind/nice man, who'd stop you on the street and talk to you as if he was a real human being" (Story 61). Her high school crush on her science teacher repeatedly overwhelmed her so that she blacked out. She has been unable to perform intercourse because she becomes too frightened and tense. Her night at the disco comes to a crashing halt with an apocalyptic vision and "regret."

One of the most disturbing series of images—in which caresses turn to slaughter—came to her on a night when she stayed in the apartment of her most recent boyfriend, after her family's insistence they get married and his insistence they have intercourse had soured their relationship. She was sleeping fitfully in his bed, and he on the couch, and in the wee hours of the morning she picked up a pen and paper to write:

When I started writing, I felt my hands very cold and trembling, and *alors* (Fr., then) I imagined *j'ai envie de lui* (Fr.: I wanted/needed him), *de le contacter* (Fr.: to touch him), *enfin de faire l'amour* (Fr.: and in the end to make love) or something *avec lui* (Fr.: with him). I imagined how I'd treat my body since he was sleeping downstairs: it was like a body that was sleeping, but it wasn't sleeping properly, it was all hunched/huddled up like this, and my left hand was braiding my hair, like this. *Alors*, I was like this [fitfully hunched/huddled up] when I went to bed, and imagined how the fingernails were scaring/frightening this body. And that fear started, the nails made fear start from here, from the skull, and fear penetrated the whole body, and when that fear penetrated *le corps* (Fr.: the body), the fear became a kind of coldness that ran from the top to the bottom. My legs were cold, and that's how fear penetrated my whole body.

Then after a while my body was like this [demonstrating open], my body was free/relieved, it wasn't hunched up anymore, it became stretched. Once it was stretched/extended, I put it down like a *farisa* (victim/prey), and suddenly she became surrounded: the fox came to eat, the dog came to eat, they all gathered around her. *Alors*, I felt many hands, different hands, a soft hand caressing you, then I felt a hard/rough hand, then again a cold hand, and a hot hand—

everything was touching/stroking that *corps* (Fr.: body). After a while the sweat started streaming down, the sweat, all the blood was coming down, of the *farisa* (victim/prey), the blood was beginning to cover all the victim. Then you could see axes and knives all around. It was a frightening, terrifying scene: it wasn't love any more, that woman wasn't making love any more, the scene turned into a slaughterhouse. It became a slaughterhouse, blood was all over, there were lots of knives and axes, and a lot of blood. It was a slaughterhouse, no more caresses. (Story 69)

The variety of these stories shows the kind of componential structure Lévi-Strauss insists characterizes systems of myth: it is as if Khadija were exploring the range of responses vulnerable women might make to predatory men in a patriarchal world. Her stories trace out a detailed sexual politics, according to which a woman might be erotically naive and "backward," numbly "dead," an unwilling "meal" for a man or "prey" for slaughter, full of desire that she must "hide," delinquently indulgent of "her own *plaisir*," manipulatively scheming, or—perhaps—"liberated" to seek fulfillment with lovers of her choosing. Many of these may have been Khadija's experiences; all remain her possibilities.

An underlying script often appears in which she responds to feelings of vulnerability or abuse with beautification and erotic imaginings, which then get spoiled by intruding images of violation and catastrophe. She makes it clear that she yearns for love rather than just sex, but love, safety, power, and rejection all have become highly sexualized, leaving her, as she says, disturbingly "complexed about sex." In many passages, Khadija speaks of erotic matters in ways that straightforwardly convey sexual desire, but many others show impulses to beautify, attract attention, and manipulate that articulate more defensive strategies for creating control in the face of vulnerability, for rehabilitating a sense of worth in the face of denigration, and for eliciting affection in the face of loss.

Cataclysm

Many of Khadija's romantic flights end in cataclysmic visions—grotesque and terrifying manifestations of the *fitna* (chaos/disorder) Mernissi maintains is deeply associated with women's sexuality. But cataclysms do not occur only in sexualized contexts, and they seem especially to threaten at night or during transitions to sleep and wakefulness—in liminal times traditionally regarded as dangerous because of exposures to chthonic forces. She recalls her dreams of escape turning into nightmares:

I'd dream I was going to some open/empty space or to a garden, and I'd sit alone next to a tree or something. But after a while, I'd look around and notice an old woman with a really ugly face, holding a stick. And she'd follow me and try to hit me. I'd run, but it was like you'd run and run and run and not move, like you're standing in your place. That happened so many times. Someone or a dog would follow me from behind, or some snake would climb/crawl up on me. I'd be sleeping and start screaming and my mother would come running. (Story 60)

Such dreams were probably triggered by Khadija's fear of beatings, but the widespread use of jinn, devil, and ogre stories to frighten children into obedience probably shaped them as well. Like Hussein, she often "externalizes" anxiety and feels herself vulnerable to attack by chthonic beings (even though she doesn't "believe in" them) and malevolent humans. She recalls awakening from sleep as a child and imagining "someone was holding a knife to me" (Story 118), she felt frightened of hearing her mother's dawn prayers, and even now fears the call to prayer:

It still really scares me, especially during Ramadan when their numbers grow. I don't like it at all when I hear that in the morning. . . . I imagine it's some kind of huge man who starts howling like that. I feel that something bad is going to happen. (Story 90)

She also feared the *jinniya* (female demon) Aisha Qandisha, known primarily for seducing men and then rendering them impotent:

They used to tell me a lot of stories about Aisha Qandisha. They'd say Aisha Qandisha is like a mule but also like a woman with wild hair and protruding teeth. Some woman would tell me that Aisha Qandisha had come upon her and did this or that, and I couldn't sleep alone, I always had to have someone to hold on to. I'd always *kantkhayel* (dream/imagine) that she'd come upon me. (Story 61)

As an adult, she continually pictures herself dying by accident or in a war or earthquake:

Surtout par accident (Fr.: Especially by accident). I always visualize it in an accident, in *la guerre* (Fr.: a war). I always fear wars will kill us. . . . I think that we could have an unexpected death, that it will happen haphazardly, for example, that there could be *un tremblement de terre* (Fr.: an earthquake), or a fire in the house, or something like that. Sometimes I'll be sleeping and I'll jump out of bed and run to the kitchen to make sure that the Butagas bottle is shut. So what does this mean? It means I'm scared of death. I'm afraid it'll be open and someone will strike a match and it'll explode and everybody in the house will die. (Story 81)

Responding to a TAT drawing of a figure slumped by a couch, she says it could depict either *la misere* (Fr.: misery) that leads to suicide or *la guerre* (Fr.: war):

"this is how they find *la victim* [Fr.], falling, how he's dying on the porch of his house or in the street." Pointing to the picture she says, "*Voilà! La misere!* This is where you end up with *la misere*: everyone *'infajer* (explodes), one way or another, by killing himself or going crazy or doing something *ghriba* (strange/bizarre)" (Story 79).

Cataclysmic imagery appears associated with tensions that build unbearably toward what she often terms *'infijar,* which might best be rendered "explosive release." The *'infijar* may take shape as flood, flaming explosion, bloody slaughter, suicide, divine judgment—or sexual fantasy, arousal, and release. Although fear often takes over the scene and she (or someone with whom she identifies) becomes the victim, she also can imagine herself the agent, as she does when the tension turns erotic or when her righteous rage at the bourgeoisie enables her to wish she might "wipe them out" and "burn down and blow up their villas" (Story 135). It is sometimes disturbingly unclear who brings about the apocalypse, but it threatens both from without and from within.

Core-Level Personality ❀

The affective tensions most prominently organizing Khadija's genotypic or core-level personality appear characteristic of trauma-related syndromes: pervasive fearfulness (hypervigilant arousal), flights of imagination and sometimes fainting (dissociative numbing), and cataclysmic imagery (intrusive reexperiencing).[12] To these general features we can add her fear of abandonment, her deep well of agitated sadness, and the erotic character of her flights. In addition, her accounts of *la crise* indicate that she can be overwhelmed by the arousal this can bring on, and her failed attempts to have intercourse testify that she indeed suffers from intense anxiety about sex.

Several features of this constellation correspond to the personality style conventionally labeled "hysterical," in which sexuality comes to be nonconsciously used to defend against anxiety.[13] That is, when she responds to feelings of fear, vulnerability, and abandonment with defiant impulses to beautify and seductively display her body to attract admiration and affection, she may enact a "hysterical" style. Feminist psychologists have both criticized the term *hysteria* and documented how the phenomenon tends to develop in patriarchal cultures, where conversion symptoms often can be interpreted as the body's attempt to speak what oppression silences.[14] Janice Boddy thus insists that Sudanese women's possession trances should not be seen as hysterical symptoms but as articulating a counterhegemonic discourse, in which antiselves emerge to exhibit behaviors and demand indulgences forbidden to women by hegemonic Islam.[15] But writing from an orthodox psychoanalytic framework, Alan Krohn argues for the validity of "hysteria" as a syndrome that varies from culture to culture, its essence consisting of nonconscious enactments of the culture's core "myth of passivity" in response to oppressive "emotional straitjacketing" of the sort that typically confines women to a greater degree than men.[16]

We need not term Khadija's sexualization of experience and desire to beautify *hysterical*, but psychodynamic accounts of the process may shed light on features of her core-level personality that often have been observed to develop—especially among women—in highly patriarchal societies. As Foucault insists, oppression does not so much repress sexuality as construct it.[17] Does Khadija's eroticized style ultimately empower her or trap her within a "myth of passivity"? We cannot say. She describes it as motivating courageous defiance, which then renders her vulnerable to the ravages of gossip, to men's predations, and to threats from traditional authorities.

We can indeed see that this style animates a counterhegemonic discourse, that she, unlike the "spirit-possessed" women described by Boddy, seeks to live as her authentic self. Whether or not it ultimately empowers her, it enables her to defiantly affirm her desires for autonomy, respect, and bodily pleasure. As sometimes occurs in response to childhood abuse, Khadija's dissociative flights, her withdrawals into solitude, and her eroticization of relationships may well have helped preserve positive features of her personality from culturally mandated suppression, so that as a young adult she can struggle against her culture to live by them as her "principles." In another poem, she writes:

> The sun comes out and illuminates all, driving away the clouds,
> engraving the day's beauty in my memory.
> I open the windows and find nature sublimely embellished by the
> sun's beauty.
> I feel the warmth of the sun after the coldness of the universe on my
> breast. . . .
> I find the flowers opening and opened my heart to them.
> I found the rivers running and ran with them after I couldn't move.
> I felt overcome before nature, I smiled with happiness, I sang of love.

Social Personality ❀

If Khadija narrates her life story as a struggle with solitude, sexuality, and romance, she equally tells it as a struggle for honor, reputation, and respect. Again and again, this conflict takes shape as one of exposure versus concealment: of her body, her feelings, and her thoughts. She portrays herself and others in situations tempting exposure and demanding concealment with the sort of automaticity with which Hussein constructs relational triangles and Rachida positions herself within her honorable household and polluting body. Unlike Rachida, Khadija's experience is focused not so much on "dirtiness" associated with her womb and reproductive powers as on the surfaces of her body. Her stories cast her as someone recurrently tempted to expose herself to attract admiration, nourish love, and find release/relief; but in the face of public, divine, and inner authorities who demand she keep herself concealed. These crystallize as contrasting senses of self or subselves that form the cores of two identities she experiences as so antithetical that she says she has "two personalities."

As she eloquently points out, exposure and concealment are always public matters in which others judge her social reputation and worth. Back in Ouarzazate from the freer atmosphere of Casablanca, she finds herself trapped in the "old clothes" and "old skin" of her former reputation (Story 13). But she can swim naked "in imagination," where she says, "You have no witness over your back. Nothing would scare you. You can act in total freedom" (Story 93). She often never names those who watch and judge her but refers simply to "people" or "they." And when she does name names—her mother, her brother Farid, her sister Fadila—she casts them as society's official agents: "My older sister and mother tell me, 'Your honor is being sullied! If people see you with that man, what will they say?'" (Story 40). She hears the foul language of men in the cafés, her married bosses' clumsy seductions, and the threats of the accountant who tries to extort sex as so many voices of "Arab men." She feels herself constantly under the gaze of a patriarchal generalized Other, which has two effects at once: it preys on her, making her feel like "meat" at a meal, and it condemns her, plunging her into "regret" and self-insult. That is, the gaze promises to honor and threatens to dishonor her—and the imperatives of exposure versus concealment emerge in her narrative as an internalization of the honor-modesty system's demand that she conceal her body, feelings, and ideas in accordance with the principles of modesty.

Khadija is hardly unusual for her imaginary flights of romance and exposure, or even for daring to turn some daydreams into realities. Traditional culture celebrates love and romance, even sometimes at the cost of scandal: as a child, she listened to the region's popular Romeo-and-Juliet folktales, and her mother warned her about singing popular love songs. Novelist Naguib Mahfouz's Cairo is certainly a world rife with loves and lusts that escape concealment. But the romantic traditions of Arab and then European culture have provided her an alternate Generalized Other, one she perceives to love beautification and exposure, which encourages her to flee and violate the norms of modesty. Many Moroccan women experience this duality, but she stands out for the intensity of her ambivalence and also for her unwillingness to compromise.

Exposure and Concealment

Khadija explicitly casts herself as embroiled in a lifelong struggle with society's agents, who demand she conceal what she would expose and reveal what she would conceal. She rages at men's harassment on the street, at her bosses' attempts to touch and seduce her, at a coworker's claim that he has photos of her naked, and at the custom of displaying a bride's bloody underwear as proof of her virginity. She recalls her mother so frightening her about guarding her virginity that she could not talk to boys at school or wash herself at home. Yet while her mother beat her for slight indiscretions, her father gave her money to cut her hair and buy pants and blouses and taught her the advantages of European ways over Moroccan. In the home of her well-off uncle, she tasted freedoms she associates with a European way of life: she dressed in pants and blouses, went with them to parks and beaches, and developed one of her first crushes on their son.

At nearly the same time, she spent a summer in the home of her fundamentalist uncle and learned to cover herself, retreat from contact with men, and fear the tallying of her sins on Judgment Day. She recalls sitting in the women's section of the mosque, listening to the imam's sermon over loudspeakers:

> He'd tell us about a woman who was touched by a foreign man and said that wherever the woman is touched that place will be burnt—that on Judgment Day, burning coals will be put on her there. *Alors,* that image terrified me, and I thought that what he was saying was true. As he began reciting from the Quran, I started crying, I was so scared! How could that be? I realized that I had greeted so many men, and that I was always uncovered, and that I did so many other things. I was crying in the mosque, and when I turned around, I saw the women were all crying. (Story 87)
>
> I kept asking them, "Is there a way to erase the sins I've committed? Will God absolve them? Will God forgive me?" . . . They said that God disgraced any woman who wore men's clothes: that God will inflict pain on any woman who wears pants. I'd worn pants, since I was little. Your hair, your hands, your legs must not be uncovered. What topped it all was the beach, because you shouldn't wear a bathing suit and uncover yourself before people. *Alors,* I committed all of those. (Story 88)

From elementary school, she says she daydreamed herself naked with boys she liked, and now wants to take lovers of her choosing and wishes she could run naked and free on French beaches (Story 32). Yet dancing at the disco, visions of cataclysm bring her back to what she perceives as the greater strengths of the "Moroccan" Khadija who would live by the rules of concealment.

The tension of exposure versus concealment deeply shapes her perception of her body and the world, and often inspires the images and metaphors she uses to represent herself. She continually focuses attention on the surfaces of bodies, their clothing (or lack of it), their postural and gestural styles, their makeup and hair styling—all of which Islamic tradition insists be covered. This appears in her Rorschach responses in her desire to decorate and beautify surfaces and entrances, and in her TAT stories in the detailed attention she gives to the sexual meanings of women's postures, facial expressions, and fashion styles. And it appears in several early memories. Recall that in her earliest memory—of the quarrel that led both of her parents to abandon the children—she said she began caring for her siblings, "even though I was still small and still needed someone to *igheṭini* (cover/care for me)." And when, after long accounts of deprivation and abuse, I asked if she had a happy childhood memory, she recalled celebrations of the "Little Feast" at the end of Ramadan, "when we'd put on our new clothes" and "my mother and father would be happy—he'd tickle her and laugh with her and she'd just keep laughing." The same went for the Great Feast:

> We'd be really happy at those times, because the atmosphere of the house would change: there'd be plenty of food and everyone would eat their fill, the house would be spotlessly clean, we'd be wearing all new clothes. I'd wish I could make the celebration last longer. (Story 56)

She says she always finds sacrifices disturbing and "I hardly eat at all," but she loves getting new clothes:

> I have to have clothes. . . . You have to go out and show off your new clothes. If you don't get new clothes, you regret it until the end of time. I always had that idea: I must wear some new clothes during a feast. . . . (Story 56)

And like many young Moroccans, Khadija imagines that studying *informatique* (Fr.: computer programming) or *compatibilité* (Fr.: accounting) would have gotten her on a more certain track to a modern life, but she also recalls wishing her family would have paid for her to study *la modèliste* (Fr.: modeling) (Story 120). All of these passages testify to the delight she takes in presenting herself attractively, fashionably dressed in public, that appears as a prototypic form of positive affect she remembers, imagines, and seeks.

The Dancer

She also tells of an encounter with a pair of French tourists, in the equivalent of U.S. eighth grade, which she presents as the turning point in her struggle over what kind of life to live. She had stayed the summer with her conservative uncle in Casablanca, and "that year I decided I was going to be like an *'ikhwania* (a Muslim sister). I'd fight with my brother and sister, and tell them they should pray." Then back in Ouarzazate:

> One day my brother Ahmad invited home some Christians, a *nasraniya* (European woman) and her boyfriend. They came to our apartment, and she had *waḥed la taille men dak shi* (Fr. and Arabic: a physique that was really great)! She was wearing jean pants, you know, and I

looked her over and kept looking at her and *bghit nḥmaq* (I nearly went crazy) over that girl! I couldn't wait for her just to stand up, and I just kept staring at her *la taille* (Fr.: waist/physique)—I still can't forget it now! She was wearing blue jeans and *une chemise* (Fr.: a blouse). As I told you, I was praying at that time, and I'd decided that I had to keep away from all that. But at the same time I didn't think—I no longer kept thinking about God.

I just kept staring at that girl, just waiting for her to stand up. She was tall, and *la taille ᶜndha mgada ou souple* (Fr. and Arabic: her figure was lean/thin and supple/lithe), and I kept staring at her like this [in amazement]. . . . She told us she studies *la danse classique* (Fr.: ballet), and she even showed us some of her pictures: she was wearing those things they dance in, and when I saw her in them, I wished I could be like her, like that, that I could dance. And I thought that if I practiced that *la danse classique* (Fr.) I'd be like her, I'd have *la taille* (Fr.: figure) like hers.

When I told my sister about her, I told her that she was *nari* (wow!), *ᵏaḍama* (really stupendous), and that sort of thing, that she was so beautiful, and my sister said, "Are you crazy? One who prays mustn't be like that! Are you crazy?" So I was really upset. I thought about some place where there would be only girls, *shi salle* (Arabic and Fr.: a room) where there'd be only girls, where there'd be no men, and then I could do that kind of dancing. (Story 33)

Again, she minces no words, straightforwardly wishing she could become the French woman: that she might show off a lithe figure like hers, become a dancer, and choose her lover. At a time when she was struggling with sin and practicing concealment—"I didn't know whether that religion was *zwina* (beautiful/good) or *khayba* (ugly/bad)" (Story 88)—the tourists opened to her a world that valued exposure. After their visit, Ahmad told her, "It's they who know what life is. Here we don't know what life is" (Story 33), and from this point, she says, she has wanted a European life.

She has had to pursue this style of life in a hostile environment, and it now angers her that she must conceal so much of what she wishes to reveal:

> We live in such dependence on other people's attitudes. We don't live the way we want, not at all! If you want to live your own way, you have to hide from people, so they won't see you. But I can't bear to hide those *les choses* (Fr.: things): if I like someone and build a relationship with him, I must go out [in public] with him. I can't bear to hide it, understand? But the situation makes you hide things —you mustn't expose/reveal them. (Story 41)

She condemns girls who resort to duplicity and conceal their Western-style indulgences:

Especially in Casablanca, you'll find girls who leave home totally veiled, so you'd think she's a devoted Muslim girl, and then heads for another *quartier* (Fr.: neighborhood), to the hairdresser's or a friend's, where she'll exchange her uniform for a fancy dress and fix her hair. She transforms into an unrecognizable person and then goes out and does whatever pleases her. She'll spend the evening or the night, and when she comes back home, she'll be the same veiled girl who left earlier. Once home, as if nothing had happened, she'll perform her ablutions and pray. They can fabricate things even in Islam. That's something I don't agree with at all! (Story 98)

But her ambivalence about exposure emerges again as she voices suspicion about what decoration may conceal, dislikes the false look that heavy makeup gives women, and condemns women who fall for slick-looking men:

She'll look over a young man and his appearance strikes her as *wahed zwaq* (well-appointed), and he strikes her as something like she's dreamed: *bien coiffée, bien maquillée, oula bien, meqad mezwin* (Fr. & Arabic: well groomed and well built), and he's driving a car, even though it's not his. It's an appearance on a stage, a mere appearance. . . . How many girls become victims of guys like that! What does she see: he's the son of so-and-so or he's really handsome or beautiful or he dresses well—it's just *zwaq* (decoration/adornment). Underneath that, you'll find everything's ripped and dirty, but on top of that, he'll wear a nice leather jacket *pour attire l'attention d'une fille* (Fr.: to attract a girl's attention). (Story 126)

These passages show Khadija delineating an ethics of principled exposure. She defines herself in contrast to those who conform to the honor-modesty system's rules of concealment but also to hypocrites, to those who falsely dress up sullied interiors. More positively, she identifies herself with courageous self-expression. She finishes the sentence completion stem "What they liked about her" with "is that she's a person of honesty and decisiveness," which she explains means that she will go out in pants and a sweater if she wants, even though her parents tell her to wear an ankle-length and long-sleeved djellaba. She knows many girls who stay quietly under their father's and brothers' control, but in a remarkable passage, she praises courageous defiance:

A girl should appear, *rah*, powerful. She should appear as a personage in the house, even though she's *mziyera* (squeezed/pressured) by her father and mother and all that. She nonetheless must always *tbeyin rasha* (show herself), that she, too, has a role in the house! She mustn't become *fashela* (defeated) or become *khayfa* (frightened). Even under the stick, even if he beats her with the stick, *l'essential* (Fr.: the important thing) is that those people know: here I am, here's who I am! Here are my ideas! Here is my life! Here's what I hope/wish for! (Story 108)

Khadija thus portrays herself as a girl who was both too frightened to reveal and too weak to conceal herself, who has grown into a woman who demands the right to resist seclusion and to expose her body, her affections, and her ideas in accordance with her principles. She appears to seek a kind of vindicating purity in exposure—a purity of affections and intentions. But even when she defies her parents and brother, the amorphous "they" and their internalized spokeswoman, the harsh "Moroccan" Khadija, always hover nearby to shame her into silence and concealment.

As an internalization of the honor-modesty system, the exposure-concealment configuration integrates many of the affective tensions of Khadija's core-level personality. Abandonment and love, security and anxiety, strength and weakness, pride and regret, relief and apocalypse, honor and dishonor, salvation and damnation all come to hinge on matters of exposure and concealment. She feels nearly continuously fixed in the predatory gazes of men who would undress her, in the shaming gazes of traditionals and traditionalists who condemn her partial undress. Yet she also feels powerfully called by the potentially admiring, loving gazes of a modern man and by the desire to dress fashionably to attract him. All these gazes interrogate her as to her essence and worth, constructing her as a person who cannot help but define herself by acts of exposure and concealment. She has fashioned an identity around each of these imperatives, which she struggles mightily to reconcile.

Identity ❧

When it comes to her identity, Khadija once again provides her own psychological analysis: she lives the contradiction of being "two Khadijas," one European and one Muslim. At least since her early teen years, she has tried to live as the European Khadija, except for about a year under her fundamentalist uncle's influence when she was fourteen and perhaps for the few months of her arranged marriage. It appears that she passed through a "moratorium" or "crisis" period in her midteens and has consolidated this identity—both in that it provides a well-articulated value system and in that she has assembled a life structure that enables her to live by it as a modern young career woman. In spite of these developmental successes, though, she finds herself thwarted at many turns by her hostile social milieu and by the inner voice of the Muslim Khadija. It often becomes disturbingly unclear to her which of these is her "true" or authentic self. Hear how she describes this struggle in yet another passage:

> When I see myself as a European, like, I picture/imagine myself in *Europa*, and I'll be in a swimming pool naked, *par example* [Fr.], smoking a cigarette and drinking a beer. *Au même temps* (Fr.: at the same time), I think about God, about Islam, because at that time

Islam affects me, understand? I regret it: Why did I insult God? It's as if I'd mocked God. At that moment it's the stronger Khadija who's a Muslim, a believer, and she reproaches the weaker one who made that error, who got drunk, who smoked, who went swimming naked.

That Khadija would say *nari* (goodness)! God says this and that and commands that you must not *katʿri* (expose your body), you must not dress in men's clothes, you must not even greet men. And death: the day I die, I'm going to be burned, you'll go into the fire. Then the other Khadija, it's like she has nothing to say. She'll keep quiet. She'll answer, but her answer will be *semt* (mute), always speechless, silenced. Her silence would be the only answer she'd give. [pause] Her answer would be silenced; her silence would be the only answer she'd give.

[Like it's your mother's voice?] Like that, my mother's voice. That voice is like the imam in the mosque. Where did I hear that? From the one who gives the sermon. So then I appear to myself like I'm covered up, wearing the veil, understand? And I cry, and I get goose pimples, and I say, "Why did I do that?" [The accusing Khadija says:] "Why did you do that?" [pause] It's like I'd become sick, I'd become psychologically sick. And when I'd at last come out of it, the Khadija who was shouting, *raḥ*, it's she who'd be the right/good one. So I'd regret it: I mustn't have that thought! I shouldn't have thought that. . . . How many times have I thought like that and gotten up and put on a djellaba, and I'll pray and I'll fast and so forth.

But I don't stay with it. . . . Something so *simple* [Fr.] comes along, like I'll read a book or a magazine and find pictures, and say: *Allah! Allah!* It's so beautiful, *a la coup de shaʿr* (Fr. & Arabic: such a cut/style of hair), how beautiful! God! Such beautiful makeup, how beautiful! *Ṣafi*, that matter of Islam and God vanish! (Story 32)

Like Hussein, Khadija has differentiated her discourses of identity along the fault line of modernity versus tradition, though with a much stronger association of modernity with the West and tradition with "Muslims" and "Arabs" —and with much more jarring and disorienting shifts between the two.

The European Khadija

Khadija traces her preference for European ways to her father, who grew up in a French-run orphanage and told her the French had treated him better than his own countrymen ever had. He also encouraged her adoption of Western styles. At the age of fourteen, however, she was in turmoil. A summer's stay with her fundamentalist uncle had frightened her onto the "straight path," even though she harbored doubts about God's existence. Back in Ouarzazate, her afternoon with the French dancer turned everything upside down: "I no longer thought about God. . . . I wished I could be like her" (Story 33). "Ahmad and I, we wanted to live a *Europiya* [Fr.] life," she says:

> We wanted to create it in our house and in every way. We started doing everything to become another family, a new family. But here you run into a lot of problems. [pause] If only you could go back and have a different father. [chuckling] Go back and get a different mother: *Suzanne* or *Christine*. [laughing] *Alors*, my mother's not going to come back like that, *jamais* (Fr.: never). (Story 129)

She returned to school that fall, in the equivalent of U.S. ninth grade, with "awful complexes" (Story 5), and inspired by her science teacher, she developed a love for science, especially biology. She recalls this as an exciting time of discovering European ideas: "In French I'd read about *la nature* [Fr.], or something far away, something *romansia* (Fr.: romantic), or something about *les femmes actualment* (Fr.: modern women), or something *scientifique* [Fr.]." She continues:

> I enjoy science very much. . . . One studies the things you live: when you were born into life—you must learn for yourself from what you were created, how many bones there are in you, the organs you have, what's in you, what you should eat, what you should drink. . . . If you know a lot of these things, you know how to talk intelligently about what a human being is, what it means to be human *ga*ᶜ. That's why I like *science* [Fr.]. (Story 37)

A humanities class built on her new scientific understandings and "liberated" her:

> What really opened my eyes was that year I had a teacher who taught philosophy, and he'd analyze things deeply with us. He introduced us to radical ideas, and my view of things turned around dramatically, and I no longer kept up with those other things [the religious outlook]—which came to appear to me as superficial, as having no meaning whatsoever.
>
> [What ideas did you pick up?] He would analyze reality, the material world. He'd give an analysis, *voilà*, of what the planet Earth is like and how it was created. We'd analyze things scientifically. It no longer appeared to me that it was God who does things. I'd thought that the rain was like God showering us, those were the ideas I had! That it was God who does everything. But when I started reading all those books and studying *science* [Fr.], everything appeared to me as something ordinary, *c'est normal, la nature qui parle, voilà* (Fr.: normal, that it's nature that speaks): how things sprout and blossom, how the fog settles, how the weather changes. And so I'd

say to myself, *raḥ*, there isn't another power which *katehakem* (controls/rules) all that; *koul ḥaja ḥakma f-rasha* (Everything controls/rules itself [f.]). (Story 29)

Many of the pious students in the class refused to talk about these things, she recalls, and hated their teacher.

> But for me it was the opposite. I liked him. He'd give us assignments, and I wouldn't want to put the pen down from my hand. I'd write pages and pages, I liked it all. And he noticed that, he liked me for my work, and he'd bring me books, and I'd read them and summarize them for him and give them back to him. That man, I'll never forget him. . . . [Did you feel like you were getting a little freedom?] *Justement* (Fr.: exactly). Like *kayliberit* (Fr. & Arabic: it liberated me), I found a kind of *liberation* [Fr.]. (Story 29)

Science shows her a world devoid of the forces her mother and uncle and all of the traditional authorities had taught her to fear: no jinn spirits to "hit" her, no God to burn her, no font of pollution inside her to conceal. For Khadija, science possesses the liberating power the Enlightenment promised. There isn't "another power" that rules, she says, using the term *ḥakem*, which means political and religious rule, as well as familial authority. Everything rules itself, she declares, using the feminine conjugation that clearly applies this principle to herself.

Though she is hardly a political activist, her belief that everything should rule itself becomes explicitly political in some of her poems. There she writes of the "sadness" she shares with others of the "lower" or "backward" social orders, attributing it to poverty, hunger, and the "denial of freedom" (Story 135). As often as she feels fearful of jinn spirits and the devil, she doesn't believe chthonic beings actually exist, and she says she really fears the predations of the rich and powerful *bourgeoisiyin* and threats from the authorities who act as their agents—such as the gendarmes who recently came calling on a friend of hers after she began dating an American Peace Corps volunteer. "I see myself in the lower class," she says. "My salary doesn't last more than two weeks, and then I do without. . . . I'll wake up and there'll be no breakfast to eat. If you buy a loaf of bread, you have to share it with everybody. I live in *la misère* (Fr.: poverty)." She says she's hardly alone:

> Millions of people suffer from this poverty. . . . The *bourgeoisiyin* have suppressed us, they suppressed us in the streets and suppressed us at home. We'll always remain on the bottom. . . . They try to divert our attention. They make us dance with the radio, the television, the newspapers, so we won't speak our minds. We'll never speak up, we'll always keep silent! They stop us. They give us all those Egyptian movies to deaden our minds, so we won't think, because if we start to think, the people will rise up. Nobody can speak with this

oppression. Who's going to speak? I can't stand up and say, "Why does this inequality exist?"—I'd disappear. The authorities do whatever they want with the lower class. (Story 135)

Then she reads a poem in which she again draws on the image of the *farisa* (victim/prey) to describe herself:

I ask myself: Do I keep silent? Life has taught me to speak up!
This life hasn't taught me to remain silent,
but to shout like a lamb being killed by a butcher.
It struggles to run away—as do I in my life.
Do I remain silent?
Life has taught me to shout and to speak up like a lamb
that doesn't want to be killed by the butcher.
I speak up against death. I refuse death like the lamb that doesn't
    want to die.
I speak up against injustice,
against the *bourgeoisiyin* doing injustice to us. (Story 135)

And she vents her rage:

Those people in the *bourgeois* class who live comfortably and have everything they want, *franchement* (Fr.: honestly), I don't like those people. I wish I could wipe them out. They shouldn't exist. Personally, if I pass a villa (Fr.: mansion), *surtout a Casa* (Fr.: especially in Casablanca), and I see a Mercedes parked in front of it and a doorman and all that, I wish I could burn it down and blow it up. How can they live so comfortably and know about the people who live beneath them and not even give them what they give to their dogs? (Story 135)

She even borrows a few lines from the Islamists, a note of irony creeping into her voice: "This is a Muslim society, and Islam doesn't teach that! Does Islam say, 'You eat bread and I stare at you?' Islam doesn't teach that. So why is there a discrepancy? Why shouldn't everyone be equal?" (Story 135).

If the Enlightenment's demystification of the world thus provides the abstract, ideological framework for Khadija's European identity, her concrete self-representations consist of exemplars drawn from Western popular culture that display her beauty and embody her freedom: the French ballet dancer she yearns to resemble, the young, stylish, women she admires on magazine covers and sees checking into local tourist hotels, herself in European fashion or naked in the sunshine or alone with her lover. Her eating, hygiene, and grooming habits are thoroughly Western, and she eschews many of the self-care practices grounded in religion: she does not purify or pray or fast during Ramadan. More poetically, she likens herself to the butterfly who spreads her *multicoulour* wings in springtime and, above all, the European

Khadija who would take flight and display her honorable purity by exposing her body in trust.

This discourse draws much of its meaning from opposed antiself images of traditional covered, concealed, and oppressed women, such as her mother, her sister Fadila, the high school acquaintance dishonored at her wedding, herself at puberty in the mosque, and herself at the cusp of adulthood as Hassan's wife. More poetically, she likens herself to the "dark child" of sadness and to a slaughtered *farisa* (prey), which certainly represents the vulnerable, beaten, scarred child she was at her mother's hands and gives shape to the fear she feels in response to the threats permeating her milieu. Here she draws on the wealth of traditional associations linking females with vulnerable beasts: from the term *ṣiyyid* (hunting) used by and for men who cruise the streets for girls, to the frequency with which women refer to themselves as *bhaym* (livestock), to the widespread use of eating metaphors to describe exploitation. Elaine Combs-Schilling has even called attention to the many ways in which the defloration ritual at traditional marriage ceremonies echoes sacrifice,[18] and it is precisely the passive presentation of a girl/woman to a man that so infuriates Khadija.

The Muslim Khadija

The Muslim Khadija would keep God in mind, keep herself secluded and covered in public, and avert her gaze from men. She says she lived this way for two brief periods in her life, but she mainly experiences this self as the internalized surveillance and voice of traditional authorities—of her mother, her uncle, the imam, and the diffuse "they" of traditional and traditionalist convention. As we have seen, this voice intrudes without warning, scolding and insulting her, and she often perceives it to issue from the stronger of her selves because it makes her see things in light of the impending Judgment Day. It is death, she says, more than punishment or ostracism, which terrifies her: "What frightens me is the end. It's death. . . . Islam says that you're going to be judged" (Story 27). The cataclysm she imagined at the disco forced mortality upon her: "What's the meaning of life? It's limited. I'm waiting for the day of death, so I mustn't laugh, because I'm going to die." Whenever she hears Quranic verses recited, she thinks of death (Story 88) and *ᶜzra'il*, the angel of death, "who will come to you at the break of dawn and ask you who you are, and order you to recite the Quran" (Story 28). The macabre figure drawn in a cemetery in a TAT card reminded her of *ᶜzra'il*:

> This is how I hear it, and this has been in my mind since I was little: that when a person dies, when he is buried, at that moment *kaywaqef ᶜlih ᶜzra'il* (the angel of death comes upon him), and this picture shows a wild, frightening person, someone who isn't normal—the way I picture him in my mind. *Voilà, c'est ça* (Fr.: Here it is), this is

it, they name him ʿzra'il, the angel of death. . . . When they cover one with dirt, he comes and starts questioning him: Who are you? Do you know the Quran? . . . If the person has committed crimes in his life, if he was bad with people and he didn't pray and didn't fast, ʿzra'il transforms himself into someone who is bad, who is ugly and frightening, and they say his teeth stick out. If he's been good in life, and prays and worships God and fasts and does good deeds, he appears to him as a wise old man with a kindly appearance. (Story 81)

Later she comments:

The most terrifying and threatening thing that occupies my mind is death, which is the end. I constantly think, while I'm walking or sitting or sleeping, that one day I'll find myself dead in my sleep. Death is an end, as if death stands as a failure for a person. I feel thwarted. I tell myself I'm going to die without accomplishing what I've wanted to do in life. My goals seem so far away from me; and death will keep me from achieving them. (Story 88)

When it comes to the truth of the religious account, however, she says again and again, in both Arabic and French, "I don't know," and then laughing says, "God knows whether ʿzra'il exists or doesn't."

Only once does she seem to find positive feelings in religion, when she perceives the older man at prayer in a card I added to the TAT sequence to be deep in a kind of transcendent rapture or reverence. "It's as if God is holding you in his hands," she explains, "protecting you from everything. While you are praying, you are in direct contact with God, so you have nothing to fear" (Story 87). She goes on:

Reverence is when you transcend your actual l'état (Fr.: state), when you don't feel it any more, as if you're gone. You're focused on the world of the dead or of God, or I don't know what world, the world of heaven. You go far away.

She says the man could be a religious scholar or a Sufi, but then quickly returns to her modernist view:

He's not an emancipated person . . . he's a peasant who lives in the countryside. . . . Those people can't achieve anything, they have no education, they can't keep up with the times. They have a very strong faith. . . . Their thought is always with God. They're waiting for the day when God makes everything come true. . . . Why is he praying here? Because he thinks that one day he will die. Once dead, he will be buried, and once buried, the day of judgment will come. He's waiting for the day when God will judge him, to see if he will go to heaven or hell. (Story 87)

But then again she thinks maybe his simple faith could be the answer: "When I set aside the *point d'interrogation* (Fr.: question mark) I've put on that field, I realize that he's right. It's right. This is what should be. *Bon*, I think that I must pray, that I should do what he's doing, that he's following the right path."

The Muslim Khadija speaks mainly of sin, punishment, repentance, death, and final judgment and views God as offering a refuge from sin. But she still associates mosques, imams, and prayers with fear rather than security. She feels terrified by the threats of being burned in hell, and the emotions summoned forth in her uncle's mosque evoke her wish to flee:

> The imam would reach a section of the Quran that would touch his emotions, and he'd begin to cry. Especially when he'd talk about the revival day, judgment, the death day—it was too much. You found everyone crying, everybody was in reverence/rapture. There was a sort of terrifying, frightening atmosphere hovering over people. It'd affect you to the point that you'd want to run away from that place of terror. (Story 87)

For Khadija, God does not offer to shelter the orphan, as Mohammed finds in Daybreak, nor the promise of prowess Hussein sees in stories of the prophets' lives, nor the vision of heaven's bounty Rachida finds amid the warnings of Al Raḥman. And so she finds she cannot long keep God in her thoughts without taking flight.

Key Symbols

A discourse of identity takes shape through the linkage of abstract concepts and concrete symbols—the concepts explaining the symbols and the symbols enlivening the concepts with affect and demonstrating how they might apply to the world. Both Khadija's modernist-European and her traditionalist-Muslim discourses are well articulated in terms of their abstract concepts and principles. After all, she is an intelligent woman who spends her leisure reading serious literature and writing short stories and poetry, and although she has not memorized the Quran, she can give quite solid accounts of Islamic schools and trends. She thinks a good deal about the meaning of freedom and death, and both personalities keep up their side of the *ḥiwar* (dialogue) by appealing to ultimate principles.

Her body surface—concealed or revealed—appears as the key structurally ambiguous symbol defining an octavelike relation at the core of each discourse. Within each discourse, covering and exposure evoke powerful emotions: imprisonment and fear versus freedom and joy for the European Khadija; security and redemption versus terror and pain for the Muslim Khadija. At the same time, the acts of covering and exposing represent moral principles: *covering* shows the Muslim Khadija's modesty and strength but the European Khadija's confinement and timidity; *exposure* demonstrates the European Khadija's beauty and purity of heart but the Muslim Khadija's sin. Many other symbols delineate this opposition as well, perhaps the most prominent being the butterfly and *farisa* (prey/victim), which are powerfully evocative but do not appear to build on the sort of structured ambiguity as do many key self-representations (except perhaps in the case of her "bat"- "butterfly" responses to the Rorschach blot). She also threads terms built from the root $f * j * r$ throughout the narrative to describe either the self-destructive "explosion" or floodlike "release/relief" that tensions build toward—and these appear to establish an octavelike relationship between her traditional mother's "crazy" explosions of rage and the modern woman's romantic/erotic *plaisir*. Interestingly, *fejar* also means "to split or cleave" and *fujur* "to act immorally, sin, live licentiously, lead a dissolute life, live in debauchery, to commit adultery"[19]—and as we have seen, *fajr* means "break of dawn" that she dreads. This cluster of terms thus serves as a self-representational "motif," as does Hussein's use of chiaroscuro images and $w * q * f$ derivatives, and Rachida's *rahim* (womb)–*rahem* (uterine kin)–*al rahman* (the Merciful) imagery. The European Khadija's discourse loosely follows a hero epic schema, as do Mohammed's and Hussein's, though its genre more closely approximates romance than epic.

Language also plays a crucial role in differentiating her two personalities, as the European Khadija laces her speech with much more French— especially concerning romantic, erotic, and scientific matters—than does the mainly Arabic-speaking Muslim Khadija. Educated Moroccans continually "code switch" between French and Arabic, often mixing words and phrases and using Arabic conjugations to fit French verbs into sentences in playful and creative ways. Most of my respondents studied the Quran and classical literature in Arabic but learned science and Western popular culture in French, which certainly invites differentiation of subselves along tradition versus modernity, European versus Moroccan lines. Khadija did much more of this code shifting than the others I interviewed, and I suspect that her binguality facilitates the dissociation between her European and Muslim personalities.

Surprisingly, she writes almost entirely in classical Arabic. She says she has tried to write in French but finds it more difficult to express herself. Indeed, judging from the dozen or so poems she read to me, her poetry appears to combine feelings, images, and ideas in novel ways, sometimes weaving together meanings that her two discourses otherwise keep separate—such as one in which images of purifying cataclysm lead not to repentance but to a "breaking out" to the "joyful life" and a "waking up" to "freedom and hope." She describes her writing:

> When I have something in my heart and nobody who understands me, the only solution is to put it down on a sheet, to draw words on

a sheet. . . . The pencil becomes part of my hand, like one of my fingers. . . . It's my mind I write about, I write about all the struggle I live inside, the contradictions. All the words that flutter over the sheets form the principles I embrace and believe in, and sometimes I even worship them. (Story 136)

Drawing again on the theme of concealment, she says she writes from honest self-exposure: "I talk about myself as I appear in front of me, something which is uncovered, which appears as it truly is. I don't lie to myself, I don't deceive myself, I don't make it seem more beautiful than it is" (Story 136). This all suggests that her writing allows her to explore forms of integration that transcend the sharp dichotomies of her two personalities.

Dialectic of Modernity

Beneath all Khadija's experience lies the sadness of the "dark child," the hemmed-in, beaten, silenced child who would fly into destructive rage and create cataclysms.[20] Her modernist discourse orchestrates these affective tensions, emplotting them in time, space, and characters, conferring meaning on them, and working their gray textures into melodies she hopes will burst forth with color and hope—as she writes of the setting sun's ocher-red rays dissipating the dark gray clouds and their sadness. As tensions build, this discourse guides her to take flight into erotic excitement that seeks love and "relief/release" rather than "explosion." She beautifies herself and exposes her physique in Western styles on city streets, in bikinis on beaches, and in nakedness to her lovers; she writes her sometimes suicidal despair into poetry she hopes some day to publish; she courageously demands her share of public space and paid employment. By these works (or by variants on the melodic line of beautification and exposure), she creates the European Khadija, whose dreams dissipate her fears and repair the damage done by blows to her skin and insults to her spirit, and whose exposures reveal the purity of her heart and intentions. The dark child's rage surfaces in revolutionary daydreams, as she likens her voice raised in protest to the *farisa*'s (prey/victim's) screams of resistance and struggle for escape, and as she imagines laying waste to the villas of the *bourgeoisiyin* who cause the sadness of people like her.

But her mounting fears also readily bring on images of apocalypse that expand the temporal framework of her experience to cast the present under the spell of death and *ʿzra'il*'s interrogation on Judgment Day, where beauties, sensual joys, and even earthly loves look shallow, ephemeral, and ultimately sinful. This sudden, flaring shift of the temporal parameters brings into play an entirely different world of beings, forces, and values and calls to life the seemingly stronger Muslim Khadija. Here the dark child's rage rekindles the imam's and her mother's terrorizing words, which, spit out as accusations and insults, silence the now-weaker European Khadija. "Regret" reigns with concealment. Inevitably, however, the temporal framework contracts again, God slips from her mind, and exposures of rebellious thoughts and libidinous feelings slip nonconsciously through walls of concealment that feel increasingly claustrophobic. The rudiments of the European Khadija "hysterically" enact themselves and then coalesce as she takes control, deploys science to sweep her world clean of fearsome chthonic forces, opens her *multicolour* wings, and takes flight in search of love. The cycle begins anew (see Figure 6-1).

In a poem discussed earlier, she becomes a butterfly lost in a desert of sadness and addresses pleas to an ambiguous "you" who ignore her: "I want to know where you are, when I can see you." Waiting in solitude, "I smother the sadness of my days." The "you" becomes men—"I was born with you, I grew up with you, I have a brother and a father, I grew up in a world of men"—and then materializes as a man she hopes "can save me" (Story 137). In another, she describes watching a gray, cloudy sunset heavy with sadness, when rays of sun break through, "spreading a red glow over the gray clouds and changed it from sadness into love and beauty." She explains: "The sun keeps setting until you get angry, and if you concentrate on that scenery a lot of problems tumble onto you. . . . So I changed that scenery from sadness, I took off the sadness and gave to it beauty, love and beauty" (Story 140). The cycle continues with a poem about setting sail to a "wild island," written about her lover in Casablanca after he shunned her to marry someone else. "I let myself fall in love with him *bêtement* (Fr.: stupidly/like a beast)," she commented. "How many times have my relationships ended like that!" She explained: "The island is a person to whom I gave everything. I gave all my life to him."

> I boarded a small boat and engraved the image of a drowning person in my mind,
> I headed toward an island that my friends had spoken of

Figure 6-1 Khadija's European and Muslim identities

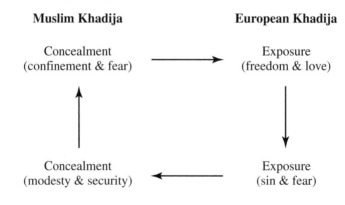

I began building dreams in my imagination until I reached the
  island.
When I arrived, I wondered what would become of me:
  I was frightened of wild animals, frightened to die
  It was a wild island, and I couldn't live there alone.
Why had I come?
I wished I hadn't sailed the sea.
Why did I bring nothing?
Why didn't I stay on land?
This is what happens to a person who undertakes the impossible,
  and doesn't think about going wrong.
This is my fate. (Story 141)

CHAPTER 7

Conclusions

Anthropologists are no longer surprised when new evidence is brought forth of the existence of full-fledged individuality among primitives. In the heyday of folk theory it was glibly assumed that the primitive individual was literally submerged, that no room was left for personality or self-expression in a society ridden by tradition, dominated by established habits and dogmas, shot through with inflexible patterns. No one any longer believes this. We know now that the very uniformity of primitive patterns should not be taken literally.

—Alexander Goldenweiser, 1936[1]

Scholars today reject the word *primitive*, but they have not given up the notion that non-Western peoples are submerged in their collectivist social relationships and lack the individuality of Westerners. So above all, these life narratives show "full-fledged individuality" flourishing in Morocco, as it undoubtedly does throughout the Middle East, even in its most traditional milieus. The young Moroccans I interviewed cannot be said to have relationally defined "mosaic" selves that contrast with Americans' "bounded" selves, as Geertz and others have suggested. They indeed value family loyalty, make personal sacrifices to maintain extended family ties, and protect their household's honor. Many of them also feel a kind of matrifocal interdependence, resembling the *amae* (or "indulged dependence") Takeo Doi describes for Japan,[2] that rarely appears in interviews with young middle-class Americans. These are psychological differences that make a difference, but they do not construct sociocentric *selves*. My interviewees also experience themselves as bounded individuals, as striving for autonomy as well as connectedness, and in important respects as alienated from their social groups as embedded in them.

The life narratives, in fact, show that cultural psychologists cannot simply theorize about culture and self because individuals have neither *a* culture nor *a* self. They live in environments created by cultural regions that intersect in southern Morocco: basic infant care practices resemble those of Africa and South

Asia; circumcision rites for men are Middle Eastern; the honor-modesty system is circum-Mediterranean; prayer, fasting, and the pollution-purification system are spread throughout the Muslim world; gender representations are Middle Eastern but extend throughout the "purdah zone" into northern India; and the contrasts of tradition versus modernity have been shaped by Morocco's distinctive colonial history, French-Arabic bilingualism, and the tourism industry. Further, my interviewees' culture is characterized by dispute rather than consensus about core values and concepts of personhood, dispute animated especially by the millennia-old tension between the principles of honor-modesty and those of religion and by the century-old tension between Moroccan-style tradition and Western-style modernity. Most important, individuals develop multiple and often contrasting senses of self, subselves, or identities: Mohammed as *jahel* (wild/delinquent) versus ʿ*skeri* (soldier) versus *fqih* (religious scholar); Hussein as modern versus traditional versus devout; Rachida as possessed of ʿ*qel* (intelligence/maturity) and *klem* (voice) versus *wesekh* (dirt) and *fitna* (chaos/disorder); Khadija as Moroccan versus French.

In all of the narratives I recorded, shifts among this sort of subselves and identities show a mixture of sociocentric and egocentric self-representations. Recall Mohammed's sociocentric *fqih* (devout) identity versus his egocentric *jahel* (delinquent) self; Hussein's ambivalence over leaving his traditional family behind versus more fully enmeshing himself in it; Rachida's abrupt shifts between egocentric boasts that she runs her own life and sociocentric subordination to the rule of her male relatives; and Khadija's split into an egocentric French self and a sociocentric Moroccan one. Turkish psychologist Cigdem Kagitcibasi believes that the "relational" components of self are more strongly developed in Middle Easterners (and in most non-Western, "majority" cultures) but hardly crowd out the individualist components. She argues that individualism and group loyalties typically coexist, sometimes conflicting but often converging to animate a "socially-motivated achievement motivation."[3] Suad Joseph makes similar observations based on her studies of Lebanese families: "Connectivity exists side by side with individualism in the same culture, and perhaps even in the same person," she writes; "these are not oppositional polarities."[4] This conclusion—that egocentric *and* sociocentric senses of self coexist within most Middle Easterners—fits with the more recent models of acculturation and self-conceptions described in chapter 1 and with the conclusion reached by Oyserman and colleagues after their meta-analysis of individualism-collectivism studies.[5] And if Triandis is correct that these are rooted in modes of subsistence, it also fits with the historical development of North African and Middle Eastern cultures from the interaction of collectivism-fostering peasant agriculture and individualism-fostering nomadic pastoralism.[6]

The coexistence of egocentric and sociocentric orientations contradicts the "boundary permeability" model of self advanced by Markus and Kitayama but is consistent with their "repertoire of schemata" view.[7] And it is not inconsistent with the view of Oyserman and colleagues[8] and other researchers[9] that cultures differ because social situations sample individuals' more independent versus more interdependent self-conceptions. But the life narratives show much more than this: they show a small number of identity-defining *narratives* or *discourses*, each of which brings into play a worldview with its own moral imperatives and space-time-causality coordinates. As Ewing suggests, each discourse can create an "illusion of wholeness," so that individuals do not feel divided even as they shift between contradictory identities. Cultures differ because they provide distinctive materials from which individuals construct these discourses.[10] Cultural psychology therefore needs to view the shaping of selves as a *developmental* process[11] and not only a social psychological one: culture influences the emotional tensions comprising core personality, it inculcates the etiquettes of social interaction and self-care practices that shape social personas, and it provides the symbolic, ideological, and narrative materials that individuals selectively use to fashion identities.

Viewed developmentally, the young adult Moroccans I interviewed appear to be psychologically *individuating* along the lines described by Jung and Erikson, though in dramatically different social and cultural conditions than prevail in Western societies. They may not be trying to achieve autonomy by breaking family and kin loyalties or by taking contractual views of what they give and get in their personal relationships, as may be common in Western societies. And economic and political underdevelopment certainly denies them opportunities for psychological development that are available to many Westerners. But they clearly are seeking to compose personal identities as their own idiosyncratic variations on their culture's main themes, just as Americans do.[12] Further, this sort of individuation does not appear to be a Western import, as shown by Dwight Reynolds's recent study of 140 premodern Arabic autobiographies.[13] Against the prevailing view that autobiography arose in Europe as an expression of an emerging individualistic "Western self"[14] and develops in other cultures only as a consequence of Westernization, Reynolds shows that an Arabic autobiographical genre was established by the eleventh century and that many writers used its formulaic literary conventions to convey distinctive life stories and personalities. Recent studies of premodern Chinese, Japanese, and Tibetan autobiographical writings reach similar conclusions.[15]

Eighty years ago, Edward Sapir likened the acquisition of culture to the mastery of a musical instrument and genre. There can be no expression of individuality, he argued, without first subordinating personal idiosyncrasies to acquire the skills and formal principles of a cultural heritage. Only after achieving proficiency can one innovate and develop a distinctive style. He believed that "genuine" cultures—which today would be classed as collectivist—tend to provide aesthetically more coherent heritages, and therefore richer materials with which to individuate, than do "spurious" modern cultures, which fragment spheres of life and co-opt individuation into hollow consumerism.[16] As Goldenweiser recognized, "full-fledged individuality" does not simply mean getting the life one wants, and in spite of the travails faced by those I interviewed, Moroccan culture appears to provide a great many genuine resources for individuation.

These life narratives document the "intense struggle" among "conflicting value orientations" that Halim Barakat argues has historically shaped Arab culture: a struggle of innovation with tradition that sets individuals on diverging developmental trajectories and divides them within themselves.[17] This differs sharply from the Geertz-Eickelman-Rosen view, which portrays a general consensus on core principles and focuses on how these are negotiated in practice. The narratives especially contradict Geertz's conclusion that Moroccans' "selfhood is never in danger" because their "location in the general mosaic" of social categories leaves "the substantive content of the categories . . . aside as something properly concealed in apartments, temples, and tents."[18] All those I interviewed felt their selves very much endangered, not only by limited opportunities to live their dreams but also by relentless scrutiny of their values, intentions, and mettle.

Again, this does not appear to be a recent consequence of colonialism, education, or mass media. The informal life histories I collected from uneducated men and women in remote High Atlas villages showed similar struggles to stake claims to public identities that embody private sentiments, though cast in more fully "traditional" idioms. Ethnographies of other Middle Eastern milieus also show threatened selves struggling for identities,[19] as do North African life histories,[20] autobiographies,[21] and novels.[22] The crucial issue for cultural psychology, especially for anyone seeking to understand contemporary North African and Middle Eastern cultures, concerns how conflicts between personal ambitions and family loyalties have ceased being matters of individual struggle and become reconfigured in terms of the identity politics spawned by globalization and underdevelopment, in which "the West" now represents egocentric strivings and "authentic tradition" represents sociocentric responsibilities.

Overall, then, these life narratives indicate that young Moroccans and Americans differ not in the *process* of identity formation but in the *content* of the self-representations they employ and in the *affective tensions* these organize. Where Americans appear to differentiate identities primarily along the lines of social class, ethnicity, gender, and subcultural styles, young Moroccans prominently employ axes of tradition versus modernity (often equated with Morocco versus Europe), religion (both Muslim versus non-Muslim and devotion versus delinquency), and gender (mainly in the forms of reason versus chaos, authority versus compassion, and concealment versus exposure). In addition, Moroccan childcare practices and social institutions appear to cultivate feelings—especially those related to matrifocal interdependence, to vulnerability to chthonic beings and the evil eye, to cycles of purity and pollution, to the honor-modesty system, and to religious piety—that shape culturally distinctive sentiments, motives, and senses of self that identities organize.

Perhaps most important, the narratives show the play of *mimesis* described by Taussig and Pamuk in the construction of identity (see chapter 1): the simultaneous attempt to "magically" acquire powers by copying some cultural Others and to expel vulnerabilities by rejecting other cultural Others. Here the Middle East's historical struggle among conflicting value orientations has come to be played out in terms of globalization-era identity politics: across the Mediterranean and Atlantic stands the modern Westerner; across the deserts to the South and East the traditional Moroccan and Muslim believer. These archetypal Others mix thoroughly in the sights, sounds, and interactional textures of daily life, forming a new culture of dispute and dialogue. Young Moroccans may identify with the Western Other as progressive and liberating and disidentify with the traditional Other as backward and encumbering, or they may reject this "Euromanic" stance and identify with the traditional Other as authentic, healthy, and upright and disidentify with the Western Other as alien, corrupt, and degenerate. As the life narratives show, most shift between variants of these identities. The crucial question observers can pose—but young Moroccans must live—concerns whether this dualism pitches them into "schizophrenic" dispute or engages them in creative dialogue.

In this chapter, I review what the study of these lives can tell us about personality organization, about self-representation, about psychological development in Middle Eastern societies, and about relations of culture and self.

Personality Organization ❀

Like American life narratives, these interviews show that identity coalesces as a configuration of multiple discourses or subselves, in much the manner Ewing described for the Pakistanis she interviewed.[23] They show personality to be complex and fluid: to shift continually among subselves within an identity-defining discourse (e.g., Mohammed and Rachida) and sometimes also among two or three discourses (e.g., Hussein and Khadija). On the whole, personality and self have been seen as stabilizing and often conservative forces in culture. This is especially true in the Middle East, where frustration with setbacks to democratization have led a surprising number of scholars to view personality as a repository of authoritarian tradition that subverts modernization.[24] There indeed can be a conservatism to personality, especially when individuals rigidly embrace cultural conventions to defend against "abject" senses of self[25]: Mohammed as *jahel* (wild/rabid), Hussein wasting away in three prisons of darkness like al-Ma'arri, Rachida as *wesekh* (dirty/impure), Khadija as *farisa* (prey). But life histories show personality to be what the American culture-and-personality school saw it as: a source of variation and innovation that must be standardized by culture, often coercively and at great cost to those whose temperaments poorly fit their culture's configuration.

Levels of Personality Organization

LeVine's theory of culture-and-personality[26] and my own analysis of American life narratives[27] convinced me of the need to distinguish between genotypic and phenotypic levels of personality organization (see chapter 1), which I have termed *core personality* and *identity.* The Moroccan life narratives further demonstrate the importance of this distinction, as only a layered model of this sort can account for how an individual's contrasting identities may configure the same core-level affective tensions into dramatically different patterns, as in the cases of Hussein and Khadija. It also takes a layered model to describe how an individual's identity may be organized to maintain one sense of self and disintegrate another, as in the cases of Mohammed and Rachida. Of equal importance, only a layered model can account for developmental discontinuities, such as the early shaping of externalized readings of anxiety followed by later disbelief in chthonic beings, which appears to bring many of those I interviewed frightening intimations of unknown or fantastic forces.

But these life narratives also suggest that a third level of organization must be added to the model, in a sense "between" core-level personality and identity. It was Hussein's narrative that first led me to postulate this level of organization, as I found I could not fully account for his personality with a two-level model. In particular, the relational triangle (i.e., tyrant, victim, and challenger/defender) shows too much complexity and performs too important an integrative role to regard it as a feature of core-level organization. I tried to treat it as an identity-defining discourse of honor, but this also proved untenable. A search of his narrative showed that he rarely uses the explicit rhetoric of honor, which I knew lives on in more "tribal" High Atlas communities. Instead, I found many instances in which he initially construes a test of honor but then defines the unfolding actions and relationships in modernist, traditionalist, or religious terms. Only in characterizing his difficult relationship with his father does he make much use of the idiom of honor. In addition to falling short of defining an identity, then, the relational triangle seemed repeatedly to put Hussein in a dilemma that he resolved by other discourses. I therefore concluded that although honorable manhood is nearly always at issue for him, he has not drawn on the region's traditional rhetoric to formulate a *discourse* of honor.

By breaking his narrative into story segments, I discovered that the relational triangle organizes episodes illustrating his modernist outlook, its traditionalist inversion, and his religious worldview. As I began to regard these broader outlooks as discourses, the triangular configurations increasingly appeared to serve as building blocks: they construct experiences, feelings, and relationships as concerning honor and modesty, but these then require larger frameworks to confer specific self-representational meanings. This organization increasingly suggested developmental discontinuity: that by internalizing the honor-modesty system, Hussein was well prepared to grow into the rural tribal world of his grandfathers. But he grew up instead in the mind-opening but worry-filled atmosphere of school, facing Casablanca and Rabat and Paris and turning his back on the isolated villages and rugged ranges of the pre-Saharan hinterlands. Had he lived in his grandfather's day and fully developed a discourse of honor and the Muslim self-care system of which he now practices only parts, I do not believe I would have found myself puzzling over features of his narrative that seemed neither core-level nor identity. But after internalizing the relational paradigm central to the region's traditional honor-modesty and patron-client systems, the Hussein I interviewed sought to redefine it in terms of achievement in the modern, urban world, in terms of religion, and ultimately in terms of a "calling."

Emotional displacements suggesting an intermediary level of organization also appear prominently in Rachida's narrative, such as those by which she construes intimations of rejection and fragmentation to be matters of propriety and piety associated with her household's honor and bounty, and by which she assimilates feelings of menstrual distress to religiously based sentiments of pollution and purification. In many instances, these transformations take place before she develops a narrative line in which to embed and orchestrate the feelings. It is almost as if she settles on a key signature—a scale of modesty and propriety (i.e., defining the parameters of social personality)—that confers musiclike meaning on the fears of abandonment and fragmentation that first emerge as merely cacophonous sounds (i.e., core personality) and then begins a narrative composition that evokes feelings of bounty in its harmonies (i.e., identity) and gives her a sense of self-control.

Khadija narrates her life in a key of concealment and exposure, a scale of body surfaces that confers an erotic timbre to a wide range of the emotions she experiences. Like Rachida, she feels herself continually the object of judging, potentially admiring, potentially condemning gazes. "A woman exposes or conceals herself" thus takes on a type-scenic quality in her narrative: saturated with excitement, danger, and moral significance, such images beg for emplotment in larger narratives that might then turn romantic or tragic. Like the relational triangle in Hussein's narrative, the exposure-concealment schema entails much more organization and moral meaning than do core-level affective tensions, but it presents her with a challenge rather than assigning her an identity. Playing this simultaneously integrative and interrogative role, it similarly appears to comprise social personality.

The existence of integrative structures at this level in Mohammed's narrative is less clear. The three subselves or senses of self he represents as *fqih* (devout), ^c*skeri* (soldier), and *jahel* (delinquent) together may form a social personality and play an organizing role similar to that of the relational triangle in Hussein's narrative. But unlike Hussein's relational triangle, his narrative does not stage these figures together as a single configuration or prominently employ them in type-scenic form. They can be viewed as characters comprising his identity, rather than as organizing an intermediary level. I suspect that the status of these subselves remains ambiguous at least partly because Mohammed narrates his life as the most traditional of the four, perhaps as the most traditional of the Moroccans I interviewed. In spite of his years in Rabat and his considerable education, he resembles some of the young men we came to know in High Atlas villages who articulate identities in the traditional rhetorics of honor and religion.

I believe I did not recognize *social personality* in American life narratives because most of those I interviewed had not experienced this sort of discontinuity, and as an insider who didn't need to puzzle over every cultural reference, I blindly overlooked the evidence I now think many of them contain. As I look at these narratives now, they indeed show automatically constituted configurations that can be termed *social personas*. They typically center not on honor or piety but on self-esteem as described in various folk terminologies as arising from achievement, social standing, physical attractiveness, and popularity. Together these cohere to form a multidimensional system, schema, or code, analogous to the circum-Mediterranean honor-modesty code, but of a very different character. The premier traits and motives studied by American psychologists—self-esteem, intelligence, agreeableness, and needs for achievement, affiliation, and power—may yet be operationalized in a universal manner, but their inception and scholarly popularity clearly reflect the core dimensions of distinctly American social personas.

Social Persona and the Generalized Other

The building of theory should be guided by three overriding principles: parsimony, completeness, and coherence with related theories. Adding a third level to the model developed in *Self Representation* violates the principle of parsimony, and for this reason alone I feel reluctant to propose it. Genotype-phenotype (core level–identity) models are hardly in good currency among personality or cultural psychologists, and it seems unwise to muddy a two-level theory with a third level. Nonetheless, analysis of these narratives convinces me that the principle of completeness demands it. At least some of these lives show integrative structures that cannot be regarded as either core-level or identity but organize affective tensions in accordance with distinctive cultural patterns, most prominently those of the honor-modesty system and Muslim religiosity.

Because these resemble the internalized cultural patterns described by many theorists—especially Eric Wolf (social etiquettes), Pierre Bourdieu (habitus as logic, rhetoric, syntax, and sentiment), and G. H. Mead (social self shaped by the Generalized Other)—considerations of theoretical coherence tip the scale toward incorporating *social personality* or *social persona* in the model as a third level of organization. In addition, Erik Erikson gave increasing emphasis to the late childhood "ritualization" of social interaction, self-care, and daily activities, which he believed deeply internalize a sense of cultural-group membership as the foundation of identity.[28] He continued to distinguish identity formation as a later and cognitively more complex process, however, one that often substantially revises earlier group identifications. As the acquisition of ritualized social interaction sets the stage for identity, then, it appears analogous to the organization of social personality as I have described this in the narratives.

At the level of social persona, then, a society's interpersonal etiquettes, habitus, or ritualized interaction patterns can be seen to shape a culturally distinctive set of *motives*: "needs" for achievement, self-esteem, popularity, and the like in America; for honor, modesty, purification, and the like in Morocco. Each motive or need defines a range of individual differences: just as some Americans have high needs for achievement and others low, so some Moroccans would score high on a "need for honor" measure and others low. This three-level model of personality thus parallels that proposed by Dan McAdams, based on three levels of knowledge that observers may obtain about persons. His Level I consists of the "decontextualized, and relatively nonconditional constructs called 'traits,' which provide a dispositional signature for personality." This encompasses what have come to be termed the *big five personality traits*[29] and roughly corresponds to what I have termed *core personality*. Level II consists of motives, values, personal strivings, and the like "that are contextualized in time, place, or role." This encompasses what psychologists have traditionally studied as motives or needs and parallels what I have termed *social personality*.[30] Level III consists of personal identity, as embedded in a life narrative.[31]

At the same time that a society's social etiquettes are shaping universal *traits* into culturally distinctive *motives*, they also are shaping universal *emotions* in accordance with cultural display rules to form what might be labeled with the somewhat archaic term *sentiments*. This follows Bourdieu's and Abu-Lughod's use of the term and that of also American psychologist William McDougall, who in the 1920s outlined a theory of character as an organization of sentiments that he defined as "acquired conative trends."[32] McDougall chose the term to describe linkages of affect, moral principle, and action that are more complex and enduring than comparatively simple emotions or traits. He underscored the distinction between a transient emotional *state* and a more enduring *sentiment*, which entails an active pursuit or avoidance of the state and infuses the state with value. McDougall did not suggest that sentiments are culture-specific, but his theory lends itself to this view. In contrast to traits and emotions, which can be described in universal *etic* terms, motives and sentiments should be described in *emic*, culturally specific terms. Universal traits and emotions do not vanish in the formation of social personas, and they probably can be measured in ways that give the impression that most psychological processes are universal. But they take on new meanings, stylings, and linkages that may be culture-specific.

This acquisition of social etiquettes, motives, and sentiments has important consequences for self-representation, as an individual increasingly comes to see one's self—and to monitor and judge one's performances—from the point of view of a Generalized Other. In G. H. Mead's view, this consolidates various *Me* representations into a more or less coherent *social self*. Although Mead often treats this as a rather smooth process, he sometimes goes to awkward lengths to preserve the freedom of the "I" to escape being fixed by the system of social roles and mirroring that shapes the "Me." The Generalized Other thus resembles what Sartre terms the *gaze* of the impersonal social "they," or what Althusser describes as the interpolation or "hailing" of the individual by anonymous authorities,[33] as it ominously threatens to freeze one into a self not of one's making. In some passages, Mead portrays the social self as challenging the individual (the "I" pole of the self) to prove his or her social competence or to disprove what she or he has been made out to be. This is precisely what social personas seem to entail in the life narratives: integrating the person into culture and posing the questions that an identity must then answer. Early culture-and-personality theorists were thus on solid ground when they interpreted culturally distinctive interactional etiquettes as shaping personality organization, but went awry when they inferred that they form a "national character" or "basic personality." Internalized cultural etiquettes should be thought of as forming a *habitus*, a *social self*, or *social personae*, which sets the task of fashioning an identity by forcing the questions: "Who am I?" "What am I worth?" and "For what will I live?" to be answered in the culture's own terms.

This three-level model thus makes possible an important theoretical synthesis that accords with a good deal of life narrative evidence: the socialization to and mastery of social etiquettes crystallize a set of culturally distinctive motives and sentiments, on the one hand, and a set of role-based self-conceptions on the other. Together, the motives typically studied by personality psychologists, the emotional display rules studied by cross-cultural psychologists, and the self-as-a-social-structure described by G. H. Mead comprise *social personality*. For most individuals, the consolidation of social persona marks a significant modification of his or her temperament, entailing an amplification of some temperamental traits, a checking or diminution of others, and perhaps a laborious cultivating of some characteristics to which she or he is not temperamentally inclined. In addition, most individuals probably develop more than a single social persona as they internalize different social roles, contexts, or values. Thus motives, emotions, and self-conceptions are not simply specific to situations—as both social psychologists and discourse theorists are fond of insisting—but to social personas that can be flexibly deployed not only in conformity to situational pressures but also to effect resistance and innovation. Finally, social personality does not confer an *identity*, as Erikson uses this term, but defines the task of formulating one. Ideally, an achieved identity provides an integration of social personas that enables an individual to flexibly and creatively deploy them as complementary sides of his or her character.

The Moroccan life narratives I recorded suggest that the honor-modesty system and Islam provide two predominant configurations of social personality within North African culture. Most individuals internalize both, some in ways that converge (e.g., Rachida) and some in ways that conflict (e.g., Mohammed). But it is important to keep in mind that the culture provides more than two etiquette-motive systems, that individuals can differ dramatically in which of these they internalize, and that men and women likely internalize different features of both.

Culture and Personality Development

I propose this three-level model to account for the organization of adult personality as seen in life narratives, without making assumptions about how each level develops. But the observation that core-level tensions appear integrated into more complex units at the level of social personality, and social personas integrated into more complex discourses of identity, accords well with a developmental view that focuses on two biologically based transitions (one around age five to seven, the other around puberty) that cultures almost universally read as signals of readiness for crucial social role transitions. That is, core personality characteristics may be shaped mainly in early childhood (as LeVine believes), social personality primarily in later childhood (as Mead suggests in his examples), and identity in adolescence and early adulthood (as Erikson theorizes).

Yasuko Minoura recently argued that there is a critical period for assimilating cultural patterns in late childhood and presented data that children who emigrate before that period rather easily assimilate the new culture, whereas those who emigrate after that period never completely assimilate it.[34] This clearly cannot be correct, as there is compelling evidence that the learning of culture begins at birth and continues through the life course. But it may be that interactional styles and etiquettes, and the motives and emotions associated with them, do tend to be internalized in late childhood, as she suggests, and in a relatively indelible way that appears in narratives as social personality. This was when Mohammed says he lost his mother, became *niḍam* (well-bred/orderly), and learned how to fight; when Hussein says he witnessed his parents' quarrels, fled beatings at school, and took up soccer; when Rachida memorized the Quran and witnessed her mother's miscarriage;

and when Khadija says her mother often beat her, she became *timide*, and she began taking flight in erotic reveries.

Let me be clear: the hypothesis that core personality, social personality, and identity develop in early childhood, late childhood, and adolescence, respectively, is a speculative one. It cannot be evaluated with life narrative data, from which one cannot reconstruct developmental histories. But as a framework for linking life narrative and other sorts of data on the cultural shaping of personality, it has considerable appeal. First, it points beyond discussions of culture-and-self toward investigating how culture affects specific levels of personality in successive developmental epochs. This is hardly a new idea, but the importance of building *developmental* theory cannot be overstated, nor can the importance of taking account of developmental discontinuities in an era when migration and rapid social change have become ubiquitous. Further, the model nicely incorporates Erikson's view that identity develops via three processes (introjection in early childhood, identifications in middle to late childhood, and ideological belief systems in adolescence) and that culturally specific forms of ritualization play a crucial integrative role in the second. It gives increased importance to the period of late childhood, which psychologists continue to neglect in favor of early childhood and adolescence. Many lines of research now indicate that this is a crucially important period, especially for the development of social competence and a sense of self-worth. This view also converges with research on culture and emotions, as Matsumoto suggests that the basic acquisition of the cultural display rules that shape the expression of emotions probably takes place between the ages of six and ten.[35]

Finally, the model can be formulated in a way that avoids postulating a rigid developmental timetable. If the apprenticeship-competence-expertise sequence now used to characterize some developmental processes[36] were applied to these levels, a schedule of cultural influences on personality might be postulated along the lines of Table 7-1.

The use of *apprenticeship-competence-expertise* terminology has some obvious drawbacks. It suggests that affective tensions, moral sentiments, and self-representations can be regarded as *skills* and that a set of culturally useful skills

Table 7-1 Developmental periods and levels of personality organization

	Infancy	Early Childhood	Late Childhood	Adolescence	Early Adulthood
Core	apprenticeship	competence	expertise		
Social		apprenticeship	competence	expertise	
Identity			apprenticeship	competence	expertise

can be identified at each period. Even were this feasible, the analogy implies an "as the twig is bent" continuity to development[37] that focuses attention away from culturally patterned discontinuities. Yet this model also calls attention to the ways personality characteristics have strategic uses and develop as inter-personal and intrapsychic tools.[38] And it recognizes that cultures value certain affective tensions, moral sentiments, and self-representations and ignore or seek to suppress others.

Early culture-and-personality theorists like Ruth Benedict and Marga-ret Mead argued that all societies contain roughly the same range of human temperaments but that each culture favors a subset of temperamental quali-ties and cultivates them toward its ideals, in ways that often make the ideals difficult to achieve for those born with different traits.[39] Their cultural rela-tivism did not hold that human nature is so plastic that culture can mold it in any direction but that individuals who flourish in a culture that prizes their temperamental qualities might founder in one that favors those they lack and, conversely, those who become deviants in one culture might well have de-veloped into ideal men and women had they been born into another. As simple as it is, the model diagrammed in Figure 7-1 may provide a frame-work for more subtly examining the interaction of temperaments and cul-tural environments, especially because it adds an account of the emerging levels of personality organization within which temperaments must be pro-gressively integrated. Identity "expertise," then, can be viewed in the light of Sapir's, Benedict's, and Margaret Mead's aesthetic view of culture: as the ability to vary, create, and individuate, using materials provided by one's cultural heritage.

Self-Representation ❀

Multiple Identities

My investigation of American life narratives found that identity takes shape as an internal differentiation: as a splitting of subjective experience, in which some affective states or motives are egosyntonically embraced as *Me* and oth-ers egodystonically represented as *not-Me* and located in the hearts, minds, and bodies of others, who usually reside across significant social boundaries. Signs of gender, ethnicity, social class, religion, and lifestyle thus come to differentiate inner, psychological worlds as well as society, "inscribing" as Hussein put it, a map of the social order "deep inside." Yet these mappings tend not to be stable but charged with ambivalence, and American narratives show that at least some individuals shift among contrasting identities, set-ting out often contradictory differentiations of *Me* versus *not-Me*.

The Moroccan narratives show similar shifts among multiple senses of self or identities, with identity proper consisting of one or more discourses that configure subselves into *Me* versus *not-Me* contrasts. Mohammed and Rachida narrate their lives largely in terms of a single overarching discourse that transforms a dangerous or abject self (wild, ignorant, and rabid in Mohammed's case; polluted and chaos-prone in Rachida's) into controlled, honorable, pious selves. Mohammed sketches but does not fully develop a pair of contrasting discourses as he embraces his "clean" life of tradition and piety against the dangers of urban anomie and delinquency, and then casts his life in Skoura as little, backward, and boring compared with the "cleaner," modern, and grander life he sees in Rabat. Rachida begins to articulate a pair of contrasting discourses when she takes up the issue of women's nature and rights and voices both a feminist outlook rooted in her *m^{c}aqel* (rational/mature) and *naqi* (clean/pure) sense of self and a patriarchal outlook rooted in her *foḍa* (chaos)-prone and *wesekh* (dirty/polluted) sense of self. But this appears more a contradiction or dialogue within her overarching religious discourse than as a pair of identity-defining discourses. Khadija articulates a sharply contrasting pair of discourses (European and Muslim), and Hussein three potentially complementary discourses (modernist, traditionalist, religious), each orchestrating different transformations of core affective tensions into idealized selves and antiselves.

Units of Representation

Discourses define identities through linkages of abstract concepts with concrete imagery (in Hussein's narrative, for example, *irada qawiya*, or "monumental strength," with "like a lion" and "like *^{c}ntar*"). Neither concepts nor images can stand alone: concepts define abstract categories and principles but require images or symbols to show by example how they apply to the world and to show by feel how they apply to inner experience. Images evoke and are evoked by affects and so selectively bring alive features of one's larger world. They impart the sort of kinesthetic, affective, aesthetic meaningfulness that music nonconceptually evokes but require a conceptual framework to adequately specify their meanings. Discourses take shape by establishing loose, montagelike linkages between concepts and images, which give them a fundamentally poetic, rhetorical character. They aim less at scientific accuracy than at juxtapositions of concepts and images that create experiences with particular feeling tones and meanings and that can make pointed impressions on others, such as "honor," "elegance," "piety," or "innocence."

Analyzing American life narratives, I drew on the work of Claude Lévi-Strauss,[40] Clifford Geertz,[41] and Victor Turner[42] to identify the elements of self-representation, in increasing size or scope, as *symbol, metaphor,* and *myth.* The Moroccan narratives—especially Hussein's—suggest that some elements are more appropriately described as *motifs* and *type scenes,* terms used in studies of oral epics.[43] Given the importance of oral recitation in Islam and North African culture, I at first thought that Moroccans might use these devices while Americans employ symbols and metaphors. But analysis of subsequent Moroccan texts showed frequent use of symbols and metaphors, and reexamination of American narratives showed uses of motifs and type scenes that I had not initially recognized. Most narratives contain all of these elements, and no rigid distinction can be made between symbols and motifs, or even between metaphors and type scenes. But there do appear to be individual differences in the prominence of one or the other sort, which can yield differing narrative styles.

The crucial observation from both American and Moroccan narratives concerns the relation between smaller and larger elements: as Ricoeur[44] emphasizes for written narrative, symbols tend to be especially dense with meaning and powerfully evocative but require networks of metaphor to specify which of many possible meanings they are to carry. Type scenes appear to play the same role vis-à-vis motifs. The relation between smaller and larger units might also be described in terms of Silvan Tomkins's script theory,[45] as his notion of *scene* (a representation of an affect) roughly corresponds to *motif* and his *script* (a set of ordering rules that interpret, amplify, and control scenes) to *type scene*, and in terms of his notion of how larger plots, theories, and maps organize scripts into narrative or discourse.

In some instances, concepts and images link to form key symbols[46] that anchor identity by embodying the major themes of a life. In Hussein's narrative, we see how the denotative meanings of terms built from the $w * q * f$ root (*stand, stand up for, stop, be brought to a halt*) figuratively depict their connotative meanings: prowess versus impotence, courage versus cowardice, maturity versus immaturity. Embedded in a discourse, key symbols can take on the "microdot"-like character Robert Stoller has described of fantasy elements, produced by the representational compression he believes operates in all kinds of thought:

> During World War II, the Nazis devised a system for hiding messages: the microdot, "a photograph the size of a printed period that reproduced with perfect clarity a standard-sized typewritten letter." Most human behavior—the functioning of the mind—works the same way; Freud described something like this long ago. In a process comparable to the miniaturization that allows stupendous amounts of information to be stored, arranged, rearranged, and transmitted within so small an apparatus as the brain, we—our minds—use psychic mechanisms that work at high speed to compress great masses of data into amazingly small "space" in a purposeful, organized way. One might even look on the mind as the movement of these very efficient microdots: their content, the rules and mechanisms of their functioning, and their teleology—their motivation.[47]

Key symbols of this sort appear in Moroccan as well as American narratives as critical nodes through which self-representation is articulated and personality culturally constructed. Like microdots, key symbols condense enormous amounts of information, simultaneously about bodily sensations and feeling tones, strengths and vulnerabilities, social relationships and moral principles. We see this in the "home" Mohammed finds in God, in Hussein's identity-defining pronouncement that "standing up" for the falsely accused maintains "an innocent relationship with God," in Rachida's recitation of the sura al raḥman, and in Khadija's self-exposure. Like Kuhnian "exemplars," such associations of bodily movements, affective tensions, and moral values show how things work in each of these personal but also cultural universes. Key symbols do not just provide "models" of *how* things work—a role played perhaps by metaphors, type scenes, and larger plot schemas—but direct, experiential demonstrations of things *at work*, experientially demonstrating the basic types of energy and dynamic motion to be found in one's life world.

Octave Relations

Both Americans and Moroccans appear to use structurally ambiguous key symbols to link contrasting senses of self in ways that construe them as "higher" and "lower" versions of each other. Drawing an analogy from tonal music, I have termed these *octave relations* and suggested they serve as the elementary units of self-representation: they define a scalelike ontological-moral space, within which subjectivity experiences itself as in "departure from" and "return toward" the end points. As the establishment of a scale confers musical meanings on notes that by themselves have only sound properties, so the narrative establishment of a symbolic octave confers ontological and moral meanings on textures of feeling that by themselves have only affective qualities. That is, I recognize—create—who I am at any moment as my position and movement within a scalelike configuration of locations, each location a degree of departure from or return toward subself and/or antiself prototypes. A discourse establishes the scale and orchestrates melodic (*Me* versus *past-Me*) and harmonic (*Me* versus *not-Me*) movements within it, leading toward a resolution of tensions at the higher octave note. Thus Mohammed faces down death beneath the torture chamber's spotlights and attains a home in God at Daybreak, Hussein feels himself *tweqqef* (brought to a halt) by powerful tyrants and seeks the empowerment that will enable him to *waqef* (stand up) in defense of the weak, Rachida finds herself polluted by the uncontrollable powers of her *raḥim* (womb) but restored to purity in recitation of *al raḥman* (the Merciful), and Khadija repairs the scars of beatings and insults by beautification and exposure.

These structures imply a stunning degree of creative synthesis in the architecture of identity, all executed seemingly without deliberate design. Indeed, the musical analogy easily overstates the order, symmetry, and completeness of life narratives, and it would be a mistake to view self-representational systems as taking shape according to classical forms of aesthetic coherence.

Personality and identity are above all processes that fashion open, incomplete structures, and Hermans and Kempen's dialogical model better captures the sense of cacophonous dispute that often emerges from clashing inner voices.[48] But I believe that self-representation does use the higher-order cognitive processes that enable us to hear and create music and that structurally ambiguous symbols thereby come to play a privileged role in the architecture of identity. Identity emerges as the system within personality that brings order to the buzzing, blooming confusion of experience and often achieves remarkable coherence, even though moment-to-moment subjective experience may not. That is, the fact that an individual has fashioned a beautifully symmetrical self-representational system does not predict how consistently his or her experience will conform to its contours. An elegantly composed fugue can defeat a musician's effort to perform it, and identities may achieve impressive symmetries best described by musical analogies, even if their performance sounds more like awkward improvisation, dispute, or even cacophony.

I believe that as people go about the business of their daily lives, identity regularly recedes into the background while they organize thought and action to meet situational exigencies. Situations may sample a great variety of self-schemas that do not have central places in an individual's identity but guide behavior in specific contexts. As Erikson suggests, identity may fade from the actor's view precisely when she or he becomes most engrossed in enacting it. Then as immersion in situational exigencies introduces noise that disintegrates identities, people look for opportunities to reestablish or reclarify them. Many create semiritualized periods—be they daydreams, self-care practices, shopping, prayer, leisure activities, or whatever—in which they evoke and perform their primary discourse of identity in its most fuguelike form. Cultures also appear to provide identity-clarifying rituals, which I believe the cycle of daily and weekly purification-and-prayer provides to many devout Muslims. Gilbert Herdt describes how the Sambia nosebleeding ritual,[49] first traumatically forced on seven- to ten-year-old boys, often comes to be practiced privately by senior men to purify and restore their sense of vigor. This provides an elegant example of how a cultural key symbol with a shared public meaning can come to be appropriated as a personal key symbol rich in private, idiosyncratic life-historical meanings.

In his 1890 *Principles of Psychology*, William James wrote of the "division of the man into several selves," based on "the distinct *groups* of persons about whose opinion he cares." He puzzled over how the "I" could maintain a sense of continuity through the flux of changing "Me" representations and offered a seemingly silly analogy: the relationship of the "I" to its "Mes" resembles that of a rancher to the herd of cows he has branded: "The individual beasts [that is, the "Mes"] do not stick together. . . . Each wanders with whatever accidental mates it finds." But the brand "symbolizes the characters of warmth and continuity, by reason of which the judgement [of unity] is made. . . . Each brand, so far, is the mark, or cause of our knowing that certain things belong together."[50] If we give a narrative interpretation to his "*self*-brand"[51]—as the key symbols or motifs of a life history—James's analogy might well be on the right track. If the self-brands have the character of scale-defining octaves, then it is conceivable that every thought could carry the mark, not so much as a signature scrawled into a corner of each frame of consciousness as an implicitly perceived key-signature framework that makes self-representational thought possible.

The continuous nonconscious presence of musiclike building blocks of identity requires only the sort of generative structures and processes we now know underlie music, language, and vision. It is quite reasonable to posit that these provide the space-time-causality coordinates that enable us to perceive the personal significance of ordinary events by a simple shift of attention to the "soundtrack" of one's life. Here the musical analogy converges with generative[52] and multiple drafts[53] theories of the stream of consciousness—which open-ended life history interviews track more fully than any other method.

Personality in Middle Eastern Societies ※

In this section, I briefly review writings about personality in Middle Eastern societies in light of evidence from this life narrative data. My objective is not to test hypotheses with the narratives, especially because a handful of life studies cannot provide appropriate data for evaluating hypotheses about group psychological differences. Rather, my goals are (1) to put these life narratives in the larger context of the region and (2) to outline a description of personality development in the region that takes account of the multiplicity of identity, the layered character of personality, developmental disjunctions, and the primary symbolic axes along which young Moroccans appear to be defining identities. I use the core personality–social persona–identity distinctions to organize my discussion and then end with some observations about social influences on personality development. See my *The Middle East: A Cultural Psychology* for a fuller account of influences of psychological development in the region.

Much of the literature on psychological development in Arab-Muslim societies adopts some variant of a "basic personality" or "national character" model, describing culture as creating a predominant type of personality or self. The best-known treatments by outsiders (Patai's recently reprinted *The Arab Mind* and Pryce-Jones's *The Closed Circle*) focus on the honor-shame complex, which they indict as the root cause of the Middle East's economic and political woes. These authors go so far as to claim that concern with honor and shame prevent Arabs from developing rationality and mastering technology, as if Japan, generally regarded as the globe's premier shame culture, remained mired in technological backwardness. Some Arab scholars have drawn on these notions to criticize their own cultures, raising questions about the extent to which they have themselves embraced Eurocentric views.

Fuad Moughrabi sharply criticized the first generation of this literature,[54] showed the extent to which scholars driven by a variety of motives have focused almost exclusively on negative characteristics, objected to their reliance on impression and anecdote rather than data, and decried their failure to consider the range of individual variation. Halim Barakat recently updated the critique,[55] while defending the importance of examining Arab psychological development and identity as part of a broader self-criticism aimed at "awakening." He approves of the social critiques that view personality more as a consequence than the cause of underdevelopment[56] but objects to the way these give an impression that Arab populaces are mired in an inertia of tradition and portray a static cultural consensus that misrepresents the intense struggle over "opposite and conflicting value orientations"[57] animating Middle Eastern societies. If there is little quantitative research on psychological development in North Africa and the Middle East, there fortunately are writings based on careful observation that offer nuanced and provocative hypotheses, which I draw on in the following discussion.

Core-Level Personality ❁

Infant Care and Matrifocal Interdependence

In Imeghrane villages, women averaged 8.7 live births in the 1980s, and because subsistence agropastoralism still requires enormous labor inputs, few had sought birth control. The childhood morality rate (birth to age five) approached 20 percent, children were not vaccinated, and many were chronically undernourished. Few households had a supply of clean water, and many children suffered recurrent diarrhea and dehydration. The Moroccans I interviewed were born into this world. Infant and childcare strategies in these conditions tend to follow what LeVine has termed a *pediatric* model,[58] adapted to maximize survival in conditions of poor nutrition and high mortality. This contrasts with the "pedagogic" model characteristic of Western middle classes, which encourages exploration and "pseudodialogue" interactions that appear as early preparation for formal schooling. In particular, traditional Moroccan childcare maximizes nutrition with prolonged nursing on demand and minimizes caloric expenditure by soothing signs of distress, avoiding arousing interaction, and generally dampening excitement. Like most societies in the temperate zones (including all of Africa), Moroccans carry their infants in slings rather than cradles, which means they have near-continuous physical contact with their caretakers, spend minimal time alone (which is believed to invite jinn attack), and engage in relatively little face-to-face interaction.[59] Infants sleep with their mothers for months or years but not for the prolonged periods found in some polygamous societies of Africa. Polygamy is allowed but rare, North Africa does not have a long postpartum sex taboo, and nuclear families typically share a sleeping room, so infants do not have quite as exclusive a bond with their mothers as they do in many African societies.

This style of infant care has been reported by many observers to facilitate the development of an intense, secure, highly physical attachment to the mothering figure, which cultures often continue to elaborate into something like the *amae* relationship described by Doi for Japan,[60] in which the mother provides "indulged dependence" and cultivates a sense of indebtedness on the child's part. This parallels Bouhdiba's,[61] Mernissi's,[62] and Msefer's[63] accounts of mother-son bonding in North Africa and probably lays the foundation for interdependent familial and patron-client relationships throughout life. In accord with descriptions by these North African researchers, I refer to this as "matrifocal interdependence."

Weaning: Trauma or Transition?

Nursing typically continues for two or three years in pediatric models of infant care, but weaning often tends to be abrupt and signal an end to exclusive maternal care. Weaning in Morocco has been observed to be especially abrupt, with potentially traumatic consequences that have been a subject of debate by Moroccan social scientists. In Imeghrane, mothers often weaned at one to two and a half years, when they felt they had to return to agricultural and household work or when they became pregnant (as they believe a pregnant woman's breast milk poisons the nursing infant). Many women use hot or bitter herbs on their nipples to enforce avoidance, and a significant minority of infants are sent to stay with relatives in another village until the baby "forgets its mother's milk." Some infants wean themselves and others adjust with little distress, but many are weaned before they have become accustomed to eating solid foods, and the transition can be nutritionally difficult. Adults recognize weaning as a stressful event, and we saw infants ragefully crying and tearing at their mothers' chests, regressing from walking to crawling, and refusing to eat until they lost weight and became ill. Local pediatricians felt infants are especially vulnerable to diseases at that period, and our analysis of raw census data for the region suggested an increase in mortality around the age of two. LeVine's careful measurements showed a general but short-term decline in the well-being of rural Kenyan infants around the time of weaning and transfer to caretakers other than the mother.

A number of Moroccan scholars believe abrupt weaning compromises a smooth process of separation-individuation and leaves many infants with a residue of basic mistrust, anxiously dependent, and fearful of separation.[64] Interestingly, Rouchdi Chaouite argues to the contrary that other family members typically rally around to comfort and distract the infant, so that weaning more frequently provides a bridge to the extended family and to attachment to the household as a supraindividual entity.[65] Our observations in Imeghrane confirm that weaning typically is treated as a household matter, in which grandfathers, fathers, and older brothers care for and play with the child, as well as the women of three generations. It is thus plausible that weaning may be culturally organized as a critical juncture at which matrifocal interdependence is elaborated into the household attachments—with an idealized image of the household becoming a kind of "self object" (Chaouite uses the term *group self*)—that form the core of the honor system. Most likely, abrupt weaning *creates* individual differences: some infants experience losses that compromise their basic sense of security, and others experience an expanded sphere of attachments that provide security and autonomy.

Circumcision and the Making of Men

John Whiting has suggested that the pediatric childcare practices in temperate zone societies foster not only matrifocal interdependence (my term) but also an early feminine sense of self that in boys leads to a "cross-gender sex identity conflict."[66] Like Chodorow,[67] Gilligan,[68] and Herdt,[69] Whiting believes that many societies require men to build masculine identities by rejecting and turning against those "feminine" qualities—often turning misogynistically against women as they become "real men." Whiting believes that the more prolonged and intense the early feminine identification, the more work the culture must do to masculinize boys in adolescence—hence the association of long infant-mother sleeping arrangements with puberty initiations that entail genital mutilation (usually viewed as masculinizing the male body). Gilmore concurs with this view and further suggests that the more manhood entails warfare and a warrior ethos, the more intensively a culture symbolically defeminizes and hypermasculinizes its young men.[70]

No available data indicate how closely the North African pattern parallels that described by Whiting, but many of the features are present in perhaps attenuated form. In addition to cultivating an intense mother-infant interdependence, tribal North Africa was an acephalous society that lay largely outside the reach of state authorities, and each male was expected to fight for his family, lineage, village, and tribe. Throughout the Mediterranean and Middle East, a rhetoric of martial prowess, daring, cunning, and vengeance animated what Herzfeld terms the *poetics of manhood*.[71] Yet no initiation rituals are performed on either gender at puberty (female circumcision is practiced in Egypt and many sub-Saharan cultures but not in North Africa), nor are boys physically separated from their mothers and immersed in men's societies to the extent they are in many of the societies Whiting examines.[72] Puberty tends to be marked mainly by keeping the Ramadan fast. North African (and perhaps circum-Mediterranean) cultures thus may generate moderate forms of "cross-sex gender identity conflict" but leave the resolution up to individuals.

In North Africa, boys are circumcised, and the foreskin is traditionally regarded as a bit of feminine tissue that must be removed to purify him and make him marriageable. Yet this is performed not in adolescence but at an age when these meanings cannot be grasped, the potential for terror and trauma is high, and no change in status follows. Crapanzano has pondered these seemingly paradoxical features and suggested that circumcision in North Africa does not resolve or consolidate gender identity but creates a mark signifying sexual-religious maturity as a destiny that must be achieved against a background of anxiety and doubt.[73]

Externalization

Two other influences on core-level development deserve mention. First, from toddlerhood, children are taught external interpretations of internal states. That is, they are taught that a host of chthonic beings threaten or protect them, so that feelings of anxiety and security may be attributed to their presence. Traditional culture builds this externalization into a system of affective self-management, based on monitoring and modifying one's state of purity versus pollution, balancing heat versus cold, and regulating other features of one's behavior and environment that could either provoke or placate chthonic beings. From neighboring Algeria, Frantz Fanon wrote that this world of menacing invisible forces is crucial to constituting the community and providing a sense of security:

> This magical superstructure which permeates native society . . . frightens me and so takes on an undoubted reality. By terrifying me, it integrates me in the traditions and the history of my district or of my tribe, and at the same time it reassures me. . . . By entangling myself in this inextricable network where actions are repeated with crystalline inevitability, I find the everlasting world which belongs to me, and the perenniality which is thereby affirmed of the world belonging to us.[74]

In addition, rural Moroccan children experience considerably more morbidity, physical discomfort, and deaths of family members than do the Western children on whom most psychological theories of development are based. They suffer illnesses and injuries without pain-relieving medications and also endure more hunger and thirst, heat and cold, insects and itches, and chronic respiratory, intestinal, and skin infections. Parents do their best to protect and comfort their children, but often they simply can't. Western psychology knows much about the sequelae of parental neglect and abuse but very little about suffering that persists in spite of compassionate care. A heightened sense of bodily vulnerability and greater reliance on dissociation, externalization, and conscious suppression as intrapsychic coping strategies may result.

Evidence from the Narratives

The interviews suggest that matrifocal interdependence plays a prominent role in the psychic and interpersonal lives of most, though not all, young Moroccans. Hussein's narrative shows this in almost archetypal form, as do those of four other men I interviewed whose mothers remain at the center of their emotional lives, even for the two who live away from home. If Rachida's personal relationships with her mother and sisters appear somewhat distant, a deep psychological interdependence animates her attachment to her idealized household and, in her spiritual life, to the chain of uterine kin. Mohammed's life centers emotionally on the loss of his mother and subsequent "lack" of someone who might have played her nurturing, sustaining role, which he finally finds in God and the Prophet. Naima, a mother of four, described a more archetypal interdependence with her mother, who lived a few doors away. Their daily lives intermeshed, as they cooperated in childcare and household tasks, and this cooperation provided the framework for their close, though not strifeless, personal bond. Saadia[75] and her mother had a highly ambivalent interdependence: they quarreled incessantly at home, but Saadia found herself so unable to live apart that she had dropped out of the university in spite of doing well in her courses. She often was unable to shake her rather "obsessive" worries that terrible things would befall her mother if she were not there to prevent them.

There are important exceptions. Khadija appears thoroughly estranged from her mother and as having no attachment to her household as a home or as an idealized honor-bearing group. Neither Said nor Ahmad presents himself as estranged from his mother or his family, but they also show minimal emotional interdependence. An irreligious college student hoping for an engineering career, Said had been born in a hamlet of Skoura when his impoverished, illiterate father was in his fifties and his mother thirty. With his father aging and in ill health, his mother ran the family, and he recalls her acting more as disciplinarian than protector. He makes personal sacrifices to help his family and feels affection for his parents and sympathy for their plight, but he shows little emotional interdependence. Ahmad had been sent to stay with an aunt to "forget his mother's milk" when he was weaned, but his aunt and uncle had no children and his own parents were struggling to take care of several, so he stayed and grew up there. Now a tenured high school science teacher, he has moved back into a wing of his parents' home and acts in many ways as the household's head. He treats both his real and foster mothers with affection and respect, and says he feels especially grateful to his uncle for raising another man's son as his own, but he shows little emotional interdependence with either.

Observations of families and the interviews together suggest that for many and perhaps most Moroccans, pediatric infant-care practices establish a maternal bond that is cultivated into an interdependence that forms a core relational orientation within their personalities. The exceptions clearly show that this does not always happen, and some of the life narratives make it clear that interdependence may entail a good deal of conflict and strife. But I believe the literature on the Middle East, which so often emphasizes the patriarchal character of family relations, generally understates most families' matrifocal emotional ties and the psychological importance of *amae*-like interdependence. This interdependence typically focuses on the mother but may be tapped—with different etiquettes and sentiments than Doi describes for Japan—to construct a variety of senior-junior and patron-client relationships, including with saints, the Prophet, and God, as the sermon on *rahm* recorded by Antoun (see chapter 1) so eloquently shows.

As for debates about weaning and circumcision, the narratives, as expected, provide scant evidence. Having witnessed the distress and regression that often accompany abrupt weaning and the terror, rage, and loss of consciousness that not infrequently accompany circumcisions, it is difficult to believe these practices do not have enduring effects for at least a sizable minority of Moroccans.[76] I think it likely that abrupt weaning and circumcision contribute to the seemingly high levels of anxiety and vulnerability that appear in many of the narratives, but the relatively frequent deaths, serious illnesses, poorly treated injuries, divorces, and dividing households easily could account for these characteristics. Rachida's fear of fragmenting relationships and attachment to her idealized household might fit Chaouite's scenario by which extended family relationships ease and repair the trauma of weaning, but this is speculation without evidence.

The narratives do show, however, that nearly all of the young Moroccans I interviewed have disquieting experiences of "the fantastic," in which they feel themselves to be in the presence of threatening nonnatural forces that they do not want to identify as jinns, ogres, Satan, or the evil eye but cannot reject as figments of their imagination. These experiences appear to arise from childhood and adult influences: (1) learning as children to "externalize" anxiety and fear chthonic threats and (2) living as young adults in a world of "limited good" that is saturated with covert interpersonal struggles, damaging gossip, and corrupt authorities who often act capriciously.[77] Nearly all of those I interviewed appear to have internalized the first stage of this traditional anxiety-management system and readily read anxieties and fears as arising from external threats. But under the influence of their modern educations, they resist adopting many of the beliefs (in jinns, Satan, and the evil eye) and practices (wearing amulets, uttering protective phrases, purifying, etc.) that would complete the system.

I believe this developmental disjunction has important—and largely unappreciated—psychological effects for many young Moroccans who find themselves troubled by seemingly irrational fears, by vague senses of vulnerability, by depressive moods or nightmares, by lusts and losses of erotic interest, or by physical symptoms traditionally attributed to chthonic forces but that have no ready modern explanation. Minor and DeVos, in fact, found anxiety levels to be higher among urban Algerians than among village dwellers and suggested that urbanites tend to eschew the "superstitious" beliefs that buffered anxiety in rural settings.[78] Many young Moroccans at times find themselves in worlds resembling those evoked by "magical realist" writers, and I believe that the Islamist doctrine of inner jihad (struggle) against *nafs* (desire) appeals to a good number of young Moroccans because it promises to manage these kinds of disturbing experiences at the same time as it offers an account of their vulnerability to menacing but often amorphous political and economic forces.

Finally, it is important to note the organizing role played in each narrative of core-level affective tensions that appear largely idiosyncratic: Mohammed's rather obsessive-compulsive ambivalence over holding on versus letting go, Hussein's struggle with depressive lethargy, Rachida's fear of fragmenting attachments and deprivation, and Khadija's eroticized flights and intrusions of cataclysmic imagery. It is not that culture plays no role in creating these, but they probably have arisen from some combination of innate temperament and familial influences that could not easily be predicted from broad cultural patterns. These idiosyncratic tensions set Moroccans on diverging developmental trajectories, ultimately influencing how they select and refashion features of their cultural heritage as they create identities.

Social Personality ❀

Fathers and Teachers

As I discussed in chapter 4, Bouhdiba believes that although mothers almost exclusively shape early development, a distant, fearsome, and sometimes violent father often predominates over later childhood and adolescence and sometimes well into adulthood.[79] If fathers spend relatively little time with infants and toddlers, nearly all accounts describe the contact they do have as affectionate, playful, and nurturant.[80] But the traditional cultural model of child rearing prescribes that fathers adopt a more distant, formal, harsh stance with their children—especially sons—when they reach age five to seven. Given the presence of other intimidating senior men and teachers, boys at this age encounter the public world as overwhelmingly male and saturated with threat, which Bouhdiba suggests they experience as "castrating." He believes this encourages the further cultivation of *matrifocal interdependence* (again, my term) into an alliance in which mother and son strive to protect each other and conspire to circumvent patriarchal authorities, a pattern we saw prominently developed in Hussein's narrative.

This disjunction indeed fits many men's parental relationships, but not all. We observed many rural families in which fathers were not distant and threatening, and mothers do not always act as the havens of protection they are idealized to be. Edward Prothro's survey of Lebanese mothers found them to report more frequent use of physical punishment than Sears, Maccoby, and Levin's sample of middle-class American mothers.[81] Too many familial relationships do not fit Bouhdiba's description to ignore the importance of nonauthoritarian fathering, both on individual men and on the models of authority available in the culture. But Bouhdiba's account needs to be qualified, not rejected, especially because some important experiences with terrifying, brutal, and often-unjust male authorities do appear in most of the life narratives I elicited. And Bouhdiba is hardly alone among North African and Middle Eastern social scientists in emphasizing the centrality of patriarchal authority.[82] Such themes also appear prominently in many published North African autobiographies and literary works. Eickelman's life history of a *qadi* (religious judge) in Boujad portrays this sort of "stern" father:

> What I remember most of my childhood is the cane. When we were young, my brother and I were beaten three times daily by my father: morning, noon, and night. Each night he required us to stand before him and recite five *hizbs* [verses] of the Quran. Other children were expected to recite one. If we made a mistake, then we would be beaten again.[83]

In *Mountains Forgotten by God*, Brick Oussaid recounts his boyhood as a shepherd in the Middle Atlas, whose hardships of poverty, illness, and weather were only intensified by being sent to school where a "tyrannical" teacher regularly humiliated his students—"He soon had a nickname for each of us: 'Come here, you crud.' 'Get up, nigger.' 'Repeat, the ape in the back.' 'Your turn, cripple!'"—and beat them: "According to his mood, he hit us on the hand, and then, when they were swollen, came the agony of being beaten over the fingernails. . . ."[84] Eickelman tells us that as a senior man, household head, and enforcer of religious law, the *qadi* came to view his childhood beatings "as a sign of his father's concern for him." Not so Oussaid, who eventually became an engineer and emigrated permanently to France: "Our daily misfortunes made us unhappy, and our little group had no real sort of life. We just barely survived. We were grave and fearful because, hurt and mistreated, our hearts and spirits were broken."[85] And not so Abdelkrim Ghallab, a renowned nationalist leader who in *Le Passe Enterre* recalled beatings from his father and Quranic school teacher. A public square in Fes gave him and his friends a few moments of freedom between home and mosque:

> At home . . . family life was lived in submission to severe rules that the children could neither disobey nor challenge; the authority of the father who imposed these laws never would have tolerated resistance or disobedience.
>
> At the mosque, the *fqih* reigned in terror over the children; as soon as one aspired to get a little freedom, the *fqih* would order he

put his feet in the air, and beat them twice as hard with his stick, and thus return the child to the level of his terrorized classmates.[86]

Émigré writer Driss Chraibi's autobiographical novel *The Simple Past* paints horrifying images of "Lord," his father,[87] "the embodiment of Islam," and rails at the brutality of religious authorities:

> Four years at Koranic schools taught me law, dogma, the limits of dogma, and *hadiths*, with cudgel blows to the head and on the soles of my feet—administered with such mastery that even till the Judgment Day I never will forget them.[88]

Naguib Mahfouz's *Palace Walk* conveys the subtleties of fearsome paternal authority in his depiction of Ahmad Abd al-Jawad and his family:

> [At breakfast] the brothers took their places politely and deferentially, with their heads bowed as though at Friday prayers. . . . No one dared look directly at their father's face . . . their fear itself made them more nervous and prone to the very errors they were trying so hard to avoid.[89]

His youngest son, Kamal, took the long route home from elementary school, in order not to pass his father's store: "His father made him tremble with terror. He could not imagine that a jinni popping out at him would frighten him any more than his father screaming at him in anger." Yet, "he furtively took his fun behind his father's back whenever he felt like it," especially because "his mother shielded him and allowed him as much innocent play as he wanted." It hadn't always been that way:

> He was often amazed to remember that this same father had been sweet and kind to him not so long ago, when he was a small child. Al-Siyyid Ahmad had enjoyed playing with him and from time to time had treated him to various kinds of sweets. He had done his best to lighten Kamal's circumcision day, hideous though it was, by filling his lap with chocolates and candy and smothering him with care and affection. Then how quickly everything had changed. Affection had turned into severity, tender conversation into shouts, and fondling to blows. He had even made circumcision itself a means for terrifying the boy. For a long time Kamal had been confused and had thought they might inflict the same fate on what he had left.
>
> It was not just fear that he felt toward his father. His respect for him was as great as his fear. He admired his strong, imposing appearance, his dignity that swept everyone along with it, the elegance of his clothing, and the ability he believed him to have to do anything. Perhaps it was the way his mother spoke about her husband that put him in such awe of him. He could not imagine that any other man in the world could equal al-Siyyid Ahmad's power, dignity, or wealth.[90]

Many authorities deliberately cultivate distant, fear-inspiring personas. During the year we taught in a Moroccan high school, several teachers explained that our students were unruly because they did not sufficiently "fear" us and advised us to send a few haphazardly chosen troublemakers to the vice principal, who would beat them with a rubber hose. We know from observation that children are beaten in many households, in nearly all Quranic schools, and in most public schools—and several of those I interviewed said they bore scars from beatings by parents, teachers, and in the case of one woman, an older brother. In addition, policemen often beat "suspects" soon after they arrest them, sometimes in public, in order (some say) to make them more compliant in custody. Even if not present in one's family, this sort of patriarchal authority looms somewhere in nearly every child and young person's milieu.

Compliance versus Autonomy

Another global feature of child rearing probably exacerbates the tension many men (and perhaps women) experience between independence and compliance. Robert Edgerton found that pastoralist societies differ markedly from agricultural societies in valuing independence, open emotionality, and direct aggression,[91] and many ethnographers have emphasized that agricultural societies emphasize compliance, conformity, and indirect aggression.[92] Pre-Saharan societies tend to be transhumant, which means that households operate as both agricultural and pastoral entities. In combination with great ecological variability, this produces a surprisingly wide-open competition for resources and social status that requires a difficult-to-achieve blend of familial loyalty and individual initiative. Our studies of the Imeghrane lead me to believe that the agropastoral complementarity produces two contrary socialization imperatives, such that parents demand both autonomy and compliance, in often unpredictable turns.

The culture in fact celebrates the rebellious courage of youth in folktales, public rituals, and a variety of other ways. But it equally celebrates self-sacrifice for filial piety.[93] The themes of rebellion, return, and accommodation to familial authority resonate in every corner of the culture, not so much as a modal pattern of behavior as an enduring ambivalence, woven through the rhetoric of development that animates everyday conversation as well as through the life narratives. Economic underdevelopment in the region's towns may actually intensify this conflict for educated young Moroccans, as it makes definitive separation from or adherence to natal households and parental authorities problematic. But the facts that this conflict appears to chronically beset sons in the most traditional mountain villages, and that it appears prominently in folktales dating from the precolonial period, suggest that it is not simply a product of partial modernization. The crucial point is that what looks from a Western perspective like "inconsistent" child rearing may make much more sense when seen in the context of cross-cutting parental objectives. But it still may present many children with the challenge of figuring out in which contexts they should act obediently and in which they should act boldly on their own initiative. Further, the fact that obedience may be enforced in the name of Islam and independence admired in the name of honor may encourage the consolidation of contrasting orientations toward authorities, as Mohammed's narrative shows so clearly.

Honor and Blessedness

Many scholars have seen the honor code as forming the core of North African–Middle Eastern cultures, and others have seen Islam as playing that role. The relationship between these systems emerges as an especially problematic one, both for researchers and for the people who live by them. In general, their congruence has been overstated and their conflict insufficiently appreciated. As Eric Wolf has shown, Islam from its inception pitted itself as a universal brotherhood of believers against the divisive brotherhood of descent that forms the heart of lineage and tribal solidarity and of the honor-modesty system.[94] Although the powerful certainly seek to cloak exploitation and privilege in hegemonic religious rhetorics, the weak make perhaps even greater appeal to Islamic principles to plead their cases and to envision a just world.

In his often-ethnocentric *The Arab Mind*, Raphael Patai nonetheless makes the insightful observation that there appears to be a Bedouin "substratum" and an Islamic "substratum" to personality—and by "Bedouin" he essentially refers to what I have termed the honor-modesty system. Raymond Jamous's ethnography of rural northeastern Morocco, *Honneur et Baraka*, also emphasizes the pervasive interplay of these two forms of power and prestige: honor built on aggressive, intimidating masculine prowess and blessedness or bounty bestowed as a divine gift, often as the reward for piety.[95] At some times and places, honor and blessedness seem to flow as confluents, as they were archetypally fused in the life of the Prophet. At other times and places, honor and blessedness seem set against each other, as in the many hagiographies in which saints' miracles humble military strong men, sultans, and tyrants. This dialectic of contrasting yet converging frameworks certainly characterized much of the cultural life we observed in Imeghrane and in the pre-Saharan villages-becoming-towns where I conducted interviews.

Training in both systems typically begins in earnest in later childhood. Around the age of seven, boys traditionally entered Quranic school to be taught how to comport themselves in public as representatives of their households and lineages. Some girls attended Quranic schools, but most received religious instruction at home and were increasingly kept in the house and taught how to practice concealment in public. Both boys and girls learned the etiquettes of deference-modesty toward their seniors and how to exercise authority over their juniors: elder brothers to protect and defend younger; sisters to care for and control younger children. Both also began to take active roles in religious celebrations, to fast during Ramadan, and to monitor minor states of pollution and purification. The principles of honor-modesty and those of Islam are often taught in different contexts, with the evocation of different emotions, and with the use of contrasting rhetorics, especially of patrikin loyalty and gender inequality in the case of honor-modesty, and of the equality of brothers and believers in the case of Islam. Prayer and other important religious practices tend to be set apart in time and space, in aesthetic ambience, posture, and linguistic register in ways that would appear to facilitate the consolidation of contrasting social frames and psychological states. In particular, cycles of pollution and purification appear not only to manage body-based anxieties but also to orchestrate an oscillation between the "dirty" business of hierarchical, competitive, and divisive profane affairs and the innocence, equality, and security experienced in the purity of God's immanence.

Studies of child rearing throughout the Middle East make it clear that learning the honor-modesty etiquettes of social interaction and Islamic practices of self-care and worship deeply shape emotions and self-conceptions, so that they come to have an automatic or grammarlike character.[96] Yet far from simply conforming to the imperatives of ascribed kinship and gender roles or to the dictates of Islamic principles, the great majority of Moroccans commonly experience internal turmoil and debate over doing right, often tragically between the imperatives of honor and of piety.

Evidence from the Narratives

The majority of men I interviewed portrayed their fathers much the way Mohammed and Hussein did: as the kind of distant, demanding, and fearsome authority figure Oussaid, Ghallab, Chraibi, and Mahfouz describe in their writings. Like Mohammed and Hussein, they reported feeling admiration for their fathers as well as fear. And as Mahfouz captures, most recalled tender, playful, intimate times with their fathers in their early years, with entrance into public or Quranic school often marking the transformation to formality and harshness. This clearly reflects a prevailing cultural model of fatherhood. As a forty-something merchant[97] with a ten-year-old son described the "Muslim" philosophy of childrearing: "For the first seven years you're your son's slave; for the next seven, he's your slave. After that he's beyond your reach and it's up to God." Nearly all of these men described serious conflicts with their fathers, in several instances taking shape as rebellious delinquencies and blunders of the sort Mohammed describes, or generational conflict like Hussein's, in which modern-thinking sons cast themselves as struggling with traditional fathers over values, lifestyles, and career goals. Fearsome fathers do not loom quite as large in women's narratives, but I suspect I was not likely to interview the daughters of such men. Fadna and Saadia described fathers (and an uncle, in Fadna's case) who were sometimes harsh and fearsome but reported little conflict in their late teen and early adult years. Rachida had struggled against both of her parents over marriage proposals and won, and her career success and willing compliance subsequently gained her an unusual degree of freedom with them.

The exceptions again are important: Said said his older father was almost not a figure in his life but a warm and supportive one when he was. Ahmad reported that he grew up without fearing his foster father, who was rather formal and distant but never intimidated or beat him. And Khadija's father is certainly unusual in his support for her Western-facing ambitions—however ambivalently he gave it—but it is not entirely unusual for Moroccan women to say that their mothers acted as disciplinarians and their fathers treated them with a measure of kindness and informality they didn't show to their brothers. Even in remote Imeghrane villages, the variety of paternal relationships was surprising, ranging from fathers who abused and humiliated their grown, married sons to those who trustingly let sons in their early to mid-twenties take care of most of the household affairs.

There can be little doubt that these patriarch figures—threatening but protecting, punitive and generous, fear-inspiring and admirable—serve as an important and dangerous model for political leadership. As Stadtler shows, this is precisely the point of Chraibi's *Simple Past* and many other North African novels.[98] These are certainly qualities that many political authorities seek to project, from tribal sheikhs and regional *caid*s to urban *pasha*s and, traditionally, the monarch. That the *fqih*s who teach in Quranic schools and a good many public school teachers also use fear, beatings, and ridicule to control their students seems to generalize both the model and the resentment. Importantly, the narratives also show that more mentorlike prototypes of authority and more egalitarian imaginings of civic and political association—many of them equally traditional—coexist alongside authoritarian images. And many men, like Hussein and even Mohammed at points, criticize authoritarian parenting and political leadership in favor of more democratic ideals.[99] Yet as Hammoudi argues,[100] the post-Independence rehabilitation of the rural notable as both an agent of state administration and a political persona that combines these traditional qualities of manliness and the charisma of the Sufi sheikh has served to entrench authoritarian models.

Most of the narratives also show the sort of conflict over autonomy versus compliance seen in the previous chapters, and abrupt shifts between rebellious and obedient stances and between egocentric and sociocentric orientations are quite common. I use the terms *autonomy* and *compliance* deliberately to convey the important point that much of what is discussed as individualist versus collectivist orientations concerns not just whether selves are defined through autonomy or connection but orientations to authority. What the narratives show, then, are neither individualist nor collectivist selves but chronic ambivalence between sociocentric and egocentric orientations that often entails ambivalent obedience and rebellion.

Finally, nearly all of the narratives show social personas organized in accordance with the etiquettes and sentiments of the honor-modesty system and with Islamic spirituality and self-care practices. A great deal of individual variation appears here: some individuals draw primarily on one or the other, some draw on both in varying degrees of tension and confluence, and all give idiosyncratic emphasis to some features and virtually ignore others. The honor-modesty system generates individual differences, conferring honor on some, requiring some to seek honor through deference and modesty, and shaming others. Islam also sets some on the "straight path" to salvation and bounty, and others on "zigzagging" paths (as many young Moroccans phrase it) that meander perilously toward damnation. The variation this produces remains variation on recognizable themes, and this pair of cultural systems appears to quite pervasively organize the middle level of personality. Honor and Islam appear as largely *traditional* systems of sentiment and representation, and "modern" identities often must be constructed as reformulations of them, creating for many another developmental discontinuity. Nearly all of those I interviewed have educations that put them among the most successful quartile of their peers, and they seek to recast honor in modern terms of academic and career achievement and to make achievement meaningful within a religious framework.

Identity ✤

Life narratives demonstrate the great freedom individuals have to fashion identities by selecting elements from their cultural heritage and by refashioning and combining them in idiosyncratic ways. No shared values or beliefs about self make identities distinctly Moroccan—or pre-Saharan or North African. The cultural distinctiveness of identity comes, rather, from the fact that individuals draw the building blocks of self-representational systems from a partially shared lexicon of symbols and metaphors, motifs and type scenes.[101] As we have seen, identity organizes as a system of identifications and disidentifications juxtaposed in narrative episodes and dialogue. As we also have seen, narrators tend to identify with idealized in-group figures and to employ stereotypic images of disliked or pitied out-group members as *not-Me* representations of characteristics they seek to deny in themselves. But these often are reversible, so that an individual might represent the out-group as displaying admired or empowering characteristics the in-group lacks. *Not-Me* stereotypes thus also serve to define the primary boundaries across which individuals may reach to mimetically draw the power of Others into their characters. It is society's major fault lines, then, that come to define its primary axes of identity. Or to phrase this differently, adult identity tends to be built on the scaffolding of a society's predominant pattern of contested power. In the life narratives I elicited from Americans, gender, social class, ethnicity, and subcultural "lifestyle" appeared as the most prominent of these axes. In the Moroccan narratives, gender, religion, and modernization appear to define the primary axes.[102]

Gender

Gender is probably a universal dimension of identity by which personalities are internally differentiated, though this takes specific forms that vary from culture to culture. A great deal has been written on gender in the Middle East, but Audrey Shalinsky's exploration of gender ideology in northern Afghanistan makes two especially important observations about how men and women flexibly use it to organize identities.[103] First, she found that the gender ideology actually has two aspects, between which Afghans switch: one based in stereotypes about the essential "nature" of men and women and one based on contextual evaluations of specific men's and women's actions. Second, she found that the stereotypes are often linked with ethnic and human-jinn contrasts: the most negative, abject, and fearful representations tend to be attributed to women of *other* ethnic groups and to the *almasti*, a "witchlike" jinn figure resembling North Africa's Aisha Qandisha. According to the view of the psyche taught by local religious figures, desire (*nafs*) must be controlled by reason (*ʿqel*) or chaos and disorder (*fitna*) will result, and this provides the basis for judgments of morality and character that are applied to both men and women. Another facet of the ideology, however, associates men with reason and women with desire and disorder: "Men may consistently increase their *ʿaql* through their lifetime by the study of the Qur'an, while women who have more *ʿaql* in childhood lose it after marriage as their sexual desires awaken."[104] Among themselves, though, women often reverse these images, emphasizing their self-control and indicting men for being ruled by their desires.

When they speak of men and women "in the abstract," Shalinsky observes, Afghans make rich use of the stereotypes; but when they speak of "specific cases," they tend to use the basic theory in a gender-neutral way. In addition, men "do not necessarily think that their own women are as uncontrolled as the abstract statements indicate. It is the women from other ethnic groups who are the temptresses. . . ."[105] Women similarly fear the "wild and evil" men from neighboring ethnic groups. "While ethnicity and gender are differentiated realms," she writes, "they are mutual metaphorizations of each other. Negative sexuality, *nafs*, is attributed to the opposite sex or to those outside the ethnic group."[106] Men thus stereotypically associate unconstrained desire (*nafs*) with women, women often associate it with men, and both attribute it to out-groups and non-Muslim *almasti* (witch) spirits.

In the 1970s, Daisy Dwyer studied gender images—one could say *stereotypes*—in Taroudant, about 250 kilometers east of Ouarzazate and part of the same Berber-Arab cultural mixture. In addition to the view that men "develop more *'aqel* (intelligence, responsibility, rationality) while women have more *nifs* (flesh-centered desires and tensions),"[107] she reports widespread acceptance of diverging models of the life span:

> At birth, it is said, women have one hundred angels and men have one hundred devils. Each year, however, one angel moves from the female to the male and one devil moves from the male to the female until male virtue and female folly reach their ultimate actualizations.[108]

As girls mature into women, then, they develop "insatiable sexuality," a "proclivity for causing conflict," and powers "to destroy the well-being of a man."[109] Importantly, she found that while women continually criticized the view that men are more motivated by ꜥ*qel* (reason) and less by *nafs* (desire), they generally endorsed the stereotypic view of themselves. "Women, like men, subscribe to the image of raging female passion," she writes, and differ from the men mainly in viewing men as equally animal, "as possessing their own quotient of insatiability and waywardness."[110]

As discussed earlier, several of the most influential analysts of gender, including Fatima Mernissi and Abdelwaheb Bouhdiba, believe that two stereotypic images of women are particularly prominent. One is the mother as a near-sacred wellspring of nurturance and compassion. The other image is of women as a source of *fitna* (chaos/disorder), of dangerous, polluting, order-breaking sexuality and quarrelsomeness. Mernissi argues that this forms the psychological core of male attitudes toward women in Middle Eastern societies and shows how the Muslim view of women as dangerously strong (especially but not only sexually) contrasts with the Western stereotype of women as passive and weak. Men striving to achieve the self-control essential to mature manhood may thus use the role of guardian of *fitna*-prone women to help symbolically excise (as "female" qualities) the more unruly impulses in their own character.

Two figures provide ideal male prototypes: the Big Man, who embodies the fear-inspiring but also protective qualities of honor, and the saint, who displays piety and manifests *baraka* (blessedness). The contradictory forces that animate these figures are most clearly displayed in the hagiographies of saints, especially those who battle and inflict defeats on tyrannical sultans, like the seventeenth-century monarch Moulay Ismail. But ideally the strength of the big man fuses with the piety of the saint, as they do in the great politico-religious leaders. The Prophet thus appears as the archetypally ideal male figure, combining the most excellent of spiritual, martial, and husbandly powers. Abdullah Hammoudi's *Master and Disciple* explores how the path to masculinization scripted into saint-follower, master-disciple relationships typically entails a stage of submission and feminization, such that manhood is achieved in rejection of the feminine. As Chodorow, Whiting, Herdt, and others have suggested, many of the world's cultures have schemas for building manhood in contrast to rejected femininity, of which these Big Man and saint figures appear as culturally distinctive prototypes.

If women must struggle against internalizing stereotypes of themselves as sources of pollution and *fitna* (chaos/disorder), ethnographies of traditional milieus suggest that they build positive identities from their rich relationships with other women and from their powers of fecundity and nurturance.[111] This receives rich symbolic elaboration in the women's agricultural and household work, in the enclosed architecture of houses and villages, in clothing styles, in the morals and etiquettes of modesty, and in poetry and religion.[112]

North Africa and the Middle East also boast one of the world's great traditions of literary and poetic celebrations of romantic love, which together with modern cinematic figures, provides young Moroccans a rich variety of images of man-and-woman friends, lovers, and compatriots. Locally, the poignant Romeo and Juliet–like story (lovers from feuding families died trying to reach each other and were turned into small lakes named *tislit* and *isli*, bride and groom) celebrated at the annual end-of-summer festival in a nearby Middle Atlas valley testifies to the ancient character of cultural debate and inner turmoil over true love and familial loyalty. Patriarchy reigns, but not in a closed universe of unquestioned patriarchal values. Patriarchy rather reigns amid sharp dispute and a deep sense of tragedy.

Religion

The Muslim cosmology defines a series of important social boundaries, especially Muslim versus Christian and Jew and the Muslim era versus the *jahiliya,* the pre-Islamic "era of ignorance." Together with the oppositions of Prophet and Satan, saints and jinn spirits, and purity and pollution, these contrasts probably provided core axes of identity organization in precolonial North Africa. As Hamid Ammar and Michael Gilsenan report, unmarried young men in both rural and urban settings traditionally spent a good deal of time in the company of local religious sheikhs, learning details and subtleties of adult piety and sometimes acting as enforcers of morality.[113] Although many social scientists expected modernization to bring a decline in the salience of religion, precisely the opposite has occurred, as popular movements to renew and purify Islam have characterized colonial and postcolonial periods. Many young Moroccans opt for the authenticity of their own heritage by returning to Islam after periods of skepticism or delinquent laxity. Many identify strongly with the Palestinian cause and some with Islamist critiques of the West and its influence. The Christian and Jew then easily become figures of disidentification that represent rejected features of individuals' own personalities as "anti-Muslim." Islamist themes resonate powerfully for many young Moroccans who do not support Islamist groups or programs, especially Islamist criticisms of the Westernized *bourgeoisiyin.*

It also is important, however, not to underestimate the potentially progressive features of Islamist themes, many of which more closely resemble liberation theology than Western journalists typically recognize. Many envision a renaissance of a socially activist spirituality, opposed to oppression and corruption, on the one hand, and dedicated to serving the poor and disadvantaged on the other.[114] In the view of some observers, rejection of the West could free Middle Eastern societies to creatively modernize their own traditions—perhaps as have Japan, India, and other developing societies that have had more control of their own destinies. Islamism too, then, shows two faces: one dangerously totalistic, the other potentially broadening the circles of empathic identification in more inclusive ways.

Modernization

Colonization, independence, massive "guest-worker" emigration to Europe, tourism in Morocco, and the diffusion of Euro-Western culture via the educational system and mass media have transformed traditional North African culture. These influences have not so much modernized Moroccan culture as underdeveloped it—especially in more peripheral areas like the pre-Sahara, where they have created a new cultural universe built around struggles for "modernization" and defenses of "tradition." Contemporary Moroccan culture can best be understood as saturated by a "rhetoric of development": by continuous debates over the nature of modernity and tradition. Given the pervasive dualisms Krichen describes (see chapter 1), even seemingly insignificant and mundane aspects of daily life—styles of grooming, nuances of pronunciation, the wearing of a watch, eating with fingers or a fork—can suddenly become symbolic, politicized, and polarizing issues in the struggle to modernize in an authentically Moroccan, Arab, or Muslim manner.[115]

Sociologist Mounia Bennani-Chraibi had just begun a study of youth and media in Morocco when youth-led riots broke out at the end of 1990, attacking "the material symbols of 'modernity.'" Less than a year later, a series of antigovernment, anti-Western demonstrations staged in response to the Gulf War also were dominated by teenagers and young adults. She broadened the scope of her inquiry, interviewing participants in the demonstrations and some of those arrested, and three years later published her observations as *Soumis et Rebelles*. Traditional family and kin groups are decreasing in size and importance, she believes, bringing about a "birth of the individual." Individuals, however, are growing into an overpopulated world of economic underdevelopment and political oppression, where only a few can achieve the educations, careers, and living standards that are the promise of modernization. These conditions engage most young Moroccans in two related struggles: one in the social realm for the educations and steady jobs that would enable them to help support their parental families, marry, and begin families of their own, and the other in the realm of ideas, values, and meanings—for *identity*. The realm of values, she writes, has quite literally become a marketplace:

> In the marketplaces of the big cities, Oum Khaltoum [a famous Egyptian singer], Michael Jackson, and reciters of the Quran compete for people's attention. Islamist literature published in Cairo or Casablanca appears next to Playboy and La Femme Actuelle. During the month of Ramadan, the exciting nights of leisure and meeting follow austere days of fasting. In the summer, returning from the beach, young people stop to pray in one of the mosques they come upon in their path.[116]

She found young people "fascinated" with the West as "at the same time a model and a counter-model." They alternated between "attraction and repulsion," "idealizing" and "demonizing" the West. They often described Europeans as possessing all the virtues Moroccans lack:

> The West offers the image of a universe where the fulfilled individual is also an accomplished citizen. The myth of development persists with all of its paraphernalia—science, technology, medicine, the moon, rockets, undersea research. These descriptions are almost always accompanied by a phrase like, "not like in our homes," "not like here," or "not like us."[117]

At the same time, however, nearly all of those she interviewed also rejected European ways as decadent and dissolute—affirming superiority of Morocco's familial and spiritual values.

As they "compartmentalize" these contrary attitudes, many also appeared to allot "transgressive" behaviors and religious devotion their separate times and spaces. A few had become more permanently "marginalized" in their delinquencies, and some turned to Islamism to live piously all day every day. The vast majority approved of the mixing of males and females in schools, work settings, and public and wanted to choose their own spouses. But she found male-female relationships to be anxiously embroiled in conflicting values. Boys have to establish themselves financially before they can marry, but most girls still rely on marriage to provide them a place in society. For most boys, "female sexuality and the loss of virginity constitutes a defect, a taboo; on the other hand, sexual experience acquired by a man is something natural and indispensable."[118] The majority of girls concur, oppose premarital sexuality, and view "virginity as a young girl's weapon in the war of the sexes."[119] Yet many of those in their later teens and early twenties also have relationships with boys that involve some sexual play, though usually not intercourse. She quotes a twenty-five-year-old Casablanca secretary named Loubna, who argues that sex is "natural," an important part of a girl's maturation, and that girls have the same right to pleasure as boys. When the interviewer asks, "And what about virginity?" Lubna vehemently responds, "Ah, virginity before everything!" and launches into a speech on the importance of maintaining virginity until marriage, couched in terms of religious values and family obligations absent from her earlier defense of pleasure. She even justifies the killing of a daughter who loses her virginity before marriage. Bennani-Chraibi writes:

> The young girl submits herself to two value systems: one dominated by individualism and hedonism, the other fundamentally social, where the person is legitimately subordinated to the law of the collective. . . . [Yet] the two systems do not appear opposed in her eyes.[120]

She found political views to be similarly ambivalent and contradictory but not as polarized and hardened by strife as in Egypt and Algeria. Most youths were alienated from the political system, which they saw as a game of elites beyond their influence, and they voiced their resistance mainly in the large genre of political jokes that circulate in private circles. She again found side-by-side idealization and demonization of Western political systems, and many of those who condemned religious regimes (Iran, Saudi Arabia) and movements (Algeria) as "not true Islam" also idealized the state of justice that "true Islam" would bring. The demonstrations and riots united socialist, democrat, Islamist, and apolitical youth in an inchoate spirit of rebellion fueled by their forced submission and seclusion. In the end, she sees Moroccan youth as caught up in tumultuous struggle with dual identities, usually carried on beneath surfaces of cultural calm, but occasionally exploding in public as they did in the riots and demonstrations.

As many observers note, two axes of tradition versus modernity appear especially important in providing young Moroccans with prototypic identifications and disidentifications. First, a rural-urban axis stretches from hinterland areas to Casablanca and Rabat, contrasting tradition and modernity at each stop along the way. That is, Agdez looks modern in comparison with the hamlets and herding camps scattered through the rugged Saghro Mountains and up into the High Atlas but looks backward and traditional even from the perspective of Ouarzazate (the provincial capital), which in turn looks backward and traditional from downtown Marrakech or Casablanca. This axis demarcates an ancient contrast in styles of life, which the fourteenth-century historian Ibn Khaldun placed at the center of his political sociology. The twentieth century has infused this contrast with a host of new meanings and symbols, and it is rife with stereotypic images of urbanites and country folk that provide endless material for Moroccan humor but also easily become matters of political dispute. Sawsan el-Messiri traces the nuances of these images in his study of social identity among what might be termed the *working people* of Cairo, who contrast themselves to the effete Westernized elites, on the one hand, and to the "backward" rural peasants on the other.[121]

A second axis runs from traditional Morocco to modern Europe—especially to France, whose influence on North African culture has been enormous. This certainly parallels the rural-urban in many respects but differs in that France represents a civilization that differs profoundly in religion, wealth, gender relations, and a great range of styles and values. As the colonizer of Morocco, France also appears as the superior power, the oppressor, and the home to strong anti-Arab racism. The Algerian case vignettes presented by Minor and DeVos suggest that even in the 1950s and 1960s, some individuals sought to reject their backward traditional culture to take on the modern French, others to reject the Christian colonizer's culture and affirm their own authentic tradition, and others to seek syntheses or complements.

Evidence from the Narratives

The fact that I interviewed educated members of a younger generation has several important consequences. First, the narratives show perhaps surprisingly little use of the rhetoric of honor, which certainly lives on in agropastoral, peasant, and urban *populaire* milieus. It is hardly absent from the texts, but in spite of the fact that *sentiments* of honor, modesty, and shame appear ubiquitous, the *rhetoric* of honor does not emerge as the language of identity. Rather, identity appears fashioned largely in terms of gender, religion, and modernity versus tradition. Second, I did not interview any of the well-traveled, Westernized, often nonreligious members of the urban elites, nor did I interview Islamist activists, so these orientations are not represented in my data. And third, many of this generation aspire to live by more modern ideas about men and women than they perceive their parents to hold, and some of the men may have refrained from voicing views of women to me that they might have to their friends, as they easily could guess from the fact that my spouse worked and appeared in public on her own that I did not share them.

Culturally distinctive constructions of gender appear to provide an important dimension of identity in all of the narratives, though much as Shalinsky describes, in complex, flexible ways. Like Mohammed and Hussein, most of the men speak about women they love in nonstereotypic terms but then invoke the sacred and *fitna* (chaos)-prone stereotypes in figures of speech and when they reflect generally on men and women. Like the characters in Mahfouz's *Cairo Trilogy*, the interviews show how wrong it would be to view men as possessing a single constellation of patriarchal views toward women. Still, the men's narratives show the salience of the *fitna*-prone woman as an antiself representation by which they affirm their possession of ᶜqel (rationality) and self-control. As has been reported for many societies—including our own—masculinity often appears at least partially constructed as a rejection of the stereotypically feminine.

Three of the four women I interviewed see themselves as feminists and have adopted some traditionally male rhetorics: for Rachida, Khadija, and Saadia, possessing ᶜqel (rationality) and *klem* (voice) and for Khadija dressing "like a man." Yet both Rachida and Khadija appear to have deeply internalized variants of the *fitna*-prone image of women and feel highly ambivalent about their sexual and reproductive powers, as D. Dwyer noted of many women in the Taroudant region.[122] Neither anchors a positive identity in fertility and its management, as Boddy describes among the Hofriyati, and Naima—the only mother I interviewed—broke off before these issues arose. Perhaps most important, men generally appear to establish manhood via their relations with senior men and male competitors, with women serving to symbolize the sacredness they protect and the forces of chaos they control—much as Jane Schneider describes for traditional Mediterranean cultures.[123] The women, by contrast, appear to more androgynously construct themselves as composites of—or as sometimes raucous dialogues between—masculine and feminine representations.

Religion prominently defines an axis of identity in these four narratives (and in most of the others I elicited), defining alternative discourses for Hussein and Khadija and demarcating predominant self versus antiself oppositions for Mohammed and Rachida. Interestingly, the salient boundaries for Hussein and Khadija are those setting off Muslims from Christians in space and from the *jahiliya* (pre-Islamic era) in time, whereas Mohammed and Rachida highlight the contrast between pious and delinquent Muslims and leave the spatial house of Islam versus house of unbelief and temporal Islamic era versus *jahiliya* boundaries largely implicit. Most important, the self versus antiself representations set up by the latter boundaries appear readily reversible. Hussein's and Khadija's narratives clearly show this, but so do Mohammed's and Rachida's at points. Certainly the fact that the richer and more powerful "Christian" world dominates the Muslim invites mimesis of the sort Pamuk describes in his story of Master Bedii, the mannequin maker. And Islamism offers a kind of empowering mimesis that reverses this: identifying with the original community of Muslims founded at Mecca, it negates contemporary society as having declined into *jahiliya* and rejects Westernization as identification with the oppressor, the Great Satan in the Ayatollah Khomeini's famous phrase.

Modernity versus tradition emerges as perhaps the most volatile and ambivalently debated axis of identity. The young Moroccans I interviewed know well the experience of both Orhan Pamuk's journalist who ends his story about Master Bedii the mannequin maker by embracing the freedom to copy from the boulevard display windows and the silver screen. They also well understand the view of Al e Ahmed, who describes the alienation and emptiness wrought by Euromania (see chapter 1). In this context, the figures of the modern European and the traditional Muslim both serve as Others from which young Moroccans might tap sources of power by mimesis—and this readily gives rise to the experience of being both and of being neither. The tradition-modernity axis organizes contrasting identities for Hussein and Khadija and vigorous inner dialogue within Mohammed's and Rachida's religious discourses. In these and nearly all of the other narratives, modernity irresistibly beckons at one moment and repels at the next, and tradition can shift in the blink of an eye between being a repository of strength and value and an imprisoning world of backwardness and deprivation. This reflects the "tragedy of development"[124] within which young Moroccans are forging identities and lives.

Abdelkrim Ghareeb recently drew on the theories of four figures—Moroccan nationalist leader Allal al-Fasi, sociologist Paul Pascon, Freud, and Piaget—to sketch a similar picture of Moroccan youth.[125] Al-Fassi had described Moroccan youth as torn between their indigenous culture and the European implant, so that, writes Ghareeb, "the individual in Moroccan society finds himself lost and alternating in his choices and decisions."[126] But motivated by the apparent weakness of their own heritage, al-Fassi predicted youth would imitatively opt for the European model as a source of strength. Pascon similarly pointed out that fifty years of colonialism had turned Morocco into a "composite" society: a mixture of Moroccan and French cultures and of indigenous and Western orders of knowledge, manifest in the shifting, "composite" behavior of individuals. But where al-Fassi saw only contradiction and inner discord, Pascon also saw composite life as animating creativity and development. Ghareeb's Freudian analysis shows Moroccan youth alternating between two egos—a "Moroccan-culture ego" anchored in identification with their fathers and a "Western-culture ego" based on rejection of their fathers and identification with Western figures—setting up disturbingly contradictory relations with the id. And his Piagetian analysis shows youth not as passing through a brief disequilibrium at the onset of formal operational thinking but as trapped in an interminable disequilibrium caused by being embedded in the contradictory orders of indigenous and Western knowledge. Ghareeb draws these analyses together to raise the question of whether Morocco's composite culture dooms individuals to inner strife and disequilibrium, and whether this may be a "transitional" period—though now decades long—in which generations of Moroccan youth suffer and sacrifice as they work to create new forms of cultural coherence.

Stepping back for a moment to consider "composite" culture and selves in the light of contemporary models in cross-cultural psychology, the narratives suggest that young Moroccans' constructions of identity are better described by theories of acculturation and ethnic identity than by individualism versus collectivism models (even in their more sophisticated forms).[127] That is, their situation in a globalized and Western-dominated world resembles—at least in some respects—that of immigrants or ethnic minorities who seek to embrace both cultural frameworks, along a developmental path made torturous by unending battle with majority stereotypes and a potentially corrosive sense of backwardness and inferiority.[128] And recent studies of both acculturation and ethnic identity suggest that bicultural and hybrid identities may provide the psychologically healthiest response to cultural duality (see chapter 1).[129]

The Muslim Ethic and the Spirit of Modernization

Perhaps one of the most important findings from this study concerns the way many young Moroccans seek modernity not by embracing variants of secular humanism but by synthesizing honor-driven achievement and religious values. Their formulations parallel Weber's account of the Protestant ethic in many respects, including the eschatological legitimation of economic endeavor, the effort to blend faith and reason, and the emphasis on this-worldly asceticism. Like the Protestant ethic, their worldviews differ markedly from versions of Enlightenment liberalism that we commonly identify with modernity, especially by virtue of the central place accorded to faith and the primacy given to religious and familial authority over individual freedom. These narratives contain very little of the explicit rhetoric of *self*-cultivation so characteristic of American life narratives, and they are not modern in that particular twentieth-century, Western, middle-class sense of self-consciously seeking self-actualization for the sake of realizing one's human potential.

Although Khadija, Said, and Mohammed K. cast their primary identities in terms of Western-inspired ideals, Mohammed, Hussein, Rachida, Ahmad, Saadia, Mebarik, and Nasser articulated their primary identities in terms of some form of this "Muslim Ethic."[130] In no sense are these individuals a representative sample, but the numbers do roughly echo the subjective impression I developed from informally interviewing scores of Moroccans: although an important minority are consolidating individualist outlooks of the sort idealized by Westerners as modern, a much larger proportion represent their lives as callings within a "Muslim ethicist" framework. In all seven of these narratives, religious faith and practice provide not just a spiritual complement to a secular modernity but a vehicle for "becoming modern."

Robert Bellah has shown how the dissemination of the samurai class's Bushido code and emergence of new religious movements throughout the Tokugawa period facilitated Japan's modernization, as did the Protestant ethic in Europe.[131] He traces how the broad diffusion of the Bushido ethic and consequent synthesis of "Shinto Nationalism" promoted a melding of modernist social ambitions and religious values, symbolized by the mission and power of a state headed by a divine emperor who would foster development at home and expel the "barbarians" from abroad. And John Waterbury has shown how the Berbers of the Moroccan Sous region (the same Tashelhait-speaking group as those in the Ouarzazate-Agdez region) developed a Protestant ethic sort of variant of Islam as they became famously successful self-sacrificing entrepreneurs and merchants.[132] I believe this to be a crucially important underlying cultural movement that affects the entire post-Independence generation: the transformation of the traditional patriarchal, patronal, honor-modesty schema into a modernist achievement-career schema—via the linkage of the latter to religion—as a "calling." Ernest Gellner has described this sort of "Weberian ethic" in his discussion of "Algerian Puritanism,"[133] and Ellis

Goldberg has drawn attention to the ways Islamic activists resemble Protestant reformers.[134]

These parallels can be overstated, but they have an important implication: the cultural synthesis of modernism and religion has a personal side, which appears in the form of a modernist achievement orientation, and a political side, which appears as a kind of "natural" support for a number of key Islamist themes. Political Islam may be the media-visible tip of an iceberg, the submerged six sevenths consisting of the large numbers of young North Africans who have fashioned "Muslim ethicist" identities as they struggle against unfavorable odds to succeed in the educational system and open doors into the economy's modern sector. It is in this genre of discourse that many seek to resolve the conflict of individualistic achievement motives and collectivist responsibilities to kin and to synthesize potentially conflicting Moroccan and French-Western styles of life. For the Muslim ethicist, individual achievement can "honor" one's family, maintain an "innocent relationship with God," and help build the nation and the house of Islam. And it takes but a short step to turn this into religiously inspired political activism, especially for those whose dreams appear dashed or turn hollow in the hallways of modern bureaucracies.

Cultures and Selves ❀

This theory of identity based on the study of lives contrasts sharply with the simple models still employed by many anthropologists and psychologists: those that view the self as matching a culture's concept of person or its predominant value orientations, as solidly or permeably bounded, or as a collection of self-attributions inferred from regularities in one's own behavior or feedback from others. It does support models positing that individuals shift among alternative value systems and self-conceptions. The life narrative evidence does not show these coalescing as private, public, and collective selves[135] but rather as integrated into more encompassing systems akin to the cultural frames or ethnic identities studied in conjunction with acculturation.[136] And the theory proposed here goes beyond the information-processing models that hypothesize that cognitive schemas created by often faulty social inference are sampled by situations and then guide behavior. Rather, it postulates a more complex generative model, according to which Gestalt properties of symbols and metaphors and structurally ambiguous relations set up among linguistic terms and visual images are employed to organize the building, suppression, and release of tension states.[137] This enables it to describe the role of metaphors and key symbols in (1) establishing musical scalelike frameworks of meaning that individuals use to track their continually changing social-moral locations and to perform themselves in their culture, (2) endowing universal emotions with culturally specific meanings and display styles, and hence (3) integrating personality and the individual with his or her culture.

A Distributed Model of Culture

I hope this book has shown how densely culture saturates life narratives—how little of an individual's experience and the meanings she or he imparts to it can be grasped without a detailed knowledge of the several cultural regions embedding his or her life. I hope it also has shown how idiosyncratic are each individual's experiences, how selectively they draw on their cultural heritages to give them meaning, and how intensely they struggle to create coherent life projects that "stand for" something, as Hussein puts it. How can the views be reconciled that every facet of a personality appears culturally constructed but the result emerges as a highly idiosyncratic configuration of culture? This question increasingly came to trouble me as I gained fluency in Moroccan Arabic and learned enough about Moroccan families and social forces to see beyond the relatively uniform textures of interpersonal etiquettes and styles. The more I shared of the culture, the greater the individual distinctiveness I recognized—and the more culture appeared "distributed" in the ways described by Anthony Wallace[138] and Theodore Schwartz.[139]

Study of lives methods, I believe, lead an investigator inexorably along two routes toward a distributed view of culture. First, they show the great extent to which individuals find themselves at odds with their culture, thrown into experiences they do not understand, which they find incongruent with their culture's prevailing concept of personhood, and for which they resist accepting their culture's preferred interpretations. They invariably find innovative ways of using their shared language, parsed with meaningful silences, to convey emotions and senses of self that feel profoundly private, personal, and idiosyncratic. Second, the study of lives shows a tremendous range of individual variation within a culture. Even though all members of a culture ultimately may draw on the same heritage to interpret and configure their idiosyncrasies, they do so in such highly selective and divergent ways as to render them potentially as alien to each other as to outsiders. Here the dictum of the early configurationists (Ruth Benedict, Edward Sapir, Margaret Mead) that culture is "personality writ large" may be reversed to yield the more appropriate dictum that personality is "culture writ small."

The configurationists viewed a culture as selectively borrowing a subset of traits from those distributed through a large culture area and then refashioning these in accordance with a guiding aesthetic or sense of life's overriding purposes. Life narratives similarly show individuals to develop personalities by selectively borrowing and refashioning elements from their larger cultural heritage. Each person thus comes to carry a portion of his or her culture, weaving an identity from details that others glimpse but dimly at the horizon of their experience or, in some cases, from details unknown even to their neighbors, spouses, and friends. Although a diligent ethnographer may succeed in accessing enough life domains to assemble an elegant account of "the culture," life narratives show that this culture is in fact distributed, portioned out to individuals.

Figure 7-1 seeks to depict this sort of distribution by comparing some major features of shared Islamic culture selected and elaborated in the life narratives of Hussein and Rachida.

An ethnographer describing Moroccan-Muslim culture might write about the elements forming the ellipse (perhaps also including elements I have omitted). Both Hussein and Rachida have at least superficial familiarity with all the elements forming the ellipse and therefore share an Islamic cultural heritage in a way that most Americans do not. But Hussein has developed a detailed knowledge and intense emotional investment in elements (indicated by the arrows projecting from "Hussein") that remain peripheral to Rachida's concerns, and she has done likewise, creating personalized versions of their shared culture. Further, the diagram could be expanded to show each highly "cathected" element opening a passage to an ellipse of details at a second level (Figure 7-2).

Figure 7-1 Cultural configuration and identity

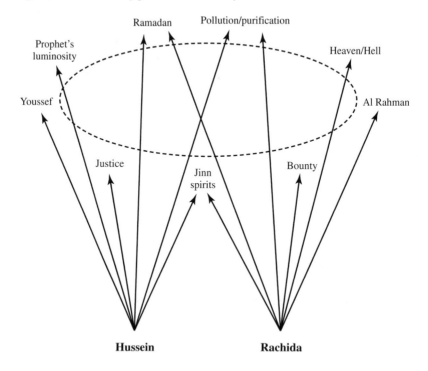

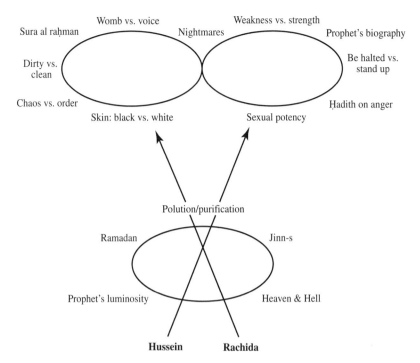

Figure 7-2 Individualized configurations of "shared" elements

Although Hussein and Rachida "share" their culture's pollution-purification complex, each has internalized it in an idiosyncratic form and developed expertise in regions that the other knows only by hearsay or as a novice. And precisely because they lack access to each other's areas of expertise, they do not share this "hypertext"-like diagram of their culture that only an ethnographer could construct. All of the elements Hussein has selected and woven into discourses would represent his map of his "culture writ small," and those Rachida has selected similarly would map her version of *the* culture.

These observations make much—perhaps too much—of the obvious range of individual differences to be found within a culture. And too many psychologists still fail to appreciate the extent to which culture as shown in Figure 7-1 shapes thought, feeling, and development. Economic and political forces indeed may forge a *cultural integration* of the elements depicted in the ellipse of Figure 7-1, and this may entail a hegemonic concept of personhood that affects all members of the society. Every able-bodied person may participate in public performances that articulate this configuration, whether in the everyday ritual of interpersonal etiquettes or in the big rituals of seasonal and life-cycle transitions. But as Melford Spiro[140] argues, perhaps few or none internalize this pattern as the organization of their personalities, selves, or identities. Study of lives methods indicate that *psychological integration* entails not only shared cultural frameworks of the sort depicted in Figure 7-1 but also expertise in fine details and idiosyncrasies of meaning that no sane ethnographer would aspire to incorporate into a general account of the culture. That is, it often appears that elements at the second, less widely shared levels (the upper ellipses of Figure 7-2) play crucial roles in organizing self-representation. The Muslim men praying in unison at the outdoor ʿyd al adha service may all affirm the (lower ellipse level) cultural configuration from the depth of their hearts, but then they also ask forgiveness for profoundly different sins and plead for profoundly different kinds of intercession from a God they recognize as showing different faces to each believer. Hussein draws on light-and-shadow symbolism from several shared cultural sources to link identities to his fascination with *ḥaraka ʿshwa'iya* (random/haphazard movement), but he does not share this particular kinesthetic sense of excitement and apprehension with any of the other Moroccans I interviewed. Many Moroccans feel moved by recitation of the sura *al raḥman*, but do not find the specific meanings that bring Rachida to tears.

In the writings of both psychologists and anthropologists, the "culture constructs self" view has often overshot its mark, giving the illusion that individuals are confined within a "prison-house of language"[141] or values or cognitive styles, with no latitude to evade or resist the voices that assail them. We need not postulate an autonomous subject who remains somehow free of culture to give an account of persons or selves as under-determined by "their" culture. We need only recognize that an individual's psychological processes may select different cultural elements than do societal-level economic and political forces and synthesize them in accordance with different aims.

The relationship between culture and individual thus entails two distinct processes of variation and selection. Individuals continually create new variants of cultural elements, and economic and political interests select those congruent with their hegemonic construction of culture or with the construction they may be pitting against competing groups.[142] At the same time, culture provides each individual with a great variety of symbolic elements and themes, from which she or he selects materials for fashioning an identity. The interests and motives guiding these two processes differ in important ways, so even though the mythopoetic human mind creates both culture and personality, these differ in fundamental respects.

Culture, by this view, exists in two forms. There is the public, global, "big" version (the ellipse of Figure 7-1) traditionally studied by anthropologists that is put on public display in interpersonal etiquettes, myths, rituals, and religious doctrines, where it is often reaffirmed and sometimes contested. And there are distributed, idiosyncratic, "little" versions of culture, as many as there are individuals to write their public culture small. (Figure 7-2 represents but a first step toward depicting Hussein's and Rachida's "little" versions of their culture.) The disjunction between these forms of culture must not be minimized, as the linguistic analogy—that culture is like language—often has encouraged. The fact that everyone learns and shares "the language" can give a mistaken impression of the extent to which everyone learns and shares "the culture." A person's linguistic competence is generally not thought of as organized around idiosyncrasies of pronunciation, vocabulary, or shades of meaning, whereas an individual's character is appropriately seen as organized precisely around such idiosyncrasies of experience and self-presentation. These considerations lead to two important conclusions: (1) individual personality develops through a process of writing culture small, such that every personality takes shape as a version of the culture, and (2) culture writ small according to the principles of psychological integration will never *simply* mirror culture writ large, and individuals may write their culture small in such divergent ways as to chronically baffle and misconstrue one another.

The Variation Paradox

A real paradox emerges here that presents formidable problems to cultural psychologists who wish not only to measure how cultures differ on universal traitlike behavioral, emotional, or cognitive dimensions but also to identify culturally specific psychological structures. Let me describe an example. One bright spring day, we observed a village circumcision ceremony held for a dozen or so boys aged two to five. Several hundred villagers assembled in an open area between long-feuding lineages, the men forming a group to one side, the women a group to the other side, the *ḥraten* ("black") barber-circumciser in the center beneath a tent of white shawls, and anxious and curious older children scattered around the periphery. Amid dense incense smoke (to placate and ward off jinn spirits) and the din of top-of-the-lungs chanting (to drown out the unbearable cries of the children's fear and pain), mothers one at a time brought their sons on their backs and handed them over to a male relative (fathers would feel too much compassion to do their duties), who held the boy's legs apart for the razor's cut. Wrapped and returned to their mothers' backs, the purified boys were whisked back to their homes to be comforted and recover.

The boys shared this culturally prescribed experience, which we suspected—and as Cansever's and Ozturk's studies[143] indicate—many found "traumatic." Boys in cultures that circumcise at birth, that circumcise adolescents as tests of courage, or that do not circumcise share profoundly different experiences, and so it seems natural to ask: What effect does this style of circumcision have on the psychological development of Moroccan and Middle Eastern men? But even a little closer look shows that the boys' experiences differed in the extreme. At two or three years of age, the youngest clearly had no understanding of what was happening to them or why. At five to six, the older ones knew something, but some had been told the lie that the ceremony would be performed only on others, some had been prepared for what they would undergo, and some had been told by their older play-mates that their penises would be cut off. Some appeared to experience moderate distress and rapidly regain composure, but we were told others screamed inconsolably and had nightmares for weeks. We saw two who lost consciousness from fear or pain. Some healed quickly; others developed infections and had long and painful recoveries. Some of the adult men I spoke with that day remembered their circumcision, but others did not. Some claimed "it was nothing," some recalled only having been treated like a prince in the following days, and some recalled a terror that made them shudder fifty years later.

Certainly, divergent experiences arising from temperament, birth order, household composition, inequalities in wealth, divorces, illnesses and deaths, and other factors generate and amplify individual variation. But every culturally distinctive shared experience that might be assumed to produce homogeneity among individuals (duration of nursing, circumcision, religious instruction in Quranic school, trips to the public bath, etc.) also differentiates them and directs them along divergent developmental trajectories. This is the variation paradox: How are we to conceptualize cultural influences on development when each major widely shared influence *generates* variation between individuals?

The "personality writ large" approach taken by most anthropologists—including many who would never explicitly endorse this dictum—assumes that the influence (a child-rearing practice, a family pattern, an ethical ideal, or the like) has roughly the same effect on everyone and it therefore errs in ignoring important individual variation. The contrasting "individual difference" approach taken by most psychologists assumes that the influence produces variation in some naturally occurring universal trait (e.g., self-esteem, introversion-extroversion, individualism-collectivism) and errs in ignoring the formation of culturally distinctive characteristics. A theory of cultural influences on development therefore must begin with a recognition that each culturally patterned influence may both affect population means on universal traits and create *culturally distinctive motives and sentiments that define ranges of individual variation.*

Although I have spoken in highly voluntarist terms about individuals "selecting" the elements of their cultural heritage as if they were turned loose to shop a great mall of culture, influences like large families, childhood circumcision, and memorization of the Quran under a *fqih*'s stick clearly generate variation by impelling individuals along divergent trajectories that may not be of their choosing. Here the efforts of authorities to instill and select in accordance with hegemonic concepts of personhood run into individuals' efforts to selectively make use of some features of their cultural heritage and avoid others—an encounter that often entails more clashing than confluence. Surprisingly, many individuals eventually compose identities and life structures that appear to epitomize cultural ideals but only after long years of delinquency (such as my interviewee Mohammed) or rebellion (such as the

Moroccan patriarch interviewed by Kevin Dwyer and the Lebanese imam studied by Richard Antoun). Naguib Mahfouz's Nobel Prize-winning *Cairo Trilogy* astutely explores the variations generated within a single family in reaction to powerful standardizing pressures, shaping its members into a microcosm of Egyptian society. The key point is that standardization and variation occur as obverse and reverse of the "cultural construction of self," creating *culturally distinctive ranges of variation.*

Ego, Self, and Subject

The affective, conceptual, and symbolic *content* of these Moroccans' self-representational systems differ dramatically from those of Americans I have interviewed but not their *formal* organization. That is, they differentiate personality into *Me* versus *not-Me* contrasts and integrate discourses via structurally ambiguous symbols. Like Americans, they narratively shift, in a quantumlike manner, between space-time-causality systems that, after the manner of key changes in music, redefine the meanings of events and thereby transform affects and moods. Does this add up to a modernist, monadic, coherent self, consisting of a perhaps rigidly integrated ego? Or does it imply a postmodern, decentered self, consisting of multiplex flows of desire, partially frozen into illusory stabilities by the rhetorics of extended conversation with an American interlocutor?

Neither. I have deliberately avoided the terms *self* and *ego* because we do not need them. They may prove useful in other discussions and inquiries, especially of psychopathology and therapy. But life narrative methods cut a path past both Enlightenment and counter-Enlightenment projects, to a world of integrated multiplicity. That is, life narratives show a profoundly musiclike world, characterized by protomathematical relations that generate a wide domain of play and freedom. Whatever it is that generates and plays in this domain—let us use "Mohammed" or "Khadija" rather than Mohammed's "self" or Khadija's "ego"—can produce fuguelike or symphony-like works that look as classical and modern as any Enlightenment project. It also can produce jazzlike improvisations that look as free form and fluid as any postmodern mélange of genres. But all the improvisation is structured and integrated, and life narratives show a few reconfigurable identities, not many.

A final, important point on subjectivity and change. These Moroccans' self-representational systems provide discourses by which they strive to interpret their subjective experience. But their experiences are hardly confined to the meanings the discourses articulate. Indeed, their experiences continually break through the bounds of their discourses, and they live in a near-continual state of dissonance, as do we all. They cannot always masterfully perform the melodic and harmonic scores they have written (or find "inscribed"), and this creates lapses, lacunae, silences, and innovations that can spur them to refashion elements of their representational system as well as to cling to them. In addition, their discourses project them out into the world, toward new encounters and novel experiences, some of which may not "fit" the meanings their identities provide and which may well lead to change and transformation.

A life narrative collected at a single point in time yields but a still photograph and cannot be used to assess how open or closed a person may be to change, development, or involution (as the epilogue about these four respondents testifies). I believe that no cross-sectional investigation can do that, because too much fluidity is built into personality—much more than recognized by most psychologists—to predict how an individual will respond to novelty. As a system of integrated multiplicity, personality remains fundamentally open. Not only do contrasting identities organize our personalities as dialogue and dispute but also our subjective experience continually eludes, escapes, and overflows the confines of the discourses we design to render it meaningful. As Erikson recognized, identity guarantees no stability, and at some historical and life-historical moments, it leads beyond its own boundaries.

Yet all this emphasis on freedom, play, transformation, and the sheer beauty of narrative self-representation should not blind us to identity's crucial and often conservative role in accommodation to social hierarchies, economic and political underdevelopment, and nature's stubborn forces. One day we visited an especially picturesque village perched on the edge of a flood-carved gorge and were stopped in our tracks by the hauntingly beautiful voices of four women singing as they were trudging back from the rocky hinterlands with seventy-pound bundles of fuelwood shrubs on their backs. It was near noon, near a hundred degrees, and we knew they had set off before dawn. A middle-aged man walked up behind us, puffing steadily on a cigarette. "It sounds beautiful, doesn't it?" We agreed. "Just keep in mind: they're singing to forget their pain."

Epilogue

In December 1999, I returned to Morocco for a brief visit. During the few days I spent in the south, I contacted some of those I had interviewed ten years earlier, or their families. Though I am not given to making predictions, I expected to find that Mohammed had moved to join his brother in Rabat, that Hussein had finally found a job in one of Morocco's large cities, and that Rachida had stayed at home, unmarried. I feared that Khadija's life had continued along its troubled, chaotic trajectory. All of my hunches were wrong.

Mohammed returned to his family and father in Skoura after his ulcer treatment in Rabat, and stayed. He continues to manage the agricultural co-op and plays a prominent role in local religious affairs. Hussein eventually took the advice his father had given him before he went to the university and entered an Agriculture Ministry training program for extensionists. He worked unhappily for three years in village agricultural stations and then helped his brother start a consumer electronics shop in Agdez, just as a rural electrification project moved into high gear. They prospered, he quit his extensionist job, and they recently opened a second store in the provincial capital, Ouarzazate. He married a year ago.

Two years after I left, Rachida met an equally devout male teacher, and about a year later they married and set up their own household. She now has two children and continues to teach elementary school in Agdez. A year after I left, Khadija's younger sister was admitted to an engineering program at a university in Belgium, with the help of a young Belgian man she had met when he came to Morocco as a tourist. Khadija joined her there, finished high school, and then went through a professional nursing program. She now works in a large city hospital. She and her sister help support their parents and younger siblings in Taznakht, and two years ago she married a Belgian man.

NOTES

INTRODUCTION

1. See especially Spiro, "Is the Western Conception of the Self 'Peculiar' within the Context of the World Cultures?"; Murray, "What Is the Western Concept of the Self? On Forgetting David Hume"; Holland and Kipnis, "Metaphors for Embarrassment and Stories of Exposure: The Not-So-Egocentric Self in American Culture"; and Rosenberger, "Dialectic Balance in the Polar Model of Self: The Japan Case."

2. See LeVine, "Infant Environments in Psychoanalysis: A Cross-Cultural View."

3. Triandis, *Individualism and Collectivism.*

4. Kagitcibasi, "Individual and Group Loyalties: Are They Compatible?"

5. Philipchalk, *Invitation to Social Psychology*, p. 48.

6. Matsumoto, "Culture and Self: An Empirical Assessment of Markus and Kitayama's Theory of Independent and Interdependent Self-Construals."

7. Takano and Osaka, "An Unsupported Common View: Comparing Japan and the U.S. on Individualism/Collectivism."

8. Oyserman, Coon, and Kemmelmeier, "Rethinking Individualism and Collectivism."

9. Bond, "Reclaiming the Individual from Hofstede's Ecological Analysis—A 20-Year Odyssey"; Fiske, "Using Individualism and Collectivism to Compare Cultures—A Critique of the Validity and Measurement of the Constructs"; Kitayama, "Culture and Basic Psychological Processes—Toward a System View of Culture"; and Miller, "Bringing Culture to Basic Psychological Theory—Beyond Individualism and Collectivism."

10. Gjerde, "Culture, Power, and Experience: Toward a Person-Centered Cultural Psychology."

11. Oyserman et al. write that "we propose that a dichotomized way of thinking about cultures as either individualistic or collectivistic be replaced by the assumption that all societies socialize for both individualistic and collectivistic ways of construing situations" (Oyserman, Kemmelmeier, and Coon, "Cultural Psychology, A New Look," p. 4).

12. On culture and emotion, see Ekman, "Universals and Cultural Differences in Facial Expression of Emotion" and "Biological and Cultural Contributions to

Body and Facial Movement in the Expression of Emotions"; Izard, "Basic Emotions, Relations among Emotions, and Emotion-Cognition Relations"; Shweder, "The Cultural Psychology of Emotion"; and Matsumoto, "Culture and Emotion." On shifting "cultural frames" and biculturalism, see LaFromboise, Coleman, and Gerton, "Psychological Impact of Biculturalism"; Tasi, Ying, and Lee, "The Meaning of 'Being Chinese' and 'Being American'"; Oyserman, Sakamoto, and Lauffer, "Cultural Accommodation"; Benet-Martinez et al., "Negotiating Biculturalism"; Haritatos and Benet-Martinez, "Bicultual Identities"; and Hong et al., "Boundaries of Cultural Influence."

13. Geertz, "From the Natives' Point of View."
14. Oyserman, Kemmelmeier, and Coon, "Cultural Psychology, A New Look," pp. 13, 18.
15. Kagitcibasi, *Family and Human Development across Cultures.*
16. Joseph, *Intimate Selving in Arab Families.*
17. Lindholm, *The Islamic Middle East.*
18. See also Imamoglu, "Individualism and Collectivism in a Model and Scale of Balanced Differentiation and Integration."
19. Philipchalk, *Invitation to Social Psychology,* p. 49.
20. Antoun, *Muslim Preacher in the Modern World.*
21. Murray, *Explorations in Personality.*
22. White, *Lives in Progress.*
23. Smith, Bruner, and White, *Opinions and Personality.*
24. Erikson, *Childhood and Society.*
25. Levy, *Tahitians.*
26. See, for example, Hofstede, *Culture's Consequences;* Markus and Kitayama, "Culture and Self"; and Nisbett, *The Geography of Thought.*
27. Geertz, "From the Native's Point of View," pp. 123–136.
28. Anderson, "Sentimental Ambivalence and the Exegesis of 'Self' in Afghanistan."
29. Caton, "The Poetic Construction of Self."
30. These have led her to a model of culture and self congruent with that proposed here. See especially Ewing, "The Illusion of Wholeness: Culture, Self, and the Experience of Inconsistency" and "The Dream of Spiritual Initiation and the Organization of Self Representation among Pakistani Sufis."
31. See especially the 2002 edition of Raphael Patai's *The Arab Mind* and David Pryce-Jones's *The Closed Circle.*
32. See Moughrabi, "The Arab Basic Personality: A Critical Survey of the Literature," and Barakat, "Beyond the Always and the Never: Critique of Social Psychological Interpretations of Arab Society and Culture."
33. Patai, *The Arab Mind,* p. x.
34. A centuries-old confederation of eight Tashelhait-speaking *taqbilt*s, a term that, with some inaccuracy, is often translated "tribe."
35. I offered to pay two respondents who appeared to live more "on the make" lives. They accepted, but they are not among the four presented here. I gave unexpected gifts to the others at the end of the interviews.
36. Murray, *Explorations in Personality;* White, *Lives in Progress.*
37. Deutsch and Murphy, *The Clinical Interview.*
38. I parse each narrative into "story segments" that loosely correspond to psycholinguist James Gee's notion of a "Part" (Gee, "A Linguistic Approach to Narrative").

39. The narratives will be archived at the Foley Center for the Study of Lives at Northwestern University. In this book, I reference longer passages with their story segment numbers.

40. See especially the cases of Dora, the "Rat Man," and the "Wolf Man."

41. Coles, *Children of Crisis*.

42. Coles, *Migrants, Sharecroppers, Mountaineers*.

43. Abu-Lughod, *Veiled Sentiments*.

44. Wikan, *Tomorrow, God Willing*.

45. Dwyer, *Moroccan Dialogues*.

46. Behar, *Translated Woman*.

47. Oyserman et al., "Cultural Psychology: A New Look," p. 116. Emphasis mine.

CHAPTER 1

1. A few years earlier, villagers stopped performing a wintertime sacrifice for the almond crop after a prominent elder convinced them that it was a folk "innovation" that went against strict Muslim practice. That year, a late frost damaged the buds and led to one of the poorest harvests anyone could recall. The following year, the villagers reinstituted the ritual.

2. Munson, *The House of Si Abdullah*.

3. Ibid., pp. 21–22.

4. Ibid., pp. 23, 48.

5. Krichen, "Les problemes de la langue et l'intelligensia." Quoted in Burgat and Dowell *The Islamic Movement in North Africa*, p. 45.

6. Geertz, "From the Native's Point of View," pp. 123–136.

7. Boddy, *Wombs and Alien Spirits*.

8. Hofstede, *Culture's Consequences*.

9. Shweder and Bourne, "Does the Concept of the Person Vary Cross-Culturally?"

10. Geertz, "From the Natives' Point of View," p. 126.

11. Markus and Kitayama, "Culture and Self."

12. LeVine, "Infant Environments in Psychoanalysis."

13. Spiro makes this criticism of both social psychological and anthropological approaches (Spiro, "Is the Western Conception of the Self 'Peculiar' within the Context of the World Cultures?").

14. Triandis recently reemphasized that "a culture should not be characterized as individualist or collectivist. That kind of characterization is simplistic" (Triandis, "Individualism and Collectivism," p. 40).

15. Matsumoto, "Culture and Self."

16. Triandis, "The Self and Social Behavior in Differing Cultural Contexts."

17. See especially chapters by Sinha and Tripathi, Ho and Chiu, and Triandis in Kim et al., eds., *Individualism and Collectivism*.

18. Oyserman and Markus, "Possible Selves and Delinquency," and Cross and Markus, "Possible Selves across the Life Span."

19. Triandis, "The Self and Social Behavior in Differing Cultural Contexts."

20. Trafimow, Triandis, and Goto, "Some Tests of the Distinction Between the Private Self and the Collective Self," and Ybarra and Trafimow, "How Priming the Private Self or Collective Self Affects the Relative Weights of Attitudes and Subjective Norms."

21. La Fromboise, Coleman, and Gerton, "Psychological Impact of Biculturalism."

22. See Tasi, Ying, and Lee "The Meaning of 'Being Chinese' and 'Being American'" and Oyserman, "The Lens of Personhood."

23. Oyserman, Sakamoto, and Lauffer, "Cultural Accommodation: Hybridity and the Framing of Social Obligation," and Hermans and Kempen, "Moving Cultures."

24. Phinney, "Ethnic Identity in Adolescents and Adults: Review of Research."

25. Hong et al., "Multicultural Minds."

26. Verkuyten and Pouliasi, "Biculturalism among Older Children."

27. McAdams, *Power, Intimacy, and the Life Story*; Bruner, *Acts of Meaning*; Gregg, *Self Representation*; Hermans and Kempen, *The Dialogical Self*; Rosenwald and Ochberg, *Storied Lives*; and McAdams and Ochberg, eds., *Psychobiography and Life Narratives*.

28. See, for example, Schank, *Tell Me a Story*.

29. See Spence, *Narrative Truth and Historical Truth* and Carr, *Time, Narrative, and History*.

30. Bruner, *Acts of Meaning*.

31. Hermans and Kempen, *The Dialogical Self*.

32. Gregg, *Self Representation*.

33. McAdams, *Power, Intimacy, and the Life Story*.

34. *Nomothetic*: comparing individuals on characteristics they are presumed to share.

35. *Idiographic*: identifying characteristics distinctive of specific individuals.

36. Kelly, *The Psychology of Personal Constructs*; Maher, ed., *Clinical Psychology and Personality: The Selected Papers of George Kelly*.

37. Rosenberg and Gara, "The Multiplicity of Personal Identity"; Rosenberg, Van Mechelen, and DeBoeck, "A Hierarchical Classes Model"; and Rosenberg, "Self and Others: Studies in Social Personality and Autobiography."

38. Hermans and Kempen, *The Dialogical Self*, and Raggatt, "Mapping the Dialogical Self."

39. See Obeyesekere, *The Work of Culture*.

40. Foucault, *The Order of Things*.

41. See Matsumoto, "Culture and Emotion."

42. Benedict, *Patterns of Culture*.

43. Erikson, *Childhood and Society* and *Identity: Youth and Crisis*.

44. I could use the less provocative term *rhetoric*, which would emphasize the poetic and aesthetic character of self representation while retaining the sense that it is designed to persuade.

45. Goffman, *The Presentation of Self in Everyday Life*.

46. The concepts are Erikson's; the terms *Me* versus *not-Me* are mine.

47. Erikson, *Young Man Luther*.

48. Ibid., p. 236.

49. Lévi-Strauss, *The Savage Mind*, *Structural Anthropology*, and *The Raw and the Cooked*.

50. Freud, "Negation."

51. Adorno et al., *The Authoritarian Personality*.

52. See Aboulafia, *The Mediating Self* and Crossley, *Intersubjectivity*.

53. See McAdams, *Power, Intimacy, and the Life Story*, and Hermans and Kempen, *The Dialogical Self*.

54. See chapter 8 of *Self Representation* for a discussion of the unresolved tension in Mead's writings between a view of the "Generalized Other" as a kind of Rousseauian, harmony-producing General Will and as a kind of Marxian conflict-perpetuating struggle of opposed groups (Mead, *Mind, Self, and Society*).
55. See Bonner, *On Development,* and Dawkins, *The Extended Phenotype.*
56. Mischel, *Personality and Assessment.*
57. Ekman, "Universals and Cultural Differences in Facial Expression of Emotion."
58. Matsumoto, "Culture and Emotion."
59. Levy, *Tahitians,* p. 324.
60. Stern, *The Interpersonal World of the Infant.*
61. Horowitz, *States of Mind.*
62. LeVine, *Culture, Behavior, and Personality.*
63. Ibid., p. 116.
64. Ibid., pp. 121–122.
65. Ibid., pp. 122–123.
66. Bourdieu, *Outline of a Theory of Practice.*
67. McAdams, "What Do We Know When We Know a Person?"
68. Ricoeur, *Freud and Philosophy.*
69. Freud, *The Future of an Illusion,* p. 71.
70. Obeysekere, *The Work of Culture.*
71. Gee, *Social Linguistics and Literacies,* p. xv.
72. Tversky points out that his "feature-matching" theory of similarity predicts circumstances in which a pair of objects will be judged to be both the most similar and the most different of a larger set of objects. I believe this property confers on such objects a particularly important information-processing capacity, as their shared and nonshared features can represent different and even opposed meanings (Tversky, "Features of Similarity").
73. Shurtleff and Aoyagi, *The Book of Tofu.*
74. Lehrdahl and Jackendoff, *A Generative Theory of Tonal Music.*
75. Jackendoff, *Consciousness and Computational Mind,* p. 243.
76. Jackendoff, *Languages of the Mind.*
77. Dennett, *Consciousness Explained.*
78. Eickelman, *The Middle East,* pp. 178–179 (italics added).
79. Geertz, "The Meanings of Family Ties."
80. H. Geertz, C. Geertz, Eickelman, and Rosen use the phrase *patron/client relations* only occasionally, but they clearly describe patterns of noncorporate, hierarchical, dyadic reciprocity that others take to be quintessentially patronal and clientalist. I will use these terms freely because I believe they describe an important feature of social relations in this region.
81. Geertz, "Suq: The Bazaar Economy in Sefrou."
82. Rosen, *Bargaining for Reality,* p. 4.
83. Eickelman, *Moroccan Islam,* p. 123.
84. Ibid., p. 124.
85. Montagne, *Les Berberes et le Makhzen dans le Sud au Maroc.*
86. Gellner, *Saints of the Atlas.*
87. Hart, *The Aith Waryaghar of the Moroccan Rif, Dada 'Atta and His Forty Grandsons,* and *The Ait 'Atta of Southern Morocco.*
88. Gregg and Geist, "Socio-Economic Organization of the Ait Imeghrane."

89. The homogeneity of Middle Eastern rural societies should by no means be over-emphasized. In particular, arrangements that resemble feudalism—with large landowners and landless laborers—prevail in numerous regions.

90. Rosen, in fact, presents a remarkable example, in which a challenge to a local big man is resolved when state officials arrive in the middle of the night and overturn the election, and a Royal Air Force flyover shows the reach of the favored candidate in the subsequent one.

91. For an excellent description of this practice, see Fuad Khuri's *Tents and Pyramids*.

92. Hammoudi, *Master and Disciple*.

93. Eickelman, "Traditional Islamic Learning and Ideas of the Person in the Twentieth Century," p. 37.

94. Eickelman, *Knowledge and Power in Morocco*, pp. 56, 59.

95. Ibid., p. 58.

96. Geertz, "From the Natives' Point of View," pp. 124, 125.

97. Ibid., p. 132.

98. Ibid., p. 135.

99. Ibid., p. 132.

100. Ibid., p. 133.

101. Ibid., p. 134.

102. See Jacques-Meunie, "Hierarchie Sociale au maroc Presaharien."

103. Hart, *Dada 'Atta and His Forty Grandsons* and *The Ait 'Atta of Southern Morocco*.

104. Geertz, *The Interpretation of Cultures*.

105. Ibid., p. 90.

106. Ibid., p. 131.

107. See his "Person, Time, and Conduct in Bali" in *The Interpretation of Cultures*.

108. See Schimmel, *Islamic Names*.

109. I keep the male terms, because this process differs for women.

110. Geertz, *Islam Observed*.

111. Minor and DeVos, *Oasis and Casbah*, p. 126.

112. Ibid., pp. 185–186.

113. Ibid., p. 189.

114. Ibid., p. 148.

115. Ibid., p. 156.

116. Crapanzano, *Hamadsha* and *Tuhami*.

117. Crapanzano, *Hamadsha*, p. 229.

118. Reprinted as chapter 3 in his *Hermes' Dilemma and Hamlet's Desire*.

119. Crapanzano, "Rite of Return: Circumcision in Morocco."

120. Ibid., p. 279.

121. Ibid., p. 280.

122. Hammoudi, *Master and Disciple*.

123. Ewing, "The Illusion of Wholeness."

124. Ibid., p. 259.

125. Ibid.

126. Ibid., p. 260.

127. Ibid., p. 261.

128. Ibid., p. 253.

129. Ewing, "The Dream of Spiritual Initiation and the Organization of Self Representation among Pakistani Sufis," p. 59.

130. Ibid., p. 69.

131. Lerner, *The Passing of Traditional Society*, p. 112.

132. Olson, quoting Lewis, *The Emergence of Modern Turkey*, p. 268.

133. Gole, *The Forbidden Modern*, p. 15.

134. Ibid., quoted on pp. 57–58.

135. Ibid., p. 15.

136. Poulton, *Top Hat, Grey Wolf and Crescent*, p. 318.

137. Ibid., p. 163.

138. Mottahedeh, *The Mantle of the Prophet*, p. 60.

139. Vaziri, *Iran as Imagined Nation*, p. 197.

140. Mottahedeh, *The Mantle of the Prophet*, p. 311.

141. Ibid., p. 327.

142. Ibid., p. 329.

143. Ibid., p. 312.

144. Ibid., p. 296.

145. Ibid.

146. Ibid., p. 299.

147. Vaziri, *Iran as Imagined Nation*, p. 208, 211.

148. Taussig, *Mimesis and Alterity*.

149. Ibid., pp. xiii, xviii, 62.

150. Ibid., pp. 33, 7.

151. Ibid., p. 129.

152. James, *Principles of Psychology*, p. 372.

153. Carnes, *Secret Ritual and Manhood in Victorian America*.

154. Pamuk, *The Black Book*, pp. 53–56.

CHAPTER 2

1. King Hassan II, who died in 1999 after ruling since 1957. His son, Mohammed VI, then ascended the throne.

2. By 2003, a crackdown on unofficial guides had greatly reduced their presence in the city and the "harassment" tourists felt they experienced.

3. Alison Geist's research in Imeghrane found that each household needs about one kilogram of fuel shrubs per member per day.

4. Morocco has the world's third largest deposits of phosphate (used in the manufacture of fertilizers), but the United States and the former Soviet Union have enormous deposits, and the international price has not been especially high.

5. In the 1990s, the birth rate began a significant decline.

6. A 1988 Gillies MacKinnon film called *Hideous Kinky*, starring Kate Winslet, offers some of the best views of Marrakech and the High Atlas, including a harrowing truck ride on the road from Marrakech to Ouarzazate.

7. See chapter 2 of my *The Middle East: A Cultural Psychology* for a fuller overview of social organization in rural Middle Eastern societies.

8. Evans-Pritchard, *The Nuer*.

9. Connelly, *Arab Folk Epic and Identity*.

10. See chapter 3 of my *The Middle East: A Cultural Psychology* for a fuller discussion of the region's "code of honor."

11. Maxwell, *Lords of the Atlas.*

12. See Hart, *Dada ʿAtta and His Forty Grandsons* and *The Ait ʿAtta of Southern Morocco.*

13. Leveau, *La Fellah Marocain.*

14. Although it still has a "last outpost" feel, Ouarzazate has grown substantially in the last fifteen years, with new upscale residential and shopping areas and also the decline of some traditional neighborhoods into slumlike areas.

15. And now, a development of upscale villas sited around the fairways of a golf course, sustained with water that used to flow to oases along the Drᶜa River.

16. Jacques-Meunie, "Hierarchie Sociale au Maroc Presaharien."

17. The previous *caid* had been transferred after he sold a truckload of grain shipped in to feed poor villagers during a drought.

CHAPTER 3

1. *Ḥadiths* are narratives about deeds or sayings of the Prophet that can be taken to indicate his approval of exemplary actions. I will use the phrase "sayings of the Prophet."

2. See H. Geertz, "The Meanings of Family Ties"; Maher, *Women and Property in Morocco*; and Gregg and Geist, "Socio-Economic Organization of the Ait Imeghrane."

3. Because first-born sons customarily are named Mohammed after the Prophet, this story clearly emphasizes the importance of the namer.

4. People often express fear and disdain for dogs, which run wild in packs, are regarded as impure, often are *jahel* (rabid), and may be jinns (spirits/demons) in disguise.

5. The sequence of memories moves from picturing a "pre-Oedipal" harmony in the shrine, through its rupture and the emergence of a parricidal wish during his parents' quarrel, to a veiled "castration" image in the bicycle accident, and finally to a strong paternal identification and desire to be a man among men.

6. Antoun, *Muslim Preacher in the Modern World.*

7. Dawood, translator, *The Koran,* p. 428.

8. Dawood, translator, *The Koran,* p. 420.

9. See Nelson, *The Art of Reciting the Quran.*

10. Doi, *The Anatomy of Dependence.*

11. Rank, "The Myth of the Birth of the Hero."

12. Campbell, *The Hero with a Thousand Faces.*

13. Jung, *Man and His Symbols.*

14. Raglan, "The Hero: A Study in Tradition, Myth, and Drama (Part II)."

15. Propp, *Morphology of the Folktale.*

16. Propp presents his scheme as the morphology of folktales in general, but as Dundes points out, it more accurately "might be said to outline the typical biography of a hero or heroine as it is found in fairy tales" (Dundes, "The Hero Pattern and the Life of Jesus," p. 186). Raglan and Propp's schemas also do not fit tales from other regions as well as those from Russia and Europe.

17. Erikson, *Young Man Luther.*

18. Hermans and Kempen, *The Dialogical Self.*

19. See Lord, *The Singer of Tales;* Alter, *The Art of Biblical Narrative, The Art of Bib-*

lical Poetry, and *The World of Biblical Literature*; Raglan, "The Hero"; Connelly, *Arab Folk Epic and Identity*; and Renard, *Islam and the Heroic Image*.

20. Langer, *Philosophy in a New Key*, p. 153.
21. Ortner, "On Key Symbols."
22. See Schimmel, *And Muhammed Is His Messenger*.
23. And *priest*, *preacher*, and *monk* are not equivalents to *fqih* in any but the most minimal, irrelevant senses.

CHAPTER 4

1. See Behar, *Translated Woman*.
2. See Inkeles and Smith, *Becoming Modern*.
3. *Waqef* can be used to mean erection, but *qowm/qaym* is the most common term.
4. Hussein probably saw me as potentially a similar patron figure, as the French colonist had been to his father.
5. These are central notions in both traditional and legal justice systems, whose terms we will see thread throughout his narrative.
6. Mernissi, *Beyond the Veil*.
7. Abou Zeid, "Honour and Shame among the Bedouins of Egypt," p. 246.
8. Ibid., p. 253.
9. See especially Hamady, *Temperament and Character of the Arabs*; Patai, *The Arab Mind*; Pryce-Jones, *The Closed Circle*; and Mackey, *Passion and Politics*. Pryce-Jones even writes that "shame-honor ranking is unsuited to a technical context because it prevents reason being an agreed value" (p. 51)—as if Japan, perhaps *the* prototypic shame culture, has remained mired in technological backwardness.
10. Abou Zeid, "Honour and Shame among the Bedouins of Egypt," p. 247.
11. Herzfeld, "Honour and Shame: Problems in the Comparative Analysis of Moral Systems," p. 339.
12. Herzfeld, *The Poetics of Manhood*, p. 16.
13. Bourdieu, *Outline of a Theory of Practice*, p. 197.
14. Ibid., pp. 204, 208.
15. Ibid., pp. 216–217.
16. Ibid., pp. 231–232.
17. Abou Zeid, "Honour and Shame among the Bedouins of Egypt," p. 259.
18. Abu-Lughod, *Veiled Sentiments*.
19. Ibid., pp. 87–88.
20. Ibid., p. 113.
21. Schneider, "Of Vigilance and Virgins," p. 2.
22. Ibid., p. 11.
23. Ibid., p. 17
24. Ibid., pp. 21–22.
25. Geertz, Rosen, and Geertz, *Meaning and Order in Moroccan Society*.
26. Eickelman, *The Middle East: An Anthropological Approach*, p. 240.
27. Wolf, "Kinship, Friendship, and Patron-Client Relations in Complex Societies," p. 176.
28. Fromm and Maccoby, *Social Character in a Mexican Village*. See especially p. 16.

29. Mead, *Mind, Self, and Society.*
30. See Aboulafia, *The Mediating Self.*
31. Bouhdiba, *Sexuality in Islam*, pp 212–230.
32. Ibid., p. 221.
33. Ibid., p. 220.
34. Ibid., pp. 221, 223.
35. Msefer, *Sevrages et Interdependence.*
36. Mernissi, *Beyond the Veil*, p. 69.
37. For an excellent ethnography of adolescents in a Moroccan small town, see Davis and Davis, *Adolescence in a Moroccan Town.*
38. See Devereux, *Reality and Dream.*
39. Greenwood, "Cold or Spirits? Choice and Ambiguity in Morocco's Pluralistic Medical System."
40. This echo also appears in Mohammed's narrative but not in those of the other men I interviewed.
41. Bellakhdar, Honda, and Miki's *Herb Drugs and Herbalists in the Maghreb* reports one herbalist as saying that ambergris is "used in case of chill and paralysis"(p. 147); Akhmisse's *Medicine Sans Medecins* reports that "L'ambre gris et utilise comme aphrodisiaque" (p. 182). Greenwood reports: "The hottest known substance, ambergris, is taken by old men to restore their sexual vigour when they take young wives, but it should never be taken by those under the age of forty, as it produces boils and eruptions" (p. 227).
42. Writing and passing secret love letters, followed perhaps by conversations on the way to and from class, is the main form "dating" takes among Moroccan students.
43. Inkeles and Smith, *Becoming Modern.*
44. Weber, *The Protestant Ethic and the Spirit of Capitalism.*
45. Ortner, "Is Female to Male as Nature Is to Culture?"
46. The figure may also represent his own mother, associating her aging with the forces of modernity.
47. *nira* (flame/glow) can be derived either from *nar* (fire) or *nur* (divine illumination).
48. Smoor, *Kings and Bedouins in the Palace of Aleppo as Reflected in Maari's Works.*
49. Kritzeck, *Anthology of Islamic Literature*, p. 128.
50. See especially Krichen, "Les problemes de la langue et l'intelligensia," and Barakat, *The Arab World.*
51. Burgat and Dowell, *The Islamic Movement in North Africa*, p. 48.
52. El Messiri, *Ibn al-Balad: A Concept of Egyptian Identity.*
53. Ibid., p. 85.
54. Williams, *The Country and the City.*
55. Ibn Khaldun, *The Moqqademah.*
56. It is unclear to what extent Hussein may have deliberately drawn his characterizations from Ibn Khaldun and to what extent he took them from the popular debate about urban and rural ways of life that has permeated North African popular culture for centuries.
57. "The others will be true just 30 or 40 percent of the time, as those could just be from Satan, or from the unconscious," he comments.
58. Wolf, "The Social Organization of Mecca and the Origins of Islam."

59. Rodinson, *Muhammad*, p. 70.

60. Ibid., p. 73.

61. This is verse 35 of the sura Al Nur (The Light). Verses 45–47 of the sura Al Furqan (The Criterion) are of nearly equal importance.

62. Ali, trans., *The Holy Quran*, pp. 876–877.

63. Ibid., pp. 878–879. Ali notes that "one above another" is to contrast with "light upon light" used later in the Light verse, which similarly invites the reader or listener to "contemplate the Glory of Allah by a parable of the subtle play of Light and Shade in Allah's creation."

64. Schimmel, *And Muhammed Is His Messenger*, p. 129.

65. Ibid., p. 187.

66. Nandy, *The Intimate Enemy*.

67. Accad, *Sexuality and War*.

68. Similar to *amae* as analyzed by Doi in *The Anatomy of Dependence*.

69. Marcia, "The Empirical Study of Ego Identity."

70. Levinson et al., *The Seasons of a Man's Life*.

71. Todorov, *The Fantastic*, pp. 25, 31.

72. Pirandello, "Six Characters in Search of an Author," pp. 266–267.

73. Ibid., pp. 231–232.

74. Yet his ability to construct a world of complex characters and relationships, to find sources of creativity and strength even in the depths of his despair, and to reflect both seriously and lightheartedly on his predicament all testify to his considerable psychological strengths.

CHAPTER 5

1. Amrouche grew up in a village in the Kabyle region of Algeria, received an education in French-run orphanages, and wrote her autobiography in the 1940s. See Gregg, "Culture, Personality, and the Multiplicity of Identity."

2. See Ewing, "Can Psychoanalytic Theories Explain the Pakistani Woman?"

3. Mernisi, *Beyond the Veil*.

4. Though *ḥameq* can refer to symptoms not attributed to jinns.

5. Krohn, *Hysteria: The Elusive Neurosis*. It is important to keep in mind that even regions of Morocco differ dramatically in the kind and degree of restrictions placed on women.

6. There are many versions of this tale, and Rachida's is an especially abbreviated and idiosyncratic one. Many show the lambs' cleverness in defeating the ogre, and others show the ogre's terrifying craftiness. None I know make it into an object lesson about obeying one's parents—though folktales are often told for this purpose.

7. Her use of color and movement as "additional" cues suggests that she has a potentially richer emotional life than she expresses—that she has emotional needs that are not currently integrated into her personality or identity.

8. Rachida's projective tests make her appear more deeply troubled than does her life history, which in turn makes her look more disturbed than the impression I formed of her during the course of the interviews. She took the initiative to build a trusting relationship with me, a non-Muslim male outsider, in which she reflectively talked over her personal struggles, expressed curiosity about herself and the world of secular ideas, and showed flashes of humor about her

life and peculiarities. She also possesses formidable intellectual abilities that empower her determination to advance and defend herself, and if she rarely feels playful or finds sensual forms of pleasure, she experiences a strong sense of efficacy and pride in her accomplishments. Within the rather ascetic confines she embraces, she appears capable of experiencing bounty, plenitude, and fulfillment. And when she leaves these confines to travel, she describes herself as experiencing an enlivening sense of freedom and enjoyment. In the end, it remains difficult to assess the gravity of her turmoil, especially in that I am not a clinician.

9. See LeVine et al., *Child Care and Culture: Lessons from Africa,* and chapter 7 in this book.

10. Chaouite, "L'enfant marocain: Horizon d'une pensee psychologique."

11. She literally says, "I feel its body moving/shaking," which may refer to her body, figuratively to the body of the Quran, or to her unity with it in recitation.

12. Antoun, *Muslim Preacher in the Modern World.*

13. Dawood, translator, *The Koran,* pp. 376–378.

14. Though the Hans-Wehr dictionary (Cowan, ed.) gives "pitch dark" as the translation, p. 296.

15. See especially Boddy, *Wombs and Alien Spirits*; Delaney, *The Seed and the Soil*; and Wikan, *Behind the Veil in Arabia* and *Tomorrow, God Willing.*

16. Cattle have great practical and symbolic value in this region's agropastoral way of life. Dairy products are prized as blessed foods, and a household is really complete only when each senior woman has her own cow, from which she nurtures its members.

CHAPTER 6

1. I have made minor abbreviations in some passages.

2. Goiter is endemic in the region, which uses salt from quarried local mines that lacks iodine.

3. This phrase could mean "didn't have intercourse with me" or just "stayed away from me."

4. *Salem ᶜlikoum* (may peace be upon you) is a formal greeting, *ṣbaḥ l-khir* (good morning) an informal one.

5. Herman, *Trauma and Recovery.*

6. Remarkably, she recalls two of her most terrifying memories—the quarrel that led both her parents to leave the children alone and her mother's cutting her brother's head with a thrown bowl—as occurring during rare Saharan rain storms.

7. Herman, *Trauma and Recovery.*

8. Mernissi, *Dreams of Trespass.*

9. Note that she shifts to "we" here, as if she imagines we together are beautifying the scene.

10. Khadija was always serious and not flirtatious during our conversations, but she clearly was revealing herself to me and hoping (I don't know how consciously) I might rescue her.

11. Najib Mahfouz repeatedly applies this analogy to men's lust in *Palace of Desire.*

12. See Herman, *Trauma and Recovery.*

13. See Fenichel, *The Psychoanalytic Theory of Neurosis* and Shapiro, *Neurotic Styles.*

14. See Mitchell, *Psychoanalysis and Feminism*; Kahane, "Introduction" to Bernheimer and Kahane, *In Dora's Case*; Moi, "Representation of Patriarchy"; and Sprengnether, "Enforcing Oedipus: Freud and Dora."
15. See Boddy, *Wombs and Alien Spirits*.
16. See Krohn, *Hysteria: The Elusive Neurosis*.
17. Foucault, *The History of Sexuality*.
18. Combs-Schilling, *Sacred Performances: Islam, Sexuality, and Sacrifice*.
19. J. M. Cowan, ed., *A Dictionary of Modern Written Arabic*, p. 697.
20. "Anything I write is always about sadness and failure" (Story 137).

CHAPTER 7

1. Goldenweiser, "Loose Ends of a Theory on the Individual, Pattern, and Involution in Primitive Society."
2. Doi, *The Anatomy of Dependence*.
3. Kagitcibasi, *Family and Human Development across Cultures*, p. 55. In one passage, however, she contrasts the West's "self-contained" self with the "relational" self of many non-Western cultures (p. 55).
4. Joseph, "My Son/Myself, My Mother/Myself," p. 189
5. Oyserman, Kemmelmeier, and Coon, "Cultural Psychology, A New Look."
6. See Triandis, "Individualism and Collectivism," and Edgerton, *The Individual in Cultural Adaptation*.
7. Markus and Kitayama, "Culture and Self." See chapter 1 for a discussion of these models.
8. Oyserman, Kemmelmeier, and Coon, "Cultural Psychology, A New Look."
9. See Trafimow, Triandis, and Goto, "Some Tests of the Distinction between the Private Self and the Collective Self" and Ybarra and Trafimow, "How Priming the Private Self or Collective Self Affects the Relative Weights of Attitudes and Subjective Norms."
10. Ewing, "The Illusion of Wholeness."
11. A developmental perspective does not require speculating about individuals' pasts, only investigating their current developmental "tasks."
12. See my *Self Representation*.
13. Reynolds, *Interpreting the Self*.
14. Many scholars regard St. Augustine's *Confessions* as the originating work of Western autobiographical consciousness, apparently ignoring that he was a North African Berber.
15. Wu, *The Confucian's Progress: Autobiographical Writings in Traditional China*; Rousseau, Hakuseki, and Hakuin, "Paradigms of Self in Three Autobiographies"; and Gyatso, "Autobiography in Tibetan Religious Literature," cited in Reynolds, *Interpreting the Self*, p. 32.
16. Sapir, "Culture, Genuine and Spurious."
17. See Barakat, "Socio-Economic, Cultural and Personality Forces Determining Development in Arab Society," "Beyond the Always and the Never: Critique of Social Psychological Interpretations of Arab Society and Culture," and *The Arab World*.
18. Geertz, "From the Natives' Point of View," p. 133.
19. See Abu-Lughod, *Veiled Sentiments*; Boddy, *Wombs and Alien Spirits*; Wikan, *Behind the Veil in Arabia* and *Tomorrow, God Willing*; Gilsenan, *Recognizing*

Islam and *Lords of the Lebanese Marches*; Bourdieu, "The Sentiment of Honour in Kabyle Society"; Crapanzano, *Hamadsha* and *Tuhami*; and Jamous, *Honneur et Baraka.*

20. See especially Dwyer, *Moroccan Dialogues* and Munson, *The House of Si Abdullah.*

21. See Amrouche, *My Life Story*; Ghallab, *Le Passe Enterre*; and Oussaid, *Mountains Forgotten by God.*

22. See especially Ben Jalloun, *The Sacred Night*; Chraibi, *The Simple Past*; and Khatibi, *Love in Two Languages.*

23. Ewing, "The Illusion of Wholeness."

24. See especially Khuri, *Tents and Pyramids,* and Chaqueri, *Beginning Politics in the Reproductive Cycle of Children's Tales and Games in Iran.*

25. See Kristeva, *The Powers of Horror.*

26. LeVine, *Culture, Behavior, and Personality.*

27. Gregg, *Self-Representation.*

28. Erikson, *Toys and Reasons.* Erikson repeatedly pondered the problem of how more "wholistic," tolerant, and egalitarian identities might be built on foundations of group alignments that cannot but foster ethnocentrism.

29. For more than fifty years, researchers have used factor analytic techniques to identify the dimensions underlying people's use of trait adjectives to describe themselves and others, and recently they have reached a broad consensus that human personality is composed of five basic traits: I surgency (or extroversion), II agreeableness, III conscientiousness, IV emotional stability (or neuroticism), and V culture (or intellect or openness to experience). See Wiggins, ed., *The Five-Factor Model of Personality* and Wiggins and Trapnell, "Personality Structure: The Return of the Big Five." Increasing evidence indicates that these may be at least partly heritable, and researchers have sought to name them with nonculturally specific terms. A growing body of studies from non-Western societies—including Turkey—supports the universality of this so-called Big Five structure of traits. See Somer and Goldberg, "The Structure of Turkish Trait-Descriptive Adjectives."

30. A few psychologists have distinguished *traits* (like the Big Five) from *motives* (like needs for power, affiliation, and achievement) as different kinds of psychological structures, exerting different effects on behavior and life trajectories. Winter and his colleagues recently published findings from longitudinal studies of personality that underscore the importance of distinguishing motives from traits. They argue that traits should be seen as behavioral styles through which higher-order motives are expressed. See Winter et al., "Traits and Motives: Toward an Integration of Two Traditions in Personality Research," especially p. 238.

31. McAdams, "What Do We Know When We Know a Person?"

32. McDougall, *An Outline of Psychology,* p. 418. Other psychologists have used this term to describe larger or more "molar" constellations of emotion and value, including Pradines, "Feelings as Regulators"; Peters, "The Education of the Emotions"; and Murray and Morgan, "A Clinical Study of Sentiments."

33. See Althusser, *Essays on Ideology,* and Aboulafia, *The Mediating Self.*

34. Minoura, "A Sensitive Period for the Incorporation of a Cultural Meaning System."

35. Matsumoto, *Unmasking Japan,* p. 48.

36. See Rogoff, *Apprenticeship in Thinking.*

37. See Whiting, *Culture and Human Development.*

38. See Vygotsky, *Mind in Society.*

39. See Benedict, *Patterns of Culture,* and Mead, *Sex and Temperament in Three Primitive Societies.*

40. Lévi-Strauss, *The Savage Mind, Structural Anthropology,* and *The Raw and the Cooked.*

41. Geertz, *The Interpretation of Cultures.*

42. Turner, *The Forest of Symbols.*

43. See Lord, *The Singer of Tales;* Alter, *The Art of Biblical Narrative, The Art of Biblical Poetry,* and *The World of Biblical Literature;* Raglan, "The Hero"; Connelly, *Arab Folk Epic and Identity;* and Renard, *Islam and the Heroic Image.*

44. See Ricoeur, *The Rule of Metaphor* and *Time and Narrative.*

45. Tomkins, *Exploring Affect.*

46. Ortner, "On Key Symbols."

47. Stoller, *Observing the Erotic Imagination,* pp. 165–166.

48. Hermans and Kempen, *The Dialogical Self.*

49. Herdt, "Sambia Nosebleeding Rites and Male Proximity to Women."

50. James, *Principles of Psychology,* pp. 319–320.

51. Ibid.

52. Jackendoff, *Consciousness and Computational Mind.*

53. Dennett, *Consciousness Explained.*

54. Moughrabi, "The Arab Basic Personality: A Critical Survey of the Literature."

55. Barakat, "Beyond the Always and the Never: Critique of Social Psychological Interpretations of Arab Society and Culture."

56. See as Yassin, *Al-Shakhsiyya al-'arabiyya* (The Arab Personality); Sharabi, *Neopatriarchy;* Zayour, *al-Tahlil al-Nafsi lil-Zat al-'Arabiyyah* (Psychoanalysis of the Arab Ego); Auda, *Takiyif u Moqauma* (Adaptation and Resistance); and Hijazi, *al-Takhaluf al-ijtima'i* (Underdeveloped Society).

57. Barakat, "Beyond the Always and the Never: Critique of Social Psychological Interpretations of Arab Society and Culture," p. 147.

58. LeVine et al., *Child Care and Culture.*

59. See Whiting, *Culture and Human Development.*

60. Doi, *The Anatomy of Dependence.*

61. Bouhdiba, *Sexuality in Islam.*

62. Mernissi, *Beyond the Veil.*

63. Msefer, *Sevrages et Interdependence.*

64. Ibid.; Chamcham, "L'enfant marocain"; and Dachmi, *De La Seduction Maternelle Negative.*

65. Chaouite, "L'enfant marocain: Horizon d'une pensee psychologique."

66. Whiting, *Culture and Human Development.*

67. Chodorow, *The Reproduction of Mothering.*

68. Gilligan, *In a Different Voice.*

69. Herdt, "Sambia Nosebleeding Rites and Male Proximity to Women."

70. Gilmore, *Manhood in the Making.*

71. Herzfeld, *The Poetics of Manhood;* see also Meeker, *Literature and Violence in North Arabia.*

72. Whiting, *Culture and Human Development;* see also Herdt, *Guardians of the Flutes* and "Sambia Nosebleeding Rites and Male Proximity to Women."

73. Crapanzano, "Rite of Return: Circumcision in Morocco."

74. Fanon, *The Wretched of the Earth*, pp. 55–56.

75. Saadia worked sporadically for over a year and a half with my colleague and spouse as a research assistant. I conducted informal, nontaped life-history interviews with her, which I summarized in extensive notes.

76. Again, circumcision affects only men, as North African women are not circumcised.

77. See Foster, "Peasant Society and the Image of Limited Good" and "The Anatomy of Envy." See also Garrison and Arensberg, "The Evil Eye: Envy or Risk of Seizure? Paranoia or Patronal Dependency?"

78. Minor and DeVos, *Oasis and Casbah*.

79. Bouhdiba, *Sexuality in Islam*.

80. See chapter 6 of my *The Middle East: A Cultural Psychology* for a summary.

81. Prothro, *Child Rearing in Lebanon*, and Sears, Maccoby, and Levin, *Patterns of Child Rearing*.

82. See especially Sharabi and Ani, "The Impact of Class and Culture on Social Behavior: The Feudal-Bourgeois Family in Arab Society" and Sharabi, *Neopatriarchy*.

83. Eickelman, *Knowledge and Power in Morocco*, pp. 50–51.

84. Oussaid, *Mountains Forgotten by God*, pp. 48, 50.

85. Ibid., p. 47.

86. Ghallab, *Le Passe Enterre*, p. 73 (my translation).

87. Constance Stadler describes how the power of this work derives from the fact that it is both highly autobiographical and an allegorical critique of the relationship of subject to king (Stadler, *The Nation as Idea*).

88. Chraibi, *The Simple Past*, pp. 2, 3.

89. Mahfouz, *Palace Walk*, p. 19.

90. Ibid., p. 50.

91. Edgerton, *The Individual in Cultural Adaptation*.

92. See Foster, "Peasant Society and the Image of Limited Good" and Roberts, "Belief in the Evil Eye in World Perspective."

93. See Gregg, "Underdevelopment in a North African Tribe: Toward a Psychology of Peripheral Social Orders."

94. Wolf, "The Social Organization of Mecca and the Origins of Islam."

95. Jamous, *Honneur et Baraka*.

96. See chapters 5 and 6 of my *The Middle East: A Cultural Psychology*.

97. I conducted about three hours of life-history interviews during the course of many informal conversations with this merchant in his shop near our apartment in Ouarzazate, which I summarized in notes. He had run away from home at the age of twelve after being beaten bloody by his father, sought refuge in Nasseriyine *zawiya* (brotherhood) in Zagora, and remained there working for his keep and studying the Quran and *fqih* sciences until he came of age.

98. Stadtler, *The Nation as Idea*.

99. For a fuller discussion, see Gregg, "Themes of Authority in Life-Histories of Young Moroccans."

100. Hammoudi, *Master and Disciple*.

101. *Symbols* to refer to representations of all sorts, including motifs, images, metaphors, type scenes, and epic schemas.

102. Ethnicity plays an often salient role in Moroccan culture, but only became prominent in Rachida's narrative. Ethnic contrasts were not especially politicized in the 1980s when I conducted the interviews.

103. Shalinsky, "Reason, Desire, and Sexuality."

104. Ibid., p. 326.

105. Ibid., p. 330.

106. Ibid., p. 332.

107. Dwyer, *Images and Self-Images: Male and Female in Morocco*, p. 152.

108. Ibid., p. 60.

109. Ibid., p. 4.

110. Ibid., pp. 151—152.

111. See especially Boddy, *Wombs and Alien Spirits*; Delaney, *The Seed and the Soil*; Bourdieu, "The Kabyle House or the World Reversed"; and Abu-Lughod, *Veiled Sentiments*.

112. See chapter 8 of my *The Middle East: A Cultural Psychology* for a fuller account of studies of women's identities in both traditional and modernizing milieus.

113. See Ammar, *Growing Up in an Egyptian Village*, and Gilsenan, *Lords of the Lebanese Marches*.

114. See, for example, Geneive Abdo's account of the Muslim Brotherhood's activities in Egypt in the 1970s and 1980s (Abdo, *No God but God*).

115. Krichen, "Les problemes de la langue et l'intelligensia."

116. Bennani-Chraibi, *Soumis et Rebelles Les Jeunes au Maroc*, pp. 11, 12, my translation.

117. Ibid., p. 76, my translation.

118. Ibid., pp. 116–117, my translation.

119. Ibid., p. 125, my translation.

120. Ibid., p. 123, my translation.

121. El Messiri, *Ibn al-Balad*.

122. Dwyer, *Images and Self-Images*.

123. Schneider, "Of Vigilance and Virgins."

124. Berman, *All That's Solid Melts into Air*.

125. Ghareeb, "Ai namoudaj al-twafiq al-da al-shebab mathrebi" (What Model for Moroccan Youth?).

126. Ibid., p. 127.

127. See Triandis, "The Self and Social Behavior in Differing Cultural Contexts"; Trafimow, Triandis, and Goto, "Some Tests of the Distinction between the Private Self and the Collective Self"; and Tsai, Ying, and Lee, "The Meaning of 'Being Chinese' and 'Being American.'"

128. See Phinney, "Ethnic Identity in Adolescents and Adults: Review of Research"; Oyserman, Gant, and Ager, "A Socially Contextualized Model of African American Identity"; La Fromboise, Coleman, and Gerton, "Psychological Impact of Biculturalism: Evidence and Theory"; and Verkuyten and Pouliasi, "Biculturalism among Older Children."

129. See La Fromboise et al., "Psychological Impact of Biculturalism"; Tasi et al., "The Meaning of 'Being Chinese' and 'Being American'"; Oyserman, "The Lens of Personhood: Viewing the Self and Others in a Multicultural Society"; Oyserman, Sakamoto, and Lauffer, "Cultural Accommodation: Hybridity and the Framing of Social Obligation"; Hermans and Kempen, "Moving Cultures: The

Perilous Problems of Cultural Dichotomies in a Globalizing Society"; Hong et al., "Boundaries of Cultural Influence. Construct Activation as a Mechanism for Cultural Differences in Social Perception"; and Verkuyten and Pouliasi, "Biculturalism among Older Children: Cultural Frame Switching, Attributions, Self-Identification, and Attitudes."

130. Three others whose narratives I taped cannot be said to adopt either.

131. Bellah, *Tokugawa Religion: The Values of Pre-Industrial Japan.*

132. Waterbury, *North for the Trade: The Life and Times of a Berber Merchant.*

133. Gellner, "The Unknown Apollo of Biskra: The Social Base of Algerian Puritanism."

134. Goldberg, "Smashing Idols and the State: Protestant Ethic and Egyptian Sunni Radicalism."

135. Triandis, "The Self and Social Behavior in Differing Cultural Contexts" and Trafimow, Triandis, and Goto, "Some Tests of the Distinction between the Private Self and the Collective Self."

136. La Fromboise, Coleman, and Gerton, "Psychological Impact of Biculturalism"; Verkuyten and Poulissi, "Biculturalism among Older Children"; and Oyserman, Gant, and Ager, "A Socially Contextualized Model of African American Identity."

137. See especially Lehrdahl and Jackendoff, *A Generative Theory of Tonal Music*; Jackendoff, *Consciousness and the Computational Mind*; and Jackendoff, *Languages of the Mind.*

138. Wallace, *Culture and Personality.*

139. Schwartz, "Distributive Models of Culture in Relation to Societal Scale" and "Where Is Culture? Personality as the Distributive Locus of Culture."

140. Spiro, "Is the Western Conception of the Self 'Peculiar' within the Context of World Cultures?"

141. Jameson, *The Prison-House of Language.*

142. Cultures may even develop institutions like the modern fashion industry, whose business is to selectively harvest expressions of deviance created by the alienated and impoverished and transform to them into haute couture.

143. Cansever, "Psychological Effects of Circumcision" and Ozturk, "Ritual Circumcision and Castration Anxiety."

REFERENCES

Note: Transliterations of Arabic names and words are those used in my *The Middle East: A Cultural Psychology* and follow the indexing systems of several libraries. They are not always consistent, and often an apostrophe (') is used for the ع rather than a superscript *c* (ᶜ), as in this book.

Abdo, Genieve (2000). *No God but God.* New York: Oxford University Press.

Aboulafia, Mitchell (1986). *The Mediating Self.* New Haven, CT: Yale University Press.

Abou Zeid, Ahmed (1966). "Honour and Shame among the Bedouins of Egypt." In J. G. Peristiany, ed., *Honour and Shame.* Chicago: University of Chicago Press, pp. 243–260.

Abu-Lughod, Lila (1986). *Veiled Sentiments.* Berkeley: University of California Press.

Accad, Evelyne (1990). *Sexuality and War.* New York: New York University Press.

Adorno, T. W. et al. (1950). *The Authoritarian Personality.* New York: Norton.

Akhmisse, Mustapha (n.d.). *Medicine Sans Medecins.* Casablanca: Benchara.

Ali, Abdullah Youssef, trans. (1997). *The Holy Quran.* Beltsville, MD: Amana Publications, 1997.

Alter, Robert (1981). *The Art of Biblical Narrative.* New York: Basic.

Alter, Robert (1985). *The Art of Biblical Poetry.* New York: Basic.

Alter, Robert (1992). *The World of Biblical Literature.* New York: Basic.

Althusser, Louis (1984). *Essays on Ideology.* London: Verso.

Ammar, Hamid (1954). *Growing Up in an Egyptian Village.* London: Routledge & Kegan Paul.

Amrouche, Fatima (1988). *My Life Story.* New Brunswick, NJ: Rutgers University Press.

Anderson, Jon (1985). "Sentimental Ambivalence and the Exegesis of 'Self' in Afghanistan." *Anthropological Quarterly.* 58(4):203–211.

Antoun, Richard (1989). *Muslim Preacher in the Modern World.* Princeton, NJ: Princeton University Press.

'Audah, Mahmud (1995). *al-takayyuf wa al-muqawamah* (Adaptation and Resistance). Cairo: al-majlis al-a'la lil-thaqafah.

Barakat, Halim (1976). "Socio-Economic, Cultural and Personality Forces Determining Development in Arab Society." *Social Praxis.* 2(3–4):179–204.

Barakat, Halim (1990). "Beyond the Always and the Never: Critique of Social Psychological Interpretations of Arab Society and Culture." In H. Sharabi, ed., *Theory, Politics and the Arab World*. New York: Routledge, pp. 132–159.

Barakat, Halim (1993). *The Arab World*. Berkeley: University of California Press.

Behar, Ruth (1993). *Translated Woman*. Boston: Beacon Press.

Bellah, Robert (1957). *Tokugawa Religion: The Values of Pre-Industrial Japan*. Boston: Beacon Press.

Bellakhdar, Jamal, Honda, Gisho, and Miki, Wataru (1982). *Herb Drugs and Herbalists in the Maghreb*. Tokyo: Institute for the Study of Languages and Cultures of Asia and Africa.

Benedict, Ruth (1934). *Patterns of Culture*. Boston: Houghton Mifflin.

Benet-Martinez, V., Leu, J., Lee, F., and Morris, M. (2002). "Negotiating Biculturalism: Cultural Frame Switching in Biculturals with Oppositional versus Compatible Cultural Identities." *Journal of Cross-Cultural Psychology*. 33(5):492–516.

Ben Jelloun, Tahar (1987). *The Sacred Night*. San Diego: Harcourt, Brace.

Bennani-Chraibi, Mounia (1994). *Soumis et Rebelles Les Jeunes au Maroc*. Paris: Editions le Fennec.

Berman, Marshall (1982). *All That's Solid Melts into Air*. New York: Praeger.

Boddy, Janice (1989). *Wombs and Alien Spirits*. Madison: University of Wisconsin Press.

Bond, Michael (2002). "Reclaiming the Individual from Hofstede's Ecological Analysis—A 20-Year Odyssey." *Psychological Bulletin*. 128(1):73–77.

Bonner, J. (1974). *On Development*. Cambridge: Harvard University Press.

Bouhdiba, A. (1985). *Sexuality in Islam*. London: Routledge & Kegan Paul.

Bourdieu, Pierre (1966). "The Sentiment of Honour in Kabyle Society." In J. Peristiany, ed., *Honor and Shame: The Values of Mediterranean Society*. Chicago: University of Chicago Press, pp. 171–190.

Bourdieu, Pierre (1970). "The Kabyle House or the World Reversed." In *Algeria 1960*. Cambridge: Cambridge University Press, pp. 133–153.

Bourdieu, Pierre (1985). *Outline of a Theory of Practice*. Cambridge: Cambridge University Press.

Bruner, Jerome (1990). *Acts of Meaning*. Cambridge, MA: Harvard University Press.

Burgat, Francois, and Dowell, William (1993) *The Islamic Movement in North Africa*. Austin: University of Texas Center for Middle Eastern Studies

Campbell, Joseph (1949). *The Hero with a Thousand Faces*. Princeton, NJ: Princeton University Press.

Cansever, Gocke (1965). "Psychological Effects of Circumcision." *British Journal of Psychology*. 38:321–331.

Carnes, Mark (1989). *Secret Ritual and Manhood in Victorian America*. New Haven, CT: Yale University Press.

Carr, David (1991). *Time, Narrative, and History*. Bloomington: Indiana University Press.

Caton, Steven (1985). "The Poetic Construction of Self." *Anthropological Quarterly*. 58(4):141–150.

Chraibi, Driss (1990). *The Simple Past*. Washington, DC: Three Continents Press.

Chamcham, Rouchdi (1987). "L'enfant marocain: Entre la dependance d'hier, la detresse d'aujourd'hui et l'autonomie de demain." In Dernouny, M., ed., *Enfance Maghrebines*. Casablanca: Afrique Orient, pp. 67–79.

Chaouite, Abdellatif (1987). "L'enfant marocain: Horizon d'une pensee psychologique." In M. Dernouny and A. Chaouite, eds., *Enfance Maghrebines*. Casablanca: Afrique Orient, pp. 41–66.

Chaqueri, C. (1992). *Beginning Politics in the Reproductive Cycle of Children's Tales and Games in Iran*. Lewiston, NY: Edwin Mellen Press.

Chodorow, Nancy (1978). *The Reproduction of Mothering*. Berkeley: University of California Press.

Coles, Robert (1964). *Children of Crisis*. Boston: Little, Brown.

Coles, Robert (1967) *Migrants, Sharecroppers, Mountaineers*. Boston: Little, Brown.

Combs-Schilling, M. E. (1989). *Sacred Performances: Islam, Sexuality, and Sacrifice*. New York: Columbia University Press.

Connelly, Bridget (1986). *Arab Folk Epic and Identity*. Berkeley: University of California Press.

Cowan, J. M., ed. (1976). *Hans Wehr Dictionary of Modern Written Arabic*, 3rd ed. Ithaca, NY: Spoken Languages Services.

Crapanzano, Vincent (1973). *Hamadsha*. Berkeley: University of California Press.

Crapanzano, Vincent (1980). *Tuhami*. Chicago: University of Chicago Press.

Crapanzano, Vincent (1981). "Rite of Return: Circumcision in Morocco." In W. Muensterberger and L. Boyer, eds., *The Psychoanalytic Study of Society*. New York: International Universities Press, vol. 9, pp. 15–36.

Crapanzano, Vincent (1992). *Hermes' Dilemma and Hamlet's Desire*. Cambridge, MA: Harvard University Press.

Cross, Susan, and Markus, Hazel (1991). "Possible Selves across the Life Span." *Human Development*. 34:230–255.

Crossley, Nick (1996). *Intersubjectivity*. Thousand Oaks, CA: Sage.

Dachmi, Abdeslam (1995). *De La Seduction Maternelle Negative*. Rabat: Faculte des Lettres et des Sciences Humaines.

Davis, Susan, and Davis, Douglas (1989). *Adolescence in a Moroccan Town*. New Brunswick, NJ: Rutgers University Press.

Dawkins, Richard (1982). *The Extended Phenotype*. Cambridge: Cambridge University Press.

Dawood, N., translator (2003). *The Koran*. 5th ed. New York: Penguin.

Delaney, Carol (1991). *The Seed and the Soil: Gender and Cosmology in Turkish Village Society*. Berkeley: University of California Press.

Dennett, Daniel (1991). *Consciousness Explained*. Boston: Little, Brown.

Deutsch, Felix, and Murphy, William (1955). *The Clinical Interview* (2 vols.). New York: International Universities Press.

Devereux, George (1951). *Reality and Dream*. New York: International Universities Press.

Doi, Takeo (1973). *The Anatomy of Dependence* (J. Bester, Trans.). New York: Harper & Row. (Original work published 1971)

Dundes, Alan (1980). "The Hero Pattern and the Life of Jesus." In R. Segal et al., *In Quest of the Hero*. Princeton, NJ: Princeton University Press, pp. 177–223.

Dwyer, Daisy (1978). *Images and Self-Images: Male and Female in Morocco*. New York: Columbia University Press.

Dwyer, Kevin (1982). *Moroccan Dialogues*. Baltimore: Johns Hopkins University Press.

Edgerton, R. (1971). *The Individual in Cultural Adaptation*. Berkeley: University of California Press.

Eickelman, Dale (1981). *The Middle East: An Anthropological Approach.* Englewood Cliffs, NJ: Prentice-Hall. (1st edition)

Eickelman, Dale (1981). *Moroccan Islam.* Austin: University of Texas Press.

Eickelman, Dale (1985). *Knowledge and Power in Morocco.* Princeton, NJ: Princeton University Press.

Eickelman, Dale (1991). "Traditional Islamic Learning and Ideas of the Person in the Twentieth Century." In M. Kramer, ed., *Middle Eastern Lives.* Syracuse, NY: Syracuse University Press.

Ekman, Paul (1972). "Universals and Cultural Differences in Facial Expression of Emotion." In J. R. Cole, ed., *Nebraska Symposium on Motivation.* Lincoln: University of Nebraska Press, pp. 169–249.

Ekman, Paul (1980). "Biological and Cultural Contributions to Body and Facial Movement in the Expression of Emotions." In A. Rorty, ed., *Explaining Emotions.* Berkeley: University of California Press.

El Messiri, Sawsan (1978). *Ibn al-Balad: A Concept of Egyptian Identity.* London: E. J. Brill.

Erikson, Erik (1950). *Childhood and Society.* New York: W. W. Norton.

Erikson, Erik (1958). *Young Man Luther.* New York: W. W. Norton.

Erikson, Erik (1968). *Identity: Youth and Crisis.* New York: W. W. Norton.

Erikson, Erik (1977). *Toys and Reasons.* New York: W.W. Norton.

Evans-Pritchard, E. E. (1940). *The Nuer.* New York: Oxford University Press.

Ewing, Katherine (1990). "The Illusion of Wholeness: Culture, Self, and the Experience of Inconsistency." *Ethos.* 18(3):251–278.

Ewing, Katherine (1991). "Can Psychoanalytic Theories Explain the Pakistani Woman?" *Ethos.* 19(2):131–160.

Ewing, Katherine (1991). "The Dream of Spiritual Initiation and the Organization of Self Representation among Pakistani Sufis." *American Ethnologist.* 17(1):56–74.

Ewing, Katherine (1997). *Arguing Sainthood.* Durham , NC: Duke University Press.

Fanon, Frantz (1963). *The Wretched of the Earth.* New York: Grove.

Fenichel, Otto (1945). *The Psychoanalytic Theory of Neurosis.* New York: Norton.

Fiske, Alan (2002). "Using Individualism and Collectivism to Compare Cultures: A Critique of the Validity and Measurement of the Constructs." *Psychological Bulletin.* 128(1)78–88.

Foster, George (1965). "Peasant Society and the Image of Limited Good." *American Anthropologist.* 67:293–315.

Foster, George (1972). "The Anatomy of Envy." *Current Anthropology* 13(2): 165–202.

Foucault, Michel (1971). *The Order of Things.* New York: Pantheon.

Foucault, Michel (1978). *The History of Sexuality.* New York: Pantheon.

Freud, Sigmund (1925). "Negation." In S. Freud, *Collected Papers*, vol. 5. London: Hogarth, pp. 181–185.

Freud, Sigmund (1964). *The Future of an Illusion.* Garden City, NY: Doubleday.

Fromm, Erich, and Maccoby, Michael (1970). *Social Character in a Mexican Village.* Englewood Cliffs, NJ: Prentice-Hall.

Garrison, Vivian, and Arensberg, Conrad (1976). "The Evil Eye: Envy or Risk of Seizure? Paranoia or Patronal Dependency?" In Clarence Maloney, ed., *The Evil Eye.* New York: Columbia University Press, pp. 287–328.

Gee, James (1991). "A Linguistic Approach to Narrative." *Journal of Narrative and Life History.* 1(1):15–40.

Gee, James (1990). *Social Linguistics and Literacies: Ideology in Discourses.* London: Falmer Press.

Geertz, Clifford (1968). *Islam Observed.* Chicago: University of Chicago Press

Geertz, C., Rosen, L., and Geertz, H. (1979). *Meaning and Order in Moroccan Society.* New York: Cambridge University Press.

Geertz, Clifford (1973). *The Interpretation of Cultures.* New York: Basic Books.

Geertz, Clifford (1979). "Suq: The Bazaar Economy in Sefrou." In C. Geertz, H. Geertz, and L. Rosen, eds., *Meaning and Order in Moroccan Society.* Cambridge: Cambridge University Press, pp. 123–244.

Geertz, Clifford (1984). "From the Natives' Point of View: On the Nature of Anthropological Understanding." In R. Shweder & R. LeVine, eds., *Culture Theory.* Cambridge, MA: Harvard University Press, pp. 123–136.

Geertz, Hildred (1979). "The Meanings of Family Ties." In C. Geertz, H. Geertz, and L. Rosen, eds., *Meaning and Order in Moroccan Society.* Cambridge: Cambridge University Press, pp. 315–392.

Gellner, Ernest. (1969). *Saints of the Atlas.* Chicago: University of Chicago Press.

Gellner, Ernest (1981). "The Unknown Apollo of Biskra: The Social Base of Algerian Puritanism." In *Muslim Society.* Cambridge: Cambridge University Press, pp. 149–173.

Ghallab, Abdelkrim (1987). *Le Passe Enterre.* Mohammedia: Fedala.

Ghareeb, Abdelkrim (1996). "Ai namoudaj al-twafiq al-da al-shebab mathrebi?" (What Model for Moroccan Youth?) In *a'lim al-nafs wa al-qadia al-mujtema' ma'ser* (Psychology and Issues of Modern Society). Rabat: Mohammed V University Press, pp. 117–134.

Gilligan, Carol (1982). *In a Different Voice.* Cambridge: Harvard University Press.

Gilmore, David (1990). *Manhood in the Making.* New Haven, CT: Yale University Press.

Gilsenan, Michael (1990). *Recognizing Islam.* London: I. B. Tauris.

Gilsenan, Michael (1996). *Lords of the Lebanese Marches.* Berkeley: University of California Press.

Gjerde, Per (2004). "Culture, Power, and Experience: Toward a Person-Centered Cultural Psychology." *Human Development.* 47:138–157.

Goffman, Erving (1959). *The Presentation of Self in Everyday Life.* Garden City, NY: Doubleday.

Goldberg, Ellis (1992). "Smashing Idols and the State: Protestant Ethic and Egyptian Sunni Radicalism." In J. Cole, ed., *Comparing Muslim Societies.* Ann Arbor: University of Michigan Press, pp. 195–236.

Goldenweiser, Alexander (1936). "Loose Ends of a Theory on the Individual, Pattern, and Involution in Primitive Society." In R. Lowie, ed., *Essays in Anthropology.* Freeport, NY: Books for Libraries Press, pp. 99–104.

Gole, Nilufer (1996). *The Forbidden Modern: Civilization and Veiling.* Ann Arbor: University of Michigan Press.

Greenwood, Bernard (1981). "Cold or Spirits? Choice and Ambiguity in Morocco's Pluralistic Medical System." *Social Science and Medicine.* 158:219–235.

Gregg, Gary (1990). "Underdevelopment in a North African Tribe: Toward a Psychology of Peripheral Social Orders." *Journal of Social Issues* 46(3):71–91.

Gregg, Gary (1998). "Culture, Personality, and the Multiplicity of Identity." *Ethos*. 26(2):120–152.

Gregg, Gary (1998). "Themes of Authority in Life-Histories of Young Moroccans." In S. Miller and R. Bourgia, eds., *Representations of Power in Morocco*. Cambridge, MA: Harvard University Press, pp. 215–242.

Gregg, Gary, and Geist, Alison (1988). "Socio-Economic Organization of the Ait Imeghrane." Final Report to Moroccan Ministry of Agriculture. Ouarzazate: O.R.M.V.A.O.

Gregg, Gary (1991). *Self Representation*. New York: Greenwood Press.

Gregg, Gary (2005). *The Middle East: A Cultural Psychology*. New York: Oxford University Press.

Hamady, Sania (1960). *Temperament and Character of the Arabs*. New York: Twayne.

Hammoudi, Abdellah (1997). *Master and Disciple: The Cultural Foundations of Moroccan Authoritarianism*. Chicago: University of Chicago Press.

Haritatos, J., and Benet-Martinez, V. (2002). "Bicultual Identities: The Interface of Cultural, Personality, and Socio-Cognitive Processes." *Journal of Research in Personality*. 36(6):598–606.

Hart, David (1976). *The Aith Waryaghar of the Moroccan Rif*. Tucson: University of Arizona Press.

Hart, David (1981). *Dada 'Atta and His Forty Grandsons*. Cambridge: Middle East and North African Studies Press.

Hart, David (1984). *The Ait 'Atta of Southern Morocco*. Cambridge: Middle East and North African Studies Press.

Herdt, Gilbert (1981). *Guardians of the Flutes*. Chicago: University of Chicago Press.

Herdt, Gilbert (1990). "Sambia Nosebleeding Rites and Male Proximity to Women." In J. Stigler, R. Shweder, and G. Herdt, eds., *Cultural Psychology*. Cambridge: Cambridge University Press, pp. 366–400.

Herman, Judith (1992). *Trauma and Recovery*. New York: Basic.

Hermans, Hubert, and Kempen, Harry (1991). *The Dialogical Self*. San Diego: Academic Press.

Hermans, Hubert, and Kempen, Harry (1998). "Moving Cultures: The Perilous Problems of Cultural Dichotomies in a Globalizing Society." *American Psychologist*. 53(10):1111–1120.

Herzfeld, Michael (1980). "Honour and Shame: Problems in the Comparative Analysis of Moral Systems." *Man*. 15:339–351.

Herzfeld, Michael (1985). *The Poetics of Manhood*. Princeton, NJ: Princeton University Press.

Hijazi, Mustafa (1970). *al-takhaluf al-ijtima'i*. (Underdeveloped Society) Beirut: ma'had al'inma' al-arabi.

Hofstede, Geert (1980). *Culture's Consequences*. Beverly Hills, CA: Sage.

Holland, D., and Kipnis, A. (1994). "Metaphors for Embarrassment and Stories of Exposure: The Not-So-Egocentric Self in American Culture." *Ethos*. 22(3):316–342.

Hong, Y., Benet-Martinez, V., Chiu, C., and Morris, M. (2003). "Boundaries of Cultural Influence. Construct Activation as a Mechanism for Cultural Differences in Social Perception." *Journal of Cross-Cultural Psychology*. 34(4):453–464.

Hong, Y., Morris, M., Chiu, C., and Benet-Martinez, V. (2000). "Multicultural Minds: A Dynamic Constructivist Approach to Culture and Cognition." *American Psychologist*. 55(7):709–720.

Horowitz, Mardi (1979). *States of Mind*. New York: Plenum.

Ibn Khaldun (1967). *The Moqqademah*. Princeton, NJ: Princeton University Press.

Imamoglu, E. (1998). "Individualism and Collectivism in a Model and Scale of Balanced Differentiation and Integration." *Journal of Psychology* 132(1):95–105.

Inkeles, Alex, and Smith, David (1974) *Becoming Modern*. Cambridge, MA: Harvard University Press.

Izard, Carl (1992). "Basic Emotions, Relations among Emotions, and Emotion-Cognition Relations." *Psychological Review*. 99:561–565.

Jackendoff, Ray (1987). *Consciousness and Computational Mind*. Cambridge: MIT Press.

Jackendoff, Ray (1992). *Languages of the Mind*. Cambridge, MA: MIT Press.

Jacques-Meunie, D. (1958). "Hierarchie Sociale au maroc Presaharien." *Hesperis*. 45:239–269.

James, William (1981). *Principles of Psychology*. Cambridge, MA: Harvard University Press.

Jameson, Frederick (1972). *The Prison-House of Language*. Princeton, NJ: Princeton University Press.

Jamous, Raymond (1981). *Honneur et Baraka*. Cambridge: Cambridge University Press.

Joseph, Suad (1999). "My Son/Myself, My Mother/Myself." In S. Joseph, ed., *Intimate Selving in Arab Families*. Syracuse, NY: Syracuse University Press, pp. 174–190.

Joseph, Suad, ed. (1999). *Intimate Selving in Arab Families*. Syracuse, NY: Syracuse University Press.

Jung, Carl (1968). *Man and His Symbols*. New York: Dell.

Kagitcibasi, Cigdem (1987). "Individual and Group Loyalties: Are They Compatible?" In C. Kagitcibasi, ed., *Growth and Progress in Cross-Cultural Psychology*. Berwyn, PA: Swets North America, pp. 94–103.

Kagitcibasi, Cigdam (1996). *Family and Human Development across Cultures*. Mahwah, NJ: Erlbaum.

Kahane, Claire (1985). "Introduction." In C. Bernheimer and C. Kahane, eds., *In Dora's Case*. New York: Columbia University Press.

Kelly, George (1955). *The Psychology of Personal Constructs*. New York: Norton.

Khatibi, Abdelkebir (1990). *Love in Two Languages*. Minneapolis: University of Minnesota Press.

Khuri, Fuad (1990). *Tents and Pyramids: Games and Ideology in Arab Culture from Backgammon to Autocratic Rule*. London: Saqi.

Kim, U., Triandis, H., Kagitcibasi, C., Choi, S., and Yoon, G., eds. (1994) *Individualism and Collectivism: Theory, Method, and Applications*. Thousand Oaks, CA: Sage.

Kitayama, Shinobu (2002). "Culture and Basic Psychological Processes: Toward a System View of Culture." *Psychological Bulletin*. 128(1)89–96.

Krichen, Aziz (1987). "Les problemes de la langue et l'intelligensia." In C. Michel, ed., *La Tunisie au Present*. Paris: CNRS Presses. Quoted in Burgat, F., and Dowell, W. (1993) *The Islamic Movement in North Africa*. Austin: University of Texas Center for Middle Eastern Studies.

Kristeva, Julia (1982). *The Powers of Horror*. New York: Columbia University Press.

Kritzeck, James (1964). *Anthology of Islamic Literature*. New York: Holt, Rinehart and Winston, Trans. Ameen Rihani.

Krohn, Alan (1978). *Hysteria: The Elusive Neurosis.* New York: International Universities Press.

La Fromboise, T., Coleman, H., and Gerton, J. (1993). "Psychological Impact of Biculturalism: Evidence and Theory." *Psychological Bulletin.* 114(3):395–412.

Langer, Susanne (1957). *Philosophy in a New Key.* Cambridge, MA: Harvard University Press.

Lehrdahl, Fred, and, Jacekndoff, Ray (1983). *A Generative Theory of Tonal Music.* Cambridge, MA: MIT Press.

Lerner, Daniel (1958). *The Passing of Traditional Society.* Glencoe, IL: Free Press.

Leveau, Remy (1976). *La Fellah Marocain.* Paris: Presses de la Fondation Nationale des Sciences Politiques.

LeVine, Robert (1973). *Culture, Behavior, and Personality.* Chicago: Aldine.

LeVine, Robert, et al. (1994). *Child Care and Culture: Lessons from Africa.* New York: Cambridge University Press.

LeVine, Robert (1990). "Infant Environments in Psychoanalysis: A Cross-Cultural View." In J. Stigler, R. Shweder, & G. Herdt, ed., *Cultural Psychology.* Cambridge, MA: Cambridge University Press, pp. 454–474.

Levinson, Daniel (1978). *The Seasons of a Man's Life.* New York: Ballantine.

Lévi-Strauss, Claude (1962). *The Savage Mind.* Chicago: University of Chicago Press.

Lévi-Strauss, Claude (1963). *Structural Anthropology.* New York: Basic.

Lévi-Strauss, Claude (1975). *The Raw and the Cooked.* New York: Harper.

Levy, Robert (1973). *Tahitians.* Chicago: University of Chicago Press.

Lindholm, Charles (1996). *The Islamic Middle East.* Oxford: Blackwell.

Lord, Albert (1960). *The Singer of Tales.* Cambridge: Cambridge University Press.

Mackey, Sandra (1992). *Passion and Politics.* New York: Penguin.

Maher, Brendan (1969). ed., *Clinical Psychology and Personality: The Selected Papers of George Kelly.* New York: Wiley.

Maher, Vanessa (1974). *Women and Property in Morocco.* Cambridge: Cambridge University Press.

Mahfouz, Naguib (1990). *Palace Walk.* New York: Doubleday.

Mahfouz, Naguib (1991). *Palace of Desire.* New York: Doubleday.

Marcia, James (1994). "The Empirical Study of Ego Identity." In H. Bosma et al., eds., *Identity and Development.* Thousand Oaks, CA: Sage.

Markus, Hazel, and Kitayama, Shinobu (1991). "Culture and Self." *Psychological Review.* 98:224–253.

Matsumoto, David (1996). *Unmasking Japan.* Stanford, CA: Stanford University Press.

Matsumoto, David (1999). "Culture and Self: An Empirical Assessment of Markus and Kitayama's Theory of Independent and Interdependent Self-Construals." *Asian Journal of Social Psychology.* 2:289–310.

Matsumoto, David (2001). "Culture and Emotion." In D. Matsumoto, ed., *Handbook of Culture and Psychology.* New York: Oxford University Press.

Maxwell, Gavin (1966). *Lords of the Atlas.* London: Longmans.

McAdams, Dan (1988). *Power, Intimacy, and the Life Story.* New York: Guilford Press.

McAdams, Dan (1995). "What Do We Know When We Know a Person?" *Journal of Personality.* 63(3):365–396.

McAdams, Dan, and Ochberg, Richard, eds. (1988). *Psychobiography and Life Narratives.* Durham, NC: Duke University Press.

McDougall, William (1923). *An Outline of Psychology*. London: Metheun.

Mead, G. H. (1934). *Mind, Self, and Society*. Chicago: University of Chicago Press.

Mead, Margaret (1935). *Sex and Temperament in Three Primitive Societies*. New York: Dell.

Meeker, Michael (1979). *Literature and Violence in North Arabia*. Cambridge: Cambridge University Press.

Mernissi, Fatima (1975). *Beyond the Veil*. Cambridge, MA: Schenkman.

Mernissi, Fatima (1994). *Dreams of Trespass*. Reading, MA: Addison-Wesley.

Miller, Joan (2002). "Bringing Culture to Basic Psychological Theory: Beyond Individualism and Collectivism." *Psychological Bulletin*. 128(1):97–109.

Minor, Horace, and DeVos, George (1960). *Oasis and Casbah*. Ann Arbor: University of Michigan Press.

Minoura, Yasuko (1992). "A Sensitive Period for the Incorporation of a Cultural Meaning System." *Ethos*. 20(3):304–339.

Mischel, Walter (1968). *Personality and Assessment*. New York: Wiley.

Mitchell, Juliet (1974). *Psychoanalysis and Feminism*. New York: Vintage.

Moi, Toril (1985). "Representation of Patriarchy." In C. Bernheimer and C. Kahane, eds., *In Dora's Case*. New York: Columbia University Press.

Montagne, Robert (1930). *Les Berberes et le Makhzen dans le Sud au Maroc*. Paris: Felix Alcan.

Moraldo, John (1004). "Rousseau, Hakuseki, and Hakuin: "Paradigms of Self in Three Autobiographies." In R. Ames, ed., *Self as Person in Asian Theory and Practice*. New York: State University of New York Press, pp. 57–82.

Mottahedeh, Roy (1985). *The Mantle of the Prophet*. New York: Pantheon Books.

Moughrabi, Fuad (1978). "The Arab Basic Personality: A Critical Survey of the Literature." *International Journal of Middle East Studies*. 9:99–112.

Msefer, Assia (1985). *Sevrages et Interdependence* (Weaning and Interdependence). Casablanca: Editions Maghrebines.

Munson, Henry (1984). *The House of Si Abdullah*. New Haven, CT: Yale University Press.

Murray, D. W. (1993). "What Is the Western Concept of the Self? On Forgetting David Hume." *Ethos*. 21(1):3–23

Murray, Henry (1938). *Explorations in Personality*. New York: Oxford University Press.

Murray, Henry, and Morgan, Christiana (1945). "A Clinical Study of Sentiments." *Genetic Psychological Mongraphs*. 32:3–311.

Nandy, Ashis (1983). *The Intimate Enemy*. Delhi: Oxford University Press.

Nelson, Kristina (1985). *The Art of Reciting the Quran*. Austin: University of Texas Press.

Nisbett, Richard (2003). *The Geography of Thought*. New York: Free Press.

Obeysekere, Gananath (1990). *The Work of Culture*. Chicago: University of Chicago Press.

Olson, Emelie (1985). "Muslim Identity and Secularism in Contemporary Turkey: The Headscarf Dispute." *Anthropological Quarterly* 58(4):161–170. (Quote on p. 164 from B. Lewis [1968]. *The Emergence of Modern Turkey*. New York: Oxford University Press, p. 268.)

Ortner, Sherry (1973). "On Key Symbols." *American Anthropologist*. 75:1338–1346.

Ortner, Sherry (1974). "Is Female to Male as Nature Is to Culture?" In M. Rosaldo and L. Lamphere, eds., *Woman, Culture, and Society*. Stanford, CA: Stanford University Press.

Oussaid, Brick (1989). *Mountains Forgotten by God*. Washington, DC: Three Continents Press.

Oyserman, D., Coon, H., and Kemmelmeier, M. (2002). "Rethinking Individualism and Collectivism." *Psychological Bulletin*. 128(1)3–72.

Oyserman, D., Kemmelmeier, M., and Coon, H. (2002). "Cultural Psychology, a New Look." *Psychological Bulletin*. 128(1):110–117.

Oyserman, D., Sakamoto, I., and Lauffer, A. (1998). "Cultural Accommodation: Hybridity and the Framing of Social Obligation." *Journal of Personality and Social Psychology*. 74(6):1606–1618.

Oyserman, Daphna (1993). "The Lens of Personhood: Viewing the Self and Others in a Multicultural Society." *Journal of Personality and Social Psychology*. 65(5):993–1009.

Oyserman, D., Gant, L., and Ager, J. (1995). "A Socially Contextualized Model of African American Identity." *Journal of Personality and Social Psychology*. 69(6): 1216–1232.

Oyserman, Daphna, and Markus, Hazel (1990). "Possible Selves and Delinquency." *Journal of Personality and Social Psychology*. 59(1):112–125.

Ozturk, Orhan (1973). "Ritual Circumcision and Castration Anxiety." *Psychiatry*. 36:49–60.

Pamuk, Orhan (1994). *The Black Book*. San Diego: Harcourt, Brace.

Patai, Raphael (1973). *The Arab Mind*. New York: Scribner.

Patai, Raphael (2002). *The Arab Mind*. Long Island City, NY: Hatherleigh Press.

Peters, R. (1970). "The Education of the Emotions." In M. Arnold, ed., *Feelings and Emotions*. New York: Academic Press, pp. 187–204.

Philipchalk, Ronald (1995). *Invitation to Social Psychology*. Fort Worth, IN: Harcourt Brace College.

Phinney, Jean (1990). "Ethnic Identity in Adolescents and Adults: Review of Research." *Psychological Bulletin*. 108(3):499–514.

Pirandello, Luigi (1922). "Six Characters in Search of an Author." In E. Bentler, ed., *Naked Masks: Five Plays by Luigi Pirandello*. New York: Penguin, pp. 211–276.

Poulton, Hugh (1997). *Top Hat, Grey Wolf and Crescent: Turkish Nationalism and the Turkish Republic*. New York: New York University Press.

Pradines, M. (1958). "Feelings as Regulators." In M. Arnold., ed., *The Nature of Emotion*. Baltimore: Penguin, pp. 189–200.

Propp, V. (1968). *Morphology of the Folktale*. Austin: University of Texas Press.

Prothro, Edward (1961). *Child Rearing in Lebanon*. Cambridge, MA: Harvard University Press.

Pryce-Jones, David (1989). *The Closed Circle*. New York: Harper & Row.

Raggatt, Peter (2000). "Mapping the Dialogical Self: Towards a Rationale and Method of Assessment." *European Journal of Personality*. 14(1):65–90.

Raglan, Lord (1990). "The Hero: A Study in Tradition, Myth, and Drama (Part II)." In R. Segal et al., eds., *In Quest of the Hero*. Princeton, NJ: Princeton University Press, pp. 87–175.

Rank, Otto (1990). "The Myth of the Birth of the Hero." In R. Segal et al., *In Quest of the Hero*. Princeton, NJ: Princeton University Press, pp. 3–86.

Renard, John (1993). *Islam and the Heroic Image*. Columbia, SC: University of South Carolina Press.

Reynolds, Dwight (2001). *Interpreting the Self.* Berkeley: University of California Press.

Ricoeur, Paul (1970). *Freud and Philosophy.* New Haven, CT: Yale University Press.

Ricoeur, Paul (1976). *The Rule of Metaphor.* Toronto: University of Toronto Press.

Ricoeur, Paul (1984). *Time and Narrative.* Chicago: University of Chicago Press.

Roberts, John (1976). "Belief in the Evil Eye in World Perspective." In C. Maloney, ed., *The Evil Eye.* New York: Columbia University Press, pp. 223–278.

Rodinson, Maxime (1971). *Muhammad.* New York: Pantheon Books.

Rogoff, Barbara (1990). *Apprenticeship in Thinking.* London: Oxford University Press.

Rosen, Lawrence (1984). *Bargaining for Reality.* Chicago: University of Chicago Press.

Rosenberg, S., and Gara, M. (1985). "The Multiplicity of Personal Identity." In P. Shaver, ed., *Self, Situations and Social Behavior.* Beverly Hills, CA: Sage, pp. 87–114.

Rosenberg, S., Van Mechelen, I., and DeBoeck, P. (1994). "A Hierarchical Classes Model." In P. Arabie, L. Hubert, and G. DeSoete, eds., *Clustering and Classification.* Teaneck, NJ: World Scientific, pp. 123–155.

Rosenberg, Seymour (1988). "Self and Others: Studies in Social Personality and Autobiography." *Advances in Experimental Social Psychology.* 21:57–95.

Rosenberger, Nancy (1989). "Dialectic Balance in the Polar Model of Self: The Japan Case." *Ethos.* 17(1):88–113.

Rosenwald, George, and Ochberg, Richard (1992). *Storied Lives.* New Haven, CT: Yale University Press.

Sapir, Edward (1918). "Culture, Genuine and Spurious." *American Journal of Sociology.* 29:401–429.

Schank, Roger (1990). *Tell Me a Story.* New York: Scribner's.

Schimmel, Annemarie (1985). *And Muhammed Is His Messenger.* Chapel Hill: University of North Carolina Press.

Schimmel, Annemarie (1989). *Islamic Names.* Edinburgh: Edinburgh University Press.

Schneider, June (1971). "Of Vigilance and Virgins: Honor, Shame and Access to Resources in Mediterranean Societies." *Ethnology.* 10:1–24.

Schwartz, Theodore (1972). "Distributive Models of Culture in Relation to Societal Scale." (Published in 1978 as "The Size and Shape of a Culture." In F. Barth, ed., *Scale and Social Organization.* Helsinki: Norwegian Research Council, pp. 215–252.)

Schwartz, Theodore (1978). "Where Is Culture? Personality as the Distributive Locus of Culture." In G. Spindler, ed., *The Making of Psychological Anthropology.* Berkeley: University of California Press.

Sears, R., Maccoby, E., and Levin, H. (1957). *Patterns of Child Rearing.* Oxford: Row, Peterson.

Shalinsky, Audrey (1986). "Reason, Desire, and Sexuality: The Meaning of Gender in Northern Afghanistan." *Ethos.* 14(4):323–343.

Shapiro, David (1965). *Neurotic Styles.* New York: Basic.

Sharabi, Hisham (1988). *Neopatriarchy.* New York: Oxford University Press.

Sharabi, Hisham, and Ani, Mukhtar (1977). "The Impact of Class and Culture on Social Behavior: The Feudal-Bourgeois Family in Arab Society." In L. Brown and N. Itzkowitz, eds., *Psychological Dimensions of Near Eastern Studies.* Princeton, NJ: Darwin Press, pp. 240–256.

Shurtleff, William, and Aoyagi, Akiko (1979). *The Book of Tofu*. New York: Ballantine.

Shweder, Richard (1993). "The Cultural Psychology of Emotion." In M. Lewis and J. Haviland, eds., *Handbook of Emotion*. New York: Guilford Press, pp. 417–434.

Shweder, Richard, and Bourne, E. (1984). "Does the Concept of the Person Vary Cross-Culturally?" In R. Shweder and R. LeVine, eds., *Culture Theory*. Cambridge: Cambridge University Press, pp. 158–199.

Smith, M. Brewster, Bruner, Jerome, and White, Robert (1956). *Opinions and Personality*. New York: Wiley.

Smoor, Pieter (1985). *Kings and Bedouins in the Palace of Aleppo as Reflected in Maari's Works*. Manchester, England: University of Manchester.

Somer, O., and Goldberg, L. (1999). "The Structure of Turkish Trait-Descriptive Adjectives." *Journal of Personality and Social Psychology*. 76(3):431–450.

Spence, Donald (1982). *Narrative Truth and Historical Truth*. New York: Norton.

Spiro, Melford (1993). "Is the Western Conception of the Self 'Peculiar' within the Context of the World Cultures?" *Ethos*. 21(2):107–153.

Sprengnether, Madelon (1985). "Enforcing Oedipus: Freud and Dora." In C. Bernheimer and C. Kahane, eds., *In Dora's Case*. New York: Columbia University Press.

Stadler, Constance (1996). *The Nation as Idea*. PhD Dissertation, New York University.

Stern, Daniel (1985). *The Interpersonal World of the Infant*. New York: Basic Books.

Stoller, Robert (1979). *Observing the Erotic Imagination*. New Haven, CT: Yale University Press.

Takano, Yohtaro, and Osaka, Eiko (1999). "An Unsupported Common View: Comparing Japan and the U.S. on Individualism/Collectivism." *Asian Journal of Social Psychology*. 2:311–341.

Taussig, Michael (1993). *Mimesis and Alterity*. New York: Routledge.

Todorov, Tzvetan (1973). *The Fantastic*. Ithaca, NY: Cornell University Press.

Tomkins, Silvan (1995). *Exploring Affect: The Selected Writings of Silvan Tomkins*. Cambridge: Cambridge University Press.

Trafimow, D., Triandis, H., and Goto, S. (1991). "Some Tests of the Distinction between the Private Self and the Collective Self." *Journal of Personality and Social Psychology*. 60(5):649–655

Triandis, Harry (1989). "The Self and Social Behavior in Differing Cultural Contexts." *Psychological Review*. 96(3):506–520.

Triandis, Harry (1995). *Individualism and Collectivism*. Boulder, CO: Westview Press.

Triandis, Harry (2001). "Individualism and Collectivism." In D. Matsumoto, ed., *Handbook of Culture and Psychology*. New York: Oxford University Press.

Tsai, J., Ying, Y., and Lee, P. (2000). "The Meaning of 'Being Chinese' and 'Being American.'" *Journal of Cross-Cultural Psychology*. 31(3):302–332.

Turner, Victor (1967). *The Forest of Symbols*. Ithaca, NY: Cornell University Press.

Tversky, Amos (1977). "Features of Similarity." *Psychological Review*. 84(4):325–352.

Vaziri, Mostafa (1993). *Iran as Imagined Nation*. New York: Paragon House.

Verkuyten, M., and Pouliasi, K. (2002). "Biculturalism among Older Children: Cultural Frame Switching, Attributions, Self-Identification, and Attitudes." *Journal of Cross-Cultural Psychology*. 33(6):596–609.

Vygotsky, L. S. (1978). *Mind in Society*. Cambridge, MA: Harvard University Press.

Wallace, Anthony (1961). *Culture and Personality*. New York: Random House.

Waterbury, John (1972). *North for the Trade: The Life and Times of a Berber Merchant.* Berkeley: University of California Press.

Weber, Max (1958). *The Protestant Ethic and the Spirit of Capitalism.* New York: Scribner's.

White, Robert (1952). *Lives in Progress.* New York: Dryden Press.

Whiting, John (1994). *Culture and Human Development,* ed. E. Chasdi. Cambridge: Cambridge University Press.

Wiggins, J., ed. (1996). *The Five-Factor Model of Personality.* New York: Guilford Press.

Wiggins, J., and Trapnell, P. (1997). "Personality Structure: The Return of the Big Five." In R. Hogan et al., eds., *Handbook of Personality Psychology.* San Diego: Academic Press, pp. 737–766.

Wikan, Unni (1982). *Behind the Veil in Arabia.* Chicago: University of Chicago Press.

Wikan, Unni (1996). *Tomorrow, God Willing.* Chicago: University of Chicago Press.

Williams, Raymond (1973). *The Country and the City.* New York: Oxford University Press.

Winter, D., John, O., Stewart, A., Klohne, E., and Duncan, L (1998). "Traits and Motives: Toward an Integration of Two Traditions in Personality Research." *Psychological Review.* 105(2):230–250.

Wolf, Eric (1951). The Social Organization of Mecca and the Origins of Islam. *Southwestern Journal of Anthropology.* 7(4):329–356.

Wolf, Eric (1977). "Kinship, Friendship, and Patron-Client Relations in Complex Societies." In S. Schmidt, L. Guasti, & J. Scott, eds., *Friends, Followers, and Factions.* Berkeley: University of California Press, pp. 167–177.

Wu, Pei-Yi (1990). *The Confucian's Progress: Autobiographical Writings in Traditional China.* Princeton, NJ: Princeton University Press.

Yassin, Sayyid (1974). *Al-shakhsiyya al-'arabiyya* (The Arab Personality). Cairo: Pyramid Commercial Press.

Ybarra, O., and Trafimow, D. (1998) "How Priming the Private Self or Collective Self Affects the Relative Weights of Attitudes and Subjective Norms." *Personality and Social Psychology Bulletin.* 24(4):362–370.

Zayour, Ali (1977). *Al-tahlil al-nafsi l-al-dhat al-'arabiyyah* (Psychoanalysis of the Arab Ego). Beirut: dar al-tali'ah.

INDEX